Receded
Tides
of Empire

The end of an era; the last mailship, *S.A. Vaal*, leaving Durban harbour in 1977.

Receded Tides of Empire

Aspects of the Economic and Social History of Natal and Zululand since 1910

Edited by Bill Guest
and John M. Sellers

UNIVERSITY OF NATAL PRESS
PIETERMARITZBURG
1994

'Whaling Station' by Ernst van Heerden was originally published in *Kanse op 'n wrak* (Cape Town: Tafelberg Publishers, 1982). Translated by the author, it is reprinted here with the permission of the publishers. The Epigraph is taken from 'Giovanni Jacopo Meditates (on an Alabaster Adamastor)' by David Livingstone, originally published in *Momentum: On recent South African writing*, edited by M. J. Daymond, J. U. Jacobs and Margaret Lenta (Pietermaritzburg: University of Natal Press, 1984)

ISBN 0 86980 891 5

The financial assistance of the Centre for Science Development (HSRC, South Africa) towards the publication of this work is hereby acknowledged. Opinions expressed in this publication, and conclusions arrived at, are those of the editors and contributors and are not necessarily to be attributed to the Centre for Science Development.

This book is printed on acid-free paper

Typeset in the University of Natal Press
Printed in South Africa by
The Natal Witness
Printing and Publishing Company
Pietermaritzburg

. . . Receded Tides of Empire left
A Wake:
. . . .
Now other Tides are in.

Douglas Livingstone

CONTENTS

ILLUSTRATIONS AND MAPS

ACKNOWLEDGEMENTS

The editors and publishers thank the following individuals and institutions for their assistance and for permission to reproduce illustrations in this volume.

The Local History Museum for all the photographs, with the exception of those on page 4 (Killie Campbell Africana Library) and page 209 (courtesy of M.L Sultan Technikon). Catherine Meiklejohn and Helena Margeot of the Cartographic Unit, University of Natal, Pietermaritzburg, for the considerable work involved in readying the large selection of maps for print. John Benyon of the Department of Historical Studies, University of Natal, Pietermaritzburg, for the drawing reproduced on the cover.

In 1910, following the decision of white males in a bitter referendum, the former British colony of Natal (including Zululand) became part of the Union of South Africa. The large black population in the region suffered this development in almost complete silence, while the predominantly English-speaking white minority proved reluctant to assume the new political identity imposed upon it. The ebbing tide of pro-imperial sentiment continued to find expression in periodic demands for political separatism, though these lacked a secure economic foundation. In truth, since the discovery of precious minerals in the interior from the late 1860s onwards, Natal's increasing financial dependence upon the 'overberg' trade had been drawing the region into a much more broadly based economy. The process of economic integration gathered momentum after 1910 as the earlier ties of empire correspondingly weakened.

Through specialised essays based on original research this book explores a number of the economic and social changes experienced in Natal/Zululand since Union. They reveal that much of the enterprise and exploitation which characterised the region's socio-economic life in the colonial era continued into the late twentieth century. Infrastructural development, primarily to cater for the increasing volume of traffic between the Witwatersrand and the sea, scarred the intervening landscape. The growth of local sugar, coal and manufacturing industries provided employment for the swelling ranks of job-seekers, but often at low rates of pay and under poor working conditions. The expansion of commercial agriculture confined indigenous pastoralists to overcrowded locations and forced white 'bywoners' and black tenants onto the open labour market and into the urban areas. Local patterns of urbanisation, shaped by segregationist traditions that had their roots deep in the nineteenth century, were formally entrenched by apartheid legislation.

These and other themes are not unique to the history of the Natal/Zululand region but offer points of comparison for the general reader as well as for scholars working in other southern African contexts.

Contributors

Mark Addleson
School of Business, University of the Witwatersrand

Joy Brain
Formerly of the Department of History, University of Durban-Westville

Cornelis de Jong
Formerly of the Department of Economics, University of South Africa

Paul M. Dickinson
M.A. graduate, University of the Witwatersrand

Paula A. du Plooy
Formerly of the Human Sciences Research Council, Pretoria

Bill Guest
Department of Historical Studies, University of Natal, Pietermaritzburg

Verne Harris
Deputy-Director, State Archive Services, Natal and OFS Region

Hein Heydenrych
Formerly of the Human Sciences Research Council, Pretoria

Giuseppe Lenta
Department of Economics, University of Natal, Durban

David Lincoln
Department of Sociology, University of Cape Town

Anthony Lumby
Department of Economics, University of Natal, Durban

Paul Maylam
Department of History, Rhodes University, Grahamstown

Ian McLean

Academic Planning Division, University of Natal, Durban

John M. Sellers

Formerly of the Department of Historical Studies, University of Natal, Pietermaritzburg

Trevor Wills

Formerly of the Department of Geography, University of Natal, Pietermaritzburg

The following abbreviations have been used in the text and references.

Acc. No.	Accession number
AGM	Annual General Meeting
AYB	Archives Year Book for South African History
BTI	Board of Trade and Industries
CAD	Cape Archives Depot, Cape Town
CM	Commissioner of Mines Records (Dundee)
CNC	Chief Native Commissioner
CSO	Colonial Secretary's Office (Natal) (in NAD)
DBA	De Beers Archive (Kimberley)
DC	Departmental Committee
DCCM	Dundee Coal Company Ltd, Minute Books (in NAD)
DNA	Department of Native Affairs
DNAC	Durban Native Affairs Committee
DTCF	Durban Town Clerk's Files
GMOHY	General Manager's Office, Standard Bank, Half-Yearly Letters (in SBA)
GN	Government Notice
GNLB	Government Native Labour Bureau (in TAD)
IMN	Inspector of Mines Records, Natal (Dundee)
IMNA	Inspector of Mines Natal Accident Reports (Dundee)
INSP	Inspection Reports on Branch Offices, Standard Bank (in SBA)
ISER	Institute for Social and Economic Research (Rhodes University)
K	Kommissie/Commission
LDB	Secretary for Agriculture
MDA	Mines Department Accident Files (Dundee)
MNW	Secretary for Mines and Industries (in TAD)
MVE	Ministerie van Vervoer (in TAD)
NA	Native Affairs (in TAD)
NAD	Natal Archives Depot, Pietermaritzburg
NAU	Natal Agricultural Union Records
NCLRC	Natal Coast Labour Recruiting Corporation
NCOS	Natal Coal Owners' Society, Minute Books (Talana Museum, Dundee)
n.d.	no date
NDMF	National Development and Management Foundation
NEC	Native Economic Commission
NFLC	Natal Farm Labour Committee
NLC	Natives' Land Commission
n.p.	no pagination
NRS	Natal Regional Survey
NSA	Natal Sugar Association

NTS	Naturellesake (Native Affairs) (in TAD)
OPEC	Organisation of Petroleum Exporting Countries
RP	Republic of South Africa, Government Publication
SAC	South African Collieries Ltd
SACGA	South African Cane Growers' Association
SAIRR	South African Institute of Race Relations
SAS	South African Railways Records (in TAD)
SASJ	South African Sugar Journal
SASJA	South African Sugar Journal Annual
SASYB & GD	South African Sugar Year Book and General Directory
SATS	South African Transport Services Library (Johannesburg)
SATS, AG	South African Transport Services Library, Reports of Assistant General Managers
SATS, AR	South African Transport Services Library, Annual Reports of System and Divisional (or Departmental) Officers
SATS, DS	South African Transport Services Library, Reports of Divisional Superintendent, Durban
SATS, NLS	South African Transport Services Library, Reports of Native Labour Superintendent
SBA	Standard Bank of South Africa Ltd Archives (Head Office, Johannesburg)
SC	Select Committee
SNA	Secretary for Native Affairs (Natal) (in NAD)
TAD	Transvaal Archives Depot, Pretoria
TEU	Twenty-foot Equivalent Unit
UG	Union of South Africa, Government Publication
UGG	Union of South Africa, Government Gazette
VLCC	Very Large Crude Carrier
ZPU	Zululand Planters' Union

*I*NTRODUCTION

Bill Guest and John M. Sellers

The purpose of this book is to indicate the wide-ranging research which has been undertaken into the economic and social history of the Natal-Zululand region since its incorporation into the Union of South Africa in 1910. It is also intended to reflect those aspects of the field which await the detailed investigation necessary to provide a comprehensive socio-economic analysis of the Natal province.

An important step towards a more exhaustive political history of Natal and Zululand was taken with the publication of P.S. Thompson's study of separatism in South Africa during the period 1909–61.[1] The region's economic and social historians have not yet reached a complementary milestone, though the footnotes appended to this collection of essays reflect the appearance during the last three decades of an increasing volume of books, articles and unpublished theses on various aspects of twentieth-century Natal society and, more particularly, its economic activity. Prominent among the many specialised monographs, too numerous to mention, that have been published are the Natal Regional Survey series[2] and the various reports of the Natal Town and Regional Planning Commission. These have focused the energies of researchers with a variety of expertise on several major themes, ranging from an analysis of the region's natural resources to agricultural activity, harbour development, population growth and the process of industrial expansion. These studies provide useful insights into the extent of economic and social change in Natal-Zululand since 1910, and into the nature of the relationship between that region and the broader national economy of which it officially became a part on the formation of the Union.

In 1910 the province of Natal, into which Zululand had been incorporated in 1897, comprised approximately 35 370 square miles (91 608 square kilometres) sandwiched between the Drakensberg mountains and the Indian Ocean on South Africa's north-eastern seaboard. Its northern boundaries with Swaziland and Mozambique have since remained unchanged but, following the declaration of Transkei as an 'independent homeland', Natal's southern boundary was extended in 1978 to incorporate that part of the Cape Province known as East Griqualand (see map 1), as a result of which Natal comprised approximately 7 per cent of South Africa's total surface area and remained the smallest of its four provinces.[3]

The lack of enthusiasm of Natal's whites-only electorate for the Union and for the Republic which succeeded it in 1961 is well documented.[4] It was the only South African colony in which it was considered necessary to test electoral opinion before the decision was made to join the new Union of South Africa. And, in the 1960 referendum, it was the only province to vote against the declaration of a republic, by a majority of more than 93 000 (135 598 against; 42 299 for) on a voters' roll of 192 000 in a spectacular 92,5 per cent poll. In the 1909 referendum three-quarters of the votes cast were in favour of Union, but in a low 58,2 per cent poll this constituted support from only 43,7 per cent of Natal's 25 463-strong electorate and excluded the views of the silent unenfranchised black majority who constituted almost 92 per cent of the colony's total population.[5]

In order to explain the outcome of the 1909 referendum a great deal of attention has hitherto been focused upon geographical, political and cultural factors, though it is evident that more material considerations must have weighed heavily both in the minds of those who grudgingly voted for Union and those who accepted the unavoidable by not voting at all.[6] The receding tides of Empire left in their wake a population of 1 194 043 in Natal/Zululand which, according to the first (1911) Union census, constituted just under 20 per cent of South Africa's total population of 5 973 394 persons. Natal's white community of 98 114 amounted to only 8,22 per cent of the province's population and, outnumbered by more than 11:1 by other ethnic groups, may have considered integration into a more broadly-based national economy to have more practical appeal than the pursuit of a political separatism based upon pro-imperial sentiment.[7]

Imperial ties, made manifest by the presence of Government House and the garrison at Fort Napier, were strongest in Pietermaritzburg. It was also the only one of the four colonial capitals threatened with the loss of its political status as a capital in the proposed Union and whose civil servants faced the prospect of unemployment or transfer further afield, with dire consequences for the local business community. By contrast, the Afrikaners of northern Natal were overwhelmingly in favour of unification with the former Boer republics of the interior. The leaders of commerce and industry in the Durban area were similarly almost all in favour of Union in spite of the renewed Transvaal-Mozambique *modus vivendi* agreement which allocated only 30 per cent of the Witwatersrand railway traffic to Natal and as much as 50 per cent to the Portuguese colony, for a minimum of 10 years. The Durban Chamber of Commerce, the Port Natal Agents' Association and the Natal Manufacturers' Association all adopted a pro-Unionist stance, as did the coastal sugar farmers who similarly feared losing their 'overberg' markets. Even Natal's railwaymen, initially opposed to unification out of pique against the pro-Union Natal government which had earlier crushed their strike, changed their stance out of fear of unemployment in the wake of a possible decline in railway traffic if the colony stayed out of the Union.[8]

Indeed, inclusion in the Union not only obviated the danger of declining employment, investment and property values and an increase in Natal's

Map 1   Natal/Zululand magisterial districts, 1978

African cane-cutters on a sugar estate. In a similar picture on page 190 of *Enterprise and Exploitation* all the workers are Indian. This illustrates the change in sugar-estate labour from the nineteenth to the twentieth century.

public debt and rates of taxation, it also reduced the probability of disadvantageous competition with the Cape ports for the financially vital Witwatersrand railway traffic. Pietermaritzburg was still the economic hub of the Natal midlands but had lost its function as a forwarding station for the overberg trade as early as the 1880s when the railhead advanced beyond it deeper into the interior. By contrast, Durban's commercial sector was still vitally involved in this trade and benefited enormously, though unquantifiably, from it. So too did Natal's public exchequer in the form of customs duties and railway receipts. These collectively contributed as much as 77 per cent of the colony's total revenue in the boom financial year 1902–3; and 69 per cent in 1908–9, when they accounted for a modest surplus after four years of budget deficits during the depression following the South African War.[9]

However reluctant to join the Union, Natal simply could not afford to 'go it alone'. The earlier discovery of diamonds and gold beyond the Drakensberg had made the colony more dependent than ever before upon the transit trade. Imports, the bulk of which were destined for the interior, had continued to increase, while exports and re-exports to neighbouring territories in southern Africa had risen from 19,4 per cent of the total value of her exports in 1865 to 69,7 per cent in 1909. Exports to Britain had declined from 76,2 per cent to 10,6 per cent during that period, reflecting one already weakening economic link with the Empire to complement the incoming tide of dependence upon a broader South African economy.[10]

The discovery of precious minerals in the interior of the sub-continent had also provided a strong incentive for extensive harbour development and railway construction in Natal during the last three decades of the colonial era. A combination of large-scale dredging and tidal scour through pier construction had effectively reduced 'the Bar' across the harbour's entrance to a depth which could accommodate modern steamships, while wharfage, loading and repair facilities were also improved.[11] By 1910 it was already established as southern Africa's most important port and it has continued to maintain that position even though the history of its subsequent development has been a chequered one. (Essay no. 1, Anthony Lumby and Ian McLean, *The economy and the development of the Port of Durban*.)

The Harbour Affairs (Nyhoff) Commission of 1934–35 declared that Durban harbour was still inadequately organised and equipped by international standards, but a variety of spasmodic improvements enabled it to meet a series of formidable challenges, including the modern trend towards containerised shipping freight. In the process it played a crucial role in promoting the development of Durban as the economic centre of the Natal/Zululand region, and in serving the import-export needs of South Africa's industrial-commercial heartland in the 'Vaal Triangle'. By 1979 the exportation through Durban of coal and anthracite alone amounted to 2,9 million tons a year, which was as much as the existing harbour facilities could handle. By then approximately 10 per cent of Natal's coal exports passed through Richards Bay, the new harbour on the Zululand coast (see map 1) whose construction was initiated during the 1970s specifically to cope with the export trade and whose coal terminal was by 1982 already handling the bulk of South Africa's coal exports.[12]

Harbour development was accompanied by other infrastructural improvements, which further served the needs of the Natal/Zululand region and drew it more fully into the national economy. In 1934 the Union government assumed control of privately initiated air services and began to develop a national network. The national road system was launched in the late 1930s and was followed by considerable improvements to, *inter alia*, the Durban-Johannesburg road, the tarring of which was completed in 1961.[13] The rail-link from the port to the Witwatersrand had been completed in December 1895, becoming a major income-earner for the Natal government as well as an important avenue of employment for both Indians and Africans.[14] After 1910 it continued to generate revenue and jobs on a significant scale, though its primary significance to the national economy lay in the fact that it provided the shortest railway connection over South African soil between the burgeoning industrial-commercial heartland and the coastline.

It was for this reason that a concerted effort was made by the Union government to improve the Natal main line by means of deviations, doubling and electrification. (Essay no. 2, Hein Heydenrych and Paula A. du Plooy, *Railway development in Natal, 1910–1929*.) While there was also a large-scale extension of the region's branch-line system to serve the agricultural sector, the programme of main-line electrification, which was completed through to Volksrust on the Transvaal provincial boundary by 1937, was of even greater national importance. It gave rise to the establishment in 1922 of the Electricity Supply Commission (Escom) and to the subsequent development of a national power grid which was essential for industrialisation in South Africa. In Natal this led to the erection of large coal-fired power stations at Colenso (1927), Congella (1928) and later Pinetown (1954) and Ingagane (1963), all of which were fuelled by collieries situated in the northern reaches of the province.[15]

The decision to electrify the Natal main line into the interior had been taken primarily in response to the demands of local coal-mines for an improved carrying capacity that would enable them to meet their export and bunker contracts at Durban timeously and efficiently. The advance of the railhead in 1889–90 from Ladysmith through Elandslaagte and Glencoe to Newcastle had facilitated the emergence of a large-scale coal industry in northern Natal and had marked the beginning of a mutually beneficial, though not always harmonious, relationship between the colliery owners and railway authorities.[16] The railway itself became a consumer of locally produced coal while providing access to the shipment trade through Durban and, from 1895, to the inland market on the Witwatersrand. The coal-mines eliminated the need to import coal, at great expense, for locomotive consumption, and they improved railway revenues by creating a demand for trucks that would otherwise have returned empty to the port after delivering their imported cargoes in Johannesburg.

After 1910 the Union government and the South African Railways and Harbours Administration adopted a policy of rates and rebates which was generally supportive of the export and bunker trade in coal, though the long-standing inability to keep pace with the transport demands of local collieries inhibited their expansion during phases of heavy market demand. The inadequacy of the Railways' carrying capacity was a problem that was not confined to the coal industry, as reflected by the meeting of representatives from the wattle, sugar, coal and other industries held in July 1925. Preference continued to be given to the seasonal transportation needs of maize and other perishable agricultural products, but the virtual collapse of South Africa's railway transportation system during the early 1950s revealed the extent to which railway development had failed to keep abreast of the economy's expansion.[17]

Natal's colliery companies were unanimous in their opinion that electrification of the main line had not significantly eased their plight and that a double railway line to the coast or the construction of an entirely new one would have been more immediately effective.[18] Inadequate transportation facilities do not constitute the only difficulty with which local collieries have had to contend in the twentieth century. (Essay no. 3, Bill Guest, *An introduction to the post-Union Natal coal industry*.) Other challenges included the raising of sufficient investment capital, the maintenance of output balanced against the recognition of necessary safety precautions, and the retention of an adequate supply of labour in the face of unpredictable fluctuations in the market demand for coal both domestically and abroad. All these variables contributed to the erratic pattern of prosperity and depression which has characterised the history of the Natal coal industry, even allowing for the measure of stability provided by the intrusion into it of large Transvaal companies with substantial capital resources and, in some cases, other mining interests. This trend facilitated the introduction of expensive modernisation programmes into the Natal collieries and integrated them more fully into the financial structure of a much larger South African mining industry, in contrast to their earlier control by local entrepreneurs based primarily in Durban and their sometimes heavy reliance upon British investment capital.

This process was accompanied by an increasing dependence upon the expanding domestic coal market in place of the traditional reliance upon the shipment trade, though quantitatively Natal's coal output has become progressively less significant to the South African economy than it was in 1910, as controlling companies have developed the far larger Transvaal reserves. Qualitatively, the province's coal industry assumed increasing importance to the national interest as the only supplier of true coking coal to the South African Iron and Steel Corporation (Iscor), following its establishment in 1928, and of coke to the railways and various foundries. In recent years that role has also been weakened by the discovery of additional coking coal reserves in the far northern Transvaal and by technological innovations which threaten to eliminate the use of coking coal in the manufacture of steel. As has been the case in the past, colliery closures and production cut-backs will have far-reaching implications for the economic life of northern Natal.[19]

The history of the Natal whaling industry was much shorter than that of coal and was confined to the twentieth century. (Essay no.4, Cornelis de Jong, *A history of whaling from Durban.*) The first local whaling enterprise, the South African Whaling Company, was established in 1908 with Norwegian capital and the second, the Union Whaling and Fishing Company, was floated in 1909 with British finance. There were six such companies by 1913, including the well-known English firm Messrs Irvin and Johnson, and the Eastern Whaling Company whose head office was in Johannesburg and which was subsequently amalgamated with the Premier Whaling Company of Delagoa Bay under the ownership of the New Transvaal Chemical Company.[20] This was indicative of what was to follow, as fluctuating catches, variable market demand, and later, the imposition of rigorous quotas and regulations enforced a process of amalgamation and rationalisation upon the local whaling industry. After 1930, the Union Whaling and Fishing Company was the only enterprise of its kind operating from Natal and, from the 1940s, it was controlled and financed entirely from Johannesburg.

The industry continued to rely heavily on whaleboat crews, gunners, managers and chemists recruited in Norway, but their expertise could not prevent its closure in 1976 as a result of sharply rising fuel costs, increasing public hostility towards whaling and the enforcement of reduced quotas by government in collaboration with the International Whaling Commission. Natal's whaling companies all operated out of Durban, though one, African Whales Limited, established a factory at Park Rynie and there were initial plans on the part of other companies to base themselves at Port Shepstone.

By 1910, Durban had also emerged as the main focus of the region's manufacturing sector, which subsequently expanded along the transportation corridor into the interior and developed in pockets along the coastline as far as Richards Bay/Empangeni in the north and Port Shepstone in the south. (Essay no.5, Mark Addleson, *An overview of the growth of manufacturing in Natal.*) At the time of Union, two-thirds of the region's manufacturing industries were concentrated in the Umgeni district (more particularly around Durban), which in 1908 had employed 78 per cent of Natal's industrial work-force and produced 91 per cent by value of its gross industrial output. In 1911 the province contributed 26 per cent (£4 434 562 worth) of South Africa's output of manufactured goods, though it was still heavily involved in processing its own agricultural produce.[21]

The number of local industries had increased significantly towards the end of the nineteenth century in response to the emergence of a growing overberg market. Yet there had been little active promotion of the manufacturing sector. This had been disadvantaged in competition with established foreign producers by the Natal colonial government's policy of encouraging trade (and thereby boosting its income from customs duties and railway receipts) through the imposition of lower import duties than

An aerial view of the Dunlop factory in Sydney Road, Durban, in the 1930s.

those levied at the Cape. Some protection had been provided with the introduction of heavier duties on imported manufactured articles in terms of a customs agreement with the Cape Colony in 1898. Demands for further increases that were made after the formation of the Natal Manufacturers' Association in 1905 had to contend with opposition from the commercial and mining sectors as well as reluctance on the part of the colonial government. Consequently, in 1910 the region's manufacturing sector was still very much in its infancy.[22]

Despite its slow start (only beginning to expand significantly during the 1930s and 1940s) manufacturing soon became a more prominent feature of the Natal region than it was of the national economy. By 1960 it was contributing one third of the region's gross geographical product and still as much as 30 per cent in the late 1980s, compared with approximately 23 per cent of the gross geographical product of South Africa as a whole. This prominence is attributable partly to the relatively small size of Natal's financial and mining sectors in comparison with those of the Transvaal, but it is also due to a number of other encouraging factors. These include easy access to Durban harbour and proximity to the Witwatersrand, which attracts exporters as well as those producing for the domestic market, and a readily available supply of water and cheap labour. To some extent the rating policy implemented by the South African railway authorities in 1910 encouraged industries to set up in and around Durban while the Government's import-replacement policy, induced by the economic isolation of the war years 1914–18 and 1939–45, also prompted utilisers of imported raw materials to locate near a port.[23]

Natal's manufacturing sector continued to diversify as various industries were established in the smaller towns of the province such as Pietermaritzburg, Empangeni, Port Shepstone, Umkomaas, Ladysmith, Newcastle and Dundee, though many of these were involved in processing local agricultural produce. A degree of regional specialisation became evident as the Greater Durban area was dominated by the textile, clothing, footwear, paper and chemical industries, including more than half of South Africa's paint and petroleum production and one of the largest fertiliser plants in the southern hemisphere. In 1959–60 the Umgeni district (extending from Durban to Pietermaritzburg) embraced 78 per cent of Natal's manufacturing and construction enterprises, employed 77 per cent of its industrial workforce and accounted for 79 per cent of its net industrial output. This amounted to 14 per cent of South Africa's output (18 per cent including the rest of Natal's contribution) which was far less than the 49,7 per cent produced by the Witwatersrand/ Pretoria region, but compared favourably with the Western Cape's 12,6 per cent and the 4,5 per cent generated in the Port Elizabeth/Uitenhage area.[24]

One of the earliest forms of industrial activity in colonial Natal had been sugar-milling. By 1864 there were already 60 mills in operation and in 1898 the first refinery was established at South Coast Junction. By 1910 sugar had already emerged as the major export staple of Natal's coastal lowlands, due partly to governmental assistance in the form of an initially favourable tariff structure, co-operation in the importation of indentured Indian labour, and the demarcation in 1904 of 2 613 000 acres in Zululand as white farmland. This enabled the industry to embark upon a new era of sustained growth and by 1910 more than 10 000 acres had been brought under sugar cultivation north of the Thukela. Sugar-milling facilities south of Durban were already falling under the control of C. G. Smith and Company while J. L. Hulett's South African Refineries Ltd owned several large estates on the north coast and operated the concession mill erected in 1908 at Amatikulu in Zululand.[25]

After Union, the industry continued to enjoy the assistance of the state, both in institutionalising a system of migrant labour and in providing it with an assured domestic market for its product. (Essay no. 6, Paul M. Dickinson, *The South African sugar industry, 1910–1940.*) The receding imperial connection offered preferential access to the British and Canadian markets as well, thereby further protecting the industry from the effects of world competition and overproduction. The area under sugar cultivation increased nearly fourfold between 1911 and 1940 from 107 091 acres to 383 879 acres and production more than sevenfold from 82 000 tons in 1910 to 595 556 tons in 1939. Output was also improved by more efficient milling operations and by the introduction of new cane varieties with a higher sucrose content. Domestic consumption increased and was further promoted by the marketing of a cheaper Grade 2 sugar for poorer consumers, yet an increasing proportion of output was exported with the result that by 1940 South Africa had become a net exporter rather than a net importer of sugar.

In 1961 the industry produced 994 363 tons of sugar, which amounted to a twelvefold increase over its 1911 output, with approximately 40 per cent of it coming from the Zululand mills, 45 per cent from those on the north coast and 15 per cent from the south coast mills. As much as 92 per cent of coastal farmland was under sugar cultivation and organised into estates whose average size (6 630 acres) was big by Natal standards and indicative of the fact that production was dominated by large companies practising economies of scale.[26] The introduction of cane varieties which were suited to higher altitudes had resulted in sugar also becoming a major crop on farms in the Dalton/Wartburg and Mid-Illovo/Eston zones of the Natal interior. However, for the most part, the white farming community continued to be characterised by its wide diversity of crop specialisation in accordance with the dramatic bioclimatic variations encountered in the region (see map 2). While sugar had emerged during the colonial era as the most viable crop on the coastal belt, maize, wool production, dairy cattle and wattle were found to be best suited to the mist-belt of the midlands and mixed farming, including cattle, sheep, maize, fodder crops and later wattle and cotton, was conducted in the upper northern district.[27]

In 1910 wool and sugar in combination amounted to one-third by value of Natal's exports but thereafter, as the sugar industry went from strength to strength, the importance of wool production to the region's economy declined. By contrast, the value of Natal's wattle extracts increased almost thirty-twofold between 1910 and 1961, when it reached £6 800 000, and

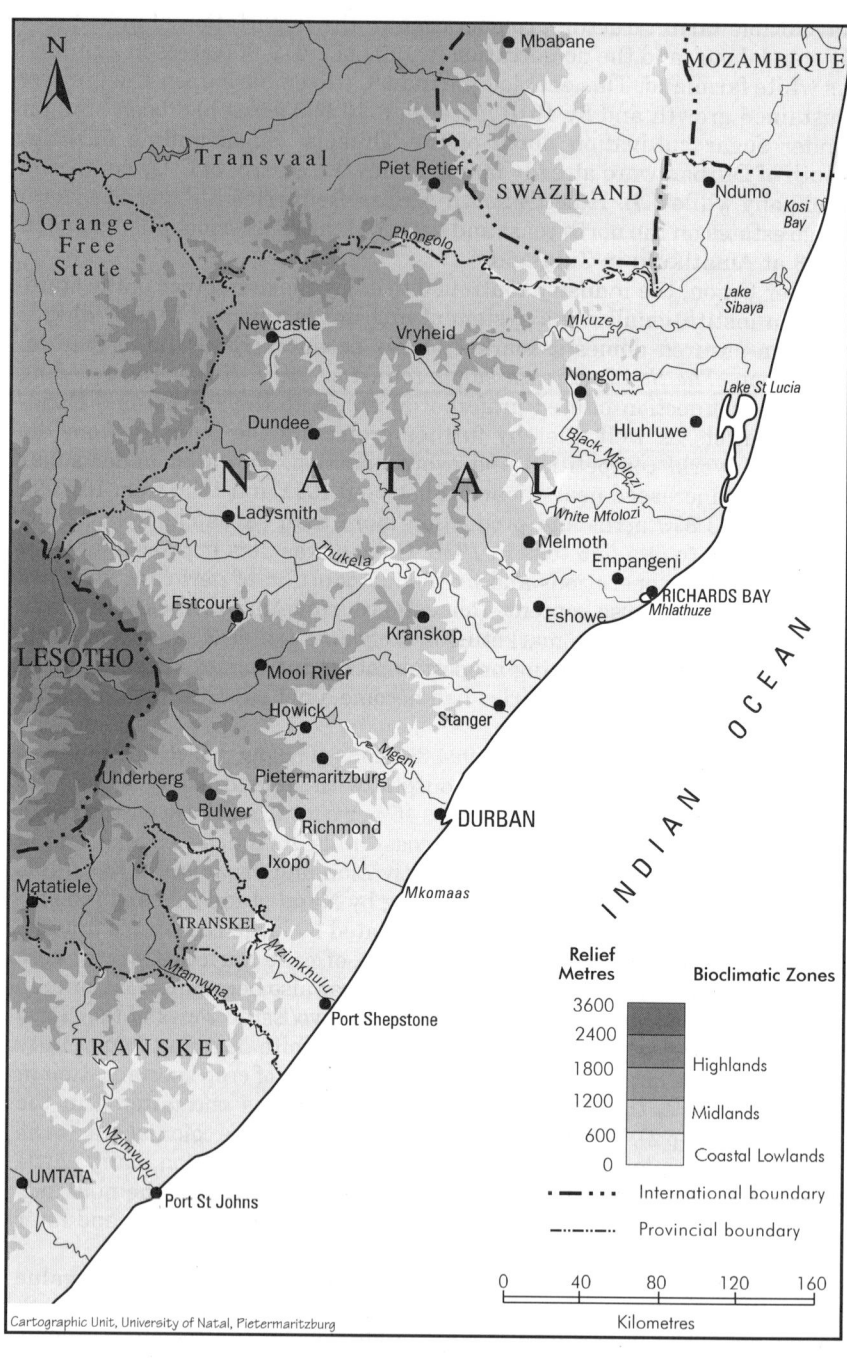

Map 2   Natal/Zululand relief and bioclimatic zones

more than 72 per cent of the total area under wattle cultivation in South Africa was to be found in the province. However, apart from sugar and wattle extracts, Natal has not become a significant exporter of agricultural produce since 1910 though its largely white commercial farming sector has catered to many of the needs of the region and, to some extent, to those of the national market as the population has increased and become more urbanised.[28]

By contrast, until the mid-1970s Natal's manufacturers continued to share in the prolonged post-war expansion of the national economy and thereafter in its subsequent decline. By then, industrial growth had already contributed significantly towards sustaining a demographic pattern of urban migration which had been gathering momentum in the region since the late nineteenth century. By 1904 more than 60 per cent of white Natalians, approximately 57 per cent of the 'coloured' community and 24 per cent of the colony's Indians were urban dwellers, with more than half of its white population living in the two main urban centres. By 1960 nearly two-thirds of the whites were resident in those cities and 89 per cent in all were urbanised, along with 86 per cent of the province's coloureds and 81 per cent of its Indian inhabitants. By 1980 more than 90 per cent of each of these three groups were urban dwellers (91,5; 90,2 and 90,2 per cent respectively).[29]

As these figures indicate, the Indians experienced a particularly marked process of socio-economic change during the course of the twentieth century. Although they became increasingly urbanised, Indians did not abandon the sugar industry altogether and some found skilled and semi skilled jobs in the mills where the wages and conditions were superior to those on the estates. By 1952 there were no more than 6 136 Indians employed in the industry, of whom 2 075 were engaged as industrial workers in the mills.[30] Nevertheless, as their numbers in the industry declined, Natal's sugar estates came into increasing competition for African labour with each other and with other employers, including the gold- and coal-mines. Land dispossession and labour tenancy arrangements along the coastal belt fell far short of meeting the labour requirements of sugar producers. In order to maintain production levels they were obliged to resort to various tactics, including the payment of wages in advance and persistent attempts to gain access to foreign labour. (Essay no. 7, David Lincoln, *The Zululand sore: migrant sugar estate labour in Natal, 1914–1939*).

Through the medium of the Natal Coast Recruiting Corporation, the Natal Sugar Association tried to recruit labour in Zululand, where members of the local Planters' Union had met with only limited success, and subsequently also in Mpondoland, the Transkei and (to a lesser extent) the northern Transvaal and Swaziland. Recruiting efforts were impeded by the low wages and poor conditions to which field-workers were subjected, but by the 1930s, when drought and economic depression flooded the labour market with unemployed blacks, Mpondoland had been established as a major source of contract labour for the larger-scale millers-cum-planters of Natal. This did not ease the plight of the smaller-scale Zululand planters north of the Thukela but, following the re-negotiation of the Mozambique Convention in 1934, they were legally able to employ an increasing number of 'malaria tolerant' labourers from the southern parts of the Portuguese territory. In this way oscillating migrancy became, with the collaboration of the state, a significant feature of the sugar industry as a whole.

The employment of Indians in the sugar industry, and the implications of their subsequent withdrawal from it, is only one aspect of their involvement in the Natal regional economy. (Essay no. 8, Joy Brain, *An economic transformation: the Indian community in Natal.*) From their arrival in 1860, Indians were employed not only in the sugar industry with which they are popularly associated, but also in a variety of agricultural occupations including the cultivation of other plantation crops like tea, coffee, cotton, tobacco and arrowroot along the coastline, and maize-growing, dairying, cattle-ranching and sheep-farming in the interior districts. Indentured and ex-indentured 'free' Indians had soon made their presence felt in non-agricultural activities such as market-gardening, fruit and vegetable hawking, commercial fishing, harbour, hotel and hospital services, and in railway construction and coal-mining.[31] Trading had begun almost simultaneously with the first arrivals, but the advent of the commercially more experienced 'passenger-class' Indians from the mid-1870s really marked the emergence of a strong local Indian trading class which posed such a threat to smaller-scale white traders.[32]

By 1885, when the Wragg Commission was appointed to investigate anti-Asiatic agitation, Natal's Indian population was almost equal to that of the white settlers in numbers and by 1904 it was larger. By 1911 Indians constituted 11,17 per cent of the region's population compared with the 8,22 per cent comprised of whites and the 0,76 per cent of coloureds. Yet the better educated 'passenger-class' Indians constituted only a small percentage of the province's Asiatics, the vast majority of whom were still illiterate and derived their income primarily from agriculture or from other forms of manual labour.[33] By 1960 only 9,7 per cent of Natal's Indians were engaged in agriculture, 33,5 per cent were employed as artisans, 22,5 per cent worked in non-manual occupations (administrative, clerical, professional and sales) and small percentages in various other capacities. As many as 78,1 per cent of them were concentrated in the Durban/Pietermaritzburg district.[34]

The continuing transformation of the Indian community into a largely urbanised and educated group that is actively involved in all sectors of the regional economy, including industry and the professions, has been achieved in spite of severe legislative restrictions imposed upon their geographical and social mobility as well as the competition provided by cheaper unskilled African labour on the one hand and politically advantaged skilled and semi-skilled whites on the other. Two significant characteristics of this process, which have had far-reaching socio-economic implications, have been the improvement in educational opportunities for Indians as a result of their own persistence in this regard and the increasing participation of Indian women in economic activities outside the home.[35]

Natal's African population has also become increasingly urbanised and geographically mobile, though less rapidly than other ethnic groups. The African farming community was not able to exploit the rising urban demand for agricultural produce, though in 1960 as many as 49,7 per cent of Africans in the region were still engaged on the land compared to 9,7 per cent of Indians, 5,1 per cent of whites and 4,7 per cent of coloureds.[36] By 1910 colonial Natal's dependence on African food producers had been reversed by a combination of natural disasters, hostile legislation and population increase which undermined the traditional homestead economy and accelerated the conversion of the peasantry into farm-serfs and oscillating migrant labourers.[37] By the 1950s ever-increasing numbers of Africans were being forced into labour migrancy or else permanently into the urban areas as a result of overpopulation, overgrazing and overcultivation in the region's so-called reserves or what in 1972 came to be officially designated as 'KwaZulu'.[38]

During the 1960s and early 1970s the annual rate of growth of the territory's agricultural industry was barely half that of the national average, yet field crop production grew at the same rate while operating at lower output yields. (Essay no. 9, Giuseppe Lenta, *Development or stagnation? Agriculture in KwaZulu, 1957–1973*.) It was the output of KwaZulu's livestock enterprises which declined during this period in spite of various attempts to improve animal husbandry in the territory. The quality of land in KwaZulu compares favourably with the rest of South Africa, in addition to which the region as a whole has several well-distributed rivers, an estimated 40 per cent of the country's total usable water resources, and is situated in that third of the subcontinent which has an average annual rainfall of more than 500 mm.[39] However, the quantity of land available in KwaZulu is very scarce relative to the population employed on it, and livestock numbers have continued to be excessive in relation to its carrying capacity, resulting in the deterioration of land resources and a decline in marketable output. The further agricultural development of KwaZulu has been restricted not so much by traditional systems of land tenure and the customary importance attached to the quantity rather than the productive capacity of livestock as by the shortage of extension officers, technical expertise and investment capital, the inadequacies of existing infrastructure and marketing facilities, the absence of a development strategy envisaged for the whole of South Africa, and the scarcity of land.

Africans living outside those areas of Natal designated as reserves and later as KwaZulu also found their access to land as owners or as tenants, increasingly restricted by hostile legislation and the continuing commercialisation of the white farming sector. The Natal colonial government had to a large extent anticipated the 1913 Natives Land Act in restraining Africans from purchasing real estate or establishing themselves as squatters on white-owned property.[40] The 1936 Native Trust and Land Act allocated 1 113 300 acres (526 000 morgen) of land in Natal for purchase by or on behalf of Africans in addition to the 11,2 million morgen already 'scheduled' countrywide for that purpose by the 1913 Land Act. However, in 1960 the purchase of the 611 083 acres (288 718 morgen) actually 'released' by the 1936 Act was still making slow progress through the agency of the South African Native Trust. In 1910 as much as 39 per cent of African-owned land in Natal was to be found in Klip River County, due to missionary-backed purchases in the 1870s. The area in question actually increased in subsequent decades, despite state efforts to the contrary, and by 1953 included approximately 50 000 acres outside the territory which had been officially released for African purchase. When, during the 1960s, the drive to remove 'black spots' from designated 'white' areas gathered momentum in Natal those in the northern districts attracted immediate attention.[41]

The population density of African-owned property in northern Natal tended to become significantly higher as white commercial farmers made increasing demands on black tenants. Even so, the impact of the market economy on labour tenancy was much more gradual in that part of the province than elsewhere. (Essay no. 10, Verne Harris, *Changing forms of agricultural labour on white-owned farms in northern Natal, 1910–1936.*) The commercialisation of agriculture in northern Natal was slower due to its remoteness from outside markets and the marginal nature of much of the available land. White share-croppers (bywoners) were the first to be affected, though some were still in evidence in the late 1950s. By the mid-1930s cash wages for African labour tenants was the accepted norm west of the Buffalo River but east of that divide, in the territory which had been annexed from the Transvaal in 1902, that practice was still the exception and tenants continued to enjoy access to land and the ownership of livestock.

By 1960 share-cropping and cash-tenancy had become far less common throughout Natal, and although there were still 42 000 registered labour tenants in the province, its white commercial farming sector was opting increasingly for mechanisation and full-time wage-labour while the state was inclined towards abolishing labour tenancy altogether.[42] Migration to the urban areas was becoming a more viable option for tenants as much as it was for many of the inhabitants of KwaZulu. Superficially, the urbanisation of Natal's African population appears to have been unspectacular, amounting to only 4 per cent in 1904, 19,1 per cent in 1960 and 23,3 per cent (Zulus only) in 1980. However, those percentages represented 36 160 persons in 1904 (compared with 64,990 urbanised whites), 420 119 persons in 1960 (compared with 302 809 white urban residents), while in the early 1980s the African population of the Greater Durban area alone numbered approximately half a million to the city's 300 000 whites who constituted 60 per cent of the province's white population.[43]

In Durban, initial attempts to establish urban segregation were directed less against Africans than Indians, whose urbanisation increased dramatically from the 1920s and was then perceived to constitute a more serious threat to white interests. Municipal authorities were more anxious to control than to segregate the African workforce, and the foundations for this were already being laid in the late nineteenth century.[44] From 1874 casual or 'togt' labourers were required to register and, from 1903, to live in municipal barracks or in private compounds. In 1869 a curfew was introduced and from 1901 all African workers in Natal were obliged to carry identification passes, registration (not only for 'togt' labourers) having been provided for in 1888. Durban's system of bureaucratic control was more effectively implemented from 1916 with the establishment of its own Native Affairs Department, financed largely from the profits generated by the municipal beer monopoly. (Essay no. 11, Paul Maylam, *The evolution of urban apartheid: influx control and segregation in Durban, c. 1900–1951.*) The various strategies of control were intensified as the push and pull factors operating in favour of the region's urban areas became stronger and the flood of Africans into the harbour-city gathered momentum.

Apart from the construction of the small Baumannville location in 1915–16, Durban did not respond to the Native Locations Act passed by the colonial parliament in 1904 to provide for the establishment of segregated locations. The 1923 Natives (Urban Areas) Act allowed for the construction of segregated African townships but it was not until 1934 that Durban's Lamont township was opened. During the 1930s demands for strict residential segregation on the part of police and ratepayers' associations led to measures which forced many Africans out of the city's central suburbs and into the shack settlements on its southern fringes or into Lamont township. Durban's fluctuating labour needs ensured that a more stringent application of influx control and urban segregation did not eventuate until after the accession to power in 1948 of the Nationalist government. The 1950 Group Areas Act represented the imposition of a much more uniform and centralised policy of segregation on South Africa as a whole but it did not, in its underlying principles, constitute a significant change from what had already been implemented less rigorously in Durban.

Pietermaritzburg also felt the effects of the new nationally applied segregationist policies, though there, too, the foundations of an 'apartheid' city had already been laid.[45] (Essay no. 12, Trevor Wills, *Segregation, separation and desegregation: Pietermaritzburg since 1910.*) By 1910 a tradition of residential segregation separated the white immigrant population from indigenous Africans (other than domestic servants) who were being drawn towards the colonial capital, and also from Indian immigrants and so-called coloureds. This segregationist pattern was still blurred in the central city area, though demands for the imposition of restrictions upon Indian trading activity and land purchases pre-dated those made in Durban and were similarly less concerned initially with African urbanisation which was largely confined to the periphery.

After 1910 Pietermaritzburg's residential growth was characterised by increasing segregation and by a process of suburbanisation which was largely the consequence of private initiative and almost entirely for the benefit of white residents, whose exclusive property rights were later endorsed by the Group Areas Act. Although the city failed to generate significant industrial growth, its African population continued to increase as more and more peasants were forced off the land. The construction of the 'Pietermaritzburg Native Village' (Sobantu) was only a partial solution and nearby Edendale soon became overcrowded as uncontrolled shack construction continued on the city's peri-urban fringes. These developments were a source of concern to local health officials, but by 1948 the central government had implemented legislation which enabled Pietermaritzburg's civic authorities, like those in Durban and elsewhere, to exercise considerable control over urban Africans as well as to curtail alleged Indian penetration into white residential areas. The advent of the Nationalist government brought in its wake Pietermaritzburg's first phase of significant industrial growth following its being declared a 'Bantustan Border Industrial Area' in 1963. As elsewhere, it also resulted in a far more rigorous division of the city into racially exclusive areas which obliged large numbers of residents, Indians in particular, to relocate themselves at inestimable cost and inconvenience. Pietermaritzburg's civic authorities, like those in Durban, did not oppose the implementation of this policy.

The dismantling of segregationist legislation gives rise to speculation as to what configuration the social geography of Natal's major urban areas will assume in the future. The reconstruction of the region's 'fragmented' cities is already the focus of careful investigation, as is the broad issue of property rights and land ownership.[46] The contributions to this book suggest several other research possibilities. The work done on harbour and railway development points the way to further research on other aspects of the region's infrastructural improvement, including road construction, and its socio-economic impact. The importance of the coal-mining industry to the economy of northern Natal demands closer scrutiny, as does the implications of colliery closures. The brief account of whaling operations from Durban points to the need for a more exhaustive investigation of fishing activities in general off the coast of Natal. The vital and increasing importance of manufacturing industry to the region has been stressed, but there is ample scope for analyses of the environmental degradation which has resulted from both mining and manufacturing enterprise. The socio-political consequences of industrialisation have yet to be fully explored, not least the role and experience of African and Indian workers, and the history of their trade union movements.[47]

The Natal sugar industry, and its labour requirements, has already attracted fairly considerable attention from historians,[48] though this prominent part of the region's agricultural sector still requires further scrutiny from a variety of perspectives, including that of its employees. The history of other agricultural activities demands closer attention, including dairy-farming, wool-production and the timber industry, whose increasing afforestation of the region is of such concern to environmentalists. The struggle of northern Natal's white farming community to wrest a living from the land has yet to be told, and the declining fortunes of Natal's and Zululand's African peasant farmers still need to be investigated in more detail.[49] The close analysis of the relationships between white landowners and African tenants in northern Natal could usefully be extended to other parts of the region, while the effect of climate and other natural phenomena on agricultural activities calls for further examination.[50]

The history of Durban and Pietermaritzburg has, to a varying extent, been investigated with particular reference to the process of African and Indian urbanisation,[51] but neither field has been exhausted and the techniques of urban studies could fruitfully be extended to the region's other urban-industrial centres such as Estcourt, Ladysmith, Newcastle, Empangeni and Richards Bay. Sectors of the economy omitted from this book and which call for in-depth research include capital formation and banking, investment and commercial entrepreneurship, informal trading and manufacturing, public and privately owned transport services, education, tourism and the hotel industry, publishing and printing, shipping,[52] and household domestic service. The role of women in the regional economy has been largely neglected,[53] while the history of numerous individual companies and specific commercial-industrial pursuits awaits the attention of business historians. The continuing integration of the Natal-Zululand region into a broader South African economy, the weakening of its imperial links and the practical viability of its separatist tradition, which persists in various forms, [54] are issues that provide a wider perspective and are likely to retain their topicality in the future.

REFERENCES

1. P.S. Thompson, *Natalians first: separatism in South Africa, 1909–1961* (Johannesburg, Southern Books, 1990).

2. The Natal Regional Survey (NRS) series was published in fifteen volumes between 1951 and 1969. Topics covered include archaeology and natural resources, population, trade unions, electricity supply, African reserves, hospital services, the Indian community, agriculture, development of the Durban/Pietermaritzburg region and the Port of Durban. A number of additional reports were also published.

3. *The Buthelezi Commission: the requirements for stability and development in KwaZulu and Natal* (Durban, Buthelezi Commission, 1982), vol. 1, pp. 77 and 147–51; vol. 2, pp. 219–44; W. Dower, *The early annals of Kokstad and Griqualand East* (Killie Campbell Africana Library Reprint Series, Pietermaritzburg, University of Natal Press, 1978), Introduction p. xix.

4. L. M. Thompson, *The unification of South Africa, 1902–1910* (Cape Town, Oxford University Press, 1960), pp. 393–96; E. H. Brookes and C. de B. Webb, *A history of Natal* (Pietermaritzburg, University of Natal Press, 1965), pp. 243–45; Thompson, *Natalians first*, pp. 1, 2, 7, 177–80; A. Duminy, 'Towards Union, 1900–1910' in Andrew Duminy and Bill Guest (eds), *Natal and Zululand from earliest times to 1910: a new history* (Pietermaritzburg, University of Natal Press, 1989), pp. 418–23.

5. Brookes and Webb, *Natal*, pp. 244–45, 248–50; Thompson, *Natalians first*, pp. 1, 7, 166–67, 177–80, 194; Thompson, *Unification of South Africa*, p. 486; T. R. H. Davenport, *South Africa: a modern history* (Bergvlei, Southern Books, 1989), pp. 298–99.

6. The economic factors in the 1909 referendum are considered more fully in Bill Guest, 'The Natal regional economy 1910–1960 in historical perspective', *The South African Journal of Economic History*, 5 (2), September 1990, pp. 16–39.

7. Union Office of Census and Statistics, *Official Year Book of the Union*, no. 1–1917 (Pretoria, Government Printer, 1918), pp. 147–57; Bureau of Census and Statistics, *Union statistics for fifty years: jubilee issue, 1910–1960* (Pretoria, Government Printer, 1960), pp. A3–A5; Thompson, *Unification of South Africa*, p. 486.

8. Duminy, 'Towards Union', p. 422; Thompson, *Unification of South Africa*, pp. 393–95; Brookes and Webb, *Natal*, p. 245; Thompson, *Natalians first*, p. 7.

9. Z. A. Konczacki, *Public finance and economic development of Natal, 1893–1910* (Durham, North Carolina, Duke University Press, 1967), pp. 57, 78, 82, 84; Thompson, *Unification of South Africa*, pp. 54, 168, 395, 492; Duminy 'Towards Union', p. 423.

10. Konczacki, *Natal, 1893–1910*, pp. 15–16, 18; D. Hobart Houghton and J. Dagut, *Source material on the South African economy*, vol. 1 (Cape Town, Oxford University Press, 1972), pp. 319, 322.

11. See Lucille Heydenrych, 'Port Natal harbour, *c*.1850–1897' in Bill Guest and John M. Sellers (eds), *Enterprise and exploitation in a Victorian colony: aspects of the economic and social history of colonial Natal* (Pietermaritzburg, University of Natal Press, 1985), pp. 17–45.

12. Lionel Capstickdale, 'South Africa's black gold', *South African Panorama*, May 1982, p. 16; P. J. Hugo, *The South African coal industry*, Report 9/83 Minerals Bureau (Braamfontein, Department of Mineral and Energy Affairs, 1983), p. 10; Ruth Edgecombe and Bill Guest, 'The Natal coal industry in the South African economy, 1910–1985', *The South African Journal of Economic History*, 2(2), September 1987, pp. 76–78.

13. Brookes and Webb, *Natal*, p. 258.

14. See Hein Heydenrych, 'Railway development in Natal to 1895' in Guest and Sellers (eds), *Enterprise and exploitation*, pp. 47–69.

15. Renfrew Christie, *Electricity, industry and class in South Africa* (London, MacMillan, 1984), pp. 79, 83–85, 89–93; Edgecombe and Guest, 'Natal coal industry in the South African economy', pp. 57, 60, 61, 66.

16. See Ruth Edgecombe and Bill Guest, 'An introduction to the pre-Union Natal coal industry' in Guest and Sellers (eds), *Enterprise and exploitation*, pp. 309–51.

17. NAD Acc. No. 1336 DCCM vol. 1/1/1/9, 13 July 1925; TAD K27 Coal Shortages Committee, vol. 1, Notule, vol. 3, File S/K 2/1; Edgecombe and Guest, 'Natal coal industry in the South African economy', pp. 55, 61, 63.

18. NAD Acc. No. 1336. DCCM vol. 1/1/1/9, 13 July and 2 December 1925, 27 April, 23 July and 25 August 1926; NCOS vol. 5, 24 November 1924; MVE vol. 354 FS 14651/10, Memorandum on the Introduction of Electric traction, General Manager, SAR & H, 3 February 1926.

19. See Bill Guest, 'Financing an infant coal industry: the case of the Natal collieries', *The South African Journal of Economic History*, 3(2), September 1988, pp. 40–60; Edgecombe and Guest, 'Natal coal industry in the South African economy', pp. 49–70.

20. See Ray Gambell, 'A short history of modern whaling off Natal', *Mercurius*, 14, 1971, pp. 37–45.

21. *Official Year Book*, 1917, p. 477; A. S. B. Humphreys and L. P. McCrystal, *Industrial development*, NRS, Preliminary Report Series, vol. 6 (Durban, Department of Economics, University of Natal, 1964), pp. 76–77; Konczacki, *Natal, 1893–1910*, pp. 5–6, 175, 183–99.

22. Humphreys and McCrystal, *Industrial development*, pp. 4, 5; Konczacki, *Natal, 1893–1910*, pp. 14–15; Bill Guest, 'The new economy' and Andrew Duminy and Bill Guest, 'The Anglo-Boer War and its economic aftermath' in Duminy and Guest (eds), *Natal and Zululand*, pp. 319–20, 354–58.

23. Natal Chamber of Industries, *Fifty years of progress: the development of industry in Natal* (Durban, The Chamber of Industries, 1956), pp. 33–36; Humphreys and McCrystal, *Industrial development*, p. 79; John Stanwix, *A study of the Natal regional economy*, Natal Town and Regional Planning Commission Report, vol. 66 (Pietermaritzburg, Natal Town and Regional Planning Commission, 1985), pp. 8, 11–12, 34–36, 41, 46.

24. Brookes and Webb, *Natal*, p. 259; Humphreys and McCrystal, *Industrial development*, pp. 79–81, 146–47, 162; see also R. T. Bell, *The growth and structure of manufacturing employment in Natal* (Durban, Institute for Social and Economic Research, University of Durban-Westville, 1985).

25. See P. Richardson, 'The Natal sugar industry, 1849–1905: an interpretative essay', *Journal of African History*, 23, 1982, pp. 515–27, reprinted in Guest and Sellers (eds), *Enterprise and exploitation*, pp. 181–97; John Laband and Paul Thompson, 'The reduction of Zululand, 1878–1904' in Duminy and Guest (eds), *Natal and Zululand*, pp. 220–21; R. F. Osborn, *Valiant harvest: the founding of the South African sugar industry, 1848–1926* (Durban, South African Sugar Association, 1964), pp. 93, 194–95; R. F. Osborn, *This man of purpose: Sir James Liege Hulett: pioneer of Natal and Zululand: a biography* (Umhlali, North Coast Sales Promotions, 1973), pp. 73–81.

26. O. P. F. Horwood (ed.) *The Umgeni-Umbilo-Umlazi rivers catchment areas: the Durban-Pietermaritzburg region*, NRS, vol. 14, part 1, (Durban, Department of Economics, University of Natal, 1967), pp. 104, 106, 109, 110, 114; *The South African Sugar Year Book, 1961–62*, pp. 204–5.

27. See Charles Ballard and Giuseppe Lenta, 'The complex nature of agriculture in colonial Natal: 1860–1909' in Guest and Sellers (eds), *Enterprise and exploitation*, pp. 121–49.

28. Konczacki, *Natal, 1893–1910*, pp. 19, 21–22; Brookes and Webb, *Natal*, pp. 258–59; Horwood (ed), *Durban-Pietermaritzburg region*, pp. 119–27.

29. *Union Statistics, 1910–1960*, p. A10; *State of South Africa Year Book*, 1962; *Population Census*, 1960; *South African Statistics*, 1980 (Pretoria, Government Printer, 1980), section 1.13; Konczacki, *Natal, 1893–1910*, p. 5; Brookes and Webb, *Natal*, pp. 257, 260; L. P. McCrystal and C. M. Moore, *An economic survey of Zululand*, NRS Preliminary Report (Durban, Department of Economics, University of Natal, 1967), p. 36.

30. Brookes and Webb, *Natal*, p. 260.

31. See Joy Brain, 'Indentured and free Indians in the economy of colonial Natal' in Guest and Sellers (eds), *Enterprise and exploitation*, pp. 199–233; Joy Brain, 'Natal's Indians, 1860–1910' in Duminy and Guest (eds), *Natal and Zululand*, pp. 249–74, and Surendra Bhana and Joy Brain, *Setting down roots: Indian migrants in South Africa, 1860–1911* (Johannesburg, Witwatersrand University Press, 1990).

32. See Surendra Bhana, 'Indian trade and trader in colonial Natal' in Guest and Sellers (eds), *Enterprise and exploitation*, pp. 235–63.

33. *Official Year Book*, 1917, pp. 147–57; *Union Statistics, 1910–1960*, pp. A3–A5; Thompson, *Unification of South Africa*, pp. 486, 489; Konczacki, *Natal, 1893–1910*, pp. 5–6, 27, 175; Brookes and Webb, *Natal*, pp. 248–50.

34. *State of South Africa Year Book*, 1962; *Population Census*, 1960; Horwood (ed) *Durban-Pietermaritzburg region*, pp. 68–69.

35. See Joy Brain, 'An economic transformation: the Indian community in Natal', essay no. 8 below; see also B. Pachai (ed), *South Africa's Indians: the evolution of a minority* (Washington, University Press of America, 1979) and V. Padayachee et al. *Indian workers and trade unions in Durban, 1930–1950* (Durban Institute for Social and Economic Research, University of Durban-Westville, 1985).

36. Horwood (ed), *Durban-Pietermaritzburg region*, pp. 68–69.

37. See J. Lambert, 'The impoverishment of the Natal peasantry, 1893–1910' in Guest and Sellers (eds), *Enterprise and exploitation*, pp. 287–307 and J. Lambert, 'From independence to rebellion: African society in crisis, c.1880–1910' in Duminy and Guest (eds) *Natal and Zululand*, pp. 373–401.

38. Surplus People Project, vol. 4, *Forced removals in South Africa* (Cape Town, Surplus People Project, 1983), pp. 29–47; Horwood (ed), *Durban-Pietermaritzburg region*, p. 157; Davenport, *South Africa*, p. 413.

39. *Buthelezi Commission*, vol. 1, pp. 77, 147–51; Stanwix, *Natal regional economy*, p. 30.

40. Laband and Thompson, 'The reduction of Zululand' and Lambert, 'From independence to rebellion' in Duminy and Guest (eds), *Natal and Zululand*, pp. 221–24, 396–97.

41. Verne Harris, 'Black-owned land, white farmers and the state in northern Natal, 1910–1936', *Journal of Natal and Zulu History*, 10, 1987, pp. 51–52; Davenport, *South Africa*, p. 293.

42. Surplus People Project, vol. 4, *Forced removals in South Africa*, pp. 29–47; Horwood (ed), *Durban-Pietermaritzburg region*, p. 157.

43. *Union Statistics*, 1960, p. A10; *South African Statistics*, 1980, Section 1.13; Konczacki, *Natal, 1893–1910*, p. 5; M. W. Swanson, ' "The fate of the Natives": black Durban and African ideology', *Natalia*, 14, 1984, pp. 59–60.

44. See M. W. Swanson, 'The "Durban System": roots of urban apartheid in colonial Natal', *African Studies*, 1976 and M. W. Swanson, 'The "Asiatic menace": creating segregation in Durban, 1870–1900', *International Journal of African Historical Studies*, 16, 1983, pp. 401–17; Swanson, 'The fate of the Natives', pp. 59–68.

45. See A. J. Christopher, 'The roots of urban segregation: South Africa at Union, 1910', *Journal of Historical Geography*, 14(2), 1988, pp. 151–69 and J. Laband and R. F. Haswell (eds), *Pietermaritzburg 1838–1988: a new portrait of an African city* (Pietermaritzburg, University of Natal Press and Shuter and Shooter, 1988).

46. See C. Heymans and G. Totemeyer (eds), *Government by the people? The politics of local government in South Africa* (Cape Town, Juta and Co., 1986); T. M. Wills, R. F. Haswell and D. H. Davies, 'The probable consequences of the repeal of the Group Areas Act for Pietermaritzburg', *Report no. 16: Pietermaritzburg 2000* (Pietermaritzburg, City Engineer's Department, 1987); T. R. H. Davenport and K. S. Hunt, *The right to the land* (Cape Town, David Philip, 1974); Tessa Marcus, *Modernizing super-exploitation, restructuring South African agriculture* (London, Zed Books, 1989).

47. See, for example, Padayachee et al. 'Indian workers and trade unions'; H. G. Ringrose, *Trade unions in Natal*, NRS, vol. 4 (Cape Town, Oxford University Press, 1951); J. Lewis, *Industrialisation and trade union organisation in South Africa, 1924–55* (Cambridge, Cambridge University Press, 1984).

48. See, for example, Osborn, *Valiant harvest*; Osborn, *Sir James Liege Hulett*; South African Sugar Association, *The Natal sugar industry* (Durban, South African Sugar Association, 1924); A. Graves and P. Richardson, 'Plantations in the political economy of colonial sugar production: Natal and Queensland, 1860–1914', *Journal of Southern African Studies*, 6(2), 1980, pp. 214–29.

49. See N. Hurwitz, *Agriculture in Natal 1850–1950*, NRS, vol. 12 (Cape Town, Oxford University Press, 1957); E. H. Brookes and N. Hurwitz, *The Native reserves of Natal*, NRS, vol. 7 (Cape Town, Oxford University Press, 1957); W. M. MacMillan, *The South African agrarian problem and its historical development* (Pretoria, State Library, 1974); C. Simkins, 'Agricultural production in the African reserves of South Africa, 1918–1969', *Journal of Southern African Studies*, 7, 1981, pp. 256–83; G. Lenta, *An area study of KwaZulu* (Stellenbosch, Unit for Future Research, University of Stellenbosch, 1982).

50. See, for example, C. Ballard, '"A year of scarcity": the 1896 locust plague in Natal and Zululand', *South African Historical Journal*, 15, 1983, pp. 34–52 and 'The repercussions of rinderpest: cattle, plague and peasant decline in colonial Natal', *International Journal of African Historical Studies*, 19 (3), 1986, pp. 421–50.

51. See, for example, R. J. Davies, 'The growth of the Durban metropolitan area', *South African Geographical Journal*, 45, 1963, pp. 15–43; Swanson, 'The Durban system', 'The Asiatic menace', 'The fate of the Natives'; P. la Hausse, 'Drinking in a cage: the Durban system and the 1929 riots', *Africa Perspective*, 20, 1982, pp. 63–75; P. Maylam, 'The "black belt": African squatters in Durban, 1935–1950', *Canadian Journal of African Studies*, 17, 1983, pp. 413–28; Laband and Haswell (eds) *Pietermaritzburg 1838–1988*.

52. See A. Porter, 'Britain, the Cape Colony and Natal, 1870–1914: capital, shipping and the imperial connexion', *The Economic History Review*, 34(4), 1981; V. E. Solomon, 'The freight rates crisis of 1907', *Journal of Natal and Zulu History*, 4, 1981, pp. 39–48; Paul Dickinson, 'Smith's coasters: the shipping interests of C. G. Smith, 1889–1966', *The South African Journal of Economic History*, 3(1), March 1988, pp. 20–32.

53. See Cherryl Walker (ed), *Women and gender in southern Africa to 1945* (Cape Town, David Philip, 1990).

54. See Thompson, *Natalians first*, and *The Buthelezi Commission*, vols 1 and 2.

ABSTRACT

There was a symbiotic relationship between the expansion of South Africa's foreign trade and domestic industry on the one hand, and the development of Durban's harbour facilities on the other. These were transformed between 1910 and 1980 as a result of the growth and diversification of the South African economy, coupled with Durban's favourable geographical position in relation to the major importing and exporting Vaal Triangle region. The period 1910 to 1924 was an important foundation phase during which the harbour's position as South Africa's premier port was maintained through the provision of additional wharfage at Maydon Wharf and the Bluff, and facilities such as a new coal-loader, oil-storage sites, a grain elevator and a graving dock. The increasing volume of international passengers and cargo, as well as coastwise traffic, continued during the subsequent 1924 to 1945 phase of rapid industrial growth in South Africa initiated by the Pact government. Further improvements, prompted partly by the Harbour Affairs (Nyhoff) Commission (1934/5), were made to Maydon Wharf, including a fish jetty and a marine airport to receive flying-boats, and the Point area, where pre-cooling chambers were erected to handle perishable goods and the new T Jetty increased wharfage by 71 per cent. During the subsequent 1945 to 1980 period of post-war economic expansion an unprecedented volume of business extended harbour development to the Bayhead area, Salisbury Island and Island View on the Bluff. During the 1960s this process was strongly influenced by the trend towards larger ships, including supertankers, and by increased exports which led to the construction of the world's largest sugar terminals at Maydon Wharf. During the 1970s provision was made at Salisbury Island for the modern trend towards containerised shipping freight, as a result of which the new Pier No 2 was developed as the largest container pier in South Africa. The port of Durban was thereby able to consolidate its position as the subcontinent's busiest and most sophisticated harbour.

THE ECONOMY AND THE DEVELOPMENT OF THE PORT OF DURBAN

Anthony Lumby and Ian McLean

Introduction

The economic history of the Port of Durban during the course of the twentieth century provides an accurate reflection of the larger changes which manifested themselves in the modern South African economy. The transformation of the national economy, including that of Natal, from its overwhelmingly agrarian and mining base to an industrialised economy and society carried with it the growth of the Bay of Natal (later Durban) from a mangrove-covered swamp to the busiest and most sophisticated harbour in Africa. That relationship, it must be stressed, was a symbiotic one: the expansion of foreign trade and domestic industry called forth the development of harbour facilities, but it was also the successful response to that challenge which assisted in the remarkable diversification of the South African economy.[1]

The Bay of Natal – 'a splendid lagoon sheltered by the Bluff and the Point'[2] – contains one of the few good harbours along the entire South African coastline.[3] Throughout the colonial history of Natal, however, a sandbar blocked the narrow entrance to the harbour and thus delayed the development of the port. It was not until the conquest of the bar in 1904, and the subsequent regular dredging of the entrance channel and the harbour in general, that the way was opened for the dramatic growth of the port.[4] And with it, of course, went the commercial, industrial and demographic expansion of Durban. Thus, as is only to be expected, there has developed an integral bond between the city and its port, making Durban the leading industrial and tertiary centre of Natal and its financial capital.[5]

Just how dramatic the growth of the Port of Durban has been is immediately apparent from a brief study of maps 1 and 2.

At the time of Union, wharf development was confined to the coaling berths at the Bluff, nine berths at the Point and four berths at Maydon Wharf, all constructed in timber. Seventy years later, in 1980, the port boasted thirteen kilometres of steel and reinforced concrete wharfage on all sides of the harbour; two sets of berths on the north side (Point and Maydon Wharf) and three sets of berths on the south side (the Bluff, Island View and Salisbury Island). More specifically, the Point had been extended by the construction of seven new berths: Q, R and the T Jetty (with L, M,

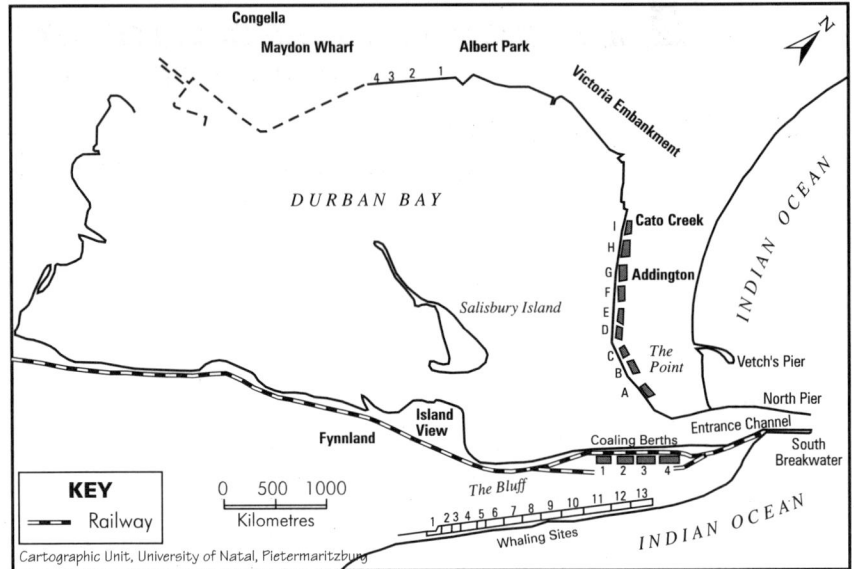

Map 1   Durban harbour in 1910

N, O and P berths which included the Ocean Passenger Terminal). At Maydon Wharf, fifteen berths had been developed, which included the largest grain elevator in South Africa, three storage terminals for handling bulk sugar exports and the Prince Edward Graving Dock for ship repair. On the south side of the harbour, at Island View, nine oil berths served the Shell and Mobil oil refineries. Finally, perhaps the most extensive and certainly the most costly development has been the construction of Pier No.1 and the container terminal at Pier No.2, both at Salisbury Island.

Further evidence of the remarkably rapid growth of the port is contained in the available statistics. The number of vessels handled by the Port of Durban increased more than fourfold from 1 632 in 1910 to the peak of 6 916 in 1970, after which the end of the long post-war boom together with the marked trend towards larger vessels reduced the total number of ships calling at the Port of Durban to 3 916 in 1980. Evidence of the growth in the size of many of those vessels is shown in the twelvefold increase in gross shipping tonnage from 6 830 000 in 1910 to 82 773 000 in 1980. As a result of this expansion, the Port of Durban has established itself as the major port of Africa. Indeed, according to B. Wiese, in 1970 the Port of Durban handled 75 per cent more tonnage than its nearest African rival, Casablanca; almost four times the tonnage handled by Cape Town; and double that of its closest South African rival, Richards Bay.[6]

There can be little doubt that the fundamental reason for this impressive growth lay not only in the concurrent growth and diversification of the South African economy, but more specifically in Durban's favourable geographical position in relation to the Pretoria/Witwatersrand/

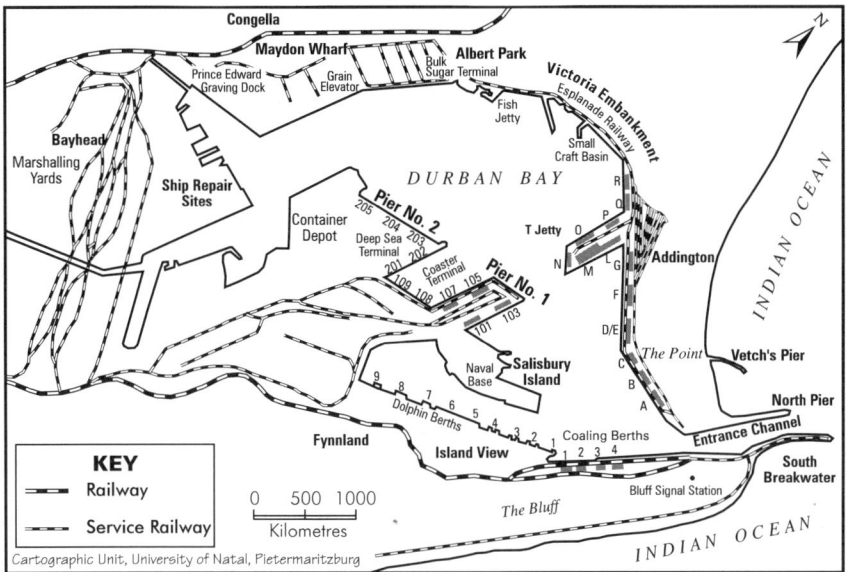

Map 2   Durban harbour in 1980

Vereeniging area. Historically, this area has constituted South Africa's major market for imports and is her major export-producing region, and Durban's proximity gave it a decided advantage over the Cape ports.[7] In addition, Durban's geographical position favoured its port for the shipment of such items as sugar from Natal, timber from the Natal midlands, citrus from Natal and the eastern Transvaal, maize from the southern Transvaal and Orange Free State, coal from northern Natal and the eastern Transvaal, steel from northern Natal and the Witwatersrand, and wool from northern Natal, the Orange Free State and south-eastern Transvaal.[8]

It would be wrong, however, to conclude from this brief overview that the growth of the Port of Durban was merely one of smooth progression. On the contrary, the history of the port's development has been a chequered one – phases of expansion alternating with phases of recession – as has been the case with the South African economy as a whole. Therefore, a proper understanding of the development of the Port of Durban requires a more detailed analysis of the major phases of its development. For this purpose, the period under review falls into three recognisably distinct phases: the foundation years from 1910 to 1924, when the economy was still dominated by agriculture and mining; the phase of rapid industrial growth from 1924 to 1945, when import substitution formed the core of the Government's industrial policy; and the long phase of post-war expansion from 1945 to 1980 – the so-called capitalist boom – which was severely punctured during the early 1970s. This historical periodisation is not only a necessary convenience, providing a form upon which to build a narrative, but it is meaningful in itself in that it reflects the broad trend of development in the international economy throughout the entire period.

At the outset, however, it is necessary to offer a word of caution with regard to some of the statistics used in the text. In the case of South Africa's foreign trade, only the free-on-board (FOB) values of imports are used because, as is evident in table 1, cost-insurance-freight (CIF) values are only available from the 1950s onwards. Furthermore, it should be noted that the values given in table 1 are stated in current prices, and therefore the apparently spectacular growth in South Africa's import-export trade should be scaled down when inflation is taken into account. This is particularly true of the 1970s onwards when inflation assumed more serious proportions. In addition, it is evident that there are some gaps in the statistics contained in tables 4 and 5; and, more seriously, the classification of cargo landed and shipped underwent major changes in the early 1970s which frustrates comparability and explains why 1970 is taken as the terminal date in these two tables. Finally, the statistics relating to the number of vessels handled by the port, contained in table 6, include a large number of smaller vessels (mainly trawlers and coasters), and therefore the gross shipping tonnage handled by the port is perhaps a better guide. Broadly speaking, then, too much reliance should not be placed on the specific statistics in these tables; they should be taken only as an indication of the general trend of development.

Table 1   South Africa's foreign trade 1910–1980 (R million)

Year	Imports		Exports		
	Total: FOB	Total: CIF	Non-Gold	Gold	Total
1910	68		44	64	108
1913	75		58	75	133
1914	63		39	41	80
1918	95		71	70	141
1920	187		104	71	175
1922	94		67	59	126
1924	132		83	80	163
1928	158		106	52	158
1932	65		41	95	136
1936	172		64	164	228
1939	182		68	184	242
1945	220		155	494	649
1950	619	670	540	222	762
1955	962	1 038	738	365	1 103
1960	1 111	1 201	884	536	1 420
1965	1 756	1 912	1 059	767	1 826
1970	2 547	2 812	1 537	837	2 374
1975	6 746	7 252	3 661	2 540	6 201
1980	14 415	15 264	9 817	10 141	19 958

Source: Department of Census and Statistics, *South African Statistics 1982*, p. 16.5.

Table 2   Percentage of overseas cargo landed and shipped at Durban, Cape Town, Port Elizabeth and East London 1910–1980 (by volume)

Year	Durban		Cape Town		Port Elizabeth		East London	
	Landed	Shipped	Landed	Shipped	Landed	Shipped	Landed	Shipped
	%	%	%	%	%	%	%	%
1910	38,9	76,1	25,3	14,6	22,4	3,7	13,4	5,6
1914	37,3	75,4	28,7	15,3	21,7	3,7	12,3	5,6
1918	51,9	67,5	33,2	23,2	9,7	4,8	5,2	4,5
1920	41,1	74,9	31,9	18,5	15,2	3,5	11,8	3,1
1924	44,6	81,8	28,1	12,4	16,1	3,1	11,2	2,7
1928	45,4	76,8	26,2	15,4	15,9	4,1	12,5	3,7
1932	44,4	68,6	34,3	16,3	11,0	8,3	10,3	6,8
1936	44,6	78,3	29,5	13,3	14,5	5,5	11,4	2,9
1939	39,8	64,9	36,1	28,4	12,9	4,6	11,2	2,1
1945	50,9	77,7	29,7	14,5	10,8	6,3	8,6	1,5
1950	42,7	71,4	30,2	19,4	17,5	6,6	9,6	2,6
1955	45,3	55,2	28,9	28,6	16,9	11,1	8,9	5,1
1960	52,4	58,4	24,4	21,9	15,6	13,6	7,6	6,1
1965	67,7	56,3	14,6	17,5	12,2	23,7	5,5	2,5
1970	54,9	49,9	21,1	16,3	17,9	27,7	6,1	6,1
1975	56,6	43,6	18,9	16,1	18,1	30,7	6,4	9,6
1980	65,5	54,7	18,4	9,3	11,0	21,7	5,1	14,3

Source: Derived from Report of the General Manager, *1910 (U.G.39/1911) – 1979–1980 (No R.P. No.)*

Note: Only the major ports of Durban, Cape Town, Port Elizabeth and East London have been included here because they are comparable in terms of the type of cargo handled. The ports of Saldanha and Richards Bay have been excluded because of their highly specialized nature, and the large volumes of iron ore, coal and aluminium handled by these ports would distort the relative performance of those ports which handled general cargo.

Table 3   Percentage of coastwise cargo landed and shipped at Durban, Cape Town, Port Elizabeth and East London 1910–1980 (by volume)

Year	Durban		Cape Town		Port Elizabeth		East London	
	Landed	Shipped	Landed	Shipped	Landed	Shipped	Landed	Shipped
	%	%	%	%	%	%	%	%
1910	4,8	84,2	77,6	11,8	7,7	1,9	9,9	2,1
1914	6,8	81,3	74,6	14,4	9,3	2,3	9,3	2,0
1918	20,6	51,7	46,6	41,5	17,6	3,4	15,2	3,4
1920	16,0	56,6	47,2	33,3	18,4	6,3	18,4	3,8
1924	13,6	60,4	45,6	32,8	19,0	3,4	21,8	3,4
1928	22,8	53,3	38,4	27,6	18,7	12,5	20,1	6,6
1932	17,2	66,0	39,8	20,7	21,1	9,3	21,9	4,0
1936	23,0	50,7	43,3	22,8	17,1	23,9	16,6	2,6
1939	22,6	55,0	43,8	21,7	17,7	21,3	15,9	2,0
1945	8,4	69,3	59,4	22,3	17,1	3,3	15,1	5,1
1950	18,0	69,3	34,4	17,1	24,6	10,4	23,2	3,2
1955	15,4	63,9	43,8	25,4	22,8	7,3	18,0	3,4
1960	13,9	69,4	45,4	20,0	24,8	7,1	15,9	3,5
1965	9,6	82,2	46,0	12,2	26,6	4,4	17,8	1,2
1970	22,9	62,5	42,1	24,1	20,2	10,9	14,8	2,5
1975	22,6	65,5	46,0	26,0	18,7	6,7	12,7	1,8
1980	17,8	72,8	49,5	19,4	18,7	4,4	14,0	3,4

Source: Derived from *Report of the General Manager*, 1910 (U.G.39/1911) – 1979–1980 (No R.P. No.)

Table 4   Overseas cargo landed at Durban 1910–1970 (1000 tons)

Year	General	Timber	Grain	Other produce	Railway goods	Coal	Oil	Explosives	Fertilizers	Sulphur
1910	759	98	8	1						
1914	669	70	12							
1918	594	82	17	3						
1920	439	69	11	3	72	2				
1924	630	141	47		80	7	11	0,8		
1928	938	166	45		64	2	174			
1932	772	95	34		37	0,7	172			
1936	1 191	168	1		54		354			
1939	1 279	167	27		95		423			
1946	1 020	125	136		41		358			
1950	1 583	133	55		30		838			
1955	1 708	173	99		46		1 421			
1960	1 995	116	238		32		2 170			
1965	2 526	121	61		30		5 619		467	105
1970	13 009	124	2		10				48	56

Source: Report of the General Manager, 1910 (U.G.39/1911) – 1969–1970 (No R.P. No.)

Table 5 Overseas cargo shipped from Durban 1910–1970 (1000 tons)

Year	General	Timber	Maize	Wool	Other produce	Coal	Grain	Fruit	Oil	Hominy chop	Ore	Skin/hides	Wattle bark	Sugar
1910	223		46		8	1 809	56							
1914	240	0,6		47	5	1 595	66							
1918	126	3	174	67	114	1 509	1							
1920	132	2	125	63	210	1 417	4							
1924	136	2	363	90	270	2 647	4	3	3					
1928	180	2	243	89	278	2 703	6	10	8	85				
1932	118	0,4	160	77	353	1 423	7	19	7	23	75			
1936	181	0,3	301	80	1	1 927	10	47	16	37	81	22	134	309
1939	149	0,1	175		1	1 726	6	65	49	15	633	21	98	377
1946	260	4		167	4	1 842	2	20	147		358	12	136	150
1950	272		14	50	53	1 372	10	45	279		925	21	169	226
1955	443	20	383	68	136	378	24	45	525	1	408	18	116	369
1960	986		411	78	186	317	89	45	957	18	857	33	144	479
1965	862	8	783	81	234	692	136	113	3 310		1 191	26	102	891
1970	5 634		483	86	460	1 177	41	130			1 382	27	75	1 008

Source: Report of the General Manager, 1910 (U.G.39/1911) – 1969–1970 (No R.P. No.)

Table 6 Vessels handled at the port of
Durban and total gross shipping
tonnage 1910–1980

Table 7 Passengers at Durban
1910–1975

Year	Total no.	Total motor vessels	Total gross tons (1000)	Arrivals	Departures
1910	1 632		6 830	30 340	20 332
1914	1 286		6 091	5 516	11 898
1918	1 283		6 601	2 680	8 120
1922	1 118		5 737	23 108	15 446
1924	1 230		6 442	20 761	12 632
1928	1 391	97	7 292	24 900	29 331
1932	1 185	193	6 791	22 759	24 371
1936	4 767	277	11 031	29 462	28 056
1939	4 396	376	12 220	33 530	30 036
1946	2 863	235	8 631	17 367	12 734
1950	4 107	327	11 246	35 096	17 167
1955	2 848	767	12 581	45 204	20 736
1960	3 796	1 187	17 490	42 210	20 760
1965	4 418	1 722	24 481	48 666	23 198
1970	6 916	3 481	53 670	46 183	32 548
1975	5 495	5 326	121 068	32 294	21 360
1980	3 916	3 799	82 773		

Source: *Report of the General Manager*, 1910 (U.G. 39/1911) – 1969–1980 (No R.P. No.)

The foundation years 1910–1924

At the turn of the century, the composition of South Africa's foreign trade reflected the country's heavy dependence upon the primary sector: agriculture and mining. C.G.W. Schumann has argued that much of the expansion experienced was the result of cyclical recovery from the South African War.[9] In those conditions of 'mild prosperity', which lasted almost until the outbreak of the First World War in 1914, the growth of the Union's foreign trade exerted pressure for the improvement and extension of harbour facilities. Thus, at the north side of the Port of Durban – the Point – 1 610 feet of wooden wharf were replaced with a 710-foot concrete quay and Berth A was extended.[10] At Congella, behind Maydon Wharf, major reclamation work was begun in order to provide commercial and industrial sites adjacent to the harbour. At the same time, discussions were held in 1912 with a view to the construction of a graving dock at Cato Creek. Although the plans were completed in 1914, construction was held in abeyance because of the outbreak of war and financial stringency.[11]

The First World War marked the first significant phase of industrial development: the disruptive effects of the war on the supply of imported goods actually forced South Africa into a phase of import substitution.[12]

Thus, according to table 1, the value of South Africa's imports fell sharply between 1913 and 1914 but had recovered by 1918, as was the case with South Africa's exports. Given South Africa's experience with war-time inflation, this phase of contraction was in fact worse than indicated in the official statistics, and it was bound to have been felt at the ports. Nevertheless, it is evident from table 2 that the Port of Durban maintained its premier position: the percentage of overseas cargo landed at Durban (of all overseas cargo landed at Durban, Cape Town, Port Elizabeth and East London) rose markedly from 37,3 per cent in 1914 to 51,9 per cent in 1918, although the share of overseas cargo shipped from Durban slipped from 75,4 per cent in 1914 to 67,5 per cent in 1918. According to table 4, gains were registered in the importation of timber and grain through the Port of Durban, and perhaps the latter came in response to the steep decline in the shipment of grain through Durban (see table 5).

Further evidence of the effects of the war is provided in tables 6 and 7. At first glance it is curious that the number of ships and gross shipping tonnage handled by the port did not experience any significant decline during the war years, but it must be borne in mind that the increased number of vessels in war service which called at Durban tended to offset the decline in commercial shipping.[13] A more accurate reflection of the impact of the war is to be found in passenger traffic: the number of passengers arriving at the Port of Durban slumped from 30 340 in 1910 to 5 516 in 1914 and declined even further to 2 680 in 1918, while the number of passengers departing from Durban showed a less marked decline from 20 332 in 1910 to 11 898 in 1914 and to 8 210 in 1918.

Despite the difficulties experienced during the war years, work on the expansion of the Port of Durban continued in certain strategic areas. For example, the importance of coal for both bunkering and the export trade was responsible for the opening in 1917 of a new coal-loading appliance at the Bluff. It comprised a dumper and a conveyor belt and was capable of discharging 600 tons per hour. At the same time, the conversion from coal- to oil-powered vessels raised the need for off-loading and storage sites for oil, as a result of which 100 acres were reserved for these purposes at Island View, of which 50 acres had still to be reclaimed.[14] Meanwhile, the Grain Elevator Committee submitted its report to the government in 1917. It recommended the construction of 36 grain elevators throughout the Union, including one at Maydon Wharf.[15] Although the government accepted these recommendations, it was not until 1919 that it authorised expenditure for the commencement of construction.[16] A further development during the war years related to the proposed graving dock at Cato Creek. As a result of difficulties with the Cato Creek site, and because Maydon Wharf appeared to be more convenient in view of the possible development of a ship-building industry in the area, it was decided to switch the location of the graving dock from Cato Creek to Maydon Wharf.[17] However, as was the case with the grain elevator, the commencement of construction was delayed until the end of the war.[18]

The cessation of hostilities in 1918 ushered in a short, sharp post-war boom in 1919–20, but once the pent-up wartime demand had been met, the boom gave way to an equally sharp post-war depression in 1921–22, from which recovery was only partially completed by the mid-1920s. These trends are reflected in the movements of South Africa's foreign trade for this period. The value of imports rose sharply from R95 million in 1918 to R187 million in 1920, fell back to R94 million in 1922, but had recovered some of the lost ground to stand at R132 million in 1924. In similar fashion, the value of South Africa's exports rose from R141 million in 1918 to R175 million in 1920, fell back to R126 million in 1922 and had almost completely recovered to R163 million in 1924. It must be stressed that the continuation of chronic inflation in the immediate post-war years has tended to overstate the real rate of growth, but the overall trend in South Africa's foreign trade remains unaffected.

In the midst of these uncertain economic conditions, extension work at the harbour commenced in earnest, and the focal point of development was Maydon Wharf. The 2 000-foot extension (Berths 6, 8 and 15 started in 1916) which had been delayed because of the war, was taken up once more and completed in 1920–21.[19] At the same time, work was begun on the construction of the graving dock at Maydon Wharf at a cost of R2 600 000. When it was completed in February 1925, and named the Prince Edward Graving Dock, it was 1 150 feet long, 110 feet broad and divisible into two chambers.[20] In addition, the government had authorised almost R2 million in 1919 for the construction of a grain elevator at Maydon Wharf. Although construction was delayed because of problems with the foundations, when it was completed and brought into operation in August 1927, it was the largest in South Africa with a capacity of 42 000 tons and capable of handling 1 000 tons per hour.[21] Meanwhile, the reclamation work that had begun at Congella (behind Maydon Wharf) before the war was continued throughout the 1920s, and this ambitious project was only to be completed in the mid-1930s.

While Maydon Wharf occupied centre-stage in harbour developments, the early 1920s also witnessed important developments in other parts of the port. Thus, in 1918, authority was given for a 780-foot eastward extension of the wharfage at the Bluff, a project that was completed in 1922–23.[22] Concurrently, good progress had been achieved with the reclamation of land at Island View for the establishment of off-loading and storage sites for oil, and by 1923 three oil tanks and three benzine tanks were in use. At the same time, work was begun on the construction of a timber wharf for oil ships at Island View.[23] Meanwhile, pressure on the limited number of berths at the Point stimulated discussions on the need for additional wharfage and sheds, and although little was achieved during the early 1920s, these ongoing discussions ultimately led to the decision to construct the T Jetty.[24]

Not surprisingly, these developments were accompanied by a heightened tempo of activity in terms of cargo and passengers handled by the port. Although the statistical evidence contained in tables 4 and 5 is fragmentary for this period, it is apparent that there was a significant increase in the landing of timber, grain and oil at Durban during the first half of the 1920s, while increased quantities of coal and maize were shipped from Durban. Furthermore, although the number of ships and gross shipping tonnage edged up only marginally, the number of passengers arriving at and departing from the port had recovered from the war-time lows. It is also apparent from table 2 that the Port of Durban's position *vis-à-vis* other South African ports had remained fundamentally unchanged. Indeed, it actually strengthened during the first half of the 1920s: the percentage of overseas cargo landed at Durban (of all overseas cargo landed at Durban, Cape Town, Port Elizabeth and East London) rose from 41,1 per cent in 1920 to 44,6 per cent in 1924, while Durban's percentage of overseas cargo shipped also rose from 74,9 per cent in 1920 to an all-time high of 81,8 per cent in 1924. These gains, it should be noted, were made largely at the expense of Cape Town.

Finally, mention ought to be made of the Port of Durban's significant role in coastwise traffic during these years. This was particularly true of the shipment of goods from Durban as she required little of the coastal traffic for her own consumption. This pattern is evident in table 3 which reveals that the percentage of coastwise cargo landed at Durban (of all coastwise cargo landed at Durban, Cape Town, Port Elizabeth and East London) declined from 16 per cent in 1920 to 13,6 per cent in 1924, while that shipped from Durban rose from 56,6 per cent in 1920 to 60,4 per cent in 1924. Virtually all of this coastal shipping was conducted by three companies: Smith's Coasters, which was primarily involved in transporting sugar between Durban and East London; African Coasters, which shipped Natal exports (such as newsprint produced from wattle bark) to the Cape and petroleum from Durban to Lourenço Marques (now Maputo); and Thesen's Steamship Company, based in Cape Town, which took supplies up the west coast.[25]

Thus, by the mid-1920s, the foundations had been laid for the development of local industry, although the Smuts Government still shied away from the adoption of a fully fledged policy of tariff protection in support of domestic industry.[26] At the same time, the foundations had also been laid for extending the Port of Durban – especially at Maydon Wharf and the Bluff – in order to maintain Durban's position at the forefront of harbour activities in the country. As will be seen, both these developments were to experience major leaps forward from the mid-1920s onwards.

Rapid industrial growth 1924–1945

The election to power of the Nationalist-Labourite coalition in 1924 proved to be a watershed in the development of the South African economy. The so-called Pact government was the first to introduce a fully fledged policy of tariff protection for the encouragement of a wide range of domestic industries.[27] The subsequent growth of local industry, including the Durban/Pinetown industrial complex in Natal, had a powerful effect upon South Africa's foreign trade: the early phase of induced industrial growth in South Africa was accompanied by a growing volume of imported raw materials and capital equipment for industry.[28] Thus it is not surprising that, as shown in table 1, the value of South Africa's imports rose

Aerial view of the T Jetty at the Point, showing the ocean terminal and office block completed in 1962.

substantially from R132 million in 1924 to R158 million in 1928, although the value of exports actually fell over the same period from R163 million to R158 million (largely because of the sharp drop in gold exports).

It was only to be expected that these developments would be reflected in the import-export trade handled by South Africa's harbours, including the Port of Durban. According to tables 4 and 5, declines were registered in the landing of grain, railway equipment and coal, but there were major gains in the landing of oil and 'general' imports which included industrial raw materials and capital equipment. In the case of shipments from the Port of Durban, the only decline registered during the second half of the 1920s was maize, for the export of all other items listed appears to have increased, especially wood and hominy chop.[29] The port was also the centre of the South African whaling industry.[30] Further evidence of the growth in business handled by Durban is shown in tables 6 and 7: there was an increase in the number of ships and gross shipping tonnage handled by the port, and there was a substantial rise in the number of passenger arrivals and departures through Durban.

This increased activity in trade and passengers was accompanied by continued construction work in the harbour. Thus, at the Bluff, the rapid conversion from coal- to oil-driven vessels and the greater demand for oil for industrial and transport usage quickened the pace of development at Island View. Construction on Berth 5 commenced in 1924 and was completed in 1929, while work was also begun on a 500-foot extension (which was to become Berth 7) in steel sheet piling.[31] Expansion also took place elsewhere in the harbour, especially at Maydon Wharf and the Point. At Maydon Wharf, approval was obtained for the reclamation of three sites and the erection of a 400-foot Fish Jetty in the vicinity of Albert Park. The construction of this jetty – begun in 1926 and completed in 1929 – encouraged the move of associated industry from the Point to Congella (behind Maydon Wharf), where considerable progress had been made in the reclamation of land for commercial and industrial usage.[32] Meanwhile, in 1926, the Perishable Products Export Control Board had recommended the erection of pre-cooling chambers at B Shed at the Point in order to handle fruit, frozen and chilled beef, eggs and butter. Construction work on this particular project was started in 1927 and the pre-cooling chambers were brought into operation in June 1930.[33]

These developments – in both foreign trade and harbour construction – ensured that the Port of Durban was able to maintain its position *vis-à-vis* other South African ports. According to table 2, the percentage of overseas cargo landed at Durban (of all overseas cargo landed at Durban, Cape Town, Port Elizabeth and East London) rose marginally from 44,6 per cent in 1924 to 45,5 per cent in 1928, although the percentage of overseas cargo shipped from Durban fell over the same period from 81,8 per cent to 76,8 per cent, largely to the benefit of Cape Town. Furthermore, it is also evident from table 3 that the established pattern of coastwise shipping remained fundamentally unaltered: Durban's favourable geographical position made it South Africa's premier port for the shipment of coastwise cargo.[34]

Meanwhile, as the 1920s drew to a close, an economic depression of unprecedented severity threatened the world economy. The general instability of the 1920s ultimately brought about a financial collapse on the New York stock exchange in October 1929, and within the year the depression set in. Although South Africa's agricultural exports suffered, the anti-cyclical expansion of the gold-mining industry cushioned the initial impact of the depression and local industry fared comparatively well.[35] For South Africa, it was the financial crisis of 1931 which severely disrupted her economy: Britain's abandonment of the gold standard and devaluation of sterling in September 1931, and South Africa's refusal to follow suit, placed the South African currency at a premium over the currencies of those countries that had abandoned gold and devalued their currencies. The inevitable result was a slump in South Africa's foreign trade.

According to table 1, the value of South Africa's imports fell sharply from R158 million in 1928 to R65 million in 1932, and although the value of total exports fell much less dramatically, from R158 million to R136 million, non-gold exports slumped from R106 million to R41 million. It was only to be expected that this contraction would have severe repercussions upon the Port of Durban. Table 4 indicates that there was a decline in all categories of imports through Durban, with timber and railway equipment amongst the worst hit; while, according to table 5, there was a decline in the shipment of most items through Durban, especially maize, coal and hominy chop. Furthermore, not only did the number of ships and gross shipping tonnage handled by the harbour experience contraction, but so did both passenger arrivals and departures.

Although the depression adversely affected the South African economy, and, through this, the volume of business handled by local harbours, it does not appear to have had a marked effect upon construction work in the Port of Durban. The likely explanation is that the funds required for construction work had been made available before the worst effects of the depression made themselves felt in 1931–32.[36] Furthermore, the effects of the crisis were short-lived, for once South Africa abandoned the gold standard and devalued her currency in December 1932, the concurrent increase in the price of gold played a crucial role in the considerable prosperity which characterised the remainder of the 1930s.[37] Within the port, the focal points of attention were once again Maydon Wharf and the Point. At Maydon Wharf, the wharfage was considerably extended between 1929 and 1933–34: Berths 9, 10, 12, 13 and 14 were constructed in timber.[38] Meanwhile, the pressure for additional facilities at the Point brought related discussions to a head in 1930. It was proposed that a 1 000-foot wharf be constructed along the length of the Victoria Embankment, but this suggestion met with a public outcry against the possible loss of bay amenities.[39] In response to this hostile reaction, the South African Railways and Harbours Administration backed down, and commenced instead with the construction of a railway-line along the Esplanade which was completed in 1938.[40]

Meanwhile, in July 1934, the government had appointed the Harbour

Affairs Commission – otherwise known as the Nyhoff Commission – to investigate the general position of harbours in the country and to recommend policy for future development. In their report, submitted in 1935, the commissioners stated at the outset that the Port of Durban was undoubtedly South Africa's most important harbour. The reason for this, they argued, was Durban's well-known advantages: the shortest rail distance to the Witwatersrand, the port of entry for traffic through the Suez Canal and, not least of all, the 'excellent natural facilities for development and extension'.[41] However, the commissioners were of the opinion that the Port of Durban lagged far behind in harbour facilities, and that the need for improvements at Durban were more urgent than the proposed improvements at Cape Town harbour. Therefore, it was recommended that the savings effected by cutting back on proposed developments at Cape Town be used for the improvement of Durban harbour.[42]

Nevertheless, the essential thrust of the Nyhoff Commission's recommendations for improvement – the deepening of all berths around the Durban harbour – was not accepted by the South African Railways and Harbours Administration because it would result in a serious loss of berthage while the necessary dredging was in operation. Instead, it was decided to develop two new berths at the Point – Berths Q and R – which would provide an additional 1 240 feet of wharfage. Construction work on these new berths began in 1936, and Berth R was completed in 1939, while Berth Q became operational in 1940.[43] Meanwhile, in 1937, a Departmental Committee of the South African Railways and Harbours Administration recommended that Berth I (which lay between Berths H and Q) should be eliminated and the wharf extended as the T Jetty. This decision required the approval of the Durban City Council for, in terms of an agreement reached in 1931, it had been decided that no structure would be permitted to protrude into the heart of the harbour. Given the urgent need for additional berthage, however, the council gave its approval and construction work on the T Jetty commenced in 1937.[44]

Alongside these developments at the Point, construction work was also in progress at Maydon Wharf. As a result of the growing popularity of air travel during the 1930s, it was decided to build a marine airport at Maydon Wharf (alongside the Prince Edward Graving Dock) in order to accommodate the flying-boats operated by Imperial Airways. Construction began in 1937 and the marine airport was completed in 1939 at a cost of R120 000.[45] At the same time, authority was also given in 1937–38 for the renewal of all berths at Maydon Wharf in steel sheet piling; but this long-term project was to be delayed by the outbreak of the Second World War, and it was only completed in the late 1960s.[46]

The remarkable phase of expansion during the 1930s is reflected in the increased volume of business conducted by the Port of Durban in those years. Table 4 indicates substantial gains in the landing of timber and railway equipment, but, above all, in oil and 'general' imports (which, as already pointed out, included raw materials and capital equipment for industry). As for the shipment of exports from Durban, table 5 shows significant increases in coal, fruit, oil and manganese ore. Additional evidence of the heightened tempo of activity in the 1930s is to be found in tables 6 and 7. The number of ships handled by the port almost quadrupled, while gross shipping tonnage almost doubled; concurrently, there was also a marked rise in the number of passengers arriving at and departing from Durban.

Notwithstanding these features of impressive growth, however, table 2 indicates a deterioration in the Port of Durban's position *vis-á-vis* other South African ports. The percentage of overseas cargo landed at Durban (of all overseas cargo landed at Durban, Cape Town, Port Elizabeth and East London) fell from 44,4 per cent in 1932 to 39,8 per cent in 1939, while the percentage of overseas cargo shipped from Durban also declined over the same period from 68,4 per cent to 64,9 per cent. This downward trend stemmed from the lack of adequate facilities at Durban harbour – a problem which had been highlighted by the Nyhoff Commission report in 1935. However, once the spate of construction work in Durban harbour reached completion in the late 1930s and early 1940s, the availability of additional facilities enabled the Port of Durban to reassert itself as South Africa's major port.[47]

Meanwhile, the Second World War intervened, and although it did not exert a seriously disruptive effect upon South Africa's foreign trade, it did affect the composition of that trade in that items of strategic importance were given preference. Thus, according to table 4, virtually all categories of items landed at Durban declined during the war. In the case of exports, table 5 shows an increase in the shipment of strategically important items such as timber, wool, coal and oil, and a fall in the shipment of nonstrategic items such as maize, grain, fruit and sugar. Furthermore, although there was a decline in gross shipping tonnage handled by the harbour, the extent of the decline in commercial shipping was masked by the increase in the number of vessels in war service that called at Durban during the war years. Further, as was only to be expected, there was a sharp contraction in the number of passengers arriving at and departing from Durban, a reflection of the extent to which passenger liners had been requisitioned for the war effort.

Despite the financial stringency of the war years, construction work continued at the Port of Durban. The projects which had been commissioned in the late 1930s now assumed strategic importance, as did the new projects initiated during the war. Thus, additional berthage was made available at Maydon Wharf (at what was to become Berth 11) with the construction of a dolphin berth – that is, a floating berth – which was brought into operation in 1942, while dolphin Berths 1, 2 and 3 were built at Island View on the Bluff in order to cater for increased shipments of oil.[48] At the Point, work continued on the building of the T Jetty, and by the end of the war it had been completed. Berths N, O and P were in full operation, but Berths M and L were only in partial use because the sheds had yet to be completed. This project represented a major step forward for the harbour, for it provided a 71 per cent increase in wharfage at the Point.[49]

Thus, during the years of rapid industrial growth in the second half of the 1920s and throughout the 1930s, the Port of Durban expanded its facilities in the service of an increasingly diversified economy. In retrospect, it is apparent that it was engaged in a struggle to cope with the pressure on berthage, especially during the late 1920s and much of the 1930s. However, the Nyhoff Commission's decision to focus attention on Durban harbour, and the subsequent spate of harbour expansion that followed in the late 1930s and early 1940s, ensured that the Port of Durban would retain pride of place amongst South Africa's ports.

The growth to maturity 1945–1980

From the late 1940s through to the early 1970s, the international economy experienced a phase of unprecedented expansion. Among the factors which account for this buoyant phase were the reformulation of the international monetary system following the Bretton Woods Conference of 1944, which established the International Monetary Fund and the World Bank; Marshall Aid, in terms of which the United States facilitated the post-war reconstruction of much of western Europe and Japan; and the General Agreement on Tariffs and Trade, which helped to free international trading relations from the protectionist strait-jacket of the inter-war years. All these factors combined to produce the so-called long capitalist boom of the 1950s and 1960s.[50]

At the end of the war, South Africa was well positioned to take advantage of these more favourable conditions. She had not suffered the same degree of physical devastation as western Europe and therefore was more able to respond to the upsurge in post-war demand. Thus the South African economy enjoyed a phase of rapid growth following the end of the war; one which spilled over into the 1950s. An indication of this expansion is contained in table 1: the value of South Africa's imports rose at an unprecedented rate from R220 million in 1945 to R619 million in 1950 and then almost doubled to R1 111 million in 1960; while, concurrently, the value of South Africa's exports increased from R649 million to R762 million and then almost doubled to R1 420 million. It was inevitable that this remarkable upsurge in South Africa's foreign trade would make itself felt at her harbours, particularly her most important port at Durban.

The direct effects were transmitted through the increased volume of business handled by the Port of Durban. Table 4 reveals that substantial gains were registered in the landing of oil and 'general' imports, which reflected the growth of domestic industry, while table 5 indicates that there were significant increases in the shipment of maize, grain, oil, manganese ore and sugar from Durban. There was, however, a steep decline in the export of coal as South Africa struggled to compete with new suppliers in the world market. Further evidence of expansion is contained in table 6: there was a sharp increase in the number of vessels handled by the harbour, and gross shipping tonnage more than doubled between 1946 and 1960. Finally, table 7 indicates that there had been a considerable rise in the number of passenger arrivals and departures, particularly the former, which not only reflected the heyday of the Union Castle mailships but also the importance of assisted immigration to South Africa during the late 1940s and early 1950s.

Meanwhile, the indirect effects of this phase of expansion were manifested in further construction work at the harbour. In 1946, the Bayhead Development Committee was established to consider the future of the Bayhead area and that portion of Salisbury Island which did not fall under Admiralty control. The Committee concluded that the Bayhead should be utilised for ship repairs, and that once the Point and Maydon Wharf had been fully developed, the pressure for additional berths could only be met at Island View and Salisbury Island.[51] In fact, this was to be the pattern of harbour development during the post-war decades. At Island View on the Bluff, a start was made in 1950 with the rebuilding of Berths 5 and 6, while the concrete platform for dolphin Berth 4 was completed for Mobil in 1953. In that same year, construction was begun on a 1 000-foot turning basin between Island View and Salisbury Island, which was completed in 1957–58.[52] At the Point, plans were drawn up in 1957 for the construction of various buildings on the T Jetty: a modern passenger terminal, pre-cooling chambers and additional sheds at Berths L and M, and a new office block for the Port Captain and the Port Goods Superintendent. This particular phase of construction was completed in 1962.[53] Meanwhile, at Maydon Wharf, work was restarted on the renewal of all berths in steel sheet piling; and between 1957 and 1959, Berths 10 and 12 were linked with a continuous concrete quay.[54]

These developments allowed the Port of Durban to retain its strong position *vis-à-vis* other South African ports, although its former dominant position was eroded. According to table 2, the percentage of overseas cargo landed at Durban (of all overseas cargo landed at Durban, Cape Town, Port Elizabeth and East London) slipped during the late 1940s from 50,9 per cent in 1945 to 42,7 per cent in 1950, but regained lost ground during the 1950s when it rose to 45,3 per cent in 1955 and then to 52,4 per cent in 1960. At the same time, however, the percentage of overseas cargo shipped from Durban evidenced a general downward trend throughout the late 1940s and the 1950s, from 77,7 per cent in 1945 to 58,4 per cent in 1960. This decline is largely explained by the sharp fall in coal exports through Durban during the 1950s, and therefore should not be interpreted as reflecting a broad-based phase of contraction for the harbour. As for the transport of coastwise cargo, table 3 indicates that the Port of Durban continued to dominate the shipment of coastal trade; and, in fact, the volume of coastwise cargo increased after the South African Railways abolished 'sea competitive rates' in 1954.[55]

In the early 1960s, South Africa's long-term phase of economic growth was severely punctured by a critical balance of payments crisis in 1960–61. Although South Africa had experienced balance of payments crises before, the crisis of 1961 was significantly different in that it stemmed from economic causes severely aggravated by political factors. Against the background of a rather weak recovery from the balance of payments crisis of 1958, the tragic consequences of the civil disobedience campaign at Sharpeville in March 1960, and the subsequent declaration of a state of emergency, led to a crisis of confidence in the South African economy and a rapid outflow of capital.[56] Contrary to expectations, however, the adoption of stringent fiscal measures and a tough political stance turned the slump of 1960–61 into a boom which lasted until 1965.[57] Thereafter, the unusually high rate of economic growth produced bottlenecks in the economy, and the adoption of restrictive fiscal measures in late 1965 engendered a slow-down in the economy that continued throughout the remainder of the 1960s.[58]

These overall trends are clearly apparent in South Africa's foreign trade. According to table 1, the value of South Africa's imports more than doubled from R1 111 million in 1960 to R2 547 million in 1970, while the value of South Africa's exports rose less markedly from R1 420 million in 1960 to R2 374 million in 1970. Looking more specifically at the import-export trade handled by the Port of Durban during the 1960s, table 4 reveals a substantial increase in oil imports, but there were declines in the importation of grain, railway equipment, fertilizers and sulphur. Of the overseas cargo shipped from Durban, table 5 shows that coal exports rose almost fourfold, fruit exports increased threefold and sugar exports doubled. Furthermore, between 1960 and 1965 alone, oil exports from Durban increased more than threefold.[59] In addition, the gross shipping tonnage handled by the harbour trebled during the 1960s, and this points to the trend towards larger ships – tankers and super-tankers – which called at Durban.

It was the last of these developments – the trend towards larger ships – which exerted a strong influence on harbour construction during the 1960s. In 1958, the Standing Committee which oversaw harbour development had put forward three recommendations for expansion at Island View: firstly, the construction of an additional dolphin berth – Berth 8 – because of the new Shell oil refinery; secondly, the deepening of Berth 7 to 42 feet LWOST (Low Water Ordinary Spring Tide) to cater for 50 000-ton oil tankers; and, thirdly, the widening of the turning basin between Island View and Salisbury Island to 1 400 feet. Work on these projects began in 1961 and was completed in stages during 1963–64, at which time work was begun on the construction of Berth 9 which was completed in 1969.[60] Meanwhile, extensions were made to the plant at the coaling berths at the Bluff in order to handle anthracite, pig-iron and other bulk products because of the growth of new markets for these items in the Far East.[61]

At the same time, the continued expansion of sugar exports through Durban led to the decision to build a bulk sugar terminal at Berth 2 at Maydon Wharf, where special storage and shipping facilities would be made available. Construction began in 1962, and when completed in 1964 it was the largest sugar terminal in the world, with a total capacity of 200 000 tons and a loading capacity of 500 tons per hour. The construction of a second storage building, adjoining the first, during the late 1960s doubled total storage capacity to 400 000 tons.[62] As important as this project undoubtedly was, it was to be overshadowed by the decision to build Pier No. 1 at Salisbury Island. As had been pointed out by the

Bayhead Development Committee in 1946, once the Point and Maydon Wharf had become fully developed, the pressure for additional berthage could only be met at Island View and that part of Salisbury Island not under Admiralty control. Given the specialised development of Island View for oil tankers, attention was turned to Salisbury Island. It was decided that a new pier would be built – Pier No. 1 – which would provide four additional berths. To this end, construction work began in 1965 and Pier No. 1 was completed and fully operational in 1969.[63]

During the course of construction of Pier No. 1, the decision was also made to accommodate the revolutionary change that was taking place in the handling of shipping freight. The conventional method of loading freight involved the movement of hundreds, perhaps thousands, of cargo 'loads' from shore to ship, a task performed by stevedores that was both time-consuming and costly. The search for an alternative method was found in containerisation, a concept that was first introduced to the ocean-carrying trade in 1965. Following this method, cargo is stored in containers of standard dimensions – Twenty-foot Equivalent Units (TEUs)[64] – which are transported in specially designed container ships, sometimes referred to as 'cellular' ships. The advantages of containerisation have been summarised by V. E. Solomon: loading is simplified, especially if the ship is a 'RoRo' (Roll-on, Roll-off) which eliminates cranage; labour costs are reduced; time is saved with a faster turn-around because 'one special container berth does the work of five conventional berths'; packing costs are reduced; and cargo enjoys greater protection and thus insurance is lower.[65]

In order to cater for containerised traffic, the decision was made to adapt Pier No. 2 – adjacent to Pier No. 1 at Salisbury Island – for containerisation. Construction work on this project, the most ambitious and costly to date, began in 1969 and was only completed in 1977 at a cost of R90 million. As will be seen, this development helped to consolidate the Port of Durban's position at a time when, according to table 2, the percentage of overseas cargo shipped from Durban fell below 50 per cent in 1970 for the first time in the twentieth century. Nevertheless, the Port of Durban maintained its dominant position in coastwise shipping; and here it ought to be noted that the pressure of rising costs in the late 1960s forced the three major coastal shipping companies to amalgamate under the name of Unicorn Lines, backed by Union Corporation and Safmarine.[66]

Meanwhile, the long boom that had characterised the international economy during the 1950s and 1960s came under increasing strain, especially as inflation assumed more serious proportions. This inflationary spiral was given a vicious upward twist when the Organisation of Petroleum Exporting Countries (OPEC) quadrupled the crude-oil price in late 1973, and the international economy entered a phase of contraction that lasted throughout the 1970s.[67] South Africa, too, was affected by the break-up of the long post-war boom, but the substantial rise in the free market price for gold went a long way towards offsetting these adverse conditions. Thus, as shown in table 1, the value of South Africa's imports rose dramatically from R2 547 million in 1970 to R14 415 million in 1980, while the value of her exports increased even more rapidly over the same period from R2 374 million to R19 958 million (half of which was accounted for by gold exports). Even when the rampant inflation of almost 150 per cent for the decade of the 1970s is taken into account, it is clear that South Africa's foreign trade experienced rapid growth, and this was reflected in the heightened tempo of business in her harbours.

At the Port of Durban, the focus of attention during the 1970s fell on the construction of Pier No. 2 at Salisbury Island. When it finally came into operation in July 1977, it was the largest container pier in South Africa, with five deep-sea container berths (Berths 201–205), seven giant ship-to-shore wharf cranes, each with a lifting capacity of 40 tons, and twenty-six hectares of stacking space for 18 838 TEUs.[68] The final phase of construction, which gave the Port of Durban its present configuration, came in the closing years of the decade when the 545-foot cross-berths (Berths 108 and 109) were built between Piers No. 1 and 2 for handling coastal container traffic.[69] There was, however, a less cheerful development during the 1970s: the worldwide shift to containerisation and rising operating costs, together with the popularisation of air travel as a means of passenger transport, dealt a shattering blow to the passenger liner, and in 1977 the mailship service between England and South Africa was phased out.[70]

Even though the 'mailboat' era had become a nostalgic memory by the 1980s, and an important part of the port's business had been lost, the decisive shift towards catering for container traffic during the 1970s had enabled the Port of Durban to reassert its dominant position amongst South Africa's ports. Thus, as is evident in table 2, the percentage of overseas cargo landed at Durban (of all overseas cargo landed at Durban, Cape Town, Port Elizabeth and East London) rose from 54,9 per cent in 1970 to 65,5 per cent in 1980. By the latter date, the percentage of overseas cargo landed at Durban was three times greater than that of Cape Town, six times that of Port Elizabeth and almost thirteen times that of East London. As for the percentage of overseas cargo shipped from Durban, not only had this recovered from the low of 49,9 per cent in 1970 to 54,7 per cent in 1980, but, at the latter date, it was six times that of Cape Town, just over four times that of East London and almost three times that of Port Elizabeth.

By the 1980s, then, the Port of Durban had consolidated its position as the busiest and most sophisticated harbour in South Africa. And in that process, not only has it contributed to the transformation of the country's economic heartland on the Witwatersrand, but the second largest concentration of industries and population has grown up around the harbour. Indeed, since the late 1960s, the Greater Durban/Pinetown conurbation has developed into a leading industrial region: principally, the Jacobs/Mobeni/Merebank complex (textiles, chemicals and food), the Maydon Wharf/Congella area (chemicals, engineering, food and clothing) and the Pinetown/New Germany area (textiles and footwear).[71] Thus the remarkable success with which the Port of Durban met the challenges of the twentieth century – from the conquest of the bar in 1904 to containerisation in the 1970s – underscores the role which the harbour has played in the development of the wider economy to which it belongs.

REFERENCES

1. F. Broeze, P. Reeves and K. McPherson, 'Imperial ports and the modern world economy', *Journal of Transport History*, 7(2), September 1986, p. 1.

2. A. F. Hattersley, *More annals of Natal* (Pietermaritzburg, Shuter and Shooter, 1936), p. 63.

3. It ought to be noted, however, that the Port of Durban remains an extremely difficult port in terms of vessel navigation: the passage of ships from heavy sea conditions immediately outside the breakwaters to the narrow entrance channel is difficult; and once inside the harbour, the stopping distance is very limited.

4. See L. Heydenrych, 'Port Natal harbour, *c.*1850–1897', in Bill Guest and John M. Sellers (eds), *Enterprise and exploitation in a Victorian colony* (Pieter-maritzburg, University of Natal Press, 1985), pp. 17–43. The conquest of the sandbar was achieved during the late nineteenth and early twentieth centuries, and the *Armadale Castle*, in 1904, was the first large vessel to enter the Port of Durban in 1904.

5. C. D. J. Atkinson, 'The pattern of industrial development in Durban: past, present and future', M.T.R.P., University of Natal, 1967, pp. 11–12.

6. B. Wiese, *Seaports and port cities of southern Africa* (Wiesbaden, Franz Steiner Verlag, 1981), p. 2.

7. See M. Boucher, 'The Cape and foreign shipping', *South African Historical Journal*, 6, 1974, pp. 3–29. The railway mileages between the four major ports and Johannesburg are as follows: Cape Town-Johannesburg: 956 miles; Port Elizabeth-Johannesburg: 712 miles; East London-Johannesburg: 665 miles; and Durban-Johannesburg: 482 miles.

8. Wiese, *Seaports and port cities*, pp. 98, 106.

9. C. G. W. Schumann, *Structural changes and business cycles in South Africa, 1806–1936* (London, P. S. King, 1958), p. 112.

10. UG 39/1911, UG 37/1912, *Report of the General Manager of Railways and Harbours*, 1910, p. 57 and 1911, pp. 67, 89. Despite the trend towards metrication since the 1960s, the construction/extension work at the harbour is given in feet because the measurements involved were precise and do not translate easily into metres.

11. UG 35/1913, UG 34/1916, *Report of General Manager*, 1912, p. 57 and 1915, pp. 63, 89.

12. A. B. Lumby, 'Industrial development prior to the Second World War' in F. L. Coleman (ed.), *Economic history of South Africa* (Pretoria, Haum, 1983), p. 201.

13. O. P. F. Horwood (ed.), *The Port of Durban*, NRS, vol. 15, (Durban, Department of Economics, University of Natal, 1969), pp. 18–19.

14. UG 56/1918, UG 59/1919, *Report of General Manager*, 1917–1918, p. 41 and 1918–1919, p. 87.

15. UG 3/1920, *Report of the Railways and Harbours Board on the Location and Design of Grain Elevators*.

16. UG 66/1920, *Report of General Manager*, 1919–20, p. 11.

17. Nevertheless, a floating dock (475 feet long and 70 feet wide) was built at the Cato Creek site, and it appears to have remained in use after the completion of the Prince Edward Graving Dock in 1925. See C. Winchester (ed.), *Shipping wonders of the world* (London, Waverley Books, n.d.), pp. 894, 897.

18. UG 59/1919, *Report of General Manager*, 1918–19, p. 87.

19. UG 42/1921, *Report of General Manager*, 1920–21, p. 56.

20. UG 43/1924, UG 50/1925, *Report of General Manager*, 1923–24, p. 7 and 1924–25, pp. 13, 112 and 140.

21. Horwood, *Port of Durban*, p. 44. See also UG 26/1924, *Report of Commission of Enquiry into Wasted Expenditure on Durban Grain Elevator*.

22. UG 43/1924, *Report of General Manager*, 1923–24, p. 68.

23. *Ibid.*

24. Apart from housing the Ocean Passenger Terminal, the T Jetty was to be the centre of Durban's export trade in fruit.

25. V. E. Solomon, 'Transport', in Coleman, *Economic history*, p. 115.

26. Lumby, 'Industrial development', p. 204, has explained that 'The government believed that it could not openly lend support to a policy of tariff protection without jeopardising its support in the commercial and gold-mining sectors, both of which depended upon imports and therefore favoured a policy of free trade.'

27. J. Nattrass, *The South African economy: its growth and change* (Cape Town, Oxford University Press, 1981), p. 163.

28. *Ibid.*, pp. 163–64, 269–70.

29. Hominy chop is ground maize prepared as a food by boiling in milk or water.

30. Winchester, *Shipping wonders*, p. 895.

31. UG 50/1929, *Report of General Manager*, 1928–29, p. 118.

32. UG 42/1926, UG 50/1929, *Report of General Manager*, 1925–26, p. 102 and 1928–29, p. 118.

33. UG 34/1927, UG 45/1930, *Report of General Manager*, 1926–27, pp. 48, 102 and 1929–30, pp. 30, 119.

34. C. Birkby, 'Cinderellas of South Africa's seas: coasters, a potential national industry, struggle for existence', *Libertas*, 5(11), October 1945, pp. 20–31; and D. R. Crookshank and S. O. Eklund, 'Coastal shipping: stepchild of South African transportation', *African Roads*, 16(1), January-February 1948, pp. 4–7.

35. L. Katzen, *Gold and the South African economy* (Cape Town, Balkema, 1964), pp. 77–83.

36. It should also be borne in mind that private enterprise had been permitted to establish itself at Maydon Wharf, and the financial resources generated from the lease of these sites were used to finance harbour developments. See T. B. Jones, 'Ports of South Africa: Durban and Richards Bay', *Africa Insight*, 20(4), 1990, p. 264.

37. Lumby, 'Industrial development', pp. 213–15.

38. UG 50/1929, UG 37/1934, *Report of General Manager*, 1928–29, p. 118 and 1933–34, p. 139.

39. UG 45/1930, *Report of General Manager*, 1929–30, pp. 38–39. This proposal was in fact a revival of a similar recommendation made by Consulting Engineers Hartley and Barry as early as 1902.

40. UG 45/1930, UG 40/1938, *Report of General Manager*, 1929–30, p. 39 and 1937–38, p. 136.

41. UG 27/1935, *Report of the Harbour Affairs Commission*, p. 43.

42. *Ibid.*, pp. 49–50.

43. UG 41/1940, *Report of General Manager*, 1939–40, p. 144.

44. UG 45/1939, RP 51/1966, *Report of General Manager*, 1938–39, p. 64 and 1964–65, p. 168.

45. UG 40/1938, UG 41/1940, *Report of General Manager*, 1937–38, p. 168 and 1939–40, p. 144. Following the recommendations in UG 32/1949, *Report of the Durban Bayhead Development Committee*, p. 8, the marine airport was closed down and converted for ship repairs.

46. UG 40/1938, RP 59/1967, *Report of General Manager*, 1937–38, p. 136 and 1966–67, p. 50.

47. 'Port of Durban foremost in Africa', *Commercial Opinion*, 34(404), September 1956, pp. 12–19.

48. UG 23/1943, UG 33/1944, *Report of General Manager*, 1942–43, p. 45 and 1943–44, p. 71.

49. UG 32/1945, *Report of General Manager*, 1944–45, p. 73.

50. P. Armstrong, A. Glyn and J. Harrison, *Capitalism since World War II* (London, Fontana, 1984), pp. 15–16.

51. UG 40/1947, *Report of the Railways and Harbours Board*, p. 12; and UG 32/1949, *Report of the Durban Bayhead Development Committee*, pp. 3–4.

52. UG 59/1950, UG 54/1954, UG 40/1958, *Report of General Manager*, 1949–50, p. 127, 1953–54, p. 136 and 1957–58, p. 150.

53. UG 40/1958, RP 65/1962, *Report of General Manager*, 1957–58, p. 152 and 1961–62, p. 80.

54. UG 46/1959, *Report of General Manager*, 1958–59, p. 137.

55. The abolition of 'sea competitive rates' – first introduced in 1911 to counteract coastwise shipping – followed the *Report of the Committee Appointed to Enquire into Railway Rating Policy in South Africa*, UG 32/1950, pars. 123–26, which recommended that such rates be raised to standard railway rates.

56. *Survey of contemporary economic conditions and prospects*, (Stellenbosch, Bureau for Economic Research, University of Stellenbosch, 1961), p. 44. During 1960 and the first half of 1961, over R12 million a month flowed out of the country.

57. D. Hobart Houghton, *The South African economy*, (Cape Town, Oxford University Press, 1967), pp. 198–210.

58. A. B. Lumby, 'The development of secondary industry: the Second World War and after', in Coleman, *Economic history*, pp. 225–26.

59. Because of the strategic importance of oil and the possible embarrassment of South Africa's customers, statistics for oil imports and exports were no longer published after 1965.

60. UG 40/1958, RP 13/1961, RP 52/1964, *Report of General Manager*, 1957–58, p. 122, 1960–61, p. 15, 1963–64, p. 52 and 1969–70, p. 64. (After 1967–68, the *Report of General Manager* was issued without an RP number). It should be noted that the commissioning of an off-shore buoy mooring for tankers off Reunion in 1970 allowed crude-oil imports to be carried in Very Large Crude Carriers (VLCCs), too large to enter the Port of Durban, and therefore the use of these Island View berths fell off substantially.

61. RP 47/1963, *Report of General Manager*, 1962–63, p. 76.

62. Horwood, *Port of Durban*, pp. 44–45. A third storage building was constructed during the 1970s.

63. RP 51/1966, *Report of General Manager*, 1965–66, p. 47 and 1969–70, p. 64.

64. A Twenty-Foot Equivalent Unit (TEU) refers to the dimensions of a standard container: 8ft x 8ft x 20ft.

65. Solomon, 'Transport', p. 119.

66. *Ibid.*, p. 115.

67. Armstrong, Glyn and Harrison, *Capitalism*, pp. 309–14.

68. *Report of General Manager*, 1973–74, pp. 17–21, 1974–75, p. 74, 1976–77, pp. 15, 53 and 1977–78, p. 49.

69. *Report of General Manager*, 1973–74, p. 19 and 1978–79, p. 54.

70. Wiese, *Seaports and port cities* p. 108.

71. *Ibid.*, p. 114.

ABSTRACT

The Natal main railway line into the interior enjoyed a great
advantage over the lines leading from other South African
ports in terms of distance to the Witwatersrand. Consequently, by 1910 the tonnage of goods handled at Durban was
already three times larger than that of South Africa's second
busiest port, Cape Town. Gradients on the Natal main line
were frequently severe but, following the recommendation of a
1913 commission, there was considerable expenditure on
improving the line by means of deviations and doubling in
preference to constructing an alternative line. In continuation
of the Natal government's active programme of railway
development during the last decade of colonial rule, the
construction of branch lines was renewed on a large scale in
the province with the result that it continued to have a far
higher number of railway miles per area than any other part of
the Union. Almost all branch lines were built to serve
agricultural interests, a notable feature being the high ratio of
narrow-gauge branch lines which were perceived as light,
inexpensive pioneer lines through which agricultural districts
in Natal could be developed. By contrast, improvements to the
main line into the interior were prompted, in part, by the
transportation needs of the northern Natal coal industry,
which was heavily dependent upon the shipment trade (exports and bunkers) through Durban. The inability of the
railway authorities to provide the swift and reliable service
needed led to the electrification of the section between Glencoe
and Pietermaritzburg, which was operational from June 1926,
and subsequently to the extension of electrification to Durban
and to Volksrust by October 1937. The need for electricity, in
turn, led to the establishment in 1922 of Escom and to the
subsequent development of a national power grid which
formed an essential foundation for industrialisation in South
Africa. The Natal railway system also provided considerable
employment opportunities and, apart from the continuous
labour shortages which it shared with some other local
employers, was characterised by a large complement of Indian
workers and a dearth of white employees prior to the introduction in 1924 of the 'civilised labour' policy.

RAILWAY DEVELOPMENT IN NATAL 1910–1929

Hein Heydenrych and Paula A. du Plooy

Introduction

At the time of Union, the Natal main railway line to the interior was already the most convenient route to the economic heart of the country, the Witwatersrand. Lourenço Marques (now Maputo) was closer than Durban, but from a national and strategic point of view Durban was preferable by virtue of the fact that it was situated on South African soil. In 1961 the relative rail distances of the four closest ports to Johannesburg were as follows:[1] Durban: 760 km (475 miles), Lourenço Marques: 570 km (356 miles), East London: 1 052 km (658 miles), Port Elizabeth: 1 126 km (704 miles). Durban's favourable position is reflected in the fact that by 1910 the total tonnage of goods handled there was more than three times higher than that of the second busiest South African port, Table Bay: 3 051 346 tons compared to 945 288 tons.[2] The Natal main line derived added importance from the fact that there were coal resources close to it.

In view of the significance of the Natal railway route in the national transportation system, concerted attempts were made to improve it through a programme of capital investment. This took the form of deviations and doubling, and finally electrification, while at the same time the branch feeder lines were steadily extended. What follows is an attempt to trace railway development in Natal in the first two decades after Union. The emphasis is on the railways as infrastructure rather than on the financial results of working, and the relationship between railway development and industrial development.

Improvement of the Natal main line

Although the Natal main line to the interior was the most convenient route to the Witwatersrand in terms of length, it was slow and tortuous. This was because the nineteenth-century engineers who designed it tried to avoid expensive bridge works and tunnels.[3] Consequently, gradients on the main line were often severe – especially on the section between Durban and Pietermaritzburg where the ruling gradient was 1 in 30. Curves with a radius of 300 feet were also not infrequent.[4] Even before 1910 the possibility of improving the route was investigated. In 1904 it was decided to improve the existing main line rather than build an alternative line. The advocates of an alternative line kept up their

Offloading electric units for the South African Railways in Durban harbour in the 1930s.

LOCAL HISTORY MUSEUM, DURBAN

agitation, but a commission appointed for this purpose again recommended in 1913 that the existing line be improved 'by constructing deviations of considerable magnitude where required' and by doubling parts of the line where necessary.[5] The main reason for this recommendation was that, if implemented, it would improve the transit and handling of coal.[6]

The first section to be improved was that between Mooi River and Estcourt. The new line, which included the 800-metre-long Stockton tunnel, was opened to traffic in September 1914.[7] A second important deviation was the Town Hill section from Pietermaritzburg to Hilton – 'one of the worst sections of the old Natal main line'.[8] The new line included two short tunnels. The new double line between Pietermaritzburg and Boughton Junction, and the connecting line from Boughton to the junction with the old main line near Blackridge were opened in May 1916. The section from Boughton to Cedara was opened in December of the same year.[9] Other important deviations were between Umlaas Road and Pentrich (opened in May 1919),[10] and between Booth Junction and Cato Ridge. This took seven years to complete and was finally opened in November 1921.[11] The estimated cost of construction for the latter deviation was £1 706 000 – an average of £42 650 per mile – which made it the most expensive section of railway in the whole South African Railways network.[12] Another big improvement was the Cedara/Nottingham Road deviation, which was opened in sections between February 1922 and March 1924.[13]

> The construction work undertaken between 1910 and 1925 amounted to building an entirely new alignment from South Coast Junction (outside Durban) to Ladysmith. Although the rail distance was increased the amount of excessive curvature eliminated in the process was the equivalent of 31 circles![14]

A special Act was passed (Act No. 30 of 1922) to validate the construction of the above deviations in Natal.

Branch-line development in Natal

Throughout the period 1910 to 1929, Natal had many more railway miles per 100 square miles (256 square km) of territory than any of the other three provinces.[15]

Table 1   Railway miles by province 1910–1929

| | Miles per 100 square miles | | | | | | |
	1910	1912	1915	1920	1923	1925	1929
Cape	1,37	1,44	1,59	1,70	1,70	1,80	1,92
Natal	3,08	3,13	3,55	3,83	4,11	4,14	4,37
Transvaal	1,57	1,99	2,26	2,40	2,40	2,54	2,87
OFS	1,97	2,20	2,52	2,67	2,67	2,87	3,13

Map 1   The Natal railway system, showing branch-line development and the coal-fields

This trend was already established by 1910. This was the result of an active programme of railway development undertaken by the Natal government after the Anglo-Boer War which saw the mileage in that colony increase from 591 (946 km) in 1901 to 999 (1 589 km) in 1910.[16] This tendency to 'over-capitalise' in terms of railway construction was continued by the Union government after 1910. Railway mileage in the Union was increased from 7 039 (11 262 km) on 31 May 1910 to 9 457 (15 131 km) by the end of 1916, and[17] by 31 March 1927 no fewer than 5 362 miles (8 579 km) had been added to the railway network.[18] Natal experienced its fair share of this railway development. As the trunk line into the interior already existed at the time of Union, and could only be improved by means of deviations, doubling and electrification, the major additions to the Natal system were in the form of branch lines. Through branch-line development, the open mileage in Natal increased from 999 (1 589 km) out of a total of 6 892 (11 027 km) in 1910[19] to 1 454, of which 247 miles (395 km) were on the two-feet (610 mm) gauge, out of a total of 12 596 miles (20 154 km) by 1929.[20]

Some important branch lines did exist in Natal by 1910 (see map 1). These were the South Coast and North Coast/Zululand lines, the Natal/Cape line from Pietermaritzburg via Donnybrook to East Griqualand, the line from Pietermaritzburg to Greytown, the branch from Glencoe to Vryheid and Hlobane, the Winterton branch, and the short lines to Weenen and Richmond. In addition, there was the line from near Umzinto on the south coast via Ixopo to Donnybrook. It is significant that, while branch lines in general were not remunerative, the tonnage of revenue-earning traffic forwarded from Natal branch lines during the first few years after Union far exceeded that from branch lines in the other three provinces put together. The tonnage figures were as follows:[21]

Table 2 Revenue-earning traffic on branch lines (tons)

	1911	1912	1913
Cape branch lines	252 902	287 955	345 765
OFS branch lines	60 567	97 934	92 284
Transvaal branch lines	336 128	370 091	393 550
Natal branch lines	1 052 315	1 048 846	1 258 283
Totals	1 701 912	1 804 826	2 089 882

The much larger tonnage in the case of the Natal branch lines was mainly attributable to coal traffic, with sugar and wattle bark playing a lesser role. In 1910, a total of 1 763 476 tons of coal was forwarded by rail to Durban, compared to 42 072 tons of wattle bark and 10 612 tons of sugar.[22]

The Union government's programme of branch-line development specifically provided for branch lines in Natal (see map 1). In 1911, twelve railway lines were authorised, of which three were in Natal: Stuartstown, as Ixopo was first named, to Union Bridge on the Cape border; an extension of the Winterton branch to Bergville; and an extension from Greytown to Krantzkop (Act No. 33 of 1911). In 1913, fourteen lines were authorised, of which five were in Natal. They were: a branch from Donnybrook to Underberg; a continuation of the South Coast branch inland from Paddock to Harding; two short branches from Dalton and Schroeders, half-way between Pietermaritzburg and Greytown, into the farming districts; and a branch from Gingindlovu on the North Coast line to Eshowe (Act No. 23 of 1913).

After the First World War, railway construction was resumed in earnest in 1922 when 22 lines were authorised. These included only two that affected Natal (see map 1): a continuation of the Natal/Cape line from Franklin to Kokstad and a branch from Franklin to Matatiele (Act No. 30 of 1922). Subsequently, in 1924, an extension of the North Coast line was authorised from Mtubatuba through Zululand to the south bank of the Phongolo River (Act No. 31 of 1924). In 1925 a further 26 lines at a total cost of over £4,5 million were authorised, including two in Natal: a branch off the North Coast line from Empangeni to Nkwaleni and one from Greytown to Rietvlei (Act No. 33 of 1925). In 1926 a short extension of the Zululand railway from the Phongolo River to the southern border of Swaziland was authorised (Act No. 48 of 1926). To these should be added the connecting line from Vryheid to Piet Retief which was opened for traffic in December 1913[23] and which completed the connection between Ermelo in the Eastern Transvaal and Vryheid, and the branch lines to Mid-Illovo and in Alfred County inland south of Port Shepstone, which had both been authorised before Union and were completed in 1911.[24]

With the exception of the Piet Retief/Vryheid line, all the above-mentioned were agricultural lines or 'light railways' intended for the conveyance of goods and produce only.[25] The reference in the South Africa Act to the promotion of the settlement of an agricultural and industrial population in the interior[26] provided the rationale for this programme of railway development. In the case of Natal, agricultural development clearly received preference during the period under review. In this regard the Union government was in complete agreement with the opinion of organised agriculture, as expressed in the resolution passed by the South African Agricultural Congress of 1911: 'That this Union is of opinion that the future prosperity of South Africa depends to a large extent on facilities for moving produce, and . . . would urge the necessity of a rapid extension of railway communication throughout the country.'[27]

Apart from the desire to promote agricultural development, there were other factors which determined the construction of branch lines in the Union as a whole, including Natal. These were petitions and requests from various districts, parliamentary advocacy, and a desire to relieve unemployment.[28] Party-political considerations may also have played a part. During the parliamentary debate on the lines finally authorised in the Act of 1913, J. W. Jagger referred to the Natal lines as 'political lines', asserting that 'most of these lines were given to districts that returned ardent supporters of the Government'.[29]

Jagger's claim remains unsubstantiated. What is evident is that agricultural interests stood to gain from all the Natal lines authorised in 1913. The branch from Donnybrook to Underberg was essentially designed to serve the farming community, while the two branches off the Greytown line from Schroeders and Dalton were intended to cater for a wattle- and dairy-farming area.[30] The branch from Gingindlovu was similarly constructed to serve the wattle farmers.[31] When Prime Minister Louis Botha entered the debate on railway construction he pleaded for every possible support to be given to the white settlers in Zululand, pointing out that they already had to cope with difficulties such as east coast fever and declaring that parliament 'should not take the hand of protection away from the white people living in Zululand' because 'these people were . . . deserving of every consideration'. [32]

In the case of the 1922 Act, the relief of unemployment played a significant role, with one clause of the Act confirming that construction work which had already been started on three lines was intended to relieve the serious unemployment that existed in the Transvaal and Griqualand West.[33] However, the two lines which affected Natal, the extension of the Natal/Cape line from Franklin to Kokstad and the branch to Matatiele, both served agricultural interests. The Zululand railway from Mtubatuba to the south bank of the Phongolo River, authorised in 1924, was specifically intended to promote the cultivation of cotton in that area,[34] although part of the line also traversed sugar estates. In this connection, reference was made to the success which had attended the extension of the railway line north of the Thukela in 1905–6. In spite of the fact that it was a malarial area the settlers in that region had fared so well that in 1923 no less than 208 000 tons of sugar cane were carried by the railway.[35]

Natal had certainly received its fair share of railway capital investment since 1910. By February 1926, expenditure in the form of new works, extensions and improvements amounting to over £20 million had been authorised, of which over £15 million had been spent.[36] When it is taken into account that between 1913 and 1925 a total of £37 703 000 was spent in the Union on new works, purchase and construction of railways *and on rolling stock*,[37] then Natal with its £15 million certainly had no cause for complaint.

A feature of Natal branch-line development was the high proportion of narrow-gauge line (2 ft wide) built – as stated before, 247 miles (395 km) out of a total of 1 454 miles (2 326 km) by 1929. The first 2-ft-gauge branch line in South Africa was the one from Kalabaskraal to Hopefield in the south-western Cape which was opened in February 1903. In the same year an engineer was requested by the Natal government to report on the possibility of adopting this gauge for some Natal lines. His report was positive and the first 2-ft-gauge line in Natal, between Estcourt and Weenen, was opened in July 1907.[38] Since then, several 2-ft-gauge branches have been added.

The reasoning behind the construction of narrow-gauge lines was that agricultural areas could be opened up by light pioneer lines, of narrow gauge and cheap construction, whenever the volume of traffic available did not justify the cost of building a standard-gauge line. It was officially estimated that the average saving in construction as compared with a standard-gauge line was £2 000 per mile.[39] However, as early as 1911 the General Manager of Railways and Harbours expressed serious doubts about the wisdom of narrow-gauge development. He pointed out that 'the advantage is a purely temporary one if the construction of a railway line at all is justified by the subsequent development of the district which it serves'.[40] The eminent railway authority, Sir David Hunter, former general manager of the Natal Government Railways, expressed similar grave reservations in this regard in 1913,[41] while the Divisional Superintendent of the Railways at Durban stated in the same year that it seemed unfortunate that 'any departure from the standard gauge should have been made'.[42] In 1934, the Natal Agricultural Union confirmed this opinion by requesting that all narrow-gauge lines be converted to the standard gauge.[43]

Two main objections were raised against narrow-gauge lines. Firstly, they were often unable to cope with the amount of traffic to be carried.[44] Secondly, there was the disadvantage that goods had to be transhipped where these lines joined standard-gauge ones. Despite a warning by the General Manager in 1911 about the delays and additional expense that this involved,[45] the construction of narrow-gauge lines was approved. In retrospect, it can be seen that the building of narrow-gauge branch lines was an expensive mistake.

The importance of the coal traffic

The coal industry responded positively to the new improved rail facilities described above. In fact, these improvements were in large measure made in response to the immediate needs of the coal industry, though they also met the wider and ultimately more important demand for a speedier service to and from the Witwatersrand – the industrial heartland of South Africa.

The importance of coal traffic in the Union as a whole is demonstrated by the fact that during 1911 more than half the tonnage of revenue-earning traffic on the South African Railways was accounted for by coal: 6 328 560 out of a total of 11 080 075 tons.[46] As the General Manager of the Railways and Harbours described it in his annual report for 1916, 'coal is a commodity easy to handle, is easily loaded and discharged, is consigned from definite centres in large and regular quantities, requires no protection or special care *en route*, and is not a source of frequent claims for compensation'.[47] Although this is largely true, many practical problems – especially the inability of the railways to provide the necessary truckage – prevented the Natal coal industry from fully exploiting the possibilities of the shipment trade (the provision of coal for bunkering and export purposes).

It was the First World War that underlined the position of Durban as the premier port of the Union,[48] and it was the war that also demonstrated 'the importance of the coal resources of the Union and the favourable position of the railways and other industries dependent upon a reliable coal supply for the continuance of their operations'.[49] However, by 1910 the Natal industry had largely abandoned the inland coal trade to the Transvaal collieries and had already started building up a lucrative shipment trade through Durban.[50] After experiments with Natal coal for bunkering yielded successful results, from 1937 all mailships started bunkering regularly at Durban.[51] By 1909 bunker coal already comprised 46,8 per cent of all Natal coal sales.[52]

In 1910 there was a general slump in the bunker and export market and, with the outbreak of the First World War, the position deteriorated further due to the disruption of shipping.[53] However, the situation gradually improved as the European coal industries were either paralysed or their production capacity was fully utilised for the war effort. Consequently, by 1916, in spite of a 6 per cent decrease in general cargo handled at Durban harbour, an increase of 63 per cent in the volume of bunkered coal over the figure for 1915 (from 930 687 tons in 1915 to 1 519 182 in 1916), resulted in a rise of 11 per cent over the previous year in the total cargo handled at the port.[54]

Table 3   Coal bunkered at and exported through Durban 1910–1928

	Tonnage
1910	1 452 695
1911	1 510 435
1912	1 383 693
1913	1 552 361
1914	1 380 886
1915	1 150 475
1916	1 684 349
1917 (January to March)	416 353
1917–18	1 472 954
1918–19	1 312 747
1919–20	1 410 812
1920–21	1 872 323
1921–22	2 073 972
1922–23	2 253 475
1923–24	2 645 929
1924–25	2 804 139
1925–26	2 635 573
1926–27	3 060 685
1927–28	2 700 676
Total	35 904 294

This favourable trend lasted until about 1920, after which the bunkering trade was subject to severe fluctuations in demand. The tonnages of coal bunkered and exported increased steadily during the 1920s and reached a peak of over three million tons in 1926–27, as can be seen in table 3, but bunker coal only comprised 1 256 276 tons of that year's total,[55] and it declined further to 1 195 598 tons in 1929. During the depression the bottom fell out of the bunker market, and thereafter it never fully recovered. By 1937–38, for instance, shipment coal handled at Durban totalled only 1 584 845 tons.[56]

The decline in the bunker trade at Durban was in large measure due to new ship designs which made steamships more fuel-efficient. While there was, therefore, a considerable increase in the tonnage of ships calling at the harbour, there was no commensurate increase in their coal requirements.[58] The other technological factor affecting the demand for bunkers was the fact that many ships burning oil instead of coal came into use during the 1920s and thereafter.[59]

The coal export trade initially experienced more or less the same pattern of demand as bunker coal. During and immediately after the First World War there was a considerable demand. During the following decade, 1920–30, exports gradually increased, with temporary upswings created by coal strikes in Britain and Australia in 1921 and 1923, respectively. By 1927, the local export trade had reached its peak at 1 811 000 tons.[60]

It is obvious that coal transportation played an increasingly important part in the working of the Natal railway system in the two decades after 1910. It is also obvious that, although the figures of coal tonnage quoted above pertain specifically to the port of Durban, that harbour formed an integral part of the railway system of Natal. In this connection N.M. Shaffer's statement comes to mind: 'A port in itself is rarely a generator of tonnage, rather it is a consequence of traffic generated by the port's hinterland.'[61] If it is further taken into account that prior to 1931 over 70 per cent of all shipped cargo at Durban was coal – in some years well over 80 per cent of all cargo[62] – then the significance of the coal traffic becomes even clearer. Consequently, the problems encountered in the transportation of this large tonnage of coal to the coast constituted the more immediate reason for the decision of the South African Railways Administration to electrify a large section of the Natal main line during the 1920s. It should not, however, be forgotten that congestion and delays on the line to Durban also adversely affected the general railway traffic to and from the Witwatersrand, further necessitating a more efficient service.

During the period under discussion Durban was, of course, not the only port which handled bunker and export coal. Lourenço Marques (Maputo) also featured in this trade. During 1926–27, when the shipment trade at Durban reached its peak of over three million tons, the corresponding figure for Lourenço Marques was 781 055 tons, consisting of 289 952 tons of bunker coal and 491 103 tons of export coal.[63] The highest previous figure for shipment coal at Lourenço Marques was 1 246 773 tons in 1920–21.[64] With regard to the shipment trade, Durban primarily served the Natal collieries, while Lourenço Marques served those of the Transvaal.

The electrification of the main line

Renfrew Christie has observed: 'Out of the difficulties of the South African Railways in transporting Natal coal came the Electricity Supply Commission.'[65] The chain of events which connects the inadequacies of the South African Railways in meeting the transport demands of the Natal coal industry with the establishment of Escom merits brief consideration.

It is ironic that while the extension of the railways – the trunk railway as well as its Dundee branch – to the interior from Durban during the nineteenth century made the establishment of a viable coal industry possible, the subsequent inability of the railways to meet the transport needs of the collieries became one of the most serious obstacles to the optimal development of that industry.[66] When, in 1886, the extension of the trunk railway line to the interior came to a halt at Ladysmith because the Colony of Natal was in dire financial straits and it was difficult to gain access to loan capital, impassioned pleas were made both by the Durban Chamber of Commerce and in the Legislative Council for the main line to be extended at least as far as the nearest coalfield, at Elandslaagte.[67] Once the line had been opened to Elandslaagte in October 1888,[68] and especially after the Natal main line had been opened to Johannesburg in 1895, the stage seemed set for the unhindered marketing of Natal coal at both the port of Durban and in the promising inland market. The shipment trade subsequently proved to be the most lucrative avenue for marketing Natal coal and by 1910 the inland trade had been left almost entirely to the more favourably placed Transvaal collieries.[69]

Before Union, the Natal government generally tried to promote the exportation of local coal through Durban by means of favourable transport rates. After 1910, the South African Railways and Harbours Administration continued this policy,[70] although higher rates and surcharges on bunker and export coal were imposed intermittently between 1916 and 1920.[71] The trade in shipment coal responded positively: in 1911 the bunkering trade at Durban increased by 13 per cent over 1910, while the tonnage of export coal in the same year was 47 per cent higher than in 1910.[72] It therefore seemed as if the shipment coal trade was set to increase by leaps and bounds.

However, the inability of the Railways Administration to meet the transport needs of the Natal collieries became chronic after 1910, especially as preference was given to the seasonal transport of maize and other agricultural produce.[73] This became an extremely frustrating phenomenon from the Natal collieries' point of view, as business was lost because of an inability to deliver consignments on time. Guest quotes several examples. Thus, for instance, during July 1914, the Dundee Coal Company had to wait 139 hours for railway trucks. That was the equivalent of one pit being closed for 14 out of 17 working days.[74] In an effort to overcome the problem in 1918, the ground stacking of coal started in earnest at the Bluff in Durban harbour. The Divisional Superintendent of the Railways at Durban admitted, however, that he regarded this as only a temporary expedient. He emphasised the seriousness of the situation by saying that the collieries at that stage expected 'to receive trucks to load 6 000 tons daily for shipment purposes . . . The maximum off-loading so far obtained by native and convict labour is about 1 500 tons per day'.[75] He expressed the hope that it would soon be possible to introduce some mechanical arrangement which would make it possible to off-load and reload coal more quickly than was possible by hand.

By 1924, however, the position had not improved. At one stage during September 1924 the Dundee Coal Company had steamships waiting in Durban harbour for 10 600 tons of coal, but had only 3 600 tons in transit and was compelled to close two pits for a day each because of a shortage of empty trucks.[76] By the end of 1925 the Railways could only meet 58 per cent of the truck requirements of the Natal collieries.[77] Under these circumstances it is not surprising that electrification of the Natal main line into the interior was considered as a possible solution. As early as 1913 all the preliminary reports on possible electrification, which had been presented from time to time, were collated and considered by the Railways Administration.[78] They were, however, found to be 'not so comprehensive as the subject demands' and the matter was postponed. In 1915 it was decided to allow such plans to stand over until after the war.[79]

In 1918, the services of a London firm of consulting engineers, Merz and McLellan, were procured and a representative of the firm was sent to South Africa to investigate the matter.[80] A report was submitted on several sections of main line as well as on some suburban lines. The main-line sections reported upon included the Natal line from Durban to Glencoe and the branch to Vryheid East, the line from Cape Town to Touws River in the Karoo, and the Transvaal coal lines from Witbank to Johannesburg and Komatipoort, respectively. The suburban lines were those from Cape Town to Sea Point and Simonstown, and from Johannesburg to Springs and Randfontein.[81]

In 1919 the electrification proposals, as set out in the report, were officially accepted in principle. In 1920, funds were voted by Parliament for electrifying the Durban/Pietermaritzburg and the Cape Town/Simonstown lines. At that time the doubling of the line north of Pietermaritzburg for steam working was in progress and a scheme existed for eventually doubling the whole line up to Tendega near Vryheid. The same firm of Merz and McLellan was appointed as consulting engineers to supervise the electrification of the section from Durban to Pietermaritzburg.[82] In 1921 the government decided to abandon the Durban/Pietermaritzburg section in favour of electrifying the Pietermaritzburg/Glencoe section.[83] The reason for this change of plan was summarised in a note prepared for the Minister of Railways and Harbours prior to the parliamentary debate:

The principal reason for deciding on electrification was the possibility of securing increased efficiency and cheaper working costs, i.e. economic development. The sections originally decided upon were selected as being suitable for securing experience in dealing with heavy goods traffic and heavy suburban traffic. Since the original decision was arrived at the Administration has been compelled by the necessities of the situation, such as the abnormal development of traffic on the Natal main line and the difficult financial position, to concentrate on the most urgent work which is the completion of the additional facilities for handling traffic on the Natal main line. At present these difficulties are met by the doubling of certain sections but as there were not sufficient funds to complete the doubling and at the same time undertake electrification, the electrification of a section not already doubled had been decided upon as the best means of securing relief at the earliest possible date.[84]

The crux of the matter was that – as the Assistant General Manager, Durban put it – 'Revenue is being lost owing to the railways not being able to accept coal which is waiting to be offered for loading.'[85] He further emphasised the point by stressing the frustration of the Natal collieries:

It is no consolation to the Natal Collieries to be told . . . that the general traffic in Natal has increased by 1 700 000 tons in the last 10 years. It is sufficient for them that during the last 10 years the coal shipped through Delagoa Bay has increased by 1 000 000 tons whereas the increase through Durban has been Nil. Moreover, the Transvaal and OFS output has increased in the same period by 3 500 000 tons while the increase in Natal has only been 600 000 tons.[86]

These arguments were further reinforced by reports submitted in November 1921 by Merz and McLellan, and by the General Manager of the Railways and Harbours, Sir William Hoy. The consulting engineers also addressed the question of the relationship between railway electrification and the general availability of power. In this regard Hoy repeated three main reasons for developing the supply of electric power in South Africa already enumerated in a report on the general supply of power submitted by Merz in April 1920 at the request of General Smuts. These were: (1) to supply electricity in bulk to existing public and private enterprises, thus the cost of electric power to existing consumers would be reduced and others would be induced to use electricity; (2) to provide for a much greater future demand from industries such as coal and iron which were at that stage operating only on a small scale; and (3) to attract and develop completely new industries, 'especially electro-chemicals, the production of fertilizers, the refinement of steel and incidentally encouraging by-product processes in connection with the distillation of coal in connection with large power-stations'.[87]

In addition to echoing all the above arguments Hoy added some of his own. The two most telling ones were, firstly, that dislocation due to delays and engine derailments consequent upon the difficult conditions on the Natal lines would be eliminated, the latter because of the different design of the electric locomotive; and secondly, that the best grade coal, which was then being used for locomotive purposes would, after electrification, be available for shipment, while low-grade coal then regarded as waste coal would be used for the power-stations.[88] He warned that, 'if electrification is not proceeded with now it will be a national calamity'.[89]

The voices of Hoy and Merz as advocates of railway electrification at that time were joined by that of the brilliant scientist, H. J. van der Bijl, who in 1920 became Scientific and Technical Adviser to the Prime Minister. In 1921 he wrote: '. . . the electrification of the Union's railways . . . can be made to be one of the most powerful factors in stimulating industrial development . . . by bringing together two of the most important requirements of most industrial undertakings, namely power and transport facilities.'[90] Charles Merz, Sir William Hoy and H. J. van der Bijl played a pivotal role in the decision to electrify the Pietermaritzburg/Glencoe section of the Natal main line, and in the establishment of Escom to make this possible. In 1922, two Acts were passed by Parliament: Act No. 30 provided, *inter alia*, for the electrification of railways and Act No. 42 for the establishment of an electricity supply commission (Escom). H. J. van der Bijl was the first chairman of Escom.[91]

A fourth individual concerned very closely with the creation of Escom as a supplier of electricity, mainly to the railways, was Sir Robert Kotze, Government Mining Engineer. In March 1920, Sir William Hoy had already observed in a confidential memorandum that the possibility had been considered of obtaining power from municipal power-stations, but that disruptions caused by strikes, such as had occurred at Johannesburg and Durban, constituted a great stumbling block.[92] Subsequently he disclosed to Kotze that the Railways Administration had considered the possibility of calling for tenders for the supply of electricity, but that the 'primary objection is again on the question of stoppages'.[93] With this in mind Kotze then outlined the various options open to the state. The one he recommended was the creation of a board of businessmen and prominent engineers to erect power-stations and supervise the supply of electricity. This recommendation was based on the model of the Ontario Electricity Commission in Canada, which was formed because of problems in connection with concessions for the use of water in Ontario.[94] The Act subsequently provided for such a board which controlled and licensed the supply of electricity, while the Electricity Supply Commission (Escom) was responsible for the

> acquisition, maintenance, and working of undertakings for an efficient supply of electricity, to Government departments, the South African Railways and Harbours Administration, local authorities, companies and other persons carrying on industrial undertakings or to any persons whatsoever in the Union.

It was foreseen, however, that the Railways Administration would be the principal customer of the undertaking.[95]

Christie points out that, in addition to the four persons mentioned above (Hoy, Merz, van der Bijl and Kotze), the creators of Escom included the then Prime Minister, General J.C. Smuts, and H. Warrington-Smyth, the Secretary for Mining; and further that, of these six, all but van der Bijl and Merz had been connected with suppressing the 1922 strike.[96] Hence their preoccupation with ensuring a supply of electricity to the railways which would be uninterrupted by strike action and industrial unrest.

Meanwhile, during 1922, the South African Railways started erecting the first power-station at Colenso, in accordance with the authority bestowed by Act No. 30 of 1922. This site on the Thukela River was chosen because it was situated right next to the section of line to be electrified, and because it was the only spot along this section where sufficient water was obtainable.[97] The little town of Colenso underwent a metamorphosis. An entire village was designed and in December 1922 work started on the construction of the 36 houses needed. At the end of March 1923 there were 347 whites and 1 872 blacks employed on the works.[98] The conversion to electricity of the 175 miles (280 km) of track between Glencoe Junction and Masons Mill, just south of Pietermaritzburg, was sufficiently advanced for a full electric service to come into operation in June 1926.[99]

The technical advantages of electric traction were soon apparent in two respects: higher speeds were attainable, especially on steep gradients, and there was a far greater availability of locomotives for active use. Whereas steam locomotives were normally available for 50 per cent of the time, the electric ones could be used for about 90 per cent of every 24 hours. Heavier individual trains could be handled at higher speeds than before. The amount of time saved was enormous: a typical goods train could cover the distance between Glencoe and Pietermaritzburg with a saving of 6 hours and 15 minutes. Whereas a heavy steam goods train between the two places took 16 hours 30 minutes to convey a maximum load of 1 000 tons, three electric units operated by one driver could now pull a load of 1 500 tons in 10 hours and 15 minutes. Coal-carrying trains were consequently speeded up considerably. The average steam coal-carrying train between Glencoe and Booth Junction had taken 34 hours and 15 minutes, but now the journey could be completed in 25 hours and 9 minutes.[100]

After building the Colenso power-station in 1926, the Railways Administration entered into an agreement whereby Escom assumed responsibility for operating the power-station, the twelve substations and the 88 000-volt cross-country transmission lines. These assets were formally handed over on 15 January 1927.[101] The original sum authorised in 1922 for the electrification scheme was £3 318 990. This amount proved quite inadequate, with the result that Parliament had to be approached in 1924 and 1925 to authorise the additional expenditure of £533 344 and £535 000 respectively.[102] This brought the total to £4 387 334. By September 1929, when the dust had settled, the total expenditure amounted to £4 421 751,[103] to which should be added £1 161 623, being the cost of 95 electric locomotives.[104]

The electrification of the railway line between Pietermaritzburg and Glencoe was a major technological feat. It put Natal far ahead of the rest of South Africa in this respect. When, by October 1937, electrification had been extended to the coast and to Volksrust[105] it constituted the longest stretch of electrified railway in the British Commonwealth.[106] The irony, however, is that while electrification had been undertaken primarily to solve the urgent transport problems of the Natal coal-mines, it did not succeed in achieving this aim. Truck shortages still persisted. In his report for the year ended March 1926, when the electrified line was already partly in operation, the Assistant General Manager, Durban, referred to the fact that the coal traffic had been lighter than in the previous year, and attributed this to 'the acute shortage of rolling stock experienced during the 12 months'. He concluded: 'In view of the money spent on improvements in Natal, it is unfortunate that we are unable to obtain full advantage of our facilities through inadequate supply of rolling stock.'[107] In the following year the same officer lamented: 'I cannot . . . see at present that we are securing the financial gain from electrification which it was stated we should attain.'[108] By 1926 the collieries were also unanimously of the opinion that a double line or the construction of a completely new line would have given more effective relief.[109]

The claim made by the Minister of Transport, C. W. Malan, in his budget speech of 1927, that 'the electrification work is an unqualified success . . .'[110] was therefore inaccurate and rash. The problem of truck shortages persisted during the 1930s and 1940s and South Africa's railway transportation system virtually collapsed during the early 1950s, when even power-stations failed to receive enough coal to generate sufficient electricity.[111] The significance of the electrification of the Natal main line therefore lies not in the provision of improved transport facilities, but rather in the fact that it gave rise to the establishment of Escom and a national power grid.

Railway labour in Natal

A prominent feature of the labour situation in Natal during the period 1910–29 was the difficulty experienced by the railway authorities in obtaining an adequate and stable work-force. Low wages, competition from the Transvaal, and the physical demands of a developing railway sector, were among the factors which contributed to the labour shortage on the Natal railways. The Natal railway system's labour force included Africans, Indians and whites. Although it is artificial to treat each group as a separate entity, they are discussed separately for practical reasons and because there were distinct trends within each of these categories.

Africans were employed largely in the construction and maintenance of railway lines. As a result of the intensive construction and railway-improvement programme undertaken in Natal there was a continual demand for African labour. In 1912 approximately 4 026 Africans were employed on the railways in Natal.[112] This number increased to 8 713 in 1920[113] and peaked at 9 565 in 1926.[114] The Natal African labour force comprised about 29 per cent of the 32 963 Africans employed by the South African Railways during that year.[115] These numbers, however, were not considered to be sufficient, for the Native Labour Superintendent (NLS) frequently complained that the supply of African labour in Natal was woefully insufficient.[116] Even in the early 1920s, when South Africa was experiencing a depression, the NLS estimated that the Natal system was 1 500 men short of its labour requirements.[117] In an attempt to relieve the shortage, surplus recruits drafted in the Transvaal and Orange Free State were sent by the railway administration to Natal.[118]

This shortfall of African labour was indicative of the negative way in which Africans perceived the Natal railways as an employer. Among the reasons for this perception were low wages, inadequate rations and poor accommodation. Railway wages in Natal were lower than those paid on the railways in the other provinces, and less than the rates paid by private enterprise.[119] Rations issued to African labourers compared poorly with those received by railway workers in the Transvaal and Orange Free State, and were considered inadequate by the Native Affairs Department.[120] When these shortcomings are combined with the physical hard work involved in the construction and maintenance of railway lines, it can be understood why railway employment was not a popular choice among Africans.

A number of different forms of employment were open to Africans which held greater attractions. Sugar plantations situated in the vicinity of Zululand had the advantage of being closer to home than many railway depots and construction works. Moreover, on sugar plantations Africans received a better supply of rations, good accommodation, some form of recreation and a nominal wage. Wages offered by the Natal collieries and Transvaal mining houses were also higher than those paid by the railway authorities and many Africans were enticed north in the hope of improving their incomes.

The NLS recognised the need to improve the Natal railway system's image. Wages were increased at various intervals, in 1912, 1917, 1919 and 1921.[122] In 1919 a bonus was offered for long service, in an attempt to induce Africans to work for longer periods and so to stabilise the labour force.[123] In 1919 the NLS also began to pay more attention to the quality of rations issued to African labourers. A number of inferior food consignments provided by contractors were returned and every effort was made to ensure that the labourers received their rations 'according to the standard scale and in good condition'.[124] Furthermore, from 1918 the NLS tried to create and maintain good relations with African chiefs and headmen in order to aid railway recruiting efforts in their districts.[125] Labourers obtained in this fashion were given preferential treatment in the hope that they would return home 'with good reports on our working conditions'.[126]

In spite of these steps it is doubtful whether the railway's popularity as an employer increased to any large extent. The African labour turnover was high and hindered the efficiency of the system.[127] During this period Africans actively protested at conditions on the railways. Unrest in Natal during 1918[128] resulted in rations being improved, while unrest during

1919 effected a pay increase.[129] The NLS adopted a paternalistic attitude with regard to African unrest. He argued that African labourers should be placed under supervision so that they could not be swayed by the whims of any 'discontented agitator'.[130] A similar attitude is evident in his dealings with Indian labourers.

Natal's was the only railway system in South Africa to employ Indians on a large scale. In the first decade of the century, Indians were the mainstay of the Natal railway labour force, as the figures for 1910 indicate: 3 262 Indians and 1 905 Africans were employed.[131] Indians filled unskilled and semi-skilled positions, such as pointsman and lampman. As was characteristic of Indian labour throughout Natal, many Indians were indentured to the railway for a number of years. The Divisional Superintendent (Durban) recognised that the indenture system was an invaluable factor in ensuring a stable labour supply, and in 1914 he recommended that Indians be encouraged to reindenture through the promise of a financial bonus.[132]

It is not clear to what extent the financial bonus had the desired effect, but a large number of Indians did reindenture. The following table reflects the number of Indians employed on the Natal railway between 1910 and 1914, as well as the proportion of free and reindentured men:[133]

Table 4   Indians employed on Natal railways

Year	Indentured	Reindentured	Free	Total
1910	1 249	1 115	898	3 262
1913	508	1 562	1 111	3 181
1914	327	823	1 525	2 675

It was not only Africans, however, who were reluctant to work on the Natal railways. There were a variety of employment opportunities available to Indians in Natal, offering higher wages and better rations than did the railways. Indians were considered to be good workers and there was always competition for their services. This competition became especially fierce after the Indian government halted Indian immigration in 1911 and the South African government started implementing its Indian repatriation scheme.

Initially, great concern was expressed by the NLS at the loss of these valuable men 'whose services could not readily be replaced'.[134] In 1912, and again in 1916, the Superintendent recommended that the wages of Indian labourers be increased in order to encourage them to remain in railway employ.[135] Despite this effort the number of Indian labourers decreased steadily until, in 1929, there were only 871 Indians employed.[136] By 1929, however, the attitude of the railway authorities had been influenced to such an extent by the Pact government's 'civilised labour' policy that satisfaction was actually expressed at the number of Indians leaving the railway service.[137]

The Pact government introduced its 'civilised labour' policy in 1924, but the South African Railways had been applying a so-called 'white labour policy' since Union. Indeed, in 1911 the White Labour Superintendent made a special effort to recruit white labourers in South Africa as a whole, the result of which was 1 385 applications for work.[138] However, the success of this policy was confined to the Cape Province, the Transvaal and the Orange Free State. The following table, presented in the *Annual Report* of 1915, indicates the number of white labourers employed by the SAR for the period 1913 to 1915 but makes no mention of Natal:[139]

Table 5   White labour on South African railways

Province	December	December	December
	1913	1914	1915
Transvaal	1 475	1 542	1 728
Orange Free State	821	770	895
Cape Province	1 552	1 511	1 537

It is not possible at this stage to pinpoint precisely the factors which made it virtually impossible for the SAR to apply a 'white labour' policy in Natal. However, Natal did have fewer white people and less of an unemployment problem than the other provinces. Moreover, white labourers would also have been attracted by the more lucrative wages offered by the mining corporations in Natal and Transvaal, and so be drawn away from railway employment. It should also be remembered that while there was scope for white labourers to perform semi-skilled work on the railways in the other provinces, Natal had Indian labourers who carried out these duties very competently.

The first mention of white railway workers in Natal was made in the 1921 Annual Report, which indicated that 28 of them were employed for that year.[140] By 1924 this number had shrunk to 14,[141] clearly indicating the failure of the SAR 'white labour' policy in Natal. However, the Pact government's determination to solve the social problem of 'poor white' unemployment by creating work for the 'civilised' section of the community at the expense of the 'non-whites', had a decisive effect on employment in the Natal railway system. In 1925 the number of white labourers employed in Natal jumped from 14 to 429.[142] Relationships between white and black labourers must have been strained by the active replacement of traditional labourers with 'poor whites'. More importantly, the additional cost of white labour placed a tremendous burden on the railway administration – not only in terms of higher wages but also in terms of supplying suitable accommodation, education and perhaps recreation.[144]

The lack of suitable housing was a nagging problem in the Natal system. This affected African and Indian labourers as well as whites, but during this period the only effort made was to solve the white housing shortage.

The white accommodation shortage was alleviated to some extent by converting African and Indian compounds into quarters for single men.[145] But there was no housing available for married men and this was an important factor in the heavy loss of white labourers. In 1929, 1 924 white labourers were employed in Natal and 610 resigned.[146] The railway administration also paid attention to the education of its white labourers. Adult education classes were held in various regions of Natal to help them to better their qualifications.[147] In this way a number of white labourers were able to improve their positions on the railways quite remarkably.

The composition of the labour force on the Natal railway system was unique in two respects. Firstly, it contained a large Indian component and, secondly, there was a notable dearth of white labourers until their number increased dramatically after 1924. A more detailed study of this aspect of railway development – in the other provinces as well as in Natal – should shed some light on the labour practices of an industrialising country.

Conclusion

At the time of Union in 1910, Durban was already established as the busiest port in South Africa, and therefore the railway system that served that port – notably the Natal main line into the interior – was the busiest system. The superior position of the Natal railway and harbour system was maintained throughout the period covered in this study. This was partly the result of its natural geographical advantages, but it was also made possible by a continuous process of improvement which took three forms: the physical improvement of the Natal main line, the extension of the branch-line system and, finally, the electrification of the main line. In the process the Natal railway system also provided employment opportunities for a considerable labour force.

The electrification of the main line must be regarded as the most significant of these developments. However, the importance of electrification lies not in its intrinsic railway value, for, as already pointed out, electrification did not succeed in its initial primary aim, i.e. to facilitate the transport of shipment coal to the harbour. The significance of electrification lies rather in the fact that it gave rise to the establishment of Escom, without which the rise of South Africa as a modern industrial state would not have been possible.

REFERENCES

1. N. M. Shaffer, *The competitive position of the Port of Durban* (Evanston, North Western University, 1965), p. 121.

2. UG 50–1929, *Report of General Manager of Railways and Harbours*, year ended 31 March 1929, p. 177.

3. L. C. A. Knowles and C. M. Knowles, *The economic development of the British overseas empire*, vol. 3 (London, George Routledge, 1936), p. 274.

4. M. H. de Kock, *The results of government ownership in South Africa* (Cape Town, Juta, 1922), p. 74.

5. UG 36–1913, *Report of the Railway Commissioners*, dated 10 December 1913, on the improvement of railway communication in the Province of Natal, p. 1.

6. *Ibid.*, p. 2.

7. UG 25–1915, *Report of General Manager*, 1915, p. 90.

8. UG 34–1916, *Report of General Manager*, 1915, p. 94.

9. UG 36–1917, *Report of General Manager*, 1916, p. 77.

10. UG 59–1919, *Report of General Manager*, 1918–19, p. 63.

11. UG 37–1922, *Report of General Manager*, 1921–22, p. 47.

12. Martin, 'Natal Railway Story', manuscript, p. 47.

13. *Ibid.*, p. 32.

14. *Ibid.*, p. 33.

15. UG 39–1911, UG 46–1913, UG 34–1916, UG 66–1920, UG 40–1923, UG 50–1925, UG 50–1929, *Report of General Manager*, 1910, p. 99, 1912, p. 115, 1915, p. 234, 1919, p. xxxviii, 1922, p. xi, 1924, p. 166, 1928, p. 144.

16. M. H. de Kock, *Selected subjects in the economic history of South Africa* (Cape Town and Johannesburg, 1924), p. 349.

17. *Ibid.*, p. 350.

18. S. H. Frankel, *The railway policy of South Africa* (Johannesburg, Hortors, 1928), p. 112.

19. UG 39–1911, *Report of General Manager*, 1910, p. 3.

20. UG 50–1929, *Report of General Manager*, 1928–29, p. 106.

21. UG 38–1914, *Report of General Manager*, 1913, p. 59.

22. UG 39–1911, *Report of General Manager*, 1910, p. 124.

23. SAS 768 G30/6/23, Part 2, Opening and naming of stations Glencoe/Piet Retief; G11551 Private and Confidential, Opening of Piet Retief/Vryheid line.

24. UG 57–1912, *Report of General Manager*, 1911, p. 6.

25. See clause 1(2) of Act No. 23 of 1913 for the description of a 'light railway'.

26. Frankel, *Railway policy*, pp. 315–16.

27. SAS 1314 RG 19/7, South African Agricultural Congress, Secretary SA Agricultural Congress to Minister of Railways, 11 December 1911.

28. UG 36–1934, *Report of the Railways and Harbour Affairs Commission*, 1934, p. 66.

29. *Debates of the House of Assembly*, January–June 1913, col. 2981.

30. *Ibid.*, cols 2824, 2985, 2986, 2990.

31. *Ibid.*, col. 2990.

32. *Ibid.*, col. 2994.

33. *Debates of the House of Assembly* as reported in the *Cape Times*, vol. vii, February-July 1922, 22 June 1922.

34. *Debates of the House of Assembly*, July–September 1924, col. 945.

35. *Ibid.*, col. 965.

36. SAS 345 FS 14651/10, Electrification Glencoe/Maritzburg, Excess cost. Memorandum on the history of the introduction of elective traction on the railways of South Africa, General Manager, 3 February 1926.

37. Frankel, *Railway policy*, table opposite p. 108. This figure of £37 703 is obtained after the deduction of the amounts for 1926 and 1927 from the total of £50 188 000 given by Frankel at the end of 1927.

38. De Kock, *The results of government ownership*, p. 7.

39. *Debates of the House of Assembly* as reported in the *Cape Times*, vol. 7, February–July 1922, 23 June 1922.

40. UG 57–1912, *Report of General Manager*, 1911, p. 50.

41. *Debates of the House of Assembly*, January–June 1913, cols 2123, 2983.

42. SATS, *Annual Reports of System and Divisional Officers*, 1913, vol. 1, *Report of Divisional Superintendent, Durban*, 1913, p. 53.

43. UG 36–1934, *Report of the Railways and Harbours Affairs Commission*, 1934, p. 87.

44. Frankel, *Railway policy*, pp. 122, 333.

45. See for instance UG 57–1912, *Report of General Manager*, 1911, p. 50 and SATS *Annual Reports of System and Divisional Officers*, vol. 1, 1913, *Report of Divisional Superintendent, Durban*, 1913, p. 53.

46. UG 57–1912, *Report of General Manager*, 1911, p. 15.

47. UG 36–1917, *Report of General Manager*, 1916, p. 51.

48. Horwood (ed.), *Port of Durban*, pp. 18–19.

49. UG 34–1916, *Report of General Manager*, 1915, p. 8.

50. W. R. Guest, 'A history of the Natal coal industry' (unpublished report, HSRC, 1987), p. 18; W. R. Guest, 'Financing an infant coal industry: the case of the Natal collieries', *South African Journal of Economic History*, 3(2), September 1988, p. 41.

51. Guest, 'Natal coal industry', p. 3.

52. *Ibid*, p. 32.

53. *Ibid*, p. 35.

54. UG 36–1917, *Report of General Manager*, 1916, p. 113.

55. UG 34–1927, *Report of General Manager*, 1926–27, pp. 181, 183; Guest, 'Natal coal industry', p. 35.

56. UG 40–1938, *Report of General Manager*, 1937–38, p. 160.

57. UG 54–1928, *Report of General Manager*, 1928, p. 80.

58. Guest, 'Natal coal industry', p. 37.

59. *Ibid.*, pp. 38–39.

60. *Ibid.*, p. 43.

61. Shaffer, *The competitive position of the Port of Durban*, p. 4.

62. *Ibid.*, p. 165 and p. 166 (graph).

63. UG 34–1927, *Report of General Manager*, 1927, p. 54.

64. *Ibid.*, p. 120.

65. Renfrew Christie, *Electricity, industry and class in South Africa* (London, MacMillan, 1984), p. 75.

66. Guest, 'Natal coal industry', p. 21.

67. D. H. Heydenrych, 'Natalse spoorwegbeleid en -konstruksie' (unpublished D.Phil. thesis, University of Stellenbosch, 1981), p. 202.

68. *Ibid*, p. 233.

69. Guest, 'Natal coal industry', p. 18.

70. *Ibid.*, pp. 18–20.

71. De Kock, *The results of government ownership*, pp. 61, 62, 66, 68.

72. UG 57–1912, *Report of General Manager*, 1911, p. 66.

73. Guest, 'Natal coal industry', p. 23.

74. *Ibid.*, p. 24.

75. SATS, *Annual Reports of System and Divisional Officers*, vol. 2, 1918–19, *Report of Divisional Superintendent, Durban*, for 12 months ended 31 March 1919, p. 499.

76. Guest, 'Natal coal industry', p. 24.

77. *Ibid.*, p. 26.

78. UG 38–1914, *Report of General Manager*, 1913, p. 40.

79. UG 25–1915, *Report of General Manager*, 1915, pp. 32–33.

80. UG 43–1918, *Report of General Manager*, 1918, p. 10; Christie, *Electricity, industry and class*, p. 79.

81. *Ibid.*, p. 79; SAS 348, F14651/3, Electrification of Railways, General and Natal, Copy of extract from the third Report of the Committee on Railways and Harbours for the year 1926, Electrification of Railways in Natal, p. 2.

82. SAS 353, F14651/5, Electrification: Natal Main Line, Select Committee Enquiry, 1926, Agreement with Merz & McLellan dated 22 December 1920.

83. SAS 348, F14651/3, Electrification of Railways, General and Natal, Copy of extract from the third Report of the Select Committee on Railways and Harbours for the year 1926, Electrification of Railways in Natal, p. 2.

84. SAS 348, F14651/2, Electrification: Maritzburg-Glencoe, Notes for Minister relative to the debate on the Part Appropriation Bill 1922–23.

85. SAS 348, F14651/3, Electrification, General and Natal, Memorandum by Mr J. R. More . . . Assistant General Manager, South African Railways, Durban, Main Line improvements, Natal – The need for rapid development, p. 5.

86. *Ibid.*, p. 6.

87. SAS 348, F14651/2, Electrification: Maritzburg-Glencoe, Merz & McLellan to Hoy, November 1921, p. 3. Also published in UG 47–1921, *Reports on the Electrification of the Natal Main Line.*

88. SAS 348, F14651/1, Electrification: Maritzburg-Glencoe, *Report by General Manager of Railways and Harbours on the Electrification of the Natal Main Line,* November 1921, pp. 10, 11. Also published in UG 47–1921, *Reports on the Electrification of the Natal Main Line.*

89. *Ibid.*, p. 13.

90. Quoted in Christie, *Electricity, industry and class*, p. 77.

91. *Ibid.*, p. 86.

92. SAS 1083, P12/131/1, Electrification of SAR, Memo for librarian, Johannesburg and Cape Town, 31 March 1920.

93. SAS 1021, P4/14, Electric Power Supply in the Union, Hoy to Kotze, 17 May 1921, p. 2.

94. SAS 1021, P4/14, Electric Power Supply, Memorandum *re* Electricity Supply for Railways and Public Purposes, 10 August 1921, pp. 1–7.

95. *Ibid.*, p. 2.

96. Christie, *Electricity, industry and class*, p. 76.

97. UG 37–1922, *Report of General Manager*, 1921–22, Annexures, p. xvi.

98. UG 40–1923, *Report of General Manager*, 1922–23, Annexures, p. xv.

99. UG 42–1926, *Report of General Manager*, 1925–26, p. 8.

100. *Ibid.*, p. 9.

101. SAS 348, F14651/3, Memorandum for Select Committee on Railways and Harbours . . . Electrification, p. 4.

102. SAS 353, F14651/5, Electrification: Natal Main Line.

103. SAS 349, F14651, Maritzburg-Glencoe Electrification Completion Certificate, Statement of Expenditure on Natal Electrification as at 30 September 1929. (This amount is the total of Escom's assets and the SA Railways and Harbours' assets under the scheme.)

104. SAS 348, F14651/3, Electrification of Railways, General and Natal, Memorandum for Select Committee on Railways and Harbours by General Manager of Railways relative to Controller and Auditor-General's Report on the Railways and Harbours Account, Financial year 1925–26, Electrification, Appendix: Electrification of Railways, 5(ii) Cost of Natal Electrification.

105. E. H. Brookes and C. de B. Webb, *A history of Natal*, (Pietermaritzburg, University of Natal Press, 1965), p. 258.

106. Christie, *Electricity, industry and class*, p. 89. Christie erroneously refers to the 'British Empire'.

107. SATS, AR, 1926, vol. II, SATS, AG, Durban, *Report*, year ended 31 March 1926, p. 72A.

108. SATS, AR, 1927, vol. II, SATS, AG, Durban, *Report*, year ended 31 March 1927, p. 5.

109. Guest, 'Natal coal industry', pp. 22–23.

110. G. B. van Zyl, *Railways*, (Cape Town, South African Party pamphlet, 1929), p. 2.

111. Guest, 'Natal coal industry' pp. 26–27.

112. ATS, AR, 1912, vol. I, SATS, AG, System 'C', p. 3.

113. SATS, AR, 1921, vol. 2, SATS, AG, Durban, *Report*, quarter ended 30 June 1921, p. 39.

114. SATS, AR, 1926, vol. 2, SATS, AG, Durban, Appendix J.

115. *Union statistics for fifty years: jubilee issue, 1910–1960* (Pretoria, Government Printer, 1960), pp. 6–15.

116. SATS, AR, 1912, vol. 2, SATS, NLS, Johannesburg, p. 3.

117. SATS, AR, 1921, vol. 3, SATS, NLS, Johannesburg, p. 1.

118. SATS, AR, 1913, vol. 2, SATS, NLS, Johannesburg; SATS, AR, 1915, vol. 2, Acting NLS, Johannesburg, p. 190.

119. SATS, AR, 1911, SATS, NLS, Pretoria, p. 3; SATS, AR, 1921, vol. 3, SATS, NLS, Johannesburg, p. 6.

120. SATS, AR, 1918, vol. 3, SATS, NLS, p. 4.

121. ATS, AR, 1918–19, vol. 3, SATS, NLS, p. 15; SATS, AR, 1927–28, vol. 3, *Report of System Manager, Durban*, p. 122.

122. SATS, AR, 1912, vol. 1, SATS, AG, System 'C'; SATS, AR, 1918, vol. 3, SATS, NLS, p. 105; SATS, AR, 1918–19, vol. 3, SATS, NLS, p. 764; SATS, AR, 1921, vol. 3, SATS, NLS, Johannesburg, p. 6.

123. SATS, AR, 1918–19, vol. 3, SATS, NLS, pp. 765–66.

124. *Ibid.*, p. 756.

125. SATS, AR, 1918, vol. 3, SATS, NLS, p. 104.

126. *Ibid.*

127. SATS, AR, 1921, vol. 3, SATS, NLS, Johannesburg, p. 6.

128. SATS, AR, 1918–19, vol. 3, SATS, NLS, p. 105.

129. *Ibid.*

130. *Ibid.*, pp. 766–68.

131. SATS, AR, 1910, DS, 1910.

132. SATS, AR, 1914, vol. 1, SATS, DS, Durban, p. 47.

133. *Ibid.*, AR, 1910, SATS, DS, Durban, p. 1.

134. SATS, AR, 1912, vol. 2, SATS, NLS, p. 5.

135. SATS, AR, 1912, vol. 1, SATS, AG, System 'C', p. 44; SATS, AR, 1916, vol. 2, DS, Durban, p. 609.

136. SATS, AR, 1928–29, vol. 2, *Report of System Manager, Durban*, p. 133.

137. *Ibid.*, p. 130.

138. SATS, AR, 1911, *Report of White Labour Superintendent, Pretoria*, p. 1.

139. SATS, AR, 1915, vol. 2, *Report of White Labour Superintendent*, p. 176.

140. SATS, AR, 1921, vol. 2, SATS, AG, Durban, *Report*, quarter ended 30 June 1921, p. 37.

141. SATS, AR, 1925, vol. 2, SATS, AG, Durban, Appendix J: Staff Statement.

142. *Ibid.*

143. This is indicated by Frankel, *Railway policy*, pp. 17, 127.

144. *Ibid.*, p. 128.

145. SATS, AR, 1927, vol. 2, SATS, AG, Durban, pp. 129–30.

146. SATS, AR, 1928–29, vol. 2, *Report of System Manager, Durban*, p. 129.

147. *Ibid.*, pp. 131–32.

ABSTRACT

In 1910 commercial coal-mining in Natal had been under way for little more than two decades. The Klip River district continued to be the main focus of mining activity until the 1930s, although railway development had already opened the way for the exploitation of the north-easterly Utrecht and Vryheid/Paulpietersburg coalfields. Between 1910 and 1980, financial control of the Natal coal industry passed almost entirely from the Durban-based entrepreneurs who had initiated it to large Transvaal-based companies, several of which had other mining interests. This transformation served to integrate Natal's collieries more fully into the much larger South African mining industry and was accompanied by the introduction on some mines of expensive modernisation programmes both below and above ground. These assisted in greatly improving safety standards, implementing more effective methods of counteracting the danger posed by the presence of coal-dust, and upgrading *in loco* medical facilities. The intrusion into the Natal mining industry of big corporations, with large capital resources and established images to maintain, was characterised also by the improved recruitment, accommodation and treatment of labour. From the 1950s it was accompanied also by increasing mechanization and the use of opencast mining methods to boost output. By 1910 the Witwatersrand market had largely, though not permanently, been abandoned to the more favourably situated Transvaal coal industry. Natal's collieries continued to concentrate their marketing efforts primarily on the shipment trade (exports and bunkers) through Durban until the early 1950s when, for a variety of reasons, that market had virtually come to an end. The 1950s and 1960s were, therefore, a difficult transitional period in which the Natal coal industry geared itself more to meeting the domestic requirements of the expanding South African economy, not least those of Escom and Iscor. During the 1970s there was a further dramatic upswing in both domestic and foreign demand, but in the 1980s coal producers experienced fluctuating fortunes, owing to the recessionary conditions, and they continue to face an uncertain future.

AN INTRODUCTION TO THE POST-UNION NATAL COAL INDUSTRY[1]

Bill Guest

The Natal coal industry in 1910

By 1910 the large-scale commercial exploitation of northern Natal's coal deposits had been under way for little more than two decades.[2] Mining activity was still concentrated primarily on the Klip River coalfield between Ladysmith and Newcastle where, for the most part, it paralleled the railway. Since 1889 the rail-link had provided vital access to the port at Durban and since 1895 to the burgeoning market on the Witwaters-rand.[3] There had been an almost seventyfold increase in Natal's coal output between 1889 (25 609 tons) and 1909 (1 786 583 tons). By that stage the north-easterly development of the railway system had facil-itated the more extensive exploitation of the Utrecht and Vryheid/Paulpietersburg coalfields (see map 1, p. 54). Klip River remained the main focus of mining operations in the province until the early 1930s, but with these further deposits, annexed from the Transvaal after the 1899–1902 South African War, Natal entered Union with vast additional reserves. These proved less hazardous to exploit than those of the fiery Klip River coalfield, where several explosions of firedamp and coal-dust had already claimed many lives, and were generally more accessible.[4]

In spite of these encouraging prospects, by 1910 the Natal coal industry faced a variety of challenges that had emerged during the first twenty years of its existence and which threatened to impede its continued expansion and profitability.

The financial structure of the industry

In 1910 the majority of Natal's colliery companies were financed and controlled by local entrepreneurs, based primarily in Durban.[5] By the 1980s there were only a few small independent coal producers still operating in the province, and financial control had passed almost entirely to the Transvaal. Investors were attracted by the superior quality of Natal coal over that of the deeper interior, and by the realisation that the northern districts of the province were South Africa's only known source of true coking coal, which was essential for the manufacture of steel. While several of Natal's colliery companies had initially relied upon British investment capital and some of the earliest had been floated and managed

Black mineworkers coming off shift at Northfield Colliery.

from London,[6] the involvement of 'up-country' capital in local mining enterprises had begun as early as the 1890s. From its establishment in 1897, the Dundee-based South African Collieries Ltd enjoyed the uniquely favourable financial support of the De Beers Company which, in keeping with its policy of encouraging a variety of deserving South African enterprises, continued to sustain it until its voluntary liquidation in 1926. Thereafter, De Beers operated its Northfield Colliery, supplying coal to the mines at Kimberley and to shipping at Durban, before eventually selling out to the Natal Navigation Collieries and Estate Company Ltd in 1934.[7]

This company, which was already outstripping its older Natal rivals by the early 1900s, had been floated with Witwatersrand capital in August 1898, so that Kimberley's financial interest in the region's coal industry was no earlier than that of Johannesburg. By 1908 the company had an impressive £400 000 sterling invested in it. By 1922 it was strong enough to absorb the London-based Vryheid (Natal) Railway Coal and Iron Company. This had been formed in 1907 to exploit the large coal deposits of Hlobane mountain and by the 1920s its Hlobane Colliery had established itself as the province's largest single coal producer.[8]

Hattinghspruit Collieries Ltd, founded in 1908, was another Natal coal-mining enterprise that enjoyed the financial support of influential Johannesburg connections which entitled it to generous overdraft facilities.[9] The Durban Navigation Collieries, established in 1903, eventually came under the control of the Union Mail Steamship Company and in 1937 was sold to the shipping agents Mann George Ltd, a subsidiary of William Cory and Son Ltd of London. In 1954 Iscor acquired a controlling interest in it to ensure a steady supply of the coking coal which was vitally necessary for the making of steel. Several other Natal mining companies that had been initiated by local entrepreneurs were eventually taken over and controlled from Johannesburg. The New Campbell and the long-lasting Natal Cambrian Collieries both fell into this category, the former being acquired by the Hamilton Company Ltd and the latter by the Johannesburg Consolidated Investment Company Ltd (JCI).[10]

In 1945 the Vryheid Coronation Colliery, incorporated in 1923 by the Victoria Falls and Transvaal Power Company and acquired in 1928 by Lewis and Marks, came under the control of the Anglo-American Corporation when it took over all the mining operations of the Lewis and Marks Group.[11] After the Second World War the advance of the Transvaal-based companies into Natal coal-mining continued to gain momentum. By the early 1980s Anglo-American had added the Indumeni mine near Wasbank, the Natal Anthracite Colliery at Hlobane and the Balgray Collieries near Utrecht to its coal-mining interests in the province. After acquiring the Durban Navigation Collieries in 1954 Iscor invested a considerable amount in upgrading its productive capacity. The General Mining Corporation did the same at Hlobane, Northfield and Kilbarchan collieries after 1963 when it succeeded Federale Mynbou, which in 1959 had absorbed the Natal Navigation Group.

While Hlobane Colliery, with its valuable coking-quality deposits, also came under the control of Iscor, and General Mining acquired the Zululand Anthracite Colliery, other large investment companies developed a stake in the Natal coal industry. Barlow Rand Ltd acquired control of the Utrecht, Umgala and Zimbutu mines in the Utrecht vicinity through its ownership of the Welgedacht Exploration Company. Lonrho's coal subsidiary, Duiker Exploration Ltd, acquired the Alpha Anthracite Company near Hlobane as well as property near Piet Retief, and Rand London took over Aloe Minerals Ltd and the Zoetmelk Mine near Vryheid, in addition to Brockwell Anthracite and Kempslust Coal Mine near Paulpietersburg. By the 1980s the Natal Ammonium Colliery, Natal Cambrian Collieries, Longridge Colliery (near Vryheid), Springlake Colliery (near Dundee) and Newcastle Platberg (at Elandslaagte) were all part of the Kangra Group (Pty) Ltd.[12] With the exception of the few remaining independent producers, Natal's collieries had therefore been thoroughly integrated into the much larger South African coal industry of which they became a part following political unification in 1910.

Few locally initiated mining enterprises were able to maintain an independent existence for long into the post-Union period. The small Natal Steam Coal Company of 1896 was a remarkable exception in surviving many financial crises prior to its eventual closure in January 1970. The Dundee Coal Company, which had been the first commercial enterprise to be launched with the specific objective of exploiting Natal's coal deposits on a large scale, also enjoyed unusual longevity. Formed in January 1889 by an astute consortium of Durban merchants and shipowners under the chairmanship of Benjamin Greenacre, it survived as an independent operation until its closure in 1962. The Company's early prominence in the Natal industry was doubtless due in some measure to its initial advantage in being the first to capitalise on the arrival of the railhead in the Klip River coalfield. Even so, its subsequent success in adapting over many years to changing market and financial circumstances owed much to those who launched it and to those who later guided its fortunes.

For all the astuteness of its directors, the Dundee Coal Company continued to be controlled by a small group of families. This promoted an inherent conservatism which ultimately worked to its disadvantage. Its fate was eventually decided by a combination of the sharp downswing in the shipment trade during the early 1950s and the difficulty experienced in maintaining a profitable level of output from its Burnside colliery, where mining conditions were becoming increasingly hazardous. In June 1953 the company's shares were listed for the first time on the Johannesburg Stock Exchange. This reflected its final abandonment of the role of a colliery producing for export and bunkers in favour of that of a manufacturing company concentrating on the production of by-products, from its By-Product Works at Wasbank, for the domestic market.[13]

The subsequent closure of the company symbolised the extent to which the Natal industry was already being dominated by companies which enjoyed the financial support, expertise and bold vision of large Transvaal-based corporations. The expensive modernisation programmes undertaken by Anglo-American at Vryheid Coronation Colliery, by Iscor at its

Durban Navigation Collieries and by the General Mining Corporation at Hlobane, Northfield and Kilbarchan collieries was indicative of the confidence which the industry's new leaders had in its future and of the resources which they had at their disposal.[14] These developments were accompanied by a gradual improvement in the living and working conditions of Natal's colliery workers, and by closer attention to the implementation of safety measures underground.

Accidents and safety regulations

By the 1980s, safety standards in the Natal coal industry had greatly improved over those in operation in 1910,[15] though the explosion which claimed the lives of 68 men at Hlobane No. 1 Colliery in September 1983, and necessitated the rescue of another 400 working elsewhere in the mine, emphasised that the industry was still not immune from major disasters. This was clearly the case even at one of the province's pre-eminent collieries which had enjoyed the benefit of a continuous process of modernisation.

In common with previous major mining accidents, the explosion at Hlobane did lead to some improvement in safety precautions, at least at the colliery concerned. New techniques were implemented to channel an adequate supply of fresh air to all the working faces, and gas detection was facilitated by the provision of more methanometers and a doubling of the number of safety lamps in use that were fitted with the Garforth modification. This was a probe attachment which made it possible to detect combustible quantities of methane gas in the layers of air immediately below the roof of each working section. Of more general significance to the industry as a whole was the agreement that self-contained rescue equipment, designed to facilitate survival in the event of any future disaster, was to be provided in all South African mines by the end of 1985.[16] The enforcement of this provision was later postponed, but its acceptance was an important milestone in the gradual improvement of safety precautions and suggested that the many lives lost in earlier colliery disasters (not least in Natal) had not been entirely in vain.

The effective implementation of such safety regulations as existed had always depended largely upon the harassed mining inspectorate and, following unification in 1910, the overstretched Mines Department (established in 1887) was reorganised. In recognition of the fiery nature and peculiar characteristics of the Natal collieries, a distinction was established between the engineering and technical aspects of mining on the one hand, and the administrative functions on the other. The latter included the legal aspects, the registration of mining titles and the collection of rents, licences, registration fees and royalties. This enabled the inspectorate to concentrate its efforts on enforcing the new Mines and Works Act (No. 12 of 1911), which now became applicable to the Natal coal industry and which was subsequently amended in the light of experience gained from further colliery accidents. It also made it possible to give closer attention to the particular problems relating to the Natal collieries and to formulate new regulations and 'special rules' for them as and when these seemed to be necessary.[17]

One of the areas in which significant improvements were effected in the post-Union period of the industry's history was in counteracting the danger posed by the presence of coal-dust. In August 1908, following the Glencoe and Cambrian explosions earlier that year, samples of coal were sent from Elandslaagte, St George's and Durban Navigation Collieries to be tested at Altoft's Laboratory in England. The tests confirmed that, even in the absence of firedamp, there was a danger of major explosions as a result of blasting in dusty Natal collieries. Three methods of prevention were recommended, i.e. dust removal, watering and stone-dusting. The last of these, being the most practical, was gradually applied to those of Natal's collieries which were recognised as 'fiery', i.e. having had specified quantities of methane gas found in them within the previous six months.

Considerable difficulty was encountered in acquiring and distributing the stone-dust but the need for even stricter precautions was emphasised by the methane gas and coal-dust explosion which wiped out an entire night shift of 124 men at the Durban Navigation No. 2 Colliery in October 1926, and which still ranks as the worst mine disaster thus far experienced in Natal. The afflicted colliery led the way in installing a system of water sprays, as well as shelves from which stone-dust could be distributed through perforated compressed-air pipes that made use of the mine ventilation. The Cambrian Colliery installed a similar system for water spraying and stone-dusting, while the Northfield Colliery began to crush shale underground and distribute the resultant stone-dust with the aid of a distributor attached to the haulage rope.[18]

By 1930 all of Natal's 'fiery' mines were being subjected to comprehensive stone-dusting, while local expertise was improved by maintaining contact with the British Safety in Mines Research Institute at Buxton in England. Tests conducted there on Natal coal samples and subsequent experience in the local industry itself showed that there was still no room for complacency. During the 1950s, as a further precaution, greater resort was made to the wet cutting of coal, as well as the wetting of broken coal following blasting operations and the washing down of haulages. In 1954 the coal owners established a central dust-sampling laboratory at Dundee and in the following year limestone dust was used in local collieries for the first time in an effort to minimise the injurious effects of stone-dusting on the health of colliery workers by reducing the free silica content of the dust to less than 3 per cent.

The mining inspectorate's persistent agitation for expenditure on more efficient systems of mine ventilation was greatly assisted in 1958 by the introduction into Natal of regulations under the Pneumoconiosis Act. This was followed, at considerable expense to the colliery companies, by the improvement of existing air passages to the working faces, the installation of more and better fans and the sinking of additional ventilation shafts. The provision of more shafts also had the effect of putting virtually all working faces within reasonable walking distance of an entrance and facilitated rescue operations in the event of accidents underground.[19]

In this connection, another significant development was the construction in 1924 of the Central Rescue Station at Dundee, equipped with proto-oxygen apparatus. The provision of this facility was delayed by years of argument between the coal owners and the Mines Department as to who was responsible for the cost. Once in place, its effectiveness in saving lives was limited by the fact that the men trained in rescue work still had to be summoned from widely dispersed mines whenever there was a colliery explosion or other major disaster. In most instances the rescue team arrived only in time to assist in the removal of corpses and the restoration of ventilation to the working faces. A team of blacks was eventually trained to undertake the heavy manual work involved, while a team of whites was organised to perform the more dangerous tasks.[20]

By 1946 the Central Rescue Station had trained 19 whites and 39 blacks in rescue work, and had at its disposal 20 sets of proto apparatus and 4 sets of Novita Oxygen equipment. None of the collieries had as yet gone to the expense of organising its own rescue teams when, in 1963, the service provided by the station at Dundee was greatly strengthened by the demarcation of four zones, each equipped with its own proto room and properly trained teams. Self-rescue equipment was prescribed as early as 1923 but, prior to the 1985 agreement concerning its mandatory use, many more lives were lost because colliery owners were reluctant to increase working costs by investing in safety devices such as the Burrell carbon monoxide mask which was available locally in the early 1940s.[21]

Prior to Union the payment of compensation for employees killed or injured in accidents was left to the discretion of employers. The Native Labour Regulation Act (No. 15 of 1911) initiated the compulsory insurance of black workers, while Indian and white employees came under the provisions of the Workmen's Compensation Act. The task of assessing the amount of compensation due to black accident victims was entrusted to the Director of Native Labour. It amounted to no more than between £1 and £20 sterling in cases of partial incapacity and between £30 and £50 in cases of death or total permanent incapacity. No compensation was payable in cases in which the victim was himself deemed responsible for the accident, although the Director of Native Labour would occasionally appeal to the employer concerned to make a 'compassionate grant'. It was only in 1934 that black miners were included under the provisions of a new Workmen's Compensation Act, which provided access to a much-improved scale of benefits in the event of death or injury as a result of a mining accident.[22]

The effects of such accidents were also ameliorated by a gradual improvement in the medical facilities available on Natal's collieries, for the quality of the first-aid treatment provided often made the difference between recovery and death. In 1915 it was reported that there were still no hospitals 'worthy of the name' on the province's mines. Elandslaagte and Hlobane Collieries had their own 'hospitals' but they were understaffed and far too small for the size of the labour force they served. It was recognised that each and every mine could not be expected to provide sophisticated medical care, but colliery managers were urged at least to set up emergency dressing-stations. The idea of a joint hospital, either at Hattinghspruit or at Glencoe Junction, was also given official encouragement, but the wide geographical distribution of Natal's mines made it difficult to agree on an appropriately central site.[23]

While accident victims and other miners in need of medical attention continued to die in the compounds, or in transit by train or horse-drawn ambulance to Dundee, little was done to improve the medical facilities on individual mines. In 1942 it could still be reported that, with two exceptions, they were 'quite inadequate and approximately similar to conditions existing on the Witwatersrand prior to the Great War'. From 1924, mine-hospital superintendents were required to hold nursing certificates but for many years little or no other medical expertise was immediately available. Even in the 1940s, few colliery workers were trained to render first aid and there was often a long delay before casualties could be brought to the surface. Nine of the ten black miners who suffered second-degree burns in the firedamp explosion at Durban Navigation No. 2 Colliery in November 1951 subsequently died of secondary shock. Some, at least, might have survived had they been given morphine injections shortly after the accident. By the late 1940s many of Natal's mines enjoyed the benefit of regular visits by local doctors and other medical personnel. In addition to their ordinary services, they were able to offer family care, maternity help and anti-venereal treatment to colliery workers and those dependants residing with them.[24]

However, such visits seldom, if ever, coincided with major emergencies and it was only in the late 1950s and 1960s that the provision of significantly better *in loco* medical facilities and more extensive first-aid training schemes for employees became evident. These developments were but a part of the improved recruitment and treatment of labour that characterised the increasing intrusion into the local mining industry of big Transvaal-based companies with large capital resources and established corporate images to maintain.

The recruitment and treatment of labour

After Union, as before it, Natal's collieries continued to encounter difficulty in attracting indigenous black labour in sufficient numbers and for long enough contractual periods to satisfy their needs. Local coal owners persisted in explaining the problem in terms of the unfair competition of unscrupulous Transvaal labour touts and traditional colonial notions of black indolence. After inspecting the local collieries in response to a plea for help from the Natal Coal Owners' Society, (formed in January 1909), the new Union government's Secretary for Native Affairs conceded in 1910 that the methods used to obtain labour for the Witwatersrand gold-mines had 'frequently been far from honest'. He nevertheless found it surprising that the province's coal industry should experience a labour crisis considering that the gold-mines were so much further inland, and that while their recruits had always been debited with the cost of their own recruitment this had not been the case with colliery recruits.[25]

The committee eventually appointed in 1918 by the Minister of Native Affairs to investigate Natal's labour shortage exposed more fundamental causes than unfair competition when it highlighted the province's excessive pre-Union reliance upon anti-tout legislation, passed by a sympathetic colonial parliament, and upon the importation of indentured Indian labour which constituted 44,5 per cent of the work-force in 1902. It suggested that, for these reasons, there had been 'less practical exploitation of labour resources in Natal than in either the Cape or the Transvaal, or indeed in any of the South African Protectorates'. It urged the province's large-scale employers to collaborate in devising more effective recruiting methods and in providing more attractive conditions of employment.[26]

The Director of Native Labour in Pretoria emphasised the need for a central recruiting organisation that represented all the collieries by pointing to the advantage enjoyed by the Transvaal gold-mines since 1912 when they had co-ordinated their recruitment programmes under the Native Recruiting Corporation (NRC). This body had grown out of the Rand Native Labour Association, formed in 1898. It focused its energies on the recruitment of labour from within South Africa and the neighbouring British Protectorates while its counterpart, the Witwatersrand Native Labour Association (WNLA), recruited in regions further afield.[27]

Within a year, the NRC had made a significant impact in draining off labour from the Vryheid district of northern Natal, yet local coal producers, several of whom claimed a labour shortfall of between 30 per cent and 50 per cent, failed to respond in the appropriate manner. The formation of a centralised recruiting agency was hinted at in 1912, when the NRC was established, and seriously mooted two years later, but the proposal was delayed because certain collieries were reluctant to participate and neither the Coal Owners' Society nor the Mine Managers' Association (established in 1903) was willing to take the initiative.[28] Both bodies anticipated that the declaration in 1924 of two 'labour districts' in northern Natal, Dundee and Vryheid, under the provisions of the Native Labour Regulation Act (No. 15 of 1911), would ease the labour crisis by prohibiting recruitment on behalf of employers situated outside those districts. The government, however, refused to provide such protection on the grounds that the total black population of the region, estimated to be 142 182 in 1912, far exceeded the labour requirements of the local collieries.[29]

The Natal Coal Owners' Society rejected the renewed suggestion that it should form for itself a combined recruiting organisation, insisting that such a step would actually increase the competition for labour unless colliery owners were permitted to extend their current fields of recruiting operations. However, the government was unwilling to allow competition with the gold industry in the recruitment of 'tropical' labour from Portuguese East Africa. In the absence of any co-ordinated recruiting scheme, Natal's coal-mines continued as before to secure their labour as best they could independently of each other, and with varying degrees of success.[30] The employment of Indians, whether indentured or 'free', was no longer a viable alternative, for although they still constituted as much as

40,58 per cent of the total labour force in 1910, their numbers dwindled steadily thereafter as all primary five-year indentures expired in 1915 and 'free' Indians demonstrated a preference for other occupations. By 1926 they constituted 8,67 per cent of the industry's total labour force and by 1965 they amounted to only 1,44 per cent.[31]

By the 1920s, if not earlier, it was clear that Natal's collieries would have to rely on indigenous black labour to satisfy their requirements. here were no officially demarcated black 'reserves' or 'locations' in northern Natal, as were to be found in the midlands and coastal belt, but the region did have the largest concentration of black-owned land in Natal, as well as several mission-owned farms which provided accommodation for colliery workers and their families. Those collieries which were situated near existing pockets of settled black population were fortunate. So too were those which owned the farms they were mining as this enabled them to encourage labourers to settle and build their own family accommodation, such properties becoming known as 'schoonplaats'.[32]

These circumstances enabled at least some of the collieries to develop a stable core of married labourers who were settled more or less permanently at or near their places of employment, and who were therefore able to become proficient in skilled tasks which had previously been performed by Indians. The creation of permanent villages or 'farm colonies' on colliery property was contrary to the 1923 Natives (Urban Areas) Act which prohibited blacks from living permanently in urban-industrial regions. Despite official disapproval and attempts to limit the proportion of married blacks in the mine labour force to 15 per cent, the presence of these settlements became a prominent feature of the Natal coal industry as colliery owners and managers increasingly appreciated the advantages of a permanently settled married work-force.[33]

However, such settlements were never sufficiently large to meet the required complement of labour. Even the small Natal Steam Coal Company, which enjoyed the advantage of a large rent-tenant population on the nearby black-owned *Stein Coal Spruit* farm right up until the closure of its mine in 1970, found it necessary to cast its recruiting net further afield. The larger colliery companies had to contend with labour recruitment and stabilisation on a much bigger scale, but for all of them the labour supply was one of those crucial variables which required constant attention on the part of management and which could adversely affect output and therefore financial performance.[34]

In addition to the labour drawn from neighbouring pockets of black settlement, Natal's coal mines also recruited through networks of agents, including country storekeepers in Transkei, Mpondoland, East and West Griqualand, Zululand, Swaziland, the Transvaal, Lesotho and, in one case, Botswana. By 1928 the industry had 227 licensed agents recruiting on its behalf all over the subcontinent with per capita premiums on the labourers provided, rates of pay and other conditions of employment varying substantially from one agent to the next. While Natal's coal mines were not permitted to compete with the Transvaal gold industry in recruiting labour from Mozambique, colliery managers were usually willing to employ illegal migrants who came through Swaziland and Piet Retief.[35]

Faced with an erratic and unpredictable labour supply, and with a decline in the numbers of its Indian employees, the Natal coal industry resorted to other ways of developing a permanent labour core for itself, or at least of postponing the loss of those workers that it was able to recruit. One method was to extend the duration of labour contracts by interpreting the term 'month' as 'a period of thirty days worked' whereas the Natal Master and Servants Act No. 40 of 1894, which included black colliers in its definition of 'servant', defined 'month' simply as 'a period of thirty days'. Furthermore, labourers were not always given tasks to perform on every working day. Consequently, a recruit who had contracted to work for six months might take as long as a year or eighteen months to fulfil his obligation, depending upon the fluctuations in market demand and output levels which, in turn, determined the number of shifts worked.

Contract labourers coming off shift often had their work-tickets marked 'togt', which meant that they were not credited with that day against their contracts. This was often done to individuals who had not filled their daily quota of coal trucks and, it was alleged, they were not paid on such occasions. It was also claimed that some mines resorted to the device of not giving labourers a formal discharge, thereby exposing them to arrest on the grounds of desertion if they sought employment elsewhere. In addition, the month's notice required on completion of contracts was often repeatedly disregarded by compound managers, compelling employees to work for several months in excess of the contracted period or risk arrest for desertion.[36]

The most ingenious method of labour retention employed on Natal's collieries was the 'token' system. This evolved by means of close collaboration between mine management and the storekeepers who held the franchise to trade on colliery property. The 'system' involved the granting of easy credit to black colliers through the issue of disc-coupons or tokens in lieu of money which had then to be redeemed on pay-day. Businesses in northern Natal towns protested that it was impossible to compete with the mine stores because they refused to redeem any tokens accepted in town from miners in lieu of cash, and because of the rural isolation of so many of the collieries. Mine store franchise-holders were able to take full advantage of their monopoly, to the extent of even being allowed to sit at the pay tables in mine offices so that they could recover debts. The collieries benefited in so far as many of their black employees became virtually tied to them after being lulled by easy credit into a more or less permanent state of indebtedness.

Various commodities could be purchased with these discs but the most contentious aspect of the token system involved the sale of beer through beerhalls and eating houses operated either by the mine stores or by the mines themselves. These were often strategically situated between the mine shaft and the compound gates to attract parched workers as they came off shift. In 1910 the Secretary for Native Affairs indicated his disapproval of such sales because they created 'the impression that the wages paid out to the Natives by the Mine Owners with the one hand, are taken back by them with the other, through the medium of these beer shops'.[37] Transkeian magistrates eventually complained that recruits from their districts had been unable to save any money after being induced to spend their pay in advance. In 1928 it was estimated that nearly five-sixths of beer sales on the collieries were being effected on credit by means of the token system or else by deductions through the pay-sheets.[38]

The sale of beer on credit did promote drunkenness among mine workers both off and on duty, but the concern this aroused was outweighed by the perceived advantage in any means of retaining a more or less permanent labour force. The token system only fell into disfavour with the colliery companies themselves when it was realised that some kraal-heads were actively discouraging potential recruits from going to Natal's mines because of the better prospects for saving money in other avenues of employment.[39] A notice officially banning the system, which appeared in the *Government Gazette* in 1934, was declared *ultra vires* following an appeal against it by Mine Stores (Natal) Ltd, a limited liability company formed in 1911 by Messrs Lazarus Brothers, which by that stage operated an extensive chain of businesses on the Natal collieries.

The days of the token system were nevertheless numbered and those who continued to operate it were warned that appropriate legislation would be introduced unless credit was limited to 45 per cent of an employee's wages. Following a commission of enquiry, the system was officially terminated as from 1 March 1938, together with other forms of credit to employees on mines and works. By then several of Natal's colliery companies had already stopped all forms of credit on their own initiative and were taking an increasing interest in the system of voluntary deferred pay. This already operated in the Transvaal as a means of attracting labour through the substantial amounts that could be saved by the end of a contract period.[40]

The Natal coal industry continued to struggle to meet its own labour requirements and the termination of the token system, coupled with the wartime increase in demand for coal and hence for greater output, again focused attention on the need for a central labour recruiting agency. The reluctance of various collieries to reveal their respective sources of labour was a major obstacle to its realisation. In 1942 there was still talk of joining either the Witwatersrand Native Labour Association, which had been permitted to supply Natal's mines with Mozambican recruits as a temporary wartime measure for the previous two years, or the Native Recruiting Corporation, which had begun to supply labour by way of compensation when that arrangement was discontinued.

In 1943 the Natal Coal Owners' Society at last took the initiative when it formed a limited liability company that was registered as the Natal Coal Owners' Native Labour Association. The Dundee Coal Company was a prominent participant, subscribing 3 512 shares after overcoming its earlier ambivalence towards the creation of such an organization. By 1945 the company had to contend with a rare labour surplus because the new

NCONLA was sending more workers than requested and none could be turned away because they were recruits and not volunteers.[41]

However, the industry's labour shortage persisted into the 1950s and encouraged the trend towards labour-saving mechanized mining methods which was gathering momentum. While it was clear that the industry's methods of recruitment, with a traditional reliance on country store-keepers, still required improvement, it was also evident that the reputation of the collieries with regard to the treatment and accommodation of employees also significantly influenced their capacity to attract sufficient manpower. This applied not only to the recruitment of blacks but also of whites, who have always constituted a small but important element in the industry's work-force. In 1909, when they constituted 4,5 per cent of those employees engaged in 'productive' (i.e. coal-getting) work, the ratio of white to black employees was approximately 1:19 (431 whites among 8 540 employed) and this was much the same in 1965 (1 409 whites in a total work-force of 27 865), compared to a ratio of 1:9,9 in the South African coal industry as a whole.[42]

The Natal collieries initially relied very heavily on British recruits to fill the supervisory and managerial posts that were so essential to the successful development of the industry. Many of them lacked the qualifications and dependability required for the responsible tasks entrusted to them, but they at least had a familiarity with coal-mining which was almost wholly lacking in southern Africa. Many of them tended to drift from one mine to another, or out of the industry altogether. Others rendered a lifetime of service, providing a vital core of experience and expertise. It was only in the 1930s that Natal's collieries began to rely increasingly upon locally recruited whites to fill positions of responsibility, though attracting and retaining suitable employees remained a perennial challenge.[43]

The Mine Managers' Association and the Coal Owners' Society explored various ways of increasing the number of white learner miners and improving the level of their training. These included recruitment talks in Natal high schools, notices in local newspapers, and the appointment of a training officer to co-ordinate training schemes at the various mines on the basis of a common curriculum. The establishment of a central training school was considered too costly and it was gradually realised that recruitment campaigns, systematic training schemes and even improved rates of pay could not obviate the need to upgrade living and working conditions in order to persuade more men to make their careers in coal-mining.[44]

Some collieries, like the Dundee Coal Company's mine at Burnside, were equipped with reasonably comfortable housing and recreational facilities for white employees as early as the 1930s. On others the living conditions were still grossly inadequate until well into the 1940s, and in some cases until the 1950s and 1960s. Expenditure on accommodation for black employees continued, as before Union, to be accorded an even lower priority and was one of the factors which encouraged Indian workers to seek more congenial avenues of employment. In January 1915 the

Inspector of Native Labour (Dundee district) reported that he could 'scarcely imagine the possibility of a worse condition of things than prevails in the married quarters on the Collieries'. By the end of 1919, as Natal's colliery managers began to appreciate the advantages of employing settled married labourers, experiments were being conducted with different types of family housing, ranging from barracks to self-contained cottages erected in village formation.[45]

The subsequent official disapproval of permanent settlements on colliery property by no means brought them to an abrupt end, but it did encourage colliery companies in their traditional tendency to be much more actively concerned with the provision of single quarters for the migrants who constituted the vast majority of the work-force. Even so, such accommodation was only gradually upgraded. The new regulations promulgated in 1915 under the Natal Health Act (No. 44 of 1901) did effect some improvements, to the extent that in 1922 the Assistant Union Health Officer declared the single quarters to be 'comparable with those existing on the Witwatersrand'. It was probably an exaggeration, for much still depended upon the persuasive ability of inspecting officials to convince colliery companies of the need to upgrade housing facilities. As Dr White, medical officer for the Enyati and Bernica mines, pointed out to the 1918 Labour Shortage Commission, the mining companies were under no obligation 'to house the boys properly, give them proper beds to sleep on, to see that the cubical [sic] space is sufficient or to prevent them taking braziers into the rooms'. The use of braziers was particularly dangerous, especially in badly ventilated barracks, because it resulted in cases of carbon monoxide poisoning.[46]

The 1915 regulations did little to establish minimum standards for sanitation and washing facilities. By 1918 the Dundee Coal Company was installing a water-borne system and septic tank on its Burnside Colliery but, in the absence of tighter reulations, this standard could not be imposed upon other collieries. Most preferred the cheaper method of disposing of bucket contents by incineration, though the practice of simply burying night-soil in the mine-dump was only reluctantly abandoned in some cases in spite of the stench to which this gave rise. The 1915 regulations were also largely ineffective in establishing a minimum scale of rations, merely indicating that 'the food and water supplied shall be of proper wholesome character and in sufficient quantity'. This gave rise to considerable variation among the Natal collieries, though in 1918 it was claimed that the average diet for black employees comprised 3 lb. of mealie meal per day, 2 lb. of meat and $1\frac{1}{2}$ lb. of vegetables per week served as a stew, as well as 2 lb. of boiled mealies and 2 pints of beer per week.[47]

There was also variation in the quantity and frequency of beer rations but by 1918 most of Natal's collieries were using this as a means of attracting recruits, quite apart from the additional sale of beer by means of the token system. Several colliery companies began to brew their own beer, though they were restricted by legislation (Act No. 30 of 1928) to a free daily issue of one pint per employee per day which was subsequently increased to 12 pints per employee per week. Following representations made by the Anglo-American Corporation, Jabula Instant Beer Powder, supplied by Jabula Foods (Pty) Ltd, was eventually used quite extensively. It consisted of pre-cooked maize that had been powdered and mixed with similarly ground 'kaffir-corn' malt and was available for consumption in 24 hours after water and brewer's yeast had been added in the recommended proportions. Complaints on the part of officials that Jabula beer exceeded the limit of 2 per cent alcohol content were readily resolved by the addition of more water to the prescribed formula.[48]

Wages, service contracts, shifts, hours of work, holidays and recreational facilities all continued to be sources of grievance well into the twentieth century. Insufficient research has been done on the Transvaal coal industry to compare its wage and cost structure with that of its Natal counterpart. It is, however, evident that wage levels on the Natal coalfields remained at least 10 per cent lower than those obtainable on the Witwatersrand and there were no significant increases for whites or blacks prior to the 1960s. In contrast to the piece-work system that was applied on the Transvaal gold-mines, the shift-system continued to operate on Natal's collieries and the length of underground shifts continued to vary according to market fluctuations, extending to 13 hours and more when demand was high or trucks were available for loading. Extended shifts gave rise to problems of feeding and sanitation underground and also led to accidents, a hazard which was further aggravated by inadequate leave provisions.[49]

It was only in 1917 that ten days' leave per annum on half-pay was conceded to white miners who had worked continuously for one year at the same colliery. Few qualified, but from 1919 all white miners were entitled to twelve days per annum on full pay and both Good Friday and Christmas Day were conceded as paid holidays. Annual leave entitlement was extended to eighteen days in 1935 and three years later a bonus of £2.10.0 per week of holiday leave due was also granted. These concessions were not extended to black mineworkers, apart from the two religious holidays. Apart from makeshift football pitches, there were virtually no recreational facilities prior to the 1940s, when some collieries built entertainment halls in which films were occasionally shown, and inter-colliery first-aid, tribal dancing and football competitions were organised. The last of these was indefinitely suspended in 1951 because of over-enthusiasm among teams and spectators which threatened at times to deteriorate into violence. There were remarkably few incidents of violence among black workers considering the limited recreational facilities available, the harsh living and working conditions and the multi-ethnic composition of the workforce.[50]

Indeed, most of the violence on Natal's collieries seems to have been inflicted by whites upon blacks, either in the form of corporal punishment or in the form of assaults by white overseers and compound managers. The mining inspectorate was virtually powerless to prevent either this or the imposition of heavy fines. Colliery companies had to strike their own balance between protecting black employees from being abused and allowing white supervisors sufficient latitude to enforce the discipline required to prevent accidents and maintain output. In 1918 it was estimated that roughly 50 per cent of the desertions from Natal's collieries were due to such violence. By the late 1920s assaults were less common, possibly because of more frequent prosecutions.[51]

Desertion nevertheless continued to be one of the most common ways in which black miners expressed their dissatisfaction with conditions on Natal's mines. The rate of desertion varied from one colliery to the next, rising to as much as 23 per cent in the case of Hlobane Colliery during the mid-1920s. Desertions increased during the Second World War when the army readily provided alternative employment, but in 1952 the overall rate was still as high as 17 per cent. This, it was claimed, was higher than the desertion rate from Transvaal gold-mines because the Natal collieries were in much closer proximity to the homes of many of their black employees. As much as 30 per cent of desertions occurred within the first six days of employment due, in part, to misrepresentation on the part of recruiting agents and misunderstanding by recruits as to the rates of pay and the nature of the work involved.[52]

In addition to desertion while under contract, black miners also expressed their dissatisfaction by not returning to the collieries on completion of contracts and by means of strike action. It is uncertain what percentage of workers declined to renew their contracts though, as with desertions, there was considerable variation among the collieries.[53] The 1911 Native Labour Regulation Act attached criminal liability to strike action on the part of black miners and, prior to the 1920s, such occurrences were rare on the Natal coalfields.

Faced with strong employer opposition and many other difficulties involved in unionizing black workers, it was not until 1943 that the Natal African Coal Workers' Union was eventually formed, followed in 1945 by the establishment of the Natal Non-European Mine Workers' Union to represent the interests of Indian and 'coloured' employees. However, both organisations were small, unregistered and easily ignored.[54] Prompted by the *Satyagraha* (passive resistance) campaign initiated in the Transvaal by Mohandas Gandhi, Indian colliery workers had at least 'inconvenienced', if not disrupted the Natal coal industry during the 1913 strike against the £3 tax, but indigenous black strikers enjoyed no such success. Colliery owners and managers stamped out any signs of disturbance and 'agitators' were quickly identified. It was not until August 1982 that black colliery workers at last acquired a meaningful voice when the first black National Union of Mineworkers was formed.[55]

White trade-unionism in the Natal coal industry was more successful, though not spectacularly so. In 1910 an unsuccessful attempt was made to form a white miners' union in the province, but three years later a local branch of the Transvaal Miners' Association was established. It was largely responsible for organising the white miners' strike of January 1914 which was part of the general strike called by the South African Federation of Trade Unions at that time. Approximately half of the industry's white employees joined the demand for shorter shifts, better pay and the provision of change-house facilities, but they were forced back to work largely on the coal owners' terms. Natal's white colliers did eventually form their own Mine Workers' Association in September 1916, linking it to the Transvaal Mine Workers' Union in May 1935, but in subsequent negotiations conducted through the Conciliation Board, established in May 1916, the coal owners continued to hold the upper hand. The reasons are not clear but may lie in the rural isolation of most collieries, the strong sense of community identity which this imposed on some, particularly the smaller ones, and the small numbers of whites employed in the industry: still only 875 in 1953 and 1 409 in 1965.[56]

Strike action and trade-unionism does not seem to have had much effect on the improvement of living and working conditions on Natal's collieries. The declaration in 1924 of the two labour districts, Dundee and Vryheid, was a step in that direction, but it did not produce a spectacular upliftment of the accommodation and other facilities provided for blacks, contrary to the expectations of the mining inspectorate that it would lead to more effective governmental control over the collieries and facilitate a 'levelling up of conditions' upon them. It had already been recognised that it was 'impossible to exercise control by mere recommendation', yet such improvements as were effected after 1924 still owed much to the frequency with which the inspectors were able to visit the various mines, and their persuasiveness. They also depended upon the extent to which the colliery companies themselves gradually recognized the advantages of providing, within their financial means, more congenial living conditions for their employees.[57] For example, despite the official declaration in August 1928 that all mine compounds were to be furnished with beds or bunks, on many collieries these were still conspicuous by their absence nearly twenty years later.[58]

Some significant improvements did become evident on certain collieries during the late 1940s when, for example, the Natal Navigation Group launched a programme of renovation and modernisation which other Transvaal-based companies were to emulate.[59] These improvements to mine properties in the province were not confined to the surface but were extended to working conditions underground.

Mining methods

By 1910 Natal collieries had already adopted as their most common method of working the pillar and stall (bord and pillar) system, which involves cutting up the coal areas leaving pillars which, once the area has been mined out, are extracted in a retreating line which allows the roof to collapse behind, thereby forming goaves. In situations where the seam being mined was less than three feet thick, the longwall method was preferable. This involves working the coal on a long face and packing the mined-out portion in order to maintain the roof. However, most colliery managers in Natal regarded the pillar and stall method as the most appropriate for their purposes in view of the many, largely unskilled workers in their employ who would otherwise have required additional costly supervision in undertaking systematic timbering, constructing pack walls and operating face conveyors.

As this suggests, by 1910 the Natal coal industry was characterised by simple hand-got mining methods, involving hand-loading and hand-tramming of the broken coal between coal-face and haulage. This continued to be the case until well into the 1950s. In some instances, where returns justified it, such as the rich coking seam at Enyati Colliery, face conveyors were installed but, for the most part, local mining companies remained reluctant to undertake the heavy expenditure involved in purchasing, installing and maintaining items of machinery. By the 1930s pneumatic picks were being introduced and by 1940 more than 75 per cent of the province's total output was undercut mechanically. Nevertheless, the industry's increased output of only 2 000 tons per day in response to the government's request for an additional 5 000 tons to meet the higher demand during the Second World War revealed the limited plant capacity of most local collieries and the low level of mechanization which they had thus far attained.[60]

Attempts to rectify this shortcoming were evident after the war and gathered momentum during the 1950s and 1960s. In 1950 the fully mechanized Ballengeich section of the Natal Cambrian Colliery was opened, the first of its kind in the province. Subsequently, at the Newcastle-Platberg Colliery, at Indumeni (near Wasbank) and at Vryheid-Coronation Colliery new sections were fully mechanized, while old ones continued to operate with traditional hand-got methods. By the 1960s the depletion of the thicker seams, which were more easily mined, highlighted the need to develop safe and economical methods of thin-seam mining, in which experience had already shown that the pillar and stall methods so widely used in Natal were inappropriate. The complete mechanization of some conventional pillar and stall operations was also attempted by means of mechanical loaders and battery-operated shuttle cars, both of which devices were first imported into South Africa in the late 1940s. One distinction to which the Natal industry could lay claim was that mechanized opencast mining methods were attempted for the first time in the subcontinent in the Gus seam horizon at Hlobane No. 1 Colliery.[61]

During the 1970s the further use of sophisticated capital-intensive techniques was more evident in the Transvaal and Orange Free State, but there were also some notable advances in Natal. In 1971, for example, the mechanization of pillar mining was introduced at Kilbarchan Colliery near Newcastle, to expedite the supply of coal via conveyor belts to the neighbouring Ingagane power station at a rate of 136 000 tons per month as originally contracted in 1959. By these means Kilbarchan was easily able to meet this commitment, until the severe drought of 1983 forced the temporary closure of the power station. It was also able to supply Iscor with about 480 000 tons per annum between 1976 and 1982, when the latter terminated the contract and began to draw all its supplies from one of its own mines.[62]

While Kilbarchan embarked upon the mechanisation of pillar mining, the Durban Navigation Colliery (DNC), which was the largest in Natal, successfully introduced mechanized longwalling after first experimenting with it in 1965. The widespread adoption of this method throughout South

Africa was precluded by the capital outlay involved, coupled with problems of roof control and operating inflexibility. However, its success at the DNC was assured through the gradual modification of the techniques involved in the light of experience there, and through the acquisition of equipment that was suited to local conditions. The two longwall faces established there in 1975 and 1976 subsequently produced 40 per cent of DNC's washed output. Production by the more conventional pillar and stall methods was also increased as part of the R29-million expansion programme embarked upon in 1974 at DNC. In spite of the high capital outlay on equipment involved in mechanized longwalling the final cost per ton proved to be marginally lower than that obtained by using other mining methods and a cleaner product, as well as a higher extraction rate, was ultimately achieved.[63]

A third modernisation programme undertaken in Natal during the 1970s was initiated by Gencor at Hlobane No. 1 Colliery, where the new Boomlager section, opened up to the west of the Alfred fault in Hlobane mountain, was fully mechanized except for the process of pillar extraction in this pillar and stall mine. The programme, estimated to cost R90 million, was planned to achieve an ultimate productive capacity of 972 000 tons per annum in response to the coking coal needs of Iscor. It was still in progress in 1983 when the world-wide crisis in the steel industry necessitated a cutback in Iscor's steel production and hence a decline in its coking coal requirements. However, Kilbarchan, Durban Navigation Colliery and Hlobane were not the only Natal mines to be exposed to modern techniques. By 1977 most of the province's collieries could boast operating sections that were mechanized or at least partly mechanized, and many were also boosting their output by means of opencast methods which in 1975 accounted for 13 per cent of South Africa's total production.[64]

The further phase of modernisation which characterised coal-mining methods in Natal during the 1950s, 1960s and 1970s was due partly to the advance of the financially well-endowed and image-conscious Witwatersrand mining houses into the local industry. It was attributable also to the sustained domestic demand for Natal's coal after the Second World War.

The marketing of Natal coal

Natal's collieries had always satisfied the needs of the immediate domestic market within the province itself but, in the absence of any significant local industrial development, that absorbed only 7,2 per cent of total output in 1909 and has never increased sufficiently to sustain the whole industry. The rapidly expanding Witwatersrand market, which had provided the rationale for railway construction into the interior, initially offered much better prospects, but in 1909 it absorbed only 8,5 per cent of Natal's coal output (compared with 14,9 per cent by the railways) and had largely, though not permanently, been abandoned to the Transvaal coal industry which had emerged during the 1890s. Its product was inferior in quality but it was able to supply the gold-mines and other industries of the

Rand more cheaply because of its closer geographical proximity, its more plentiful labour supply and its geologically more favourable mining conditions including thicker coal seams which were closer to the surface.

Consequently, by the time of Union[65] the Natal collieries had already been obliged to concentrate their marketing efforts primarily on the export and bunker trade through Durban, which in 1909 accounted for 22,6 per cent and 46,8 per cent of total output respectively. Such heavy reliance upon the shipment trade had already exposed local producers to unpredictable variations in foreign demand, as well as to the mercies of the railway and harbour authorities upon whom they depended to deliver consignments timeously. International market fluctuations had imposed an erratic pattern of prosperity and depression upon the Natal coal industry which compounded the difficulties involved in capital investment, the maintenance of output, and the retention of an adequate supply of labour. The maximisation of profits during phases of upswing in the shipment trade had been frequently impeded by congestion on the single-line rail-link to the port, by accident-induced delays or summer rain damage to the line, or by the perennial shortage of trucks which was aggravated by the seasonal preferences accorded to more perishable agricultural freight.

By the 1950s the shipment trade upon which the Natal coal industry had traditionally relied so heavily had virtually come to an end. After Union, as before, the coal trade was characterised by what the Natal Mine Managers' Association once described as 'a great struggle for existence'.[66] The fierce competition for the bunker trade was tempered by the quota system implemented by the Natal Coal Owners' Association, which had been formed in 1913, to regulate that business. However, the bunker trade continued to be heavily dependent upon the extent of shipping activity through Durban which, in turn, was strongly influenced by national economic conditions and by international business fluctuations. The disruption to international shipping caused by the outbreak of the First World War was soon followed by an increasing demand for shipment coal from Natal as each of Europe's national coal industries was either put out of commission or put to the exclusive use of the war effort.[67]

These favourable trading conditions persisted until about 1920, after which the unpredictable fluctuations of earlier years again became evident. During the depression of the early 1930s, when more than two million tons of shipping lay idle in Britain alone, the Natal collieries had virtually no bunker business at all. The problem was compounded by South Africa's adherence to the gold standard, the effect of which was virtually to make the price of coal at Durban double what was available in Britain. The end of the depression, the abandonment of the gold standard and a new agreement with the Transvaal Coal Owners' Association to minimise competition with coal supply through Lourenço Marques (Maputo) all helped to improve bunker sales at Durban. Further temporary boosts were provided by the increases in traffic resulting from the outbreak of the Abyssinian War in 1936 and the Second World War in 1939.[68]

The wartime demand proved to be wholly artificial and in 1945 Natal's bunker sales slumped to an all-time low, for the post-Union period, of 502 621 tons. In truth, the bunker trade never really recovered from the depression of the 1930s, and had actually reached its last peak in the mid-1920s when, in combination with the export trade, it absorbed 61,9 per cent of the province's coal output. These sales were ably promoted by the Natal Coal Grading Committee established in 1923 under the 1922 Coal Act to prevent the shipment of coal which was of inferior quality. There was less insistence on quality during the Second World War, though the subsequent decline in the bunker trade was much more seriously affected by other considerations. Improvements in ship design enabled coal-burning vessels to reduce their fuel requirements by up to 40 per cent and resulted in a noticeable increase in the size of the steamships calling in at Durban without a commensurate increase in demand for bunkers.[69]

Even more damaging to Natal's bunker business was the steady increase in the number of vessels burning oil or diesel instead of coal. This new trend became noticeable among the ships calling in at Durban during the 1920s and by 1930 approximately 47 acres of reclaimed land at the Island View Wharf had been occupied by the oil-storage tanks of the various oil companies. The increasing preference for oil was promoted by the needs of mailships and other passenger liners for which speed and adherence to contracted schedules of arrival and departure were of the utmost importance. The transition accelerated further during the Second World War when a high proportion of coal-fired ships were sunk by enemy action and were subsequently replaced by oil-burning vessels, which offered a more consistent performance and a cleaner, quicker turn-round capacity. By the early 1950s virtually all passenger liners and most cargo lines had made the switch in anticipation of a substantial world-wide increase in oil production with which local coal industries could not hope to compete. Moreover, the various oil companies were already transporting oil on an extensive scale in their own tankers, ensuring that their supplies at Durban, as elsewhere, were cheaper and more reliable than those of coal producers. The bunker trade had evaporated.[70] So too had the export trade, though only temporarily.

The exportation of Natal coal through Durban was almost entirely a twentieth-century development. In common with the bunker business it had also to contend with the difficulties involved in delivering consignments timeously at the port, and with the unpredictable fluctuations of international markets. Natal's natural export area was to the north-east where regular contracts were secured to supply steam coal to the Kenyan, Tanganyikan and Sudanese railways through East African ports such as Dar-es-Salaam and Port Sudan and also to the railway systems of the Philippines and Mauritius, where additional coal was supplied to the sugar estates. Bunker coal was exported to various ports, including Port Louis in Mauritius, Madagascar, Aden, Djibouti in Somaliland, Colombo in Ceylon, Karachi in Pakistan, Java, Singapore and Hong Kong.[71]

Disruptions to coal industries abroad periodically opened new if only temporary markets, such as during and immediately after the First World War (1914–20) when the only constraints upon Natal's collieries lay in their own productive capacity and in the ability of the railway authorities to provide the transport to the port that they required. The slow increase in export sales experienced during the subsequent decade (1920–30) was punctuated by brief upswings in demand arising from coal strikes in Britain and Australia, the General Strike of 1926 in Britain, and the French and Belgian occupation of the coal-rich Ruhr valley in 1923.[72]

The Natal coal industry's export trade passed its peak in 1927 when 1 811 000 tons were sold abroad. After 1929 it began to feel the effects of the Great Depression, with 1931 and 1932 proving to be the worst years it had ever experienced. There was some improvement after South Africa had followed Britain's example in going off the gold standard, but the beneficial effects were blunted by strong Indian and Japanese competition in eastern markets, by rapid increases in freight costs, and by the inability of South Africa's railway authorities to supply the Natal collieries with trucks in numbers sufficient to enable them to take maximum advantage of improved export opportunities when they presented themselves. By 1937 the transport crisis had become so chronic that the South African government imposed an embargo on export coal to ensure that domestic industries and power stations were adequately supplied.[73]

As in 1914, the outbreak of another World War in September 1939 generated an increasing international demand for shipment coal from producers, like those of Natal, who were far removed from the conflict. The local industry lacked the capacity to take full advantage of this market upswing, with the result that its shipment business only increased by 6,77 per cent between 1938 and 1945. However, the heavy wartime demand did prompt the first long-standing arrangement among Natal producers for the regulation of the export trade which had previously been conducted independently through at least four London-based shipping agents. In terms of the agreement reached in 1942 all sales were thenceforth to be arranged by the export agents of the three bigger collieries i.e. the Durban Navigation Collieries Ltd, represented and (from 1937) owned by Mann George Ltd, the Natal Navigation Group which sold all its output to Mitchell Cotts and Company Ltd, and the Dundee Coal Company which operated through Bullard King and Sons and later through A.E. Smith and Sons. No quotas were fixed as the amounts exported comprised the tonnage which was surplus to the requirements of the inland and bunker trades. As this suggests, the export trade like the trade in bunkers had by that stage already become an aspect of declining importance to Natal's coal industry in relation to its overall business.[74]

The wartime demand indeed proved to be but a temporary if prolonged respite in the overall downward trend of export sales, as it did of bunker sales. During 1946–47 there was a decline, not in foreign demand, but in the quantity of export coal which the overburdened South African Railways was capable of handling. By 1950 the SAR was quite unequal to the demands made upon it, resulting in a transport crisis which led to a country-wide coal shortage. The railways authorities themselves resorted to the expropriation of export coal for their own use before the government stepped in, as in 1937, and imposed a total embargo on the export of coal. This measure, coupled with the implementation after 1950 of import control which reduced the volume of shipping calling in at Durban, led to a spectacular 34,66 per cent decline in export and bunker sales between 1950 and 1951.[75]

One aspect of the export trade that continued to flourish was the sale of anthracite, all of which was produced in Natal, whose sales rose from 36 718 tons in 1942 to 1 334 474 tons in 1963. This spectacular increase in demand at last encouraged the development of the lower-grade Somkele and Nongoma coalfields in Zululand. The result was that in 1970 anthracite production amounted to 1,8 million tons, increasing by 1980 to 4,3 million tons, almost 75 per cent of which was exported. For the rest, the 1950s and 1960s proved to be a difficult transitional period for the Natal coal industry in which it struggled to adjust from its traditional heavy reliance upon the shipment trade and attempted to gear itself more to meeting the domestic requirements of the expanding South African economy.[76]

Some of Natal's coal producers, like the Dundee Coal Company, had always hedged their bets by competing not only for the shipment trade but also tendering for railway contracts and continuing to maintain a network of agents in the interior and in the Cape ports. The inland trade was no less cut-throat and became even more so during the depression of the early 1930s when many collieries worked only intermittently due to the spectacular decline in demand. After years of ruthless competition, with no attempt to organise that trade on a more rational commercial basis, the looming prospect of closure was averted for several of Natal's mines by the formation in 1931 of the Natal Associated Collieries (Pty) Ltd. This organisation included all the producing collieries in the province and, in addition to regulating the price and conditions of sale of all coal destined for inland consumption, it allocated such inland trade as existed on a quota basis among its members. It proved to be a turning point in the fortunes of at least some mining companies and, aided by a steady improvement in the commercial climate, was followed by a gradual increase in the sale of Natal coal on the inland market from 1 942 024 tons in 1936 to 2 678 408 tons in 1945.[77]

The sale of coal to the SAR & H actually declined as the railway administration continued to overlook the superior quality of the Natal product and to rely increasingly on supplies from the Transvaal collieries, to the extent of 36 405 800 tons between 1937 and 1946 compared with only 6 766 800 tons of Natal coal consumed during the same period. Sales to the local sugar and other industries continued to increase while the prospect of even greater domestic demand was further enhanced by the opening of the Orange Free State and Far West Rand gold-mines, South Africa's ongoing railway electrification programme, the opening of the new Van der Bijl Steel and Engineering Works at Vereeniging, and the proposal to develop a new oil-from-coal conversion industry.[78]

The most spectacular and significant increases were achieved in sales to power stations, which rose from 557 742 tons to 923 246 tons between 1936 and 1945, and in the sale of coal for coking purposes, which rose from 15 477 tons to 157 937 tons during the same period. This was reflected by the fact that Natal's inland sales of large coal (rounds and cobbles) declined from 70,87 per cent (1 007 000 tons) of total inland sales in 1936 to 61,72 per cent (1 057 000 tons) of such sales in 1945, whereas the sale of small coal (nuts, peas, mixed smalls and dross) increased from 29,13 per cent (935 000 tons) to 38,28 per cent (1 622 000 tons) during that period. It was indeed the development and increasing sophistication of the Electricity Supply Commission (Escom) and of the South African Iron and Steel Corporation (Iscor) from the 1920s which was primarily responsible for enabling the Natal collieries to improve their share of the inland market by supplying those small varieties of coal which had previously often been dumped but for which the emergence of these major industries had created a demand.[79]

Natal was already supplying small quantities of coal to municipal power stations in the Cape and in the interior, but the establishment of Escom in 1922 and the subsequent erection of several large coal-fired power stations in the absence of large domestic oil reserves ensured that henceforth coal would increasingly come to be recognised as a vital source of energy to the South African economy. The establishment of big power stations at Colenso (1927), Congella (1928) and Ingagane (1963) provided poetic compensation for the Natal coal industry in so far as its transport difficulties were an important consideration motivating the establishment of Escom in the expectation that the electrification of the province's main railway line would significantly increase its carrying capacity. By 1955 South Africa's total annual coal sales for the generation of electricity amounted to 12,9 million tons and in 1980 it had risen to 58,9 million tons, which accounted for 66 per cent of total domestic coal sales.[80]

No less important than the inauguration of Escom to the South African economy, though less extensive in its consumption of Natal coal, was the establishment in 1928 of Iscor, which produced its first steel in 1934. Steel production gave rise to an increasing demand for coke and therefore for true coking coal which, at that stage in South Africa's economic development, was obtainable only in northern Natal. Further demand for coke was generated by the requirements of the railways and of several iron foundries on the Witwatersrand. This increased even more when in 1938 Amcor took over the Union Steel Corporation and re-opened the blast furnaces at Newcastle. In 1911 Natal produced only 2 978 tons of coke but in 1955 this rose to 686 930 tons in response to market demand.[81] The province also assumed increasing importance not only as a producer of coke but also as a supplier of coking coal from the Durban Navigation Collieries (DNC) to Iscor in Pretoria, where it was blended with weaker Transvaal coking coal. By 1946 it was supplying 145 000 tons per annum for this purpose and eight years later Iscor secured this important source of supply by acquiring effective control of DNC[82]

The sustained post-war domestic demand experienced by South Africa's collieries was followed during the 1970s by a further dramatic increase in the sale of all types of coal, with total sales output more than doubling from 53,1 million tons to 111,3 million tons between 1970 and 1980. In the early 1960s the South African coal industry had been relatively small and unsophisticated, but by the late 1970s it had acquired a new-found international significance. The rapid rate of expansion experienced during the 1970s was fuelled, firstly, by a 4 per cent per annum increase in the power-generating capacity of Escom and, secondly, by a substantial revival in the export trade which had declined so dramatically during the 1950s and 1960s.[83]

The remarkable increase in foreign demand for South African coal, from approximately one million tons in the early 1970s to 29 million tons in 1980, owed much to the 'oil shock' of 1973–74 when OPEC demonstrated the strength of its oil monopoly and initiated an upward spiral of prices. This raised uncertainty in the minds of consumers world-wide as to the future long-term security of oil supplies. In view of the prevailing doubts concerning the costs involved in nuclear fuel with regard to the effective disposal of waste, coal again came to be regarded in many parts of the world as an attractive alternative source of energy. By 1976 coal was second only to gold in importance as an export earner and in 1980 it earned R688 million in foreign exchange, rising to over R900 million in 1981.[84]

The increase in domestic demand, with coal accounting for more than 80 per cent of South Africa's energy requirements by 1974, was due not only to Escom, which was responsible for 60 per cent of consumption, but also to the gold-mining and iron and steel industries with their closer links to certain collieries in order to ensure a steady supply for themselves. By the early 1980s South Africa's coal producers, including those of Natal, had reason to be optimistic about the future of their industry following more than a decade of rising foreign and domestic demand, and the establishment of a modern terminal at Richards Bay which was already handling the bulk of their exports.[85]

The Natal coal industry in the 1980s – and beyond

During the 1980s, no less than in previous decades, Natal's coal producers continued to experience fluctuating fortunes, along with their counterparts in the much larger Transvaal industry. Mechanization, improved standards of safety and greater concern for the welfare of employees had still not eliminated the ever-present danger of colliery disaster, as the Hlobane tragedy of 1983 bore witness. Moreover, for all the confidence with which local producers entered the 1980s, the coal market remained as unpredictable as ever. In mid-1982 it was estimated that South Africa had already exported 100 million tons of coal and the new loading facility at Richards Bay obligingly demonstrated its capacity to handle future export consignments of virtually any size when it established a new South African record by loading the Italian vessel *Mercurio* with 151 847 metric tons of bulk coal in a single day.[86] Escom was still the primary consumer of South African coal (approximately 40 per cent of total output) and with a power production capacity of 18 349 megawatts in 1982 it planned to double its power generation (and coal consumption) by 1990 through the construction of seven more large power stations, five of them huge coal-fired plants. A further increase in domestic coal consumption was anticipated as a consequence of the development of South Africa's oil-from-coal plants – Sasol 1, 2 and 3 – while Iscor continued to be yet another major consumer.[87]

However, during the early 1980s conditions in both foreign and domestic coal markets altered dramatically under the impact of recessionary economic circumstances. These included a substantial decline in the demand for steel, as a result of which Iscor cancelled its coking coal contracts with Indumeni, Northfield, Newcastle-Platberg and Kempslust Collieries, all of which had closed down completely by 1984. The closure of the General Mining Corporation's Hlobane Colliery near Vryheid also appeared imminent, in spite of the recent expenditure of R90 million there on the modernisation programme which had been prompted by Iscor's demand for coking coal. The mine was saved from complete closure when, in July 1983, it was placed under the control of Iscor, though mining operations there were reduced by one third and the labour force by nearly 17 per cent which involved the dismissal of 1 000 men. Other collieries were less fortunate, for by 1983 the number of Natal coal-mines in production had declined from 44 to 21 and the province's total sales output had dropped to 9 million tons compared to 14 million in 1981. The production of anthracite, the Natal coal industry's major export item, declined by a spectacular 54 per cent during 1982.[88]

The prevailing recessionary conditions were further aggravated by a severe drought. In the Newcastle district of northern Natal, for example, the water shortage became so severe that in 1983 the Ingagane Power Station was obliged to close down temporarily, with adverse consequences for the neighbouring Kilbarchan mine which had been supplying it with 136 000 tons of coal per month and had already suffered the cancellation of its contract with Iscor.[89]

Market conditions improved again during 1984, when Natal's coal exports rose to 4,09 million tons compared with 3,01 million tons in 1983, and the number of producing mines increased from 21 to 29. By 1986 South Africa's total coal exports again exceeded 45 million tons, which amounted to 26 per cent of total output and generated R3,1 billion of the R5 billion raised from coal sales. The export trade clearly remained as vital as ever to the industry and while South African producers managed to maintain their reputation as reliable and punctual suppliers, with the assistance of the new facilities at Richards Bay, the decline of the Rand on world currency markets made South African coal prices much more competitive abroad.[90]

Nevertheless, as Amcoal's chairman W. G. Boustred observed in 1986: 'The uncertainties facing the coal industry in South Africa have probably never been greater than at the present time.'[91] Those uncertainties lie not with the domestic availability of coal itself, but rather with the availability of markets abroad and at home. Export prospects are clouded not only by the traditional fluctuations in demand, with which producers have always had to contend, and with recessionary conditions in some consumer countries, but also by the prospect of tightening international sanctions if the momentum of new political initiatives in South Africa is not maintained. The domestic market has continued to shrink as the decline in economic growth results in a lower demand for coal and for electricity generated from coal. The best prospects for any future increase in domestic consumption lie with the further expansion of Escom and with the development of the synthetic fuel industry, but Natal is not likely to benefit because it does not have the sufficiently large blocks of coal reserves required for these purposes.[92]

Indeed, in 1982 it was estimated that the province was endowed with less than 3 per cent of South Africa's *in situ* reserves of all varieties of mineable coal, while in 1975 the Petrick Commission reported that the Transvaal's reserves included 78 per cent of the country's raw bituminous coal and 75 per cent of its metallurgical coal. The subsequent exploration of the northern Transvaal reserves, particularly those of the Springbok Flats, has ensured that, in quantitative terms, Natal's coalfields will continue to be of declining importance to modern South African industry. In 1910 they yielded 40 per cent of total output, 20 per cent by the early 1950s, 16,9 per cent in 1970 and 10,9 per cent in 1981 (14 million out of approximately 128 million tons), after which record year there was a sharp decline in Natal's production.[93]

Prior to the recent discovery of coking coal reserves in the remote Limpopo/Zoutpansberg and Pafuri Fields, Natal was South Africa's only known source of true coking coal which was indispensable to the manufacture of steel. Moreover, the 1982 estimate indicated that Natal still possessed 20 per cent of South Africa's metallurgical coal reserves and 63 per cent of its marketable anthracite. These considerations underline the significant role, in qualitative terms, which the Natal coal industry has hitherto played in the South African economy, but they provide no guarantee that it will continue to do so in the future. Even if there is a revival in the demand for coking coal, the high sales levels attained during the 1970s are unlikely to be repeated. Export markets that have been lost will not easily be recovered, particularly in the prevailing climate of fierce international competition. As far as the steel industry is concerned, substitution and technological change involving the use of form coke and the direct reduction process threaten to eliminate the need for coking coal altogether and with it a vital aspect of the Natal coal industry's strategic importance to the national economy.[94]

In the absence of a significant upswing in market demand the recession experienced by the Natal coal industry during the early 1980s could recur. The unhappy effects of that recession – the closure of some collieries, the production cut-backs of others, and the retrenchment of many employees – are all-too-familiar features in the history of Natal coal-mining, far more so than the prolonged phase of upswing experienced during the 1970s.

REFERENCES

1. This article is based on a major research project on the history of the Natal coal industry undertaken in collaboration with Dr D.R. Edgecombe and financially assisted by the Research Fund of the University of Natal, the Human Sciences Research Council and Rand Mines Ltd. The opinions expressed herein are not necessarily either those of Dr Edgecombe, or of the sponsors.

2. The early years of coal-mining in Natal are described in Ruth Edgecombe and Bill Guest, 'An introduction to the pre-Union Natal coal industry' in Bill Guest and John M. Sellers (eds), *Enterprise and exploitation in a Victorian colony: aspects of the economic and social history of Natal* (Pietermaritzburg, University of Natal Press, 1985), pp. 308–51.

3. See Hein Heydenrych, 'Railway development in Natal to 1895' in Guest and Sellers, *Enterprise and exploitation*, pp. 58–64.

4. 'Firedamp' is a colourless, tasteless and odourless gas which is composed of carbon and hydrogen in chemical combination. It is given off by coal as well as strata in the coal measures and, when mixed with air in sufficient quantities, it is explosive. See A. Lupton, *Mining: an elementary treatise on the getting of minerals* (London, Longmans, Green, 1889), p. 255; see also *Map: Coalfields of Natal*.

5. The financial structure of the early Natal coal industry is examined in Edgecombe and Guest, 'Pre-Union Natal coal industry', p. 317 and in Bill Guest, 'Financing an infant coal industry: the case of the Natal collieries', *The South African Journal of Economic History*, 3(2), September 1988, pp. 40–60.

6. SBA GMO 3/2/1/1 HY, Letters 1890–96, Joint General Managers to Secretary, Standard Bank, London, 6 July 1890, pp. 44–45; INSP 1/1/251, Newcastle Branch 1902–28, 26 December 1901, p. 9, 8 August 1906, p. 11, 19 December 1908, p. 13; INSP 1/1/367, Newcastle Branch, N to P 1937, 17 November 1937, p. 13; Guest, 'Financing an infant coal industry', pp. 42–45.

7. SBA INSP 1/1/46, Dundee Branch 1890–99, Attached Statements of Liabilities as at 24 December 1898, p. 16, 15 November 1900, pp. 5, 22(a); INSP 1/1/208, Dundee Branch 1902–28, Attached Statement of Liabilities as at 19 May 1904, pp. 6–8, 23 October 1909, p. 7, 2 June 1917, p. 13; DBA SAC22, The South African Collieries Ltd Liquidation Report and South African Collieries Ltd Director's and General Manager's Reports for 1918–1925; *De Beers Consolidated Mines Ltd Annual Reports*: 35th Annual Report, Year ending 30 June 1923 – 35th Ordinary General Meeting, 30 November 1923, p. 30 (reference supplied by Dr M.H. Buys, De Beers Archivist); H.A. Chilvers, *The story of De Beers* (London, Cassell, 1939), pp. 276–77.

8. GN no.1, *Natal Government Coal Commission Report of 1898*, 1899, p. 4; *Annual Report of the Commissioner of Mines*, 1909, pp. 7, 63; *The Natal Navigation Collieries and Estate Company Limited Jubilee Brochure*, n.d., n.p.; TAD K154, *Coal Commission*, 1946/47, File RS 27, Natal Navigation Collieries and Estate Co. Ltd.

9. SBA INSP 1/1/209, Durban Branch 1905–27, Return of Liabilities as at 17 July 1909, p. 14 and as at 31 July 1910, p. 14; INSP 1/1/229, Johannesburg Branch 1907–28, Statement of Liabilities of Parties as at 16 October 1909, pp. 9, 19, 33, 39, 46.

10. SBA INSP 1/1/83, Johannesburg branch 1896–99, Attached Statement of Discount and other Liabilities as at 7 October 1899, p. 97; INSP 1/1/209, Durban Branch 1905–27, Return of Liabilities as at 20 March 1905, pp. 8–9 and 18 July 1908, p. 11; INSP 1/1/251, Newcastle Branch 1902–28, Return of Liabilities as at 12 August 1905; INSP 1/1/301, Dannhauser Branch, D to F 1930, 7 November 1930, n.p.; INSP 1/1/338, Du to G 1933–35, 30 May 1933, p. 22; M. Murray, *Union Castle chronicle* (London, Longmans, Green, 1953), pp. 277–79; Ruth Edgecombe and Bill Guest, 'The Natal coal industry in the South African economy 1910–1985', *The South African Journal of Economic History*, 2(2), September 1987, p. 64.

11. TAD K154, *Coal Commission*, 1946/47, vol. 3, File 29; *Dante's Inferno: the history of Vryheid Coronation Colliery, 1923–1983*, n.p., n.d.; see also Edgecombe and Guest, 'Natal coal industry in the South African economy', pp. 49, 60.

12. IMN *Annual Reports*, 1962–64; 'Who's Who in Natal coal', *Prospect*, 21(1), 1982, p. 15; 'ZAC opens in royal glory', *Gencorama*, 5(6), July 1986, pp. 2–4; *Rand Daily Mail*, 13 September 1983; *Operating and developing coal mines in the Republic of South Africa*, Directory 2/87, (Braamfontein, Minerals Bureau, 1987), pp. 1–24.

13. NAD Accession no. 1336, Dundee Coal Company Ltd Minute Books (DCCM); Guest, 'Financing an infant coal industry', pp. 45–51.

14. TAD K154, *Coal Commission*, 1946/47, vol. 3, File 29; *Dante's* Inferno: *Vryheid Coronation Colliery*; IMN *Annual Reports*, 1962–64; Edgecombe and Guest, 'Natal coal industry in the South African economy', pp. 60, 64–65, 69.

15. For an analysis of working conditions in the Natal collieries prior to 1910, see Edgecombe and Guest, 'Pre-Union Natal coal industry', pp. 331–35.

16. *Rand Daily Mail*, 13 September 1983; C.A. Frost, 'Colliery disasters and the Press' (unpublished B.A. (Hons) essay, University of Natal, Pietermaritzburg, 1985), pp. 70–115; *The Natal Industrialist, April 1985* (Supplement to the *Sunday Tribune* 31 March 1985).

17. *Annual Report of the Commissioner of Mines*, 1909, p. 25; Ruth Edgecombe and Bill Guest, '"The coal miners' way of death": safety in the Natal collieries, 1910–1953', *Journal of Natal and Zulu History*, 8, 1985, pp. 63–64.

18. UG 34–1911, p. 120, UG 30–1927, pp. 72–73, 192–4, UG 34–1928, p. 177, *Annual Reports of the Mining Industry*; MNW 853, File 2410/26, p. 394; Union Government Gazette, vol. 109, no. 2460, 11 August 1937, p. 380; Edgecombe and Guest, 'Coal miners' way of death', pp. 68, 71–72.

19. MNW 612, File 757/22, Inspector of Mines Report, 13 July 1922; UG 36–1955, p. 24, UG 30–1956, p. 104, UG 47–1959, p. 84, RP 18–1962, pp. 43, 74, *Annual Reports of the Mining Industry*; F.A. Steart, 'Coal in Natal' (Paper presented to the Third [Triennial] Empire Mining and Metallurgical Congress, South Africa, 1930), pp. 43, 49, 53, 54, 57, 61, 63, 65, 69–70.

20. UG 17–1931, *Annual Report of the Mining Industry*, p. 69; Edgecombe and Guest, 'Coal miners' way of death', p. 72.

21. MDA 173/23, Hlobane Colliery, 22 October 1923; UG 41–1947, p. 111, RP 24–1964, p. 19, *Annual Report of the Mining Industry*; *The Natal Industrialist*, IMNA 420/41, Utrecht Colliery, 20 November 1941 and 550/44, Hlobane No. 1 Colliery, 12 September 1944; Edgecombe and Guest, 'Coal miners' way of death', p. 73.

22. NTS 2102, File 224/280, Memorandum on Workmen's Compensation Bill in its relation to Natives, 1 March 1932; DCCM vol. 1/1/1/11, 24 June, 12 and 26 August 1930.

23. GNLB 82, File 3154/12/77, Inspectors Whitehead and Falwasser (Dundee) to Director of Native Labour, 19 February 1912 and Inspector I.W. de Jager's Report, 2 January 1915; GNLB 102, File 729/13/D87, J. Burn Wood (District Surgeon, Vryheid) to Resident Magistrate (Vryheid), 19 January 1916; GNLB 223, File 348/15/D25, Acting Director Native Labour to Inspector (Dundee), 27 July 1915 and Mines Medical Inspector S.V. van Niekerk's Report, 28 July 1915; GNLB 262, File 464/16/D154, R. Hyde-Smith (Manager, Hlobane Colliery) to Inspector Native Labour (Vryheid), 19 November 1914; Ruth Edgecombe and Bill Guest, 'The black heart of the beautiful mountain: Hlobane Colliery, 1898–1953', *South African Historical Journal*, 18, 1986, pp. 210–11.

24. NA 33, File 1810/F551, vol. 1, Director of Native Labour to Secretary for Native Affairs, 8 May 1913, enclosing S.V. van Niekerk's Report on Natal mines, 17 April 1913; GNLB 82, File 3154/12/77, Inspector I.W. de Jager's Report, 2 January 1915; IMNA 917/51, Durban Navigation Colliery, 1 November 1951; Edgecombe and Guest, 'Coal miners' way of death', pp. 73, 83; Edgecombe and Guest, 'Hlobane Colliery, 1898–1953', p. 217.

25. NA 233, File 1810/F551, vol. 1, Report by Secretary Native Affairs on visit to Natal Collieries, 2 February 1910; See also Edgecombe and Guest, 'Pre-Union Natal coal industry', pp. 327–31.

26. NA 233, File 1810/F551, vol. 1, Report and Recommendations of the 'Labour Shortage' Committee, 14 October 1918.

27. GNLB 253, File 357/16/98, Notes of Meeting between Director Native Labour and Deputation from Natal Mine Managers' Association, 11 August 1920; Jill Nattrass, *The South African economy: its growth and change*, (Cape Town, Oxford University Press, 1981), p. 137.

28. GNLB 130, File 244/3/13/53, B. Colenbrander (Magistrate, Vryheid) to Chief Native Commissioner (Natal), 6 November 1913; NTS 2067, File 138/280, E. Dower, Dept. Native Affairs to Minister Native Affairs, 27 April 1911, enclosing Memo. on Native Labour in Natal and Zululand; NA 233, File 1810/F551, vol. 1, Dept. Native Affairs to J. Henderson MLA, 14 March 1912 and Report and Recommendations of the 'Labour Shortage' Committee, 14 October 1918; DCCM vol. 1/1/1/5, 7 April 1914 and vol. 1/1/1/6, 14 August 1918; Edgecombe and Guest, 'Hlobane Colliery, 1898–1953', pp. 208, 214–15.

29. NA 233, File 1810/F551, vol. 1, W. H. Royston (Secretary Coal Owners' Society) to Acting Chief Native Commissioner (Natal) 16 October 1912; Chief Native Commissioner (Natal) to Secretary Native Affairs, 12 September 1912; J. Barrett (Dept. Native Affairs) to Secretary Native Affairs, 28 January 1913; NTS 2067, File 77/280, Acting Secretary Native Affairs to Director Native Labour, 27 October 1923, and Chief Native Commissioner (Natal) to Secretary Native Affairs, 20 June and 11 November 1923, with Annexures; GNLB vol. 297, File 291/18/78, Chief Native Commissioner (Natal) to Director Native Labour, 1 November 1923.

30. NTS 2071, File 144/280, Part 1, Natal Coal Owners' Society to Secretary Native Affairs, 19 December 1925 and 19 January 1926, Secretary Native Affairs to Natal Coal Owners' Society, 13 January 1926; NCOS vol. 6, p. 299, Address by Director Native Labour (Major Cooke) to Mine Managers' Association, 1928; NTS 2091, File 209/280, Director Native Labour to Secretary Native Affairs, 19 May 1928; DCCM vol. 1/1/1/10, 8 May 1928.

31. GNLB vol. 81, File 3154/12/D77, Natal Sugar Association to Director Native Labour, 18 December 1913; NTS 2067, File 77/280, Report on Natal Coal Mines by Chief Native Commissioner (Natal) and Assistant Medical Officer of Health, 17 May 1918 and 14 June 1923; UG 34–1911, p. 58, UG 30–1927, p. 19 and UG 36–1955, p. 34 *Annual Reports of the Mining Industry*; Edgecombe and Guest, 'Coal miners' way of death', pp. 65–66.

32. GNLB vol. 82, File 3154/12/77, I. W. de Jager, Inspector Native Labour (Dundee) to Director Native Labour, 2 January 1915; NTS 2067, File 77/280, Chief Native Commissioner (Natal) to Secretary Native Affairs, 17 May 1918, enclosing Joint Report (undated), and 20 October 1923, enclosing Joint Report by Assistant Medical Officer of Health and himself; NTS 2067, File 138/280, Chief Native Commissioner to Secretary Native Affairs, 1 April 1926.

33. GNLB vol. 102, File 729/13/D87, Secretary Native Affairs to Director Native Labour, 20 October 1919, enclosing Joint Report 25 September 1919; NTS 2067, File 77/280, Director Native Labour to Secretary Native Affairs, 17 November 1925; Secretary Native Affairs to Secretary Public Health, 10 December 1925; NCOS vol. 7, 30 July 1931, pp. 182, 193, Director Native Labour to Secretary NCOS, 22 August 1931 and R. Campbell to Mr Jones, 2 November 1931.

34. Oral interviews with F. W. Hatton (Mine Secretary, Natal Steam Coal Co. 1934–70) and J. Anderson (Miner and Mine Captain, Natal Steam Coal Co. 1948–79), 13 March 1982; DCCM vol. 1/1/1/1, 4 March, 29 April, 25 May 1898; vol. 1/1/1/2, 30 September 1902 AGM.

35. DCCM vol. 1/1/1/4, 26 March 1913; vol. 1/1/1/5, 7 July 1914, 25 January 1916; vol. 1/1/1/6, 22 January, 12 February, 27 August 1919; vol. 1/1/1/7, 26 January 1921; vol. 1/1/1/8, 10 April, 30 July 1923, 4 January, 17 April, 7 and 21 May, 11 August, 24 September, 12 November 1924; vol. 1/1/1/10, 24 April, 23 October 1928; NTS 2091, File 209/280, Director Native Labour to Secretary Native Affairs, 19 May 1928; Edgecombe and Guest, 'Hlobane Colliery, 1898–1953', pp. 208–10.

36. NA 233, File 1810/F551, vol. 1, E. H. Richardson to Secretary Native Affairs, 29 June 1911; Report by Inspectors Whitehead and Falwasser, 16 February 1912; Report by District Native Commissioner, Vryheid, August 1911.

37. NA 233, File 1810/F551, vol. 1, Report by Secretary Native Affairs on visit to Natal Collieries, 2 February 1910.

38. NA 233, File 1810/F551, vol. 1, Report by Inspectors Whitehead and Falwasser, 16 February 1912; NTS 2091, File 209/280, Report by Major H. S. Cooke, Director Native Labour, 19 May 1928; GNLB vol. 218, File 199/15/339, H. A. Guy to Inspector Native Labour, 2 August 1928, and Inspector Native Labour to Chief Native Commissioner (Natal), 31 August 1928; Edgecombe and Guest, 'Hlobane Colliery, 1898–1953', p. 207.

39. NTS 2119, File 227/280, 1938; NCOS vol. 9, pp. 59, 60, 94, 138, 180; Edgecombe and Guest, 'Hlobane Colliery, 1898–1953', p. 219.

40. DCCM vol. 1/1/1/4, 22 August 1911; vol. 1/1/1/13, 14 August, 23 October 1934, 8 January 1935, 10 December 1935; vol. 1/1/1/14, 27 July 1937 and 25 January 1938; NCOS vol. 9, pp. 59, 60, 94, 138, 180.

41. DCCM vol. 1/1/1/11, 20 December 1929; vol. 1/1/1/15, 20 August 1940, 7 and 21 July, 2 October, 10 November 1942, 6 April 1943, 5 July 1943; vol. 1/1/1/16, 2 February 1945.

42. NCOS vol. 13, pp. 26, 295, 534, 581; *Annual Reports of the Commissioner of Mines*, 1889–1909; UG 30–1927, p. 19 and RP 53–1966, p. 112, *Annual Reports of the Mining Industry*.

43. SBA INSP 1/1/208, Dundee Branch 1901 28, 31 January 1902, p. 14; CM File 477/1898, Tylden-Wright (Dundee Coal Co.) to Secretary Mining Laws Revision Committee, 21 October 1898; NAD CSO 2857, 1909 Mines Commission, Evidence and Papers, p. 241; *Annual Reports of the Commissioner of Mines*, 1901–1909; IMNA 550/44, 12 September 1944; Oral interviews with R. W. Hatton and J. Anderson, 13 March 1982, and with J. R. Watson (ex-Manager, Hlobane Colliery), July 1982.

44. NCOS vol. 12, pp. 151–52, 174, vol. 13, pp. 504, 505.

45. DCCM vol. 1/1/1/5, 13 January 1914, 25 April 1916; vol. 1/1/1/13, 26 March 1935; IMNA, 550/44, 12 September 1944, *passim*; GNLB vol. 82, File 3154/12/77, I. W. de Jager, Inspector Native Labour (Dundee) to Director Native Labour, 2 January 1915 and vol. 102, File 729/12/D87 Secretary Native Affairs to Director Native Labour, 20 October 1919, enclosing Joint Report of 25 September 1919.

46. NTS 2067, File 77/280, Chief Native Commissioner (Natal) to Secretary Native Affairs, 17 May 1918; Secretary Public Health to Secretary Native Affairs, 3 October 1922; Director Native Labour to Secretary Native Affairs, 17 November 1925; Secretary Native Affairs to Secretary Public Health, 10 December 1925; NA 233, File 1810/F551, vol. 1, Evidence taken by 'Labour Shortage' Committee at Vryheid, 24 August 1918; NCOS vol. 13, pp. 509–10.

47. NA 233, File 1810/F551, vol. 1, Report by Secretary Native Affairs on Natal Collieries, 2 February 1910; NTS 2045, File 61/280, unidentified inspection report on Natal Mines, April 1918; NTS 2067, File 77/280, Secretary Native Affairs to Director Native Labour, 13 June 1918, enclosing Regulations issued in GN 63 of 1915; NTS 2067, File 77/280, Report by Chief Native Commissioner (Natal) and Assistant Officer of Health, May 1918; GNLB vol. 223, File 348/15/D25, Acting Director Native Labour to Inspector Native Labour (Dundee) 19 August 1915, enclosing Mines Medical Inspector's Report, 28 July 1915.

48. NTS 2067, File 77/280, Report by Chief Native Commissioner (Natal) and Assistant Medical Officer of Health, 17 May 1918; Director Native Labour to Secretary Native Affairs, 17 November 1925; NTS 2346, File 1082/280, Public Prosecutor (Dannhauser) to Chairman, Johannesburg Consolidated Investments (Natal Cambrian Collieries) 16 September 1958; General Mines Manager (Natal Navigation Collieries) to Magistrate (Newcastle), 21 December 1959; J. R. Wilson (Director, Jabula Foods (Pty) Ltd) to Director Bantu Labour, 17 February 1960; Secretary for Justice to Secretary Bantu Administration and Development, 21 May 1960; Director Bantu Labour to Secretary for Justice, 14 July and 29 August 1960.

49. NCOS vol. 2, p. 158,   vol. 3, pp. 11, 74, 336,   vol. 4, p. 90,   vol. 5, pp. 119–20,   vol. 6, p. 12, vol. 7, p. 355, vol. 9, pp. 108, 259; NA 233, File 1810/F551, vol. 1 Report and Recommendations of 'Labour Shortage' Committee, 14 October 1918; MNW 133, File 2102/12 and MNW 214, File 4174/3. *Reports of Inspector of Mines* for June 1912 and November 1913; UG 23–1915, *Annual Report of the Department of Mines*, p. 107.

50. NCOS vol. 3, p. 150,   vol. 4, pp. 34, 36, 98,   vol. 5, p. 211,   vol. 8, p. 49,   vol. 9, p. 117, vol. 11, pp. 228, 432–4, vol. 12 pp. 14, 21, 174, 184; DCCM vol. 1/1/1/14, 30 November 1937, 26 September 1939, 6 June 1939, 6 December 1939, and vol. 1/1/1/15, Annual Report 1939; Edgecombe and Guest, 'Hlobane Colliery, 1898–1953', pp. 200, 217.

51. NA 233, File 1810/F551, vol. 1, Report by Secretary Native Affairs on Natal Collieries, 2 February 1910; Evidence taken by 'Labour Shortage' Committee at Dundee, 18 June 1918 and Vryheid, 24 August 1918; NA 135, File 2204/13/F257, Under-Secretary for Mines to Secretary Native Affairs, 3 October 1912; Chief Native Commissioner (Natal) to Secretary Native Affairs, 25 November 1912; Secretary Native Affairs to Secretary for Mines, 30 December 1912; NTS 2012, File 12/280, Divisional Inspector (Natal) to Secretary for Labour, 31 October 1927; NCOS vol. 11, pp. 228, 231.

52. GNLB 82, File 3154/12/77, Inspectors Whitehead and Falwasser (Dundee) to Director Native Labour, 19 February 1912; NTS 2067, File 77/280, Chief Native Commissioner (Natal) to Secretary Native Affairs, 5 October 1925, enclosing Joint Report by himself and Assistant Medical Officer of Health (Natal), September 1925; NCOS vol. 8, p. 287, vol. 9, p. 133, vol. 10, p. 248, vol. 11, pp. 496–97, vol. 12, pp. 336–37; Edgecombe and Guest, 'Hlobane Colliery, 1898–1953', pp. 212–13, 218.

53. NA 233, File 1810/F551, vol. 1, E. H. Richardson to Secretary Native Affairs, 29 June 1911; Report by Inspectors Whitehead and Falwasser (Dundee), 16 February 1912; Report by District Native Commissioner (Vryheid), August 1911.

54. NCOS vol. 10, p. 127; vol. 11, pp. 4, 166, 321, 322, 364, 380, 381, 385.

55. J. D. Beall and M. D. North-Coombes, 'The 1913 disturbances in Natal: the social and economic background to "Passive Resistance" ', *Journal of Natal and Zulu History*, 6, 1983; The Rand Daily Mail, 12 December 1983.

56. NCOS vol. 1, p. 141,   vol. 2, pp. 7, 231,   vol. 3, pp. 114,   276, vol. 8, pp. 24–26;   MNW 214, File 4174/3, Inspector of Mines' Report, November 1913; UG 34–1911, p. 58; UG 36–1955, p. 34; RP 53–1966, p. 112, *Annual Reports of the Mining Industry*; Edgecombe and Guest, 'Hlobane Colliery, 1898–1953', pp. 201–2.

57. NTS 2067, File 77/280, Report by Chief Native Commissioner (Natal) and Assistant Medical Officer of Health, 14 June 1923; NTS 2081, File 200/280, D. W. Hook, Sub-Native Commissioner (Benoni) and Divisional Inspector (Natal) to Secretary for Labour, 31 October 1927; NCOS vol. 8, pp. 257–60, vol. 9, pp. 131, 132, 167, 168, vol. 10, pp. 213–17.

58. DCCM vol. 1/1/1/10, 9 October 1928; 2/VRY Add. 1 3/1/1, file 2/14/7, Inspector of Native Labour (Vryheid) to Director of Native Labour, 12 May 1944; Director of Native Labour to Inspector of Native Labour (Vryheid), 1 July 1944; Assistant Health Officer for Union to Secretary for Health, 13 September 1947; Edgecombe and Guest, 'Hlobane Colliery, 1898–1953', pp. 215–16, 220–21.

59. Oral interview with J. R. Watson, July 1982.

60. *Blue Book for the Colony of Natal (Departmental Reports)*, Annual Report of the Commissioner of Mines, 1900, pp.59–61, IMN, *Annual Reports,* 1942, 1944 and 1945; *Annual Report of the Commissioner of Mines*, 1941; TAD K154, *Coal Commission*, 1946/47, vol. 3, file 31; Edgecombe and Guest, 'Natal coal industry in the South African economy', pp. 55, 58; Edgecombe and Guest, 'Pre-Union Natal coal industry', pp. 318–21.

61. UG 50–1952, *Report of the Department of Mines*; IMN, *Annual Reports*, 1962–1969; P. Scott, 'The development of the northern Natal coalfields', *South African Geographical Journal*, September 1951, *passim*; R.B. Oliver, *Steam coal in southern Africa* (The Economist Intelligence Unit, Special Report no. 122, London, April 1922), pp. 11–12; Edgecombe and Guest, 'Natal coal industry in the South African economy', pp. 59, 64–67.

62. RP 54–1972 and RP 54–1976, *Annual Reports of the Department of Mines*; 'Kilbarchan is going strong', Special report *Gencorama*, 5(6), June 1986, pp. 16–17.

63. RP 54–1972 and RP 33–1977, *Annual Reports of the Department of Mines*; Edgecombe and Guest, 'Natal coal industry in the South African economy', p. 69.

64. RP 54–1976, *Annual Report of the Department of Mines*; C.B. Szonert (comp.) *Coal mines in South Africa*, Directory no. 2/78, (Braamfontein, Minerals Bureau, 1978), pp. 2–19; *Rand Daily Mail*, 13 September 1983.

65. For a detailed account of the marketing of Natal coal prior to 1910 see Edgecombe and Guest, 'Pre-Union Natal coal industry', pp. 321–27.

66. GNLB vol. 253, File 357/16/98, Notes of Meeting between Director Native Labour and Natal Mine Managers' Association, 11 August 1920.

67. MNW 152, File 1859/13, Inspector of Mines to Government Mining Engineer, 9 and 28 September 1914, General Manager, South African Railways to Acting Secretary for Mines, 12 October 1914; UG 23–1915, *Annual Report of the Department of Mines*, p. 65, NCOS vol. 5, p. 211, vol. 8, p. 177, vol. 10, p. 66; DCCM vol. 1/1/1/5, 3 November 1916; vol. 1/1/1/12, 10 November 1931, 6 December, 12 April 1932, 28 March, 2 May 1933, TAD K154, *Coal Commission*, 1946/47, File 30.

68. DCCM vol. 1/1/1/7, 14 September, 31 October, 14 December 1921; vol. 1/1/1/10, 22 November 1927; vol. 1/1/1/11, 8 April 1930, 26 May 1931; vol. 1/1/1/12, 16 October 1931, 14 March 1931; vol. 1/1/1/13, 13 March 1934; vol. 1/1/1/15, 21 May 1940, 27 May, 17 June, 29 July 1941, 21 April, 27 May, 9 June 1942; TAD K154, *Coal Commission*, 1946/47, vol. 9, Inter-Departmental Base Mineral Committee Report on 'Export Coal and the Natal Coal Industry', 31 October 1935; Edgecombe and Guest, 'Natal coal industry in the South African economy', pp. 51, 53–54.

69. MNW 736, vol. 8, File 2388/124, NCOS to Secretary for Mines and Industries, 16 February 1925; TAD K154, *Coal Commission*, 1946/47, vol. 2, RS18, J.M. Donald (Mitchell Cotts) to Coal Commission, 17 July 1946; vol. 3, RS23, Replies to General Outline of Information Required from NCOS n.d.; vol. 3, RS26, Durban Navigation Collieries Evidence n.d.; K15 *Mining Regulations Commission 1925*, vol. 5, NCOS to Secretary Mining Regulations Commission, Durban, 10 February 1925; MVE vol. 1079, P12/80, Coal Act of 1922 and Report of the Commission, 15 April 1921; IMN, *Annual Report* 1936; Steart, 'Coal in Natal', p. 42.

70. TAD K154, *Coal Commission*, 1946/47, vol. 3, File 27, Secretary Natal Navigation Collieries to Secretary, Coal Commission, 20 December 1946; vol. 2, RS18, J.M. Donald (Mitchell Cotts) to Coal Commission, 17 July 1946; Horwood (gen. ed) *The Port of Durban*, pp. 23, 36, 39, 43, 143 (Tables IV and V); Edgecombe and Guest, 'Natal coal industry in the South African economy', p. 56.

71. DCCM vol. 1/1/1/2, 26 April 1901, 29 August 1902, AGM 1903; vol. 1/1/1/3, AGM 1904; *Natal Mercury*, 31 October 1903; MNW 152, File 1859/13, Inspector of Mines to General Mining Engineer, 9 and 28 September 1914, General Manager (SAR) to Acting Secretary for Mines, 12 October 1914; NCOS vol. 5, p. 211; UG 23–1915,

Annual Report of the Department of Mines, p. 65; TAD K154, *Coal Commission*, 1946/47, vol. 3, File 24 and vol. 2, File 18, J. M. Donald to Secretary, Coal Commission, 17 July 1946.

72. MNW 152, File 1859/13, Inspector of Mines to Government Mining Engineer, 9 and 28 September 1914, General Manager (SAR) to Acting Secretary for Mines, 12 October 1914; UG 23–1915, *Annual Report of the Department of Mines*, p. 65; NCOS vol. 5, p. 211, vol. 8, p. 177, vol. 10, p. 66; Edgecombe and Guest, 'Natal coal industry in the South African economy', pp. 51–53.

73. TAD K14, *Special Committee of Enquiry, Base Minerals Industry*, 1938, Evidence by V. H. M. Barrett, Inspector of Mines, Natal, 24 August 1938; TAD K154, *Coal Commission*, 1946/47, vol. 9, Inter-Departmental Base Mineral Committee Report on 'Export Coal and the Natal Coal Industry', 31 October 1935; vol. 2, RS18 J. M. Donald to Coal Commission, 17 July 1946; vol. 3, RS23, Replies to General Outline of Information Required from NCOS n.d.; *Annual Reports of the Department of Mines*, 1925–37; IMN, *Annual Reports*, 1925–37.

74. MNW 736, vol. 8, File 2388/124, NCOS to Secretary for Mines and Industries, 16 February 1925; TAD K15, *Mining Regulations Commission*, 1925, vol. 5, NCOS to *Secretary, Mining Regulations Commission*, Durban, 10 February 1925; TAD K14, *Special Committee of Enquiry*, Base Minerals Industry, 1938, Evidence of V. H. M. Barrett, Inspector of Mines, Natal, 24 August 1938; TAD NTS, vol. 2226, File 445/280, Memorandum by D. Smit, Secretary Native Affairs to Minister Native Affairs, 28 May 1943; TAD K154, *Coal Commission*, 1946/47, vol. 2, File 17 and vol. 4, 'Memorandum on past and present coal position in South Africa and future prospects of the industry', pp. 20–26; vol. 2, File 18, J. M. Donald to Secretary, Coal Commission, 17 July 1946; vol. 3, File 31; *Annual Reports of the Department of Mines*, 1942–45; IMN, *Annual Reports*, 1942–45.

75. *Annual Reports of the Department of Mines*, 1951 and 1952; Edgecombe and Guest, 'Natal coal industry in the South African economy', pp. 52–56, 63.

76. IMN, *Annual Reports*, 1942, 1944, 1952, 1961–63; UG, Report no. 41 of 1947; TAD K154, *Coal Commission*, 1946/47, vol. 3, File 31; Edgecombe and Guest, 'Natal coal industry in the South African economy', pp. 59–61, 66–68.

77. DCCM vol. 1/1/1/3, 9 September 1904, 18 August 1905, 21 June 1907, 14 August 1908 and 19 July 1910, vol. 1/1/1/11, 9 December 1930; TAD K154, *Coal Commission*, 1946/47, vol. 3, File 24, Replies to General Outline of Information required from Natal Associated Collieries (Pty) Ltd, 19 November 1946, vol. 19, Report, pp. 11–12; NCOS vol. 7, p. 155; Oral interviews with F. W. Hatton and J. Anderson, 13 March 1982.

78. TAD K154, *Coal Commission*, 1946/47, vol. 3, File 24, Replies to General Outline of Information required from Natal Associated Collieries (Pty) Ltd, 19 November 1946. See attached statements NAC, no. 1, no. 7; vol. 7, W. Heckroodt, Acting General Manager SAR & H to Secretary, Coal Commission, 24 October 1946 and W. M. Clark, General Manager SAR & H to Secretary, Coal Commission, 9 December 1946; SAR/SAS, vol. 1132, p. 1100, Acting System Manager to General Manager SAR & H, 12 January 1932; D. Hobart Houghton, *The South African economy* (Cape Town, Oxford University Press, 1976), pp. 105–7, 126; Christie, *Electricity, industry and class*, pp. 122, 143, 176.

79. TAD K154, *Coal Commission*, 1946/47, vol. 3, File 24, Replies to General Outline of Information required from Natal Associated Collieries (Pty) Ltd, 19 November 1946. See attached statements NAC, no. 1, no. 7.

80. Christie, *Electricity, industry and class*, pp. 79, 83–85, 89–93; Oliver, *Steam coal in southern Africa*, p. 15; Edgecombe and Guest, 'Natal coal industry in the South African economy', pp. 57, 59–61, 66.

81. TAD K154, *Coal Commission*, 1946/47, vol. 7, Minutes of Proceedings of 28th Sitting 1st July 1947, Evidence of African Metals Corporation; DCCM vol. 1/1/1/7,

30 August 1922; *Annual Reports of the Department of Mines; Dante's* Inferno, *Vryheid Coronation Colliery*; Houghton, *South African economy*, pp. 14, 105, 123; Christie, *Electricity, industry and class*, pp. 93–96.

82. TAD K154, *Coal Commission*, 1946/47, vol. 3, File 6 and vol. 5, Extract from Committee of Enquiry Report into Base Metal Industry of the Union, 1939 (GPS 3648–1940–1320) and Steart, 'Report on the Natal coalfield', 12 September 1944; IMN, *Annual Report*, 1940; Edgecombe and Guest, 'Natal coal industry in the South African Economy', pp. 61, 64.

83. Oliver, *Steam coal in southern Africa*, pp. 15, 16, 52, 53; J. Stocks, 'Fuel minerals', *Mining Annual Review* (London, June 1982), pp. 79, 85; P. King, 'Long term trends in South African coalmining', *Coal, Gold and Base Minerals of Southern Africa*, March 1979, pp. 39–45.

84. J. M. Wilcox, 'International trade in coal', (Paper presented at United Nations Symposium on Future Prospects for Coal, Poland, October 1979), Australian Dept. Trade and Resources (Canberra, 1981), pp. 1, 11–13; *Annual Report of the Department of Mines*, 25–1981; L. Capstickdale, 'South Africa's black gold', *South African Panorama*, May 1982, pp. 14–16.

85. King, 'Long term trends in South African coal mining', p. 39; Capstickdale, 'South Africa's black gold', pp. 14, 16, 18; P. J. Hugo, *The South African coal industry*, Report 9/83 (Braamfontein, Minerals Bureau, 1983), p. 10; Edgecombe and Guest, 'Natal coal industry in the South African economy', pp. 67–68.

86. *Rand Daily Mail*, 13 September 1983; Capstickdale, 'South Africa's black gold', pp. 14, 16.

87. 'Coal could displace gold as South Africa's export leader', *World Coal* (Annual Review and Buyer's Guide), 8(60, Nov/Dec. 1982, p. 107; Special Correspondent, 'Southern Africa', *Mining Annual Review*, June 1982, pp. 419, 421; Stocks, 'Fuel minerals', p. 85; Capstickdale, 'South Africa's black gold', pp. 16–18.

88. *Annual Reports of the Department of Mines*, 25–1983, 18–1984; *Rand Daily Mail*, 13 September 1983, *Natal Witness*, Industrial and Commercial Review Supplement, 11 October 1983; Edgecombe and Guest, 'Natal coal industry in the South African economy', pp. 69, 70.

89. 'Kilbarchan is going strong', *Gencorama*, 5(6), July 1986, pp. 16–17.

90. *Mining Annual Review*, 1985, pp. 105–6, and 1986, pp. 385–86; *Sunday Times*, Business Times Supplement, 25 January 1987 and *Sunday Tribune*, Financial Tribune Supplement, 8 February 1987; Edgecombe and Guest, 'Natal coal industry in the South African economy', p. 70.

91. 'Amcoal's turnover tops R1–bn', *South African Mining : Coal, Gold and Base Minerals*, August 1986, p. 71.

92. *Coal Review* (Max Pollak and Freemantle, n.p.), November 1985; *Sunday Times*, Business Times Supplements, 30 November 1986, 25 January 1987, and 11 February 1990; *Sunday Tribune*, Financial Tribune Supplement, 8 February 1987; Geoff Shuttleworth, 'Pitfalls ahead', *Finance Week*, 31(3), 16–22 October 1986, p. 169; Edgecombe and Guest, 'Natal coal industry in the South African economy', p. 70.

93. Steart, 'Coal in Natal', pp. 38–42; Edgecombe and Guest, 'Natal coal industry in South African economy', p. 49.

94. Republic of South Africa, *Annual Report of the Department of Mines*, 25–1983; 'ISCOR plant – world first', *South African Mining : Coal, Gold and Base Minerals*, April 1986, pp. 85–86; Edgecombe and Guest, 'Natal coal industry in the South African economy', pp. 49, 70.

┌─────────────── *ABSTRACT* ───────────────┐

Natal-based whaling activity began in 1908 when two Norwegians, Jacob J. Egeland and Johan Bryde, founded the South African Whaling Company. By 1913 there were six companies operating from Durban with 25 catchers but after 1930, following several fluctuations in the demand for whale products, the Union Whaling and Fishing Company (established in 1909) was the only enterprise still hunting from Natal. From 1936 the company extended its coastal operations into pelagic whaling off Madagascar and Antarctica through the purchase of a factory ship, the *Abraham Larsen*, and additional catchers. This activity ended in 1956, following successive seasons of declining catches and output, and reduced quotas imposed by the International Whaling Convention. Shore whaling off Natal continued to prosper under the direction of Dr G.C. Scully and Hans M. Knudsen, who from 1953 managed the company on behalf of the Johannesburg-based Unit Securities Trust which had acquired control of it during the Second World War. They concentrated Union Whaling's administrative and production branches on adjacent sites at the Durban Bluff and Salisbury Island, modernised its fleet with bigger, faster ships provided with radio and spotter equipment, improved whaling operations through the use of spotter planes and more selective hunting, upgraded and diversified the company's products, and developed a wider range of markets. Union Whaling became even more dependent upon decisions taken in Johannesburg when it came under the control of the Weil and Asheim Investment Corporation, and eventually closed down in 1976 as a result of rapidly changing circumstances. These included a sharp rise in fuel costs following the 'oil shock' of 1973, growing public antipathy towards whaling, and the introduction of increasingly rigorous quotas and regulations by the South African government, in co-operation with the International Whaling Commission.

└───┘

A HISTORY OF WHALING FROM DURBAN

Cornelis de Jong

The rise and decline of shore whaling 1908–1918

Modern whaling originated in Norway between 1860 and 1870, when the Norwegian shipowner Svend Foyn of Tönsberg applied the technology of the industrial revolution to the declining traditional whaling industry. He replaced the whaling ship with the land station and, later, the floating factory; the rowing boat with the steam-driven catcher vessel; the hand harpoon with the heavy harpoon and its explosive head; and the harpoon rifle with the heavy harpoon gun. He also added other devices, invented or perfected by himself, and made a great success of modern, industrialised whaling. This trade came to be dominated by Norwegians. It spread from northern Norway to all other coasts of the northern seas, extending the search for undisturbed whale stocks. In 1905, when the catches of northern whaling had declined, the whalers went south, to the coasts of Africa and to sub-Antarctic and Antarctic seas.

At that time a new era of expansion was ushered in by the discovery of large whaling areas in southern seas, and by an improvement in the international market for oils from whales, which had previously been deteriorating since 1865. The first cause of this improvement was the rapidly growing demand for organic oils and fats on the part of the soap and margarine industries. The second cause was the invention of hydrogenation, or hardening of oils to solid fats, which rendered baleen whale oil usable for the manufacture of margarine. The hardening and deodorization of whale oil were gradually perfected.[1] By the 1920s whale oil could be used as the main ingredient in margarine and soap.

There was a hectic but brief boom of whaling off the African coasts south of the Equator between 1908 and 1913, in which South Africa participated. In 1908 a Norwegian businessman at Durban, Jacob J. Egeland,[2] in association with the Norwegian whaling magnate at Sandefjord, Johan Bryde,[3] founded the South African Whaling Company. In 1908 they established the first land station at Durban and started whaling from there. In 1909 they founded the first land station at Saldanha Bay – the second whaling centre in South Africa.

The whaling products of those days were few and unrefined. They included:

113

(i) crude baleen whale oil, usually called 'whale oil', in four grades of colour, taste and purity; the best grade was used for the manufacture of soap and later margarine, the other grades for lubricating oil;

(ii) crude sperm whale oil, or 'sperm oil', in a few grades of quality, which was used for cosmetics and as a lubricant of the highest quality;

(iii) spermaceti, a waxy substance, largely obtained from the head of the sperm whale, and used for cosmetics and candles of the best quality;

(iv) baleen plates, usually called 'whalebone', obtained from the mouth of the baleen whale and up to c. 1914 used for stays in corsets, umbrellas and whips, but thereafter replaced by cheaper springsteel and mainly used for brushes until it was replaced by plastic material;

(v) ambergris, a waxy and very scarce secretion found only in the intestines of sperm whales and highly prized for use in the perfume industry and as an aphrodisiac in Eastern countries. A find of ambergris was considered a great windfall;

(vi) guano or fertilizer, made from 'grax', that is the solid remains after the extraction of the oil from the blubber, meat and bones, and from the internal organs and rotten meat of whales;

(vii) fodder, made from the best part of those solid remains.

After the first season in 1908, Egeland and Bryde parted company for unknown reasons. After leaving the South African Whaling Company, Egeland founded, in partnership with his cousin, Abraham Erik Larsen, the Union Whaling and Fishing Company using South African capital. The young Norwegian immigrant, Larsen, was a carpenter, building contractor and astute businessman. He eventually became the 'grand old man' of whaling from Durban.[4] His company started whaling in 1910 and was quite successful. Apart from a break between 1916 and 1920, it operated until 1976.

Other Natal businessmen soon followed the example of the South African Whaling Company and founded similar whaling enterprises. In 1913, during the heyday of whaling off the Natal coast, there were 6 companies with 6 land stations on the oceanside of the Bluff and 25 catchers in operation. The S.A. Whaling Company excepted, all directors and capital were South African. The first land station was situated on the bayside of the Bluff, but after one season it was moved for sanitary and safety reasons to the oceanside. A short railway was constructed from the slipway, or mooring quay, on the bayside round the promontory of the Bluff to the whaling stations on the oceanside for the transport of the whales upon flat trucks.

In 1913 the 6 stations produced 48 144 barrels of oil, largely 'whale oil' from humpbacks. In the 1914 season the catch dropped drastically. Overfishing of the whale stocks was already evident and the brief boom was over. The same applied to all African whaling stations and floating factories at that time. In 1914 Bryde's S.A. Whaling Company stopped its operation at Durban and other companies soon followed suit. The outbreak of the First World War contributed much to this general withdrawal. In other whaling areas the rapid expansion of new whaling was soon followed by a similar drastic decline in catches and a massive abandonment of the industry. After an interval of some years whaling was sometimes resumed on a reduced scale and remained profitable for several decades. This happened off the Natal coast.

However, during the First World War one company after the other, in spite of rising prices for whale products, abandoned whaling off Africa, Natal included, because labour and supplies for whaling became increasingly scarce. The use of whalers for the war effort became more profitable when the Allied Admiralties requisitioned the best catchers for war service as patrol ships or minesweepers. In 1916 Egeland and Larsen sold their 6 catchers to the French government for service in the Mediterranean Sea. Larsen himself escorted them to Port Said and had an adventurous wartime voyage. In 1918, at the end of the war, only one company, Grindrod Whaling Company, was operating from Durban with 3 old catchers.

Revival, adversity and prosperity of Natal whaling 1918-1937

During the short post-war boom, from 1918 to 1920, prices of whale products rose considerably. Two other companies were encouraged to renew whaling from Durban and reopened their land stations at the Bluff. They were the Premier Whaling Company, founded in 1913 by Lever Brothers, South Africa, a branch of the British Lever Brothers Company, and the resuscitated enterprise of Egeland and Larsen under the name of the Union Whaling Company. The international boom ended in 1920 when the prices of whale products fell sharply. Grindrod Whaling Company went into liquidation while Premier Whaling and Union Whaling also suffered severe financial losses during 1920 in spite of satisfactory catches. Nevertheless, they managed to survive the ensuing depression from 1920 to 1923. In 1923 the prices of whale products again rose and Union Whaling profited considerably by a windfall find of ambergris worth £1 500. The years 1923 to 1929 were fairly prosperous. The two companies expanded their catcher fleets from 10 to 17 in total and extended their factories.

In 1929 many international commodity prices began to fall drastically as the Great Depression got under way. Whale product prices also declined. Premier Whaling ceased operations in 1930 and thereafter, until whaling off Natal came to an end in 1975, Union Whaling was the only operating company. Thanks to good management, strict economy measures imposed by Abraham Larsen, and satisfactory catches, Union Whaling continued operations, in 1931 with 10 catchers, in 1932 with 8, and earned small profits.

In 1931 Larsen made two bold moves in spite of prevailing low prices. He acquired the majority of shares in Premier Whaling from Lever Brothers, South Africa at a bargain price and turned this competitor into an auxiliary company. He also hired the Premier shore station so that up to 1953 Union Whaling operated two land stations at the Bluff. Larsen's second step was taken in 1932, when Union Whaling took over the mechanical workshop of the Natal Marine and Engineering Company in Durban, which had been liquidated. This workshop subsequently carried out maintenance and conversion work for Union Whaling and other shipowners and served the Admiralties during the Second World War. It was closed down in 1967.

From 1934 to 1938 whale product prices improved and Union Whaling expanded again. From 1933 the company chartered an annually increasing number of catchers from Premier Whaling – ultimately 7 – and it extended its operating fleet to 16 in 1937–39. The company entered a period of energetic expansion in spite of the very great risks involved in the whaling industry and another steep fall in product prices in 1938.

Union Whaling's participation in pelagic whaling 1937–1957

In 1936 Larsen made yet another bold move when Union Whaling began to participate in pelagic whaling – that is whaling with factory ships on the high seas – following the example of the great fishing company of Irvin and Johnson based at Cape Town. This company sent the floating factory *Tafelberg* to the Antarctic Sea in 1936. Larsen bought the old, but modernised, factoryship *Fraternitas* – ex *Sir James Clark Ross* of Ross Sea fame[5] – from a Norwegian company and renamed her *Uniwaleco*. Union Whaling also bought 6 catchers and financed the new fleet with the issue of £200 000 paid-up shares. The company sent out its pelagic fleet in the summers of 1937–38 and 1939–40 (though not in 1938–39) to Antarctic seas and in the winters of 1937, 1938 and 1939 to the waters off Madagascar. The fleet was mainly in pursuit of baleen whales in Antarctic waters, but off Madagascar the catch was mostly humpbacks. In this way the company used its precious fleet during two seasons a year instead of one, as was customary among other whaling companies and as prescribed by the first International Whaling Convention in 1937. Although the South African government did not sign this convention before the Second World War, the directors of Union Whaling thought it wise not to mention its pelagic fleet and the results of its pelagic whaling in any of its annual reports.

Pelagic whaling was risky because competition by other nations grew considerably after 1935 when two new nations joined Antarctic whaling with factory ships: Japan and Germany. After a brief recovery between 1934 and 1938 many international commodity prices slumped again in 1938 and 1939. Whale products shared in this fall, though this depression was soon lifted by the Second World War. Union Whaling pulled through successfully in both pelagic and shore whaling until the war raised prices again.

The Second World War interrupted Union Whaling's pelagic activities and also curbed its coastal whaling. The experiences of the First World War were partly repeated. Whale product prices rose, but labour and stores became scarce. Admiralties commandeered most catchers. The British Admiralty requisitioned *Uniwaleco* to serve as a tanker, and the catchers of Premier Whaling, which also flew the British flag, were similarly taken over by the Navy. *Uniwaleco* was sunk by a German submarine off Trinidad in the West Indies in 1942; 13 of her crew perished. The South African Admiralty requisitioned the best catchers of the Union Whaling Company and left the company with 5 old vessels. It continued its operations with a reduced fleet and halved production on one of the two land stations at the Bluff. The catches were generally good and, in spite of many wartime difficulties, Union Whaling continued to pay handsome dividends.

After the Second World War, Union Whaling entered another period of expansion and prosperity. The British government expropriated the German factory ship *Unitas*, at that time the largest and best-equipped floating factory in the world, of 21 846 gross registered tons. She had served three summers (1936–39) in Antarctic seas. The British renamed her *Empire Victory* and leased her to Union Whaling to compensate the company for its loss of a factory ship during the war. After *Empire Victory* had been declared a prize, the British government sold her to Union Whaling. She was promptly renamed *Abraham Larsen*, in honour of the founder of the company, and in accordance with Union Whaling's tradition of naming its ships after its directors and managers.

The Admiralty and the South African Navy gradually returned the requisitioned catchers to the company. It reconverted them and converted recently purchased corvettes to catchers. It also ordered new and fast catchers from Norway and Britain. It sent the *Larsen* with 14 and later with 10 catchers for 11 seasons (1946–57) to the Antarctic sea. The first two seasons were an outstanding success, for the conditions were favourable to Antarctic whaling: catches were good after the long pause in hunting caused by the war, and prices of whale products, especially of whale oil, were high. Thereafter conditions changed, catches declined, especially of the biggest whale species, the blue whale, and prices dropped rapidly from 1952 onwards. In addition, during the last few seasons, the *Larsen* was below the average for all Antarctic whaling fleets combined of 110 to 130 barrels of whale oil, extracted from one blue whale unit,[6] by between 10 and 15 barrels. This was an indication that the *Larsen*'s efficiency had dropped below that of newer factory ships. It is true that the *Larsen* extracted about the same number of barrels of oil per sperm whale as the average for the whole fleet, namely 50, but the total output of sperm oil was much smaller than the production of whale oil.[7]

Moreover, the International Whaling Convention, which South Africa had signed after the war, regulated whaling more strictly. In 1946 it fixed the permitted catch in Antarctic seas – the main whaling ground – at 16 000 blue whale units and it reduced this quota successively for the seasons after 1950 when overwhaling became evident. For the season of 1955–56 the quota was 15 000; for the 1956–58 seasons, 14 500. Competition for whales among the Antarctic fleets became fierce and the number, size and expenses of the catchers rose considerably.

The directors of the Union Whaling Company concluded that the heyday of Antarctic whaling was over and in 1956 they decided to sell the *Larsen* and 8 of her catchers to Japan, which continued to extend her whaling activities because she needed whale meat and bought ships from other nations who abandoned whaling. Union Whaling reduced the number of the *Larsen*'s catchers to 10 along with the length of her last season (1956–57). This reduced expenses, to the extent that the profit for the last season was good, but the sale of the ships was nevertheless concluded. In 1957 they sailed to Japan where their names were changed. The *Larsen*, renamed *Nishin Maru Nr. 2*, served the Japanese in the Antarctic sea and was eventually scrapped in 1965.

The Union Whaling Company's pelagic whaling activities had come to an end. In the 1950s the gross profits of its Antarctic branch had decreased, whereas the gross profits of its shore whaling branch had increased and exceeded that of its pelagic business for the financial years of 1956 and 1957.

Prosperity and decline of shore whaling 1945–1967

During the Second World War a rapidly expanding investment company in the financial capital of South Africa, Johannesburg, the Unit Securities Trust, acquired the majority of shares in Union Whaling. Its chairman and driving force was R. K. Fraay, a Dutch immigrant who had worked his way up from junior clerk in Pretoria to manager in Durban and then to financial magnate in Johannesburg. He underwrote the share issue of £1,5 in 1946 which facilitated the purchase of the *Empire Victory* and a fleet of catchers. The majority of the shares were held in the Transvaal. Consequently the centre of decision-making shifted gradually from Durban to Johannesburg and from the grand, but now old man, A. E. Larsen, to the younger, strong-willed R. K. Fraay.

By about 1950 it became obvious that stocks of the most valuable baleen whale species were declining. They migrate annually between their feeding grounds in Antarctic seas in summer and their mating and calving grounds in subtropical and tropical seas in winter. Some of these schools of whales pass Natal on their migration: in autumn northward, in spring southward, or they winter in the sea off Natal. The depletion of whales in Antarctic seas directly affected the catch off Natal. Indeed, the declining catches of blue whales, fin whales and humpbacks forced Union Whaling to hunt smaller baleen whale species such as sei whales, Bryde whales, and sperm whales, and to obtain a greater volume of products, including the more valuable products from fewer and smaller whales.

During its years of pelagic whaling activity, Union Whaling never neglected shore whaling. On the contrary, while Antarctic whaling declined after 1950, coastal whaling prospered for several years longer, with a record year in 1965. The investment of capital and human effort on the land stations continued unabated before and after the Second World War.

New men with specialised skills were needed for the adaptation of shore whaling to the changed circumstances. Abraham Larsen was not the person to achieve this. He had made Union Whaling a prosperous enterprise and he was a good organiser and businessman, but he was no specialised technician. The resumption of Antarctic whaling was his last great achievement. He had groomed his son Ernst as his successor, but in 1953 father and son were both eased out of the management by Fraay, retiring as joint managing directors. Fraay brought in Dr G.C. Scully, a chemist and graduate of the University of Stellenbosch, manager of African Explosives and Chemical Industries and director of other companies. He became A.E. Larsen's successor as managing director in 1953. When Scully sought the services of an experienced chemist, Union Whaling contacted Anders Jahre, a business relation at Sandefjord, the centre of Norwegian whaling. Jahre found the required person in his local whale oil factory. He was the young, talented Norwegian chemist, Hans M. Knudsen. In 1965 Scully remained chairman of the board of directors and Knudsen succeeded him as managing director. He continued to improve the land station until he left in 1968.

The business policy of Scully and Knudsen was characterised by the following features:

(i) concentration of management and production at the Bluff and on Salisbury Island in the Bay of Durban;
(ii) modernisation and rationalisation of the whaling fleet and whaling operations;
(iii) upgrading and diversification of whale products;
(iv) diversification of markets.

Concentration of management and production
So far Union Whaling had operated two land stations at the Bluff: one, its own, founded in 1910 and re-established in 1920; the other, Premier Whaling's, founded in 1912 and hired from 1932 onwards by Union Whaling along with catchers belonging to that company. Only in the years 1941 to 1946 was one of the two stations out of use because of the curbing of operations caused by the war. By 1953 both land stations were over 40 years old and both needed a general overhaul. The directors of Union Whaling decided to retain the Premier station, to purchase it from the subsidiary Premier Company and modernise it, and to discard the other station. The proprietor of the sites of both stations was the South African Railways. The factory at the Premier station was extended by means of new installations to maintain production capacity.

In 1958 the South African Railways and Harbours terminated the lease of the Union Whaling Company's site at Maydon Wharf. The Company's workshop and storehouse were then moved to Salisbury Island, where the catchers were also moored, fuelled and supplied. The directors' and managers' offices were moved to a fine, new office building constructed on the former Premier station. The distance from the city to the Bluff exceeded that to Maydon Wharf, but the management of Union Whaling was thereafter better concentrated and adjacent to the factory.

Modernisation and rationalisation of the whaling fleet and whaling operations
The modernisation of the catcher fleet was a continuous process after the Second World War, when technological development was accelerated. Old coal-burning vessels sank or became redundant and were sold to scrap-yards and replaced by bigger, faster ships. Some of these were ordered from shipyards in Britain or Norway; others were purchased from companies which had used them in Antarctic waters. The highest number of catchers owned by Union Whaling was 22, of which between 13 and 15 were employed in Antarctic seas in summer and for whaling off Natal in winter, or else laid up in Durban Bay.

Each catcher was equipped with radio and a direction finder. From 1959 onwards some catchers were equipped with Asdic finder apparatus for tracking whales under water. Eventually 7 catchers were equipped with Asdic, which needed specialist operators. Whaling operations were also made more efficient by the chartering of light aircraft for the spotting of whales from the air, so that catcher crews were better informed of their presence. The first whale-spotting aeroplane was chartered in 1954 and was an immediate success. In the ensuing years the co-operation between aircraft and catchers was improved and the Union Whaling fleet operated very efficiently. From 1961–67 two aeroplanes were chartered. When the fleet was reduced in 1968, one aircraft was deemed sufficient and it served until the whaling operations were terminated at the end of 1975.

The increase in the effectiveness of the operations is apparent from the following figures. The average number of whales of all species taken per catcher, per catching day was, in 1956, 1,26; in 1957 (a very bad year) 1,14; in 1968, 1,25; in 1969, 1,73; in 1970, 1,52; in 1971, 1,87; and in 1972, 1,49.[8] The decrease in catches of big baleen whale species after 1960 compelled Union Whaling to change its hunting methods and to concentrate more on other whale species. The season was lengthened to enhance the catch of sperm whales, by then the most important booty, and was opened in February or in the first days of March. The hunting of baleen whales was commenced by additional catchers in April but the best months for the catching of baleen whales were June, July and August. The season was usually closed towards the end of September, as there were often stormy days at sea in October.

After 1960, blue whales and humpbacks became scarce, to the extent that the pelagic catch of these species was forbidden by the International Whaling Commission. Union Whaling turned its attention to fin whales, sei whales and Bryde whales, and, of course, sperm whales. From 1968, species which had been formerly ignored, were taken and processed; these included minke whales, the smallest of the baleen whale species, which produced good meat and oil, killer whales and big dolphins, e.g. *Ziphius cavitorostratus*.

Upgrading and diversification of whale products
Before the appointment of Dr Scully and Mr Knudsen the land stations marketed a limited number of crude, simple, unrefined whale products

Whaling Station

The giants are felled and hauled,
intruding on a vast dock's space;

scythes peel the bulging blubber
as from a primordial fruit,
and booted executioners
stagger through oily streams
to hook the flapping tatters of blooded meat
to fettered hooks;
whalebone gristle resists the snap,
and whirling saws sing out in triumph.

The seagulls shriek and dive
– clear-eyed and busily wrangling –
unharmed and fearless
they are suspended above
an apocalyptic
but now silenced spray.

In a monstrous head
yawns – exposed and black –
the cavern
of man's deepest wound.

Ernst van Heerden

The flensing of a whale at Union Whaling's shore station.   LOCAL HISTORY MUSEUM, DURBAN

Union Whaling Company's shore station at the Bluff, Durban.

namely crude whale oil, sperm oil and sperm wax. Most of these products were exported via brokers in Durban and London to customers in a small number of ports in Europe, such as London, Rotterdam and Hamburg. Other products were meat meal, part of which was exported, and bone meal, which was less valuable and was mostly sold locally. As already indicated, when the catch of the big baleen whale species, namely blue whales, fin whales and humpbacks, declined after 1950, the catch of sperm whales and smaller baleen whale species became more important. From about 1960 the output of crude sperm oil exceeded that of whale oil. New products were also marketed by the company:

(a) Meat-extract. The first step was the opening of a meat-extract installation in 1956 to obtain meat-extract from baleen whale meat. From 1957 sperm whale meat was also extracted, in spite of the prevailing prejudice against this type of meat. Its production rose rapidly and yielded good revenue.
(b) Vitamin oil, which contains mainly Vitamin A, and was extracted from whale livers. The extraction process was perfected by Hans M. Knudsen and the product was marketed from 1957 to 1965. In 1955 extraction plants were installed on the *Larsen* and on one of the land stations. The vitamin oil sold well, but after cheaper synthetic oil appeared on the world market Union Whaling stopped production in 1965.
(c) Whale oil. The next step was the processing of crude whale oil, until then the main product. As early as 1948, an experimental hydrogenation plant was built for the hardening of whale oil into a solid substance suitable for the manufacture of hard soap and margarine. However, special, large hydrogenation plants could perform this process more economically and, after a few years, Union Whaling closed down its small installation, but continued to sell its whale oil in a crude state, mainly grade one.
(d) Sperm oil. In contrast, the processing of sperm oil was a great success and very rewarding. This development was started in 1958 and the first product was cold filtered oil, a high-pressure lubricant. Production began in a simple way with a pilot plant and was later extended by means of a larger installation. The second product was sulphurized sperm oil, a first-rate high-pressure lubricant, made by treating cold filtered oil with sulphur. Production started in 1959. This excellent high-pressure lubricant found markets in many countries, except the USA which produced its own. Eventually, 9 grades of this article were marketed with success in more than 20 countries. The third line was sulphurated sperm oil, produced by adding concentrated sulphuric acid to cold filtered oil and neutralising with ammonia gas dissolved in water. It was used in the leather industry and marketed from 1973 in two grades: a high sulphurated oil and a low sulphurated one.
(e) Meat meal. This product, more correctly called 'carcass meal', was also improved. South African legislation forbade its use as fertilizer, so it served as fodder. To the two grades of plain meat meal a spray-dried

soluble high-protein meal was added, called energy-fodder, which was largely exported.

(f) Whale meat for consumption. In 1967 a frozen meat plant was installed. From 1968 to the end of whaling in 1975 annual contracts for the export of frozen whale meat to meat-hungry Japan were concluded. This food was for human consumption and was carefully cut and packed under the control of Japanese supervisors. The operation was profitable, but as catches of the best whales – young fin whales – declined, the hunt for minke whales was initiated in 1968. The sale of fresh and frozen whale meat for human consumption in South Africa was small, but in 1969 processing of frozen whale meat with additives for dogs and cats was started: pets relished it.

Diversification continued up to the last season of Union Whaling in 1975. Previously sperm whale meat had been regarded as unhealthy, but in 1972 experimental canning of this food, cooked with vegetables and gravy for human consumption, was initiated. In 1975 the sale of spermaceti to candle-makers in South Africa for the best quality of candles was planned. Some experiments which proved unsuccessful were stopped. They were: hydrogenation of whale oil, mentioned above, manufacture of gelatine and glue from blubber fibres, and injection of antibiotics into freshly-killed whales to retard autolysis (decomposition of body cells).

Diversification of markets
Diversification of products led to a diversification of markets. Crude whale oil was primarily sold in centres of commerce in Europe. Union Whaling exported its refined quality products, such as lubricants, to many more countries. When the USA market was closed to whale products in the 1970s the company had no difficulty in finding other markets.

The last period 1967–1976

Until 1967 Union Whaling was a very successful enterprise. Upon the basis of a few crude, simple whale products, a chemical industry and a food industry making refined quality products were built. Profits were good in many of the years from 1954 to 1966. The personnel – black, brown and white – were well paid and generally satisfied. They became a close-knit group of specialised experts. The land station at the Bluff, it is said, became the largest and most sophisticated whaling station in the world. Scientists and biologists from South Africa and abroad collected material at the land station for their research and publications, in which they paid tribute to the hospitality shown by Union Whaling. Profits increased in spite of decreasing catches of baleen whales after about 1960. This was, to a great extent, the achievement of Hans M. Knudsen and his able assistants.

In 1967 a serious reverse occurred. In the first place the catch of baleen and sperm whales was much smaller than previously. The weather was fairly good, but apparently factory ships made a desperate effort in the Antarctic sea south of Natal to obtain a full load, with the result that the stocks of baleen whales were more severely depleted than ever before. Moreover Knudsen, who was a strict man, had forbidden the capture of sperm whales below 34 feet in length so that the catch of these animals in 1967 dropped considerably. Secondly, the prices of several whale products, initially oils, fell perceptibly on world markets. Thirdly, the devaluation of sterling in November 1967 substantially reduced the money value of Union Whaling's considerable balance in London.

The combined outcome of these setbacks was a substantial drop in catches, output and revenue and a heavy loss of R473 306. Knudsen was held responsible for this reverse. The majority of the directors objected also to his policy of continuing to make large investments in the factory, because they doubted the future of whale stocks and of whaling. In vain, Dr Scully attempted to conciliate the directors. Knudsen resigned and left South Africa on 31 March 1968. It was a sad end to an outstanding career. He joined the large fishing company of Salvesen at Leith – also a great whaling company – and became manager of Salvesen's factory at Yarmouth, Nova Scotia in Canada. There he died suddenly from heart failure in 1974.

In August and September 1967, 5 of the 10 operating catchers were laid up and from 12 August only one spotter plane was used. Because of the bad season and the doubtful prospects for whaling the directors drastically curtailed operations at the end of 1967. They sold 5 of the 13 catchers to Japan, closed down the workshop on Salisbury Island (the work of which was transferred to the workshop at the Bluff), reduced the factory capacity and dismissed some of the personnel. Some Norwegians left with Knudsen. Their posts were filled with young, able South Africans who had been trained while in the employ of Union Whaling and on Antarctic whaling expeditions. Their head was Mr L. C. Surmon, who in 1972 became one of the two managing directors.

The company continued with 7 – later 6 – catchers, and further reduced both its factory capacity and its diversification of whale products and markets. The sale of frozen meat to Japan yielded good revenue and prices of whale products rose again. The bookyear of 1968 showed a small profit, which increased in subsequent years and indicated that the company had recovered from the heavy blows sustained in 1967.

A new development in the 1960s was the introduction by the South African Government of regulations for shore whaling and supervision by State inspectors, in addition to the regulations of the International Whaling Commission that were already applied by the South African government. These governed such matters as minimum sizes for captured whales and the prohibition on the capture of lactating whales and of certain endangered species. Previously, the government had been concerned only with sanitary prescriptions, such as the avoidance of pollution. The International Whaling Commission did not fix quotas for catches by land stations or the length of the hunting season; since 1966 this had been controlled by the government.[9] From 1967, the official quota of sperm whales for Union Whaling was 2 847 per year. From 1972 this was reduced to 1 824, of which, from 1973, half had to be males and half females. From 1973 a quota for fin whales – an endangered species – was fixed at 415. The company used to take the full, or almost full, quota of sperm whales but fewer than the permitted quota of fin whales. It was allowed to catch all other baleen whale species above a certain size. Union Whaling maintained its profitability in spite of the increasing regulations which made whaling one of the most strictly regulated industries in the world.

Another change was the sale of the majority of the shares in Union Whaling by the Unit Securities Trust, perhaps in connection with the retirement of Mr. Fraay, after which the Weil and Asheim Investment Corporation in Johannesburg acquired the shares. The quotation of UWC shares on the Johannesburg stock exchange and the publication of annual reports was discontinued after 1972. The management became more dependent than ever before on the decisions of financiers in Johannesburg. The decisive blow to the Union Whaling Company came fairly unexpectedly in 1973 when the world price of fuel oil began to rise steeply. Fuel oil was a substantial cost item in the company's expenditures, being essential for propelling the fast-running catchers and driving the factory engines. Fuel costs increased very considerably, but as prices of whale products remained good and the catch was satisfactory, the financial years of 1974 and 1975 still showed a profit – the exact figures were not published.

However, Johannesburg directors expected that the fuel oil price would continue to rise and that restrictions imposed on whaling by government would become more rigorous because of the growing public antipathy towards whaling. They were right. Since the establishment of the company in 1910, the directors had followed a policy of abandoning operations before sustained financial losses could be suffered. In 1916 they had sold all 6 catchers to France and terminated operations in order to earn higher profits than wartime whaling would yield. In 1957 they had sold the *Larsen* and 8 catchers to Japan and ended pelagic whaling because they expected that pelagic, *inter alia* Antarctic, whaling would become unprofitable, which indeed became true within a decade. In 1968 they had halved the catcher fleet and factory output after just one season of financial loss in 1967. After the 1975 season they decided to terminate whaling altogether and sell out, because the fuel price had rocketed and it was anticipated that quotas for whale catches would probably be further reduced by the International Whaling Commission and the South African government. The directors expected to raise a substantial amount from the sale of the company's assets. Union Whaling would exist in name only.

In the course of 1976, the last whale products were processed and stocks disposed of, the land station was gradually run down and the catchers and loose equipment sold. The personnel were dismissed one by one but, as skilled specialists, most of them had no trouble in finding other local employment. The site of the land station, which belonged to the South African Railways, was taken over by the South African Navy. Whaling off Natal had come to an end, probably for ever. Could Union Whaling have continued its operations for much longer? Two reputable cetologists confirmed in the 1970s that the company did not deplete the stock of sperm whales off Natal and that its annual catch did not exceed the maximum sustainable yield of sperm whale stocks. The company was indeed alone in the vast whaling grounds off south-east Africa even though its action radius was limited to 150 or at most 200 sea miles. The conclusion is that Union Whaling could have continued to operate for an indefinite time had it chosen to do so.

Epilogue

Whale catchers are fast ships and can ride heavy seas. They are conspicuous by their high bridge and high funnel with catwalk from bridge to bow and harpoon gun on the bow. Their departure out to sea and return, with whales fastened alongside, to the Bay of Durban was a picturesque sight. Fortunately, the best South African maritime painter was Nils Andersen of Durban, who was of Norwegian birth and the son of a whaleman who settled in South Africa. Nils has painted catchers and lively whaling scenes several times, but not the activities on a land station. The transportation of whales on flat trucks drawn by a big puffing, whistling locomotive from the slipway on the Bay to the land station at the Bluff was a unique spectacle, not to be seen on any other whaling station. The dissection of the whale carcasses on the platform, accompanied by the cries of strangely-attired black labourers and of eager seagulls – at night illuminated in stark colours by strong lamps – was a fantastic spectacle. At least one talented South African poet, Ernst van Heerden, has sketched it in words, but no painter has done so. This weird scene is now a matter of the past, a blessing for the whales, but a loss for the South African economy.

Table 1   Whaling off Natal 1908–1975

Season	Shore stations	Catchers	Whales								Baleen whale oil (barrels)	Sperm whale oil (barrels)	Total whale oils
			Blue	Fin	Humpback	Sei	Minke	Other	Sperm	Total			
1908	1	2						106[1]		106			3 240
1909	1	2						170[1]		170			7 000
1910	2	7						532[1]		532			23 400
1911	3	10						1051[1]		1051			43 944
1912	5	18	24	7	906	11		2[2]	56	1006			38 712
1913	6	25	59	263	662	1		129[3]	230	1344			48 144
1914	5	22	66	212	412	3		3[2]	365	1061			37 116
1915	4	23	79	285	122	7		1[2]	486	980			34 254
1916	3	18	57	116	83	10		2[2]	585	853			23 634
1917	2	8	36	60	7	5			68	176			6 606
1918	1	3	9	47	9	4			73	142			4 434
1919	2	11	12	145	91	3		2[2]	388	641			19 539
1920	2	15	71	159	148	15			311	704			26 076
1921	2	13	123	246	190	49		3[2]	294	905			30 944
1922	2	10	96	164	285	48		1[2]	117	711			24 880
1923	2	10	213	330	122	60			84	809			26 200
1924	2	15	170	354	187	57		2[2]	268	1038			36 500
1925	2	15	240	254	167	112			511	1284			46 896
1926	2	15	214	336	174	97		1[2]	466	1238			46 084
1927	2	15	220	287	84	89		1[2]	408	1089			44 898
1928	2	15	131	431	62	51			695	1170			38 400
1929	2	17	177	637	99	42			842	1797			70 804
1930	2	17	265	477	131	52			336	1261			57 500

Table 1 Whaling off Natal (cont.)

| Season | Shore stations | Catchers | Whales | | | | | | | | Baleen whale oil (barrels) | Sperm whale oil (barrels) | Total whale oils |
			Blue	Fin	Humpback	Sei	Minke	Other	Sperm	Total			
1931	1	10	122	466	71	29			135	873			37 086
1932	1	8	109	345	309	23		1²	256	1043			44 122
1933	2	14	85	602	162	11		2²	306	1168			53 000
1934	2	17	70	536	514	30		2²	422	1574			60 924
1935	2	17	122	536	418	90		2²	595	1753			67 008
1936	2	18	41	528	391	68			911	1849	38 562	26 008	64 570
1937	2	16	67	755	240	64			503	1629	53 108	14 871	67 979
1938	2	16	39	536	175	64			425	1239	38 729	15 623	54 352
1939	2	16	27	502	200	42			615	1386	35 446	16 083	51 529
1940	2	11	28	324	176	25			482	1035			40 419
1941	1	5	6	193	79	5			476	759			26 638
1942	1	5	2	204	156	13			123	498			19 740
1943	1	5	10	301	80	34			299	724			27 373
1944	1	5	5	127	115	24			448	819			29 380
1945	1	5	3	162	116	34			414	729			23 189
1946	1	8	12	145	93	75			659	984	11 218	19 334	30 552
1947	2	13	18	485	90	119			502	1214	30 002	14 272	44 274
1948	2	16	16	426	182	109			846	1579	29 040	20 391	49 431
1949	2	17	17	564	190	101			694	1466	31 974	20 009	51 983
1950	2	18	9	123	151	101			391	975	24 689	13 991	38 680
1951	2	20	20	289	103	247		2²	910	2071	48 702	25 744	74 446
1952	2	14	8	451	111	155			356	1081	31 923	13 238	45 161
1953	2	14	5	441	89	96			353	984	26 942	12 371	39 313
1954	1	12	10	515	27	71			400	1023	28 095	14 858	42 953

Table 1 Whaling off Natal (cont.)

Season	Shore stations	Catchers	Blue	Fin	Humpback	Sei	Minke	Other	Sperm	Total	Baleen whale oil (barrels)	Sperm whale oil (barrels)	Total whale oils
1955	1	13	6	477	49	176			602	1310	28 759	16 447	45 206
1956	1	13	5	613	36	101			474	1229	36 098	15 007	51 105
1957	1	11	5	758	34	60			763	1620	41 471	22 412	63 883
1958	1	11	3	674	39	172			738	1626	38 100	21 701	59 801
1959	1	11	3	607	38	379			824	1851	37 574	22 866	60 440
1960	1	11	6	738	36	183			1024	1937	41 226	27 510	68 736
1961	1	11	6	622	36	475			1004	2143	35 793	25 131	60 924
1962	1	11	7	489	37	319			1640	2492	27 516	40 293	67 809
1963	1	12	5	346		369		3[4]	1771	2531	24 450	44 698	69 148
1964	1	10	5	272		282			2113	2672	15 634	46 126	61 760
1965	1	12	6	361		459		4[4]	2814	3640	22 824	55 832	78 656
1966	1	12	4	199		273		6[4]	2435	2915	13 328	58 695	72 023
1967	1	10		124		66		4[4]	1626	1822	6 664	39 528	46 192
1968	1	7		62		24	97	4[4]	1211	1398	4 022	35 100	39 122
1969	1	7		150		40	112	3[4]	1885	2190	8 437	42 200	50 657
1970	1	7		47		8	171	1[4]	1824	2051	2 683	42 319	45 002
1971	1	6		64		10	199	6[5]	2068	2347	4 345	42 624	46 969
1972	1	6		51		4	135	20[6]	1640	1850	3 271	42 923	46 194
1973	1	6		41	1	4	173	16[7]	1606	1841	3 210	37 494	40 704
1974	1	6		21		4	115	11[8]	1781	1932	1 765	39 883	41 648
1975	1	5		21		2	110	6[9]	1678	1817	1 453	35 135	36 588

Table 1 Whaling off Natal (cont.)

1. Species not recorded, but probably mostly humpbacks.
2. Southern right whales.
3. Southern right whales, 3; not specified, 126.
4. Bryde whales.
5. Bryde whales, 1; killer whales, 5.
6. Bryde whales, 3; killer whales, 17.
7. Bryde whales, 6; killer whales, 8; bottlenoses, 2.
8. Bryde whales, 8; killer whales, 2.
9. Bryde whales, 2; killer whales, 4.
10. One barrel is 170 kg or about $\frac{1}{6}$ long ton; one long ton is 1016 kg.

Sources: International Whaling Statistics, Sandefjord, Norway.
   Norwegian Whaling Gazette, Sandefjord, Norway.

Table 2   Pelagic whaling by the Union Whaling Company 1937–1957

Season	Catchers	Whales						Baleen whale oil (barrels)[1]
		Blue	Fin	Humpback	Sei	Sperm	Total	
Factory ship *Uniwaleco*								
MADAGASCAR								
1937	6						1 257[4]	53 500
1938	6	1	2	1 752	2	48	1 805	83 540
1939	5					61	1 246	53 973
ANTARCTIC SEA								
1936/37								73 883
1937/38	6					4	1 089	74 570
1938/39								
1939/40	7					36	829	41 244
Factory ship *Empire Victory/Abraham Larsen*								
ANTARCTIC SEA								
1946/47	12	1 195	983			388	2 566	184 673
1947/48	14	740	1 725			493	2 958	155 182
1948/49	14	690	1 386			532	2 608	123 398
1949/50	15	451	1 194	54		183	1 882	135 221
1950/51	15	584	1 463	1		455	2 503	138 149
1951/52	16	613	1 511	8		362	2 494	166 422
1952/53	16	259	2 019	5		177	2 460	140 889
1953/54	13	348	1 717	4		157	2 226	138 951
1954/55	13	177	1 178	9		332	1 696	82 150
1955/56	15	71	1 359	149	4	601	2 184	80 586
1956/57	10	9	1 381	13	118	75	1 506	82 567

1. One barrel is 170 kilogram or about $\frac{1}{6}$ long ton; one long ton is 1 016 kg.
2. One long ton is 1 016 kilogram.
3. One blue whale unit is equal to one blue whale, or 2 fin whales, or $2\frac{1}{2}$ humpbacks, or 6 sei whales, or 6 Bryde whales.
4. Mostly humpbacks.

Sperm whale oil (barrels)	Total whale oils (barrels)	Meat meal (long tons)[2]	Whale liver (long tons)	Whale liver oil (long tons)	Barrels of oil per			
					Blue whale unit[3]		Sperm whale	
					All factory ships	A. Larsen	All factory ships	A. Larsen
	53 500							
1 210	84 750							
1 291	55 264							
287	74 170							
260	74 830							
1 966	43 210							
20 206	204 879	1 339	127		113,1			
25 874	181 056	1 391			111,2	97,4		
27 330	150 728				115,6	97,5		
10 077	145 298	2 790	294		118,6	129,0		
23 762	161 911				117,3	105,0	51,2	52,1
19 540	185 962	3 009	193		129,4	122,5	52,4	54,0
9 566	150 455	3 203	111		128,0	113,0	52,3	52,5
8 320	147 271				128,6	116,0	50,6	53,0
16 850	99 000	2 750		24,9	117,3	107,7	49,5	50,8
28 659	109 245	3 253		20,3	121,6	100,9	49,3	48,1
4 019	86 586	3 383		18,3	128,6	114,6	49,6	53,2

REFERENCES

1. J. N. Tönnessen and A. O. Johnsen, *The history of modern whaling* (translated from the Norwegian by C. Hurst & Co., London, and Australian National University Press, Canberra, 1982), pp. 231–38.

2. *Dictionary of South African biography*, vol. 5. (H.S.R.C. Pretoria, Butterworth, Durban, 1987).

3. *Dictionary of South African biography*, vol. 5.

4. *Dictionary of South African biography*, vol. 4.

5. This is a reference to the very bold whaling expeditions of the *Sir James Clark Ross*, under command of the Norwegian whaling pioneer Carl Anton Larsen, into the Ross Sea in the heart of Antarctica during the summers of 1922–23 and 1923–24. See Tönnessen and Johnsen, *The history of modern whaling*, pp. 346–51.

6. For statistical purposes and fixing of catch quotas, whale species are expressed in blue whale units in the proportion of one blue whale to 2 fin whales; 2,5 humpbacks; 6 sei whales; and 6 Bryde whales. The Norwegian cetologist Ørjan Olsen discovered a new whale species during his visit to the whaling stations of Johan Bryde's company in South Africa and called this species after the director of the company, 'Bryde' whale.

7. See the annual comparative tables on Antarctic whaling expeditions for 1946–57 in the *Norwegian Whaling Gazette (Norsk Hvalfangst-Tidende)*, (Sandefjord, 1910–68). The last table which refers to the *Abraham Larsen* is in the *NWG*, 46, 1957, season 1956–57, p. 458.

8. *Annual Report of the Union Whaling Company*, Durban, year ended 30 September 1972, p. 12.

9. The *Annual Report of the Division of Sea Fisheries* (Department of Industries, Cape Town), no. 34, 1966, p. 8 states: 'This (1966) was the first season during which South African whaling stations had operated on a quota basis, the baleen whale catch being limited to 236,8 blue whale units for Durban and 162,7 for Donkergat (Saldanha Bay), and the sperm whale catch to 2 847 individuals for Durban and 798 individuals for Donkergat.' From the 1972 season onwards the quota for Blue Whale Units remained 236,8 but the quota for sperm whales was reduced from 2 847 to 1 824. From 1973 onwards half of the permitted number of Sperm Whales, 1 824, had to be males and half females.

STATISTICAL SOURCES

Annual reports of the Union Whaling Company, Durban, 1920–1972 (last published report covers the year ended 30 September 1972).

Annual reports of the Natal Division of Fisheries Department, Pietermaritzburg, 1908–1934 (last published report 1934).

Annual reports of the Division of Sea Fisheries, Cape Town, from 1946 to 1984 and continued.

Yearbooks of International Whaling Statistics, published by the Committee for Whaling Statistics, Sandefjord, Norway, 1943 and later years, continued.

Norwegian Whaling Gazette (Norsk Hvalfangst-Tidende), Sandefjord, 1910–1968 (last volume published 1968).

LITERATURE

Ray Gambell, 'A short history of modern whaling off Natal', *Mercurius*, 14, September 1971, pp. 37–44.

Ray Gambell, *Sperm whales off Durban*, Discovery Reports, 35, (Cambridge University Press, 1972) pp. 199–358.

Sigurd Risting, *Av hvalfangstens historie* (Kristiania (Oslo), J. W. Cappelens Forlag, 1922), particularly the chapter 'Ved Afrikas kyster', pp. 470–526.

Ørjan Olsen, 'Hvaler of hvalfangst i Sydafrika', *Bergens Museums Aarbok*, 1914–1915, no. 5, pp. 3–56.

J. N. Tönnessen, *Den moderne hvalfangstens historie*, del 2, Verdensangsten 1883–1974, Part I, 1883–1914, Publikasjon nr. 22 av Kommandör Chr. Christensens Hvalvangstmuseum, Sandefjord 1967.

ABSTRACT

Manufacturing is of particular importance to Natal, contributing approximately 30 per cent of its Gross Geographic Product. The development of manufacturing industry in the province has been strongly influenced by the growth of extra-regional markets and, in particular, by Natal's proximity to the burgeoning Pretoria/Witwatersrand/Vereeniging complex. The spatial distribution of manufacturing activity in the region is characterised by an inverted T-shaped core comprising the Greater Durban area, the transportation corridor inland towards the PWV area, and pockets of development along the coastline as far north as Richards Bay/Empangeni and as far south as Port Shepstone. The emergence of Durban as the dominant manufacturing centre in the region has been due to its close proximity to the harbour, its ready access to labour, its close association with the PWV industrial heartland and, to some extent, the rating policy applied by South African Railways. While Natal's manufacturing sector became increasingly diversified a pattern of regional specialisation, similar to that of the Western Cape but quite different from that of the PWV complex, emerged as textiles, footwear, clothing, chemicals and paper became the dominant industries in the Greater Durban area. During the post-war period up to the mid-1970s the province's manufacturing sector benefited from the rapid expansion experienced by the national economy as a whole but thereafter shared in its general decline. This was attributable to a variety of factors, including low productivity, lack of business confidence following political unrest, economic volatility and slow growth, an ideologically motivated policy of industrial decentralisation that offered little prospect for self-sustaining growth, excessive government spending, an overly-protective attitude towards local manufacturers, increasing taxation, heavy wage increases and high inflation. The reinvigoration of Natal's manufacturing sector, as of the whole economy, continues to depend upon major changes in South African society.

AN OVERVIEW OF THE GROWTH OF MANUFACTURING IN NATAL

Mark Addleson[1]

Introduction

The manufacturing sector[2] is of particular importance to the Natal regional economy. Admittedly this sector is the single biggest contributor to the country's Gross Domestic Product (GDP), but in relation to the other sectors the contribution of manufacturing activity to the regional economy is even more significant, primarily because of the relatively small mining sector in Natal. Manufacturing contributes some 30 per cent of the Gross Geographic Product (GGP) of Natal,[3] compared to about 23 per cent of the GDP of South Africa.

An overview of manufacturing in Natal must obviously focus attention on the events or circumstances which have shaped the growth of industry. Any analysis involves the adoption of a particular viewpoint, encompassing certain perspectives but also rejecting others; and it is almost inevitable that an overview with a regional focus will underplay the importance of extra-regional factors as determinants of processes that have taken place within the region. The perspectives from which the growth of manufacturing is examined are liable to mislead in precisely this way. So it is important that, at the outset, the reader is reminded about the extent to which the fortunes of manufacturing in Natal depend on the economic potential of the rest of the country.

Certainly, much of the history of manufacturing is flavoured by local circumstances; but, in spatial terms, the basic ingredients of growth are much more scattered. In the case of Natal it is obvious that the growth of extra-regional markets played a dominant role in creating the foundations of a strong manufacturing base. Yet, in terms of facilitating or thwarting growth, national government policies, in respect of, say, investment in infrastructure, or influx control (and in the case of a colonial power, even transnational policies on matters such as immigration), undoubtedly are no less important.

A recent survey amongst manufacturers in Natal revealed that more than 50 per cent of the direct forward linkages (sales) of factories are to other factories in the region.[4] Events of the last few years, however, have shown just how vulnerable the Natal region is to a weak and volatile exchange rate, and to sanctions and disinvestment pressures. All these have had a deleterious effect on the manufacturing sector; and none of them can be regarded as having had an essentially regional origin, or even for that matter as having originated within the manufacturing sector.

Rather than attempting to chronicle the growth of manufacturing in Natal since 1910 – and industrialisation only began in earnest in the 1930s with the major developments occurring after 1940 – the growth is examined here from two different, though inter-related perspectives. In the next section the evolution of the spatial distribution of manufacturing activity in the region is examined, and the continuous dominance of the Durban/Pinetown metropolitan area in the development of manufacturing in Natal is highlighted. The third section shifts the emphasis to the growth of the different sub-sectors of manufacturing, which makes it possible to focus on the nature and extent of regional specialisation in manufacturing in Natal. The fourth section again deals with spatial considerations; but this time those associated with the impact of the industrial decentralisation policy which was introduced in the 1960s.

The spatial distribution of manufacturing activity that is relevant here is the evolution of the inverted T-shaped core, which includes the transportation corridor from the port itself to the Pretoria/Witwatersrand/Vereeniging complex (PWV), as well as coastal settlements to the north and south of the Durban metropolitan area.

The gradual shift of economic activity in South Africa – located initially at the ports – has been from the western to the eastern seaboard.[5] A feature of the various phases of economic development in the country has been the relative concentration of economic activity; and Durban was one of the first of these important 'pockets' of economic growth. In the pre-industrial period, activity centred on the three coastal ports of Cape Town, Port Elizabeth and Durban, while the period of industrialisation saw the extensive growth of the Witwatersrand and Johannesburg. Fairly early in the country's economic development the four main metropoles came into being; and the agglomeration advantages of these areas meant that, ever since, they have dominated the growth of manufacturing in spatial terms.

The period of industrialisation in South Africa began with the discovery of large diamond deposits at and near Kimberley towards the end of the 1860s. The major boost, however, was provided by the commencement of large-scale gold-mining on the Witwatersrand in the 1880s. Both Cape Town and Durban benefited from their role as gateways to the Witwatersrand. Durban began as an ivory-trading post in the 1820s[6], and by the 1880s had developed as a regional centre with the export of sugar to the Cape market as its principal economic activity. By virtue of its proximity to the Witwatersrand, however, it was to play an ever-increasing role in the inter-regional trade with the latter. The combination of large-scale capital investment and labour intensive methods of extraction in gold-mining created much larger forward and backward linkages than those associated with diamond mining, and Durban soon became the main beneficiary of these linkages.

The spatial distribution of manufacturing activity in Natal

An examination of the spatial distribution of current economic activity in Natal reveals that the Greater Durban area (Durban/Pinetown/Inanda) continues to dominate the picture. The core of economic activity in the region includes the Durban metropolitan area and the transportation corridor to the PWV. In addition, a tentacle from Durban, covering nodes along the region's north coast as far as Richards Bay/Empangeni, and a tentacle covering nodes along the region's south coast as far as Port Shepstone, form part of the core. This definition of Natal's core accounts for more than 87,6 per cent of regional GGP and for approximately 90 per cent of Gross Manufacturing Product.

A breakdown of the GGP of Natal for 1978, into sectors and major locations by proportion of regional GGP, shows clearly how the Durban metropolitan area dominated regional output. The area accounted for approximately 60 per cent of GGP in 1978. The extent to which activity was concentrated establishes a metropole as the focus of economic, and especially of manufacturing activity, in the region. The Durban metropolitan area and the areas encompassing the transportation corridor from Durban to the PWV, including Pietermaritzburg, Estcourt, Ladysmith and Newcastle, contributed more than 75 per cent of GGP.

This spatial grouping accounted for 85,5 per cent of regional Gross Manufacturing Product in 1978. Linkage studies[7] indicate that, in respect of first stage (direct) backward and forward linkages to and from factories, the strongest linkages in the districts along the corridor are either to the Durban metropolitan area or to the PWV; with only limited linkages into areas surrounding the nodes along this corridor. Such linkages are usually to be found in the food industry.

A transportation corridor which forms the core of economic activity in a region is a common phenomenon. Many examples are found worldwide, and the concept is particularly well documented in the study of inter- and intra-urban land use patterns. Changes to an economic system that has been associated with the growth of a transportation corridor usually result from one of two sets of factors; either from structural changes in the economies of the end-point foci of the corridor, or from changes in transportation technology.

The coastal districts adjacent to the Durban metropolitan area (lower Tugela and Richards Bay/Empangeni to the north, and Umzinto to the south) contribute approximately 8,2 per cent of total GGP, and are especially strongly represented in agriculture and in manufacturing. Once again, there are important industrial linkages to Durban and to the PWV. These coastal nodes form part of Natal's economic core. For completeness, Port Shepstone should also be included in the southern leg of the core, though its economic contribution is still relatively small.

Factors influencing the growth of the core

The main programme for developing the Durban harbour, which 'markedly affect[ed] the full exploitation of a favourable situation for trade with the Boer republics of the interior', was not implemented until after 1880.[8] It is true, nevertheless, that the development of Durban and the regional economy of Natal, from the mid-nineteenth century – when the first substantial harbour works were begun – to Union, relied on the port and an associated distributive trade with the interior. It has been noted that 'Durban has remained the premier port of entry to the Witwatersrand, as well as the hinterland of Natal . . . Since Union, the Durban harbour has handled a larger share of total cargoes shipped to and from South African ports than all other ports combined.'[9]

An additional factor, which a number of writers cite as having influenced the location of particular industrial sub-sectors in Natal (see below), is a labour force that is peculiar to the region. Not only is the Bantustan of KwaZulu (originally a 'native reserve') virtually on Durban's doorstep – facilitating the access of labour to jobs in the core when in other metropolitan areas influx control and other legislation has hampered industrialists with regard to the hiring of black labour – but for some fifty years, up to 1911, Indian immigration was welcomed and encouraged. This policy ensured that Natal would have a substantial Indian population which, by 1910, constituted nearly 50 per cent of Durban's population of just over 115 000.

After beginning as a regional centre which serviced its partially settled hinterland and undertook small-scale processing of locally produced agricultural products, Durban grew largely because of its association with the dominant PWV area. The 'spread' of manufacturing activity within the region (highly concentrated as it is) seems to have been determined by economic factors (proximity to inputs, cost of land) and the importance of the transport network linking Durban to the PWV. The spatial economic core is integrated into the national economic system by way of linkages, while the periphery to the north and south of this core in part constitutes a labour reservoir, and in part an agricultural region which is served by a loose grid of small urban centres.

For a long time the rating policy of South African Railways, which pertained from 1910 onwards, probably had a dual influence on manufacturing in the region.[10] The policy embodied both 'tapering' – where the cost per kilometre decreases with the distance travelled – and much higher tariffs on finished items than on raw materials. The effect of this system was probably to reinforce the natural tendency for industry to concentrate round Durban (rather than at 'intermediate' locations between the source of raw materials and the market), and also to encourage some manufacturers to locate outside the region entirely (and close to their markets in the PWV). It has been suggested that '"distribution" rates and "nearest port" rates contributed considerably to the development of commerce and industry in the Southern Transvaal rather than at the ports, whilst sea-competitive rates, on the other hand, encouraged industrialists to locate their plants at the ports rather than in inland centres'.[11] Officials of South African Transport Services have indicated that the policy which currently guides the introduction of new railway tariffs is that of charging

The South African Breweries buildings in Umbilo Road, Durban, 1931.

according to the cost of transporting the product, and not according to the value of the product.

Until the 1930s, the South African economy remained fundamentally agrarian in nature. At that time a number of different factors provided the impetus for the economy to become truly industrialised. Not the least of these factors was the abandonment of the gold standard in 1932. Naturally, the southern Transvaal was the main direct beneficiary of an increase in the official gold price. The Government's programme of industrialisation and import replacement gained momentum during this time and, reinforced by the dramatic effects of economic isolation during the Second World War, the economy was rapidly transformed into one in which manufacturing became the single largest sector. An examination of table 1 reveals that the share of total manufacturing employment contributed by Durban/Pinetown remained almost constant despite the underlying overall rapid growth.

Clearly, the southern Transvaal region was the main engine of industrial growth from the 1920s onwards. What must be remembered, though, is that Natal, while holding its position in relative terms and improving this position somewhat from the 1960s onwards, did so despite the improved position of the PWV. This occurred largely because of the relative decline in the position of the Western Cape and subsequently also of the Port Elizabeth/Uitenhage area. In this sense, the Durban/Pinetown/ Pietermaritzburg core has been far and away the major beneficiary of manufacturing growth in the PWV and, especially in the immediate post-war period, the manufacturing core of Natal itself grew rapidly.

In Natal, the contribution of Greater Durban to manufacturing output increased rapidly. In the period 1919–20 Durban was providing 53 per cent of Natal's value added in manufacturing. This had risen to 63 per cent at the end of the 1920s, to 66 per cent by 1939–40; and to 73 per cent by the end of the 1940s.[12]

Over the period 1945 to 1955, during which time there was a compound annual increase of about 5,4 per cent in employment in manufacturing, the manufacturing, construction and electricity sector contributed an average of 31 per cent of the Gross Geographic Product of Natal.[13] This figure rose to 33 per cent by the end of the 1950s and increased to 40 per cent of GGP by 1970.

With the growth of manufacturing, economic conditions dictated that industry would 'suburbanise'. Wilkinson[14] has analysed the rapid growth of Pinetown in the post-war period through to the early 1960s. He portrayed the growth process from the early 1950s as a natural overflow of manufacturing activity from the Durban municipal area – cheap land (in comparison to the cost of land in Durban) being primarily responsible for the initial suburbanisation of manufacturing activity. In 1961, when there were about 100 manufacturing establishments in Pinetown, the average price of land there was still only about 25 per cent of the price of comparable land in the industrial areas of Durban. Wilkinson concluded that 'relatively cheap land and more important its availability for

Table 1 Geographical distribution of manufacturing activity in South Africa by main region (percentage shares)

	1915–16*	1925–26*	1935–36*	1945–46*	1954–55*	1965–66⁺	1976⁺	1979⁺
EMPLOYMENT								
Western Cape	21	18	15	16	14	16	15	14
Port Elizabeth	3	5	5	4	6	6	6	5
Durban/Pinetown	12	12	10	11	11	13	14	14
Pretoria/Witwatersrand/Vereeniging	29	34	47	46	46	47	44	44
Rest of South Africa	35	31	23	23	23	18	22	23
Totals	100	100	100	100	100	100	100	100
NET OUTPUT								
Western Cape	21	23	18	17	14	16		
Port Elizabeth	3	5	6	6	7	7	6	
Durban/Pinetown	12	12	10	12	11	13	13	
Pretoria/Witwatersrand/Vereeniging	38	36	47	48	50	50	52	
Rest of South Africa	26	24	19	17	18	20	20	
Totals	100	100	100	100	100	100	100	

Source: *O. P. F. Horwood et. al., 'The location of manufacturing industry'.
⁺R. T. Bell, 'The growth and structure of manufacturing employment In Natal'.

Note: In the case of data obtained from Bell, all figures have been rounded to the nearest whole number. It should be noted that the data provided by Bell and Horwood sometimes show minor, but significant, variations for the years when their series overlap. For example in respect of employment, Bell (p. 9) suggests a figure of 12,5 per cent as being the contribution of 'Durban/Pinetown/Inanda' to total manufacturing employment in 1956/57, while Horwood, et al., give a figure of 11 per cent for 'Durban/Pinetown' in the period 1954/55. The differences are probably due to the fact that each of the authors has included different magisterial districts in his definition of the Greater Durban area. Bell's figures for 1979 are also based on provisional data from the 1979 industrial census provided in advance of publication.

purchase, in industrial zones . . . equipped with modern services . . . were the factors largely responsible for the establishment of manufacturing industry in the Pinetown area.'[14]

While the metropolitan core grew apace, the amount of manufacturing activity in the 'rest of Natal' declined substantially in relative terms. The proportion of South Africa's net manufacturing output contributed by the rest of Natal (i.e. excluding the Durban/Pinetown area) declined from 10 per cent in 1915–16 to 5 per cent by 1954–55; while the contribution to employment from this area declined from 14 per cent to 5 per cent over the same period.[15]

The fact that the 'rural' industries are generally small is indicated by the relatively smaller decline in the number of establishments in the rest of Natal from 8 per cent of the South African total in 1915–16 to 6 per cent by 1954–55. Commenting on the position of rural industry in Natal, McWhirter[16] suggested that the relative contribution was exaggerated by the substantial share of the sugar industry: 'That the figure should have been as high as it was thirty years ago, and as high as it is today (1959), is largely explained by the existence of the powerful sugar industry along the Natal coast.'

Between 1970 and 1979, however, it appears as if employment in manufacturing in the rest of Natal (excluding Durban/Pinetown/ Inanda) once again increased in relative terms; from 6,29 of South Africa's manufacturing employment in 1970 to 7,9 per cent in 1979. Over the same period, employment in the Greater Durban area increased from 13,6 per cent to 13,8 per cent of total manufacturing employment in the country.[17] Most of the increase in employment in the rest of Natal occurred in Pietermaritzburg during this period and, if the latter is included in the core, the increase in employment in the rest of Natal is far less dramatic; from 4,0 per cent of total manufacturing employment to 4,7 per cent in 1979.

Pietermaritzburg became a 'deconcentration point' in terms of the government's industrial decentralisation policy, and manufacturers who located there enjoyed generous financial benefits. In the fourth section the impact of industrial decentralisation policy on the location of industry in Natal and KwaZulu is evaluated. Until well into the 1960s, however, it is apparent that, overwhelmingly, the spatial growth of manufacturing activity in Natal involved the expansion of the core area prompted by natural economic forces, the harbour providing the centre of gravitation for industries which required bulky imports into the region or country as a whole. Apart from the processing of agricultural products along the coastal strip, the transport corridor to the market of the PWV provided the incentive for establishing other factories beyond Durban/Pinetown.

The dependence of the regional economy on inter-regional trade was established at an early stage and it has been argued[18] that the economy of Natal may be considered as an extension of the PWV in view of the magnitude of the linkages. This dependence is still very strong but, as noted in the introductory remarks, a major portion of the direct (first stage) forward linkages from manufacturing appear to be captured within the region. So it would seem that, by now, the primary orientation of many manufacturing units is to buyers that are in the region itself. As Katzen[19] noted, too, 'one of Durban's strongest locational advantages is bound up with market factors. Durban firms are in the best position to serve the market constituted by the town of Durban itself.' The T-shaped core referred to in the introduction is largely one market area.

In the light of the emphasis that has been placed on the dominant position of Durban/Pinetown, it is worthwhile reflecting on just how difficult it has proved to stimulate the growth of manufacturing outside this core. There has been a desire, at least since the 1950s, to industrialise the Tugela Basin. Little actually happened until the government funded extensive infrastructural development in the area and began to support industrial growth with subsidies to industrialists.

Niewenhuysen[20] offers a logical analysis of what obstacles industrialists faced when they located in the Basin, and he explains why it would be difficult to enlarge the industrial base. The problems that he foresaw at the time no doubt were valid. Manufacturing activity, though now quite extensive, does not have a natural economic base in that area. The economy is artificial and therefore very fragile. The main linkages are either to the Greater Durban regional core or are outside the region. If a few mainstays of the area, such as coal exports or phosphates, should lose their importance economically – and sanctions are placing severe pressure on all mineral exports – the local economy could be seriously weakened, much like Port Elizabeth's when some of the motor vehicle manufacturers departed.

The growth of different types of manufacturing activity

With regard to the growth of particular manufacturing sub-groups in Natal, Bell[21] provided a detailed breakdown of the location quotients for each manufacturing sub-group (Standard Industrial Classification [SIC] major group) in the four main industrial regions in 1976. In Durban/Pinetown at that time the five most important sectors (in respect of regional specialisation) were textiles, footwear, clothing, chemicals and paper. The growth of some of these sectors is briefly examined below.

As a regional economy develops its own dynamic and the forward and backward linkages within the region are strengthened, so the manufacturing base becomes more diversified. A local economy, which initially develops around activities that service extra-regional markets, becomes increasingly self-sufficient and the orientation of producers is towards the local markets. The manufacturing sector in Natal today is well diversified. It is true, nevertheless, that there is a fairly marked pattern of regional specialisation amongst the main metropolitan areas in South Africa. While both Natal and the Western Cape have similar dominant industries, the industries which dominate the manufacturing sector in the southern Transvaal (PWV) region are completely different. (See Katzen[22] for a comparison of the major industries in the main metropolitan areas and in the rest of Natal; and Bell[23] for a comparison between the main metropolitan areas.) In the case of the southern Transvaal, machinery, metals – iron and steel, as well as non-ferrous – electrical machinery and metal products are the dominant sub-groups. Bell[24] identified these industries as being more skill-intensive than the industries which are the largest employers in Natal.

The pattern of dominant industries in Natal was established early on (see Katzen[25] for a well-documented history, up to the late 1950s, of each industrial sub-sector). If we ignore construction and engineering (which were often grouped with manufacturing as part of 'secondary industry'), by 1925 chemicals was the second largest employer in the Greater Durban area, accounting for 10,8 per cent of manufacturing employees after food (13,2 per cent). Clothing, textiles, footwear and leather contributed a total of 6,1 per cent of employment; fourth after furniture which contributed 7,2 per cent.[26]

A major change occurred when, with the assistance of a higher gold price, the economy emerged from the depression in the mid-1930s. Then the clothing, textiles and footwear group of producers became the largest manufacturing employers with 15 per cent of employment in the area – rising to over 17 per cent in the 1950s. The factor which seems to have been mainly responsible for the improved fortunes of the clothing industry in Natal, relative to the rest of the country, was the availability of Indian labour. Originally 'imported' to provide labour for the burgeoning sugar industry in the 1860s, the Indian population now offered a source of cheap but productive labour, which enabled the Natal manufacturers – especially those operating at the lower end of the market – to compete effectively with Transvaal clothing manufacturers.

A textile industry was already well developed in South Africa by the end of the 1920s. The growth of cotton-blanket manufacturing occurred behind protective tariff barriers, the blanket and 'kaffir sheeting' production being aimed mainly at the cheaper end of the market. The whole industry was boosted by isolation during the war. Durban's suitability in terms of location stemmed from the importation of raw materials and from the plentiful supply of cheap Indian and black labour to the highly labour-intensive industry. Knitting and weaving mills began to be located in Durban in the 1940s. In addition to the locational factors already mentioned, a humid climate was an important requirement of the mills.

By the mid-1950s, this sector employed more than 5500 people,[27] while the growth-rate of employment for the country as a whole during most of the 1960s was an average of more than 8,5 per cent per annum.[28] Greater Durban's share of total South African employment in textiles increased from just over 20 per cent at the end of the 1950s to over 25 per cent by the mid-1970s. Over the same period the percentage of employment in this sector in the rest of Natal rose on average more rapidly, but of course from a much smaller base.[29]

The growth phase of the footwear industry, in the 1930s, was marked by an increase in the use of materials other than leather. The advantage of a Natal (Durban) location at the time appears to have been based on the fact that the materials, at least initially, were often imported. Because footwear which incorporated the newer materials required a less skilled labour force, production which previously might only have been practical in the Transvaal was now also possible in Natal. The share of the country's total employment in footwear, contributed by Natal, continued to increase right up to the late 1970s when it amounted to over 50 per cent. Greater Durban provided 18 per cent by the end of the 1950s and this rose to 32 per cent in the mid-1970s.

Today, as noted, the chemicals, rubber and plastic products sub-group constitutes the fourth-largest sector in terms of gross output. The relative importance of the sector to the GGP of Natal has declined from the mid-1950s when it was the largest contributor to total production. This sector includes paints, fertilizers, soaps, oils and petroleum products as well as plastics and rubber products.

One of the difficulties in exploring the growth of the sector is that data have been extremely difficult to obtain. The production of petroleum products is regarded as a strategic industry and information about this sector, regarded as sensitive, is not readily available under normal circumstances. The fact that multinational producers of petroleum products have been under threat overseas, because of their involvement in South Africa, has resulted in the local companies becoming secretive and has made it even more difficult to find out about recent developments in this sub-sector.

The manufacturing sub-sectors that have been mentioned, as well as the timber industry, once again show that the formation of the general pattern of intra-regional activity in Natal – this time in terms of the *types* of manufacturing activities located in the region – is attributable mainly to economic factors. The eastern region of the country, with its high rainfall, is a major timber-producing area. Industries such as clothing, textiles and chemicals all have a significant portion of imported raw materials; the value added in production generally is high in relation to the value of raw materials; and the cost of transport on finished (processed) goods is often a much smaller proportion of the value of the goods than the cost of transport on the raw materials. Production in these sectors typically would occur close to the source of raw materials (including the harbour); and the semi-processed or finished products would be transported to the main markets.

Referring to the issue of inter-regional specialisation which was noted above, Bell[30] suggested that the reasons for this specialisation were to be found also in the nature of the labour forces in the different regions: 'Durban/Pinetown tends to be specialised in sectors of low skill-intensity and . . . a large proportion of the Indian labour force is employed in these sectors.' To be sure, the relative mix of skills and resources must impact upon the types of activities which each region can undertake most efficiently; but it is difficult to assess the relative contribution of each factor to the overall pattern. It is clear that both the types of labour available in different regions and the costs of labour have played some part in the location of different manufacturing sub-groups.

The fact that Natal and the Western Cape have the same types of dominant industries in common, however, may well owe more to the historical fact that their cores are coastal cities than it does to any similarities amongst their labour forces.[31] What is clear, however, is that as they have developed over time, the relationship between the manufacturing sectors in Natal and the PWV has been largely complementary; while that between Natal and the Western Cape has been one of competition. Given the relative distances of the latter two cores from the Transvaal market area, it is inevitable that the manufacturing sector in the Cape would lose out to Natal as the main supplier to the PWV.

Manufacturing and industrial decentralisation in the 1980s

After a period of rapid growth in the 1960s and first half of the 1970s, manufacturing industry in South Africa entered the doldrums; and the manufacturing sector in Natal did not escape the general decline.[32] With hindsight, careful monitoring of the fortunes of the sector in Natal might at least have provided a forewarning of the problems that were to occur. In the early post-war period a significant proportion of exports, especially those from Durban, involved trade with Central, and East African countries. It is granted that the economic circumstances of most of these countries have changed, in some cases quite radically, but there is no doubting their subsequent unwillingness to do business with South African companies; at least not openly. The difficulty of obtaining any figures on the extent of trade, not only with African countries but also with industrial countries like Japan, is symptomatic of the pressure which South African manufacturers have faced.

Although no comprehensive industrial census figures have been published since 1979,[33] which was about the time that the manufacturing sector began to take a turn for the worse, various independent surveys suggest that manufacturing employment has declined substantially since the early 1980s. Despite a trend towards greatly increased capital intensity in manufacturing, there has also been a massive decline in real fixed investment in the sector since 1980. The factors that have contributed to what can only be described as a dismal state of affairs are manifold. They range from low productivity, to general pessimism on the part of the business community in the wake of political unrest, and great volatility of the economy combined with slow growth. The buoyancy of the gold price in the latter half of the 1970s may have done much to divert attention away from the manufacturing sector as the main future source of growth and employment. Certainly, at present, there is nothing which could be described as an over-arching policy to foster the growth of manufacturing.

The closest that the country comes to having a policy for manufacturing, is the government's industrial decentralisation policy which was introduced at the beginning of the 1960s. There is extensive literature evaluating that policy.[34] The consensus is that decentralisation policy is ideologically motivated and grossly unproductive. Indeed, the policy apparently has more critics than it has supporters and the government commissioned a major re-examination. The purpose of decentralisation policy was to provide employment for people in the Bantustans ('homelands'). Including KwaZulu, Natal (region E[35]) has a greater share of blacks than the other defined development regions. It is worthwhile, therefore, attempting an assessment of what decentralisation has done for manufacturing and for employment in Natal.

Decentralisation incentives differ amongst regions and growth points. But, on *a priori* grounds, there is reason to believe that, once the establishment and expansion of labour-intensive industries in the PWV was constrained after 1967 by the Physical Planning Act (this later became the Environment Planning Act), a significant relocation of these industries from the PWV to Natal might have occurred under the decentralisation policy. The factors which might have prompted this relocation were the proximity of Durban to the PWV and the proximity of KwaZulu to Durban – offering ready access to unskilled labour – combined with the relatively cheap and skilled Indian labour available in Natal.

The readily available statistics on decentralised activity from the Decentralisation Board,[36] are notoriously unreliable. The board publishes figures based on industrialists' applications to decentralise; and, often, these bear little resemblance to what actually happens. In addition, the board's figures exclude decentralised activity in the 'independent homelands'. A set of aggregated statistics, for homelands, was provided by the Development Bank,[37] and because the figures accord with estimates obtained from different surveys, the bank's data appear to be reliable. The position was that up to the end of 1985[38] approximately 89 000 jobs had been created in the homelands, of which 27 626 – or 31 per cent – were in KwaZulu.

The Decentralisation Board claimed that in 1986–87 alone there were 21 542 employment opportunities contained in industrialists' applications to decentralise in region E. For the record, table 2 shows the proportion of applications to decentralise, as well as the percentage of decentralised employment and the associated capital invested, in region E for the years from 1982, when the present set of more generous incentives was introduced. The table also identifies the most 'popular' decentralised growth points in the region, highlighting those which received more than 20 applications in any year. Not only does there appear to be a steady decline in the proportion of decentralised employment going to region E but, contrary to the board's claims, the 'actual' estimates suggest that the decentralised activity accruing to region E is a smaller proportion of total activity than the proportion of the total population in region E. Decentralised activity per capita is lower in region E than the average for the country as a whole.

Such comparisons, however, are probably less important than the impact of decentralisation policy on Natal itself. Arguably, because the policy involves a highly inefficient use of resources, it is detrimental to the growth of employment opportunities in the country as a whole.[39] The direct impact of the policy on Natal is more difficult to assess. As far as the location of manufacturing industry in Natal (and elsewhere) is concerned, decentralisation policy has done little to change a pattern that has been shaped by 'natural' economic forces. About one-third of the decentralised employment occurs in KwaZulu but, as table 2 reveals, the popular growth points in the region are generally in the core area.

Though it is not clear how many businesses fall into this category, surveys have revealed that a substantial number of decentralised industries are merely relocated factories, some from within Natal itself. In a comprehensive survey of the industries in KwaZulu, Smith and Coetzee[40] estimated that only about 38 per cent of the decentralised businesses in the area were wholly new concerns. The remainder were either relocations or expansions of existing concerns; and the majority of relocations were from Durban and Pinetown. In addition, like the factories in other areas, a majority of those in Natal were probably dependent upon incentives for their survival. According to Smith and Coetzee,[41] '69,81 per cent of the respondents indicated that they would not have decentralised if concessions were not provided'. Even if they were able to continue without incentives, the chances of industrialists remaining in their decentralised locations in the long term are slim. The phenomenon of firms leaving an area when their incentives expire has already been experienced at older growth points like Hammarsdale. The fact that the firms are concentrated in the clothing and textiles sub-sectors also makes them somewhat more mobile than other categories of manufacturing. The amounts which their owners invest in the businesses are usually fairly small; while the fixed capital probably has quite a good second-hand market. This means that the costs of withdrawing when the incentives fall away are relatively small.

There has been some debate about how much decentralisation has occurred spontaneously (i.e. notwithstanding the incentives), as manufacturers sought to use the cheaper labour in rural areas. Bell[42] has made a cogent case for the occurrence of a spontaneous process from the mid-1960s to the late 1970s, although survey evidence about the importance of incentives seems to negate his arguments. If Bell is correct then Natal, where manufacturers have had access to unskilled labour largely unhindered by legislation concerning influx controls and labour preference areas, should have been the major recipient of decentralised manufacturing activity.

In relative terms, the decentralised firms located in KwaZulu are small in size and even today there are only a few factories in that area. Like nearly all the factories that have been induced to locate at growth points, whatever motivated the choice of location, the firms located in the rest of Natal are also small, 'marginal' operations. So, irrespective of whether the decentralisation process has been spontaneous or was induced by the incentives, it is clear from the numerous surveys of decentralised firms that decentralisation policy does not hold out any real hope of providing employment. The types of firms being attracted to the growth points do not offer prospects for vigorous, self-sustaining growth. They are more likely to constitute a drain on the regional economy than an asset.

Table 2 Share of South Africa's decentralised applications, jobs and capital invested (R1 000) going to region E (percentage)[1]

	1982/83	1983/84	1984/85	1985/86	1986/87	'Actual' 1986/87[2]
Applications	36,1	26,5	24,5	31,6	25,0	17,4
Job opportunities	50,4	45,4	39,9	41,5	31,3	21,7
Capital investment	36,9	49,6	35,3	34,4	26,3	20,4

Places in region E receiving more than 20 approved applications

1982/83	1983/84	1984/85	1985/86	1986/87
Isithebe	Pietermaritzburg	Isithebe	Isithebe	Isithebe
Pietermaritzburg	Isithebe	Pietermaritzburg	Tongaat	Pietermaritzburg
Ladysmith	Ezakheni	Ezakheni	Stanger	Ezakheni
	Newcastle	Ladysmith	Pietermaritzburg	Empangeni
	Richards Bay	Richards Bay	Ezakheni	Verulam
	Verulam	Newcastle	Newcastle	
		Verulam	Empangeni	

Source: Extracted from M. S. Addleson, et al. *Industrial trends and prospects in Natal-KwaZulu:* Data from *Annual Reports* of the Decentralisation Board.

Note: 1. The data is based on approved applications to decentralise and excludes all applications for the independent homelands. The 1983/84 data includes 'three giant projects' which do not appear in later *Annual Reports*.

2. The 'actual' figure was obtained by including estimates for the independent homelands.

Conclusion

In the post-war period up to the mid-1970s, the manufacturing sector in Natal benefited from the rapid expansion of economic activity that occurred in the country as a whole. Economic forces both shaped the geographical location of industry and determined the nature of specialisation within the region. State policy during this period attempted to encourage the growth of domestic industry at the expense of imports and, as the important point of entry of raw materials and capital goods into the country, the manufacturing industry in Durban probably received an added boost from import substitution.

In general, economic histories of this period have failed to emphasise that the growth occurred despite, rather than because of, state policy. In the entire post-war period, economic policy in South Africa has been subservient to the 'social engineering' associated with putting apartheid ideology into practice. Apartheid is a pernicious ideology, not only because it has destroyed human dignity and adversely affected the welfare of its victims, but because it has also proved grossly wasteful of resources. While the demand for raw materials remained strong and the country attracted a high level of foreign investment, some of the economic costs of these policies could be hidden but not reduced. In a weak economy the costs became visible again. The only surprise is that, apart from Marxists who incorrectly attributed sustained economic growth to apartheid, arguing that state policy supported the interests of capital, most analysts failed to appreciate the extent to which politics and economic progress were strongly intertwined.

The factors which contributed to the decline in the manufacturing sector in the 1980s can all be linked directly to apartheid, to the economic mismanagement associated with apartheid, or to the excessive growth in government spending which has been needed to put apartheid policies into effect. The various factors include sanctions and disinvestment; an over-protective attitude towards local manufacturers (to develop 'strategic industries' and to increase self-sufficiency); an excessively volatile monetary environment; an increasing tax burden; low productivity; and a high rate of growth of wages and high inflation. Integrated as it is into the South African economy, the manufacturing sector in Natal could not escape the consequences of the decline.

A few years ago, prompted by the record of expansion of the manufacturing sector, authors looked to the future of manufacturing in South Africa with confidence. Parallels were drawn between this country and the 'achievements of Argentina, Brazil, Mexico, South Korea, Taiwan, Hong Kong, Singapore'.[43] Today, with the economy trapped in a period of long-term decline, the future of the sector looks bleak. The problems are not superficial ones, which can be rectified by calls for export promotion or import substitution, even if they are heeded. The problems have been ingrained into the structure of South African society, although, with the resources that are available, there is apparently no reason why our economic fortunes could not be reversed.

The circumstances demand effective economic management. What has been lacking, however, is an appreciation on the part of policy-makers of the far-reaching changes in the society that are a precondition for invigorating the economy once more. Until such time as we are able to detect a semblance of economic sense in the government's policies, the growth of the economy, not least in Natal, in the 25 years from 1950 onwards, will be remembered with nostalgia as 'golden years' of the manufacturing sector.

REFERENCES

1. This chapter makes use of material contained in a study undertaken on behalf of the Natal Town and Regional Planning Commission. See M.S. Addleson, et al., *Industrial trends and prospects in Natal-KwaZulu: Region E*, Natal Town and Regional Planning Reports, vol. 72 (Pietermaritzburg, Natal Town and Regional Planning Commission, 1989).

2. In this chapter the 'manufacturing sector', or 'manufacturing industry', encompasses all activities which fall within the major groups 311 to 339 of the Standard Industrial Classification (SIC) of economic activities.

3. In all references to Natal in the chapter, the bantustan ('homeland') of KwaZulu is included in the area of Natal.

4. See Addleson, et al., *Industrial trends and prospects*, esp. pp. 119–27.

5. See Pretorius, et al., 'History of industrial decentralisation (Part 1): the regional concentration of industry and the historical basis of the policy', *Development Southern Africa*, 3(1), 1986, pp. 37–49.

6. R.J. Davies, 'The growth of the Durban metropolitan area', *South African Geographical Journal*, 45, 1963, pp. 15–43.

7. A.J. Wilkinson, 'Industry in the Pinetown magisterial district', (unpublished M.A. thesis, University of Natal, Durban, 1963); J.P. Nieuwenhuysen, 'The industrialisation of the Tugela Basin', (unpublished M.A. thesis, University of Natal, Durban, 1961).

8. Davies, 'Durban metropolitan area', p. 16.

9. M. Katzen, *Industry in Greater Durban, Part 1: its growth and structure*, Natal Town and Regional Planning Commission Reports, vol. 3, (Pietermaritzburg, Natal Town and Regional Planning Commission, 1961), p. 7.

10. Nieuwenhuysen, 'Industrialisation of the Tugela Basin', pp. 345–52; O.P.F. Horwood, et al. 'The location of manufacturing industry', *Industry and Trade*, 56(3), March 1960, pp. 99–109.

11. *Ibid.*, See also Katzen, *Industry in Greater Durban*, pp. 7, 8. Differences in railway tariffs from Cape Town and Durban, on goods destined for the Central African Federation, which favoured the latter, probably also caused the manufacturing sector in Durban to grow at the expense of the Western Cape. Especially during the latter half of the 1950s and the early 1960s, when there was open and flourishing trade with the Federation and other southern African countries. McWhirter states that in terms of the tariffs (introduced in 1954) Durban was almost as well placed as the southern Transvaal for railing goods to the Federation. See D.J.L. McWhirter, *Industry in Greater Durban Part II: raw materials as a factor in industrial location*, Natal Town and Regional Planning Commission Reports, vol. 4, (Pietermaritzburg, Natal Town and Regional Planning Commission, 1959), p. 3.

12. Katzen, *Industry in Greater Durban*, p. 6.

13. John Stanwix, *A study of the Natal regional economy*, Natal Town and Regional Planning Commission Reports, vol. 66 (Pietermaritzburg, Natal Town and Regional Planning Commission, 1985), p. 46.

14. Wilkinson, *Industry in Pinetown*, p. 230.

15. Horwood, et al., 'Location of manufacturing industry'. See also J. R. Burrows, *The population and labour resources of Natal*, Natal Town and Regional Planning Commission Reports, vol. 6 (Pietermaritzburg, Natal Town and Regional Planning Commission, 1959), ch. 8.

16. McWhirter, *Industry in Greater Durban*, p. 2.

17. R. T. Bell, *The growth and structure of manufacturing employment in Natal* (Durban, Institute for Social and Economic Research, University of Durban-Westville, 1985), p. 9.

18. See G. Maasdorp, 'Co-ordinated regional development: hope for the Good Hope proposals?' in H. Giliomee and L. Schlemmer (eds), *Up against the fences: poverty, passes and privilege in South Africa* (Cape Town, David Philip, 1985).

19. Katzen, *Industry in Greater Durban*, p. 8.

20. Nieuwenhuysen, 'Industrialisation of the Tugela Basin'.

21. Bell, *Growth and structure of manufacturing employment*, p. 22.

22. Katzen, *Industry in Greater Durban*, p. 10.

23. Bell, *Growth and structure of manufacturing employment*, see Section 3.

24. Bell, *ibid., loc. cit.*

25. Katzen, *Industry in Greater Durban*, see chs. 3 to 9.

26. See Burrows, *Population and labour resources of Natal*, p. 177.

27. Katzen, *Industry in Greater Durban*, p. 55.

28. Bell, *Growth and structure of manufacturing employment*, p. 89.

29. *Ibid.*, pp. 71–74.

30. *Ibid.*, p. 31.

31. See the comments of McWhirter, *Industry in Greater Durban*, p. 3, on the factors which accounted for regional specialisation in the cases of Natal and the Western Cape. McWhirter mentions the importance of 'easily trained' Indian labour as a factor contributing to Durban's emphasis on clothing and footwear; but he also notes that 'like so many of her leading activities', the specialisation 'also springs from the fact that Durban is by far the nearest and largest port serving the Union's main market'.

32. See Addleson, et al., *Industrial trends and prospects*.

33. The lack of census data, from the late 1970s onwards, is a cause for concern; not least because the publication of these figures would force policy-makers to confront the bleak picture in the manufacturing sector.

34. See various contributions dealing with industrial decentralisation policy in R. Tomlinson and M. Addleson (eds), *Regional restructuring under apartheid: urban and regional policies in contemporary South Africa* (Johannesburg, Ravan Press, 1987); especially contributions by Bell, Dewar, Wellings and Black, and Addleson and Tomlinson.

35. Official statistics on industrial decentralisation are aggregated and published for each of the nine development regions. For practical purposes, with regard to manufacturing activity, we can treat region E and Natal (including KwaZulu) as synonymous. Although region E also includes part of northern Transkei, apart from a few sawmills there is really no manufacturing activity in the latter area.

36. See the *Annual Reports* of the Board for the Decentralisation of Industry.

37. I.J. Du Marais (comp.), *Some statistics on manufacturing industries in the TBVC and self-governing states* (Johannesburg, Development Bank of Southern Africa, 1986.)

38. For some of the bantustans the data cover the period up to 1984. In many cases small industries, with a capital investment of less than R50 000 are excluded from the bank's estimates.

39. M.S. Addleson, et al., 'The impact of industrial decentralisation policy: the businessman's view', *South African Geographical Journal*, 67, pp. 179–200.

40. J.D. Smith and S.F. Coetzee, *KwaZulu's potential to attract specific types of industries* (Johannesburg, Development Bank of Southern Africa, 1987), p. 41.

41. *Ibid.*, p. 40.

42. Bell, *Growth and structure of manufacturing employment*, see Section 4.

43. Anne Ratcliffe, 'Industry: 1980 and beyond', in J. Matthews (ed.), *South Africa in the world economy* (Johannesburg, McGraw-Hill Book Company, 1983).

┌─────────────── *ABSTRACT* ───────────────┐

Between 1910 and 1940, South Africa changed from being a net importer to a net exporter of sugar and was largely insulated both from the fluctuations of the national economy and from the overproduction crisis that was experienced in the international sugar trade. These favourable circumstances were attributable to government protection, which provided the local sugar industry with a captive home market that enabled it to finance its export losses, and to the preferential access to the British and Canadian markets arising from South Africa's continued inclusion within the Empire. In consequence, the local industry was able to expand and prosper, increasing the gross value of its contribution to the economy's agricultural output at a time when the agricultural sector's overall contribution to the Gross Domestic Product was declining. Prior to 1932 the industry was dependent upon Uba cane but, as a result of the establishment of the Mount Edgecombe Experimental Station in 1925, four new cane varieties were introduced to produce significantly higher yields with a greater sucrose content. The often-strained relationship that existed betwen sugar growers and millers necessitated periodic governmental intervention. In exchange for increased protection and a measure of self-administration, the industry agreed to a change in the basis of payment for cane from weight to sucrose content. In addition the retail price of sugar was fixed, and a lower-priced Grade 2 sugar was introduced for the benefit of poorer consumers. The milling sector of the sugar industry was characterised by continued consolidation, greater efficiency and increased profitability, despite the high cost of capital equipment. Labour was also a significant working cost, amounting to 50 per cent of the industry's recurring expenditure between 1910 and 1940. As Indian employees steadily decreased in numbers the recruitment of African labourers became an increasing challenge in competition with better paid jobs on gold- and coal-mines, and the Government's greater concern to meet the labour requirements of the gold industry.

└───┘

156

$\textbf{T}$HE SOUTH AFRICAN SUGAR INDUSTRY
1910–1940

Paul M. Dickinson

Introduction

The Natal sugar industry prior to 1910 has been examined in some detail, with Peter Richardson providing an overview of the industry[1] and Maureen Tayal examining the labour component.[2] The industry after 1910, however, has received scant attention,[3] with the exception of labour.[4] This essay attempts to redress this oversight by examining its overall progress between 1910 and 1940.

The industry has been characterised by Richardson as being linked to the fluctuations of the economy of southern Africa.[5] This essay, however, argues that in the period 1910 to 1940 the industry was increasingly insulated from the fluctuations of the economy. This was achieved by means of governmental protection which allowed the industry a captive home market. Furthermore, South Africa's inclusion within the British Empire allowed the industry preferential access to the markets of Britain and Canada. These factors allowed the industry to expand and prosper to an extent not envisaged prior to 1910.

Since 1910 the quantitative significance of agriculture in the total economy of South Africa has been reduced. Agriculture's contribution to the Gross Domestic Product (GDP) declined by 4,7 per cent between 1920 and 1940, from 24,3 per cent to 19,6 per cent. During the same period, mining's contribution declined by 5,8 per cent, secondary industry's contribution increased by 6,6 per cent and services' contribution increased by 3,9 per cent.

Table 1   Percentage composition of GDP 1920–1940[6] (Constant 1958 prices)

Year	Agriculture	Mining and quarrying	Secondary industry	Services
1920	24,3	19,8	9,5	46,4
1925	22,2	20,4	10,1	47,3
1930	23,4	19,1	10,7	46,8
1935	22,2	14,9	14,4	48,5
1940	19,6	14,0	16,1	50,3

In contrast to agriculture's decline in terms of GDP, the gross value of the contribution of sugar-cane production to total agriculture increased from 3,7 per cent in 1911 to 10,9 per cent in 1940. South Africa changed from being a net importer to a net exporter of sugar in that period. The increased importance of sugar within the agricultural sector meant that governmental assistance, when requested in the 1920s and 1930s, was granted because of the vital importance of agriculture to the economy.

Table 2	Sugar's contribution to agriculture 1911–1940[7] (R1 000)			Table 3	Acres of cane planted 1911–1940[12]		
Year ending 30 June	Sugar	Total	Sugar %	Years	Acres	% Increase	
1911	998	27 130	3,7	1911–15	107 091		
1915	1 326	34 752	3,8	1916–20	154 917	44,7	
1920	3 516	70 010	5,0	1921–25	208 522	34,6	
1925	2 772	58 570	4,7	1926–30	270 312	29,6	
1930	4 358	48 790	8,9	1931–35	325 024	20,2	
1935	5 036	50 728	9,9	1935–40	383 879	18,1	
1940	7 692	70 800	10,9				

Production

South African sugar production increased by 726,2 per cent, from 82 000 tons in 1910 to 595 556 tons in 1939. The formation of the Union in 1910 provided the industry with an assured market which led to an increase in production of 83,2 per cent between 1910 and 1918. This captive market allowed the industry to continue to expand its production in the 1920s and 1930s when sugar was confronted by a world-wide overproduction crisis.

Sugar production only declined on six occasions in the 39-year period and these reductions were all linked to natural disasters. In the 1913–14 season there was a 4 per cent reduction as a result of drought and the Indian strike.[8] In 1917–18, floods resulted in a 8,5 per cent reduction in production.[9] Drought again led to declines in production of 24,1 per cent in 1920–21, 20,7 per cent in 1924–25 and 17,1 per cent in 1931–32.[10] A red locust invasion between 1933 and 1935 led to a decrease in production of 8,3 per cent in the 1935–36 season.[11]

The acreage under sugar-cane increased 3,6 times between 1911 and 1940, from 107 091 acres to 383 879 acres. The largest increase occurred in the five-year period between 1916 and 1920, when 47 826 acres were added, an increase of 44,7 per cent. This was the period when world demand was increasing and prices were high. For the entire period, the average five-yearly increase was 29,4 per cent.

The industry between 1911 and 1932 was dependent upon one variety of cane, namely Uba. Uba had been introduced in the 1880s for its drought and disease resistance. The cane was, however, very hard and fibrous which made it more difficult, expensive and time consuming to mill. Uba's position was further entrenched by legislation which prevented other varieties from being grown between January 1927 and December 1930, in an attempt to eradicate mosaic disease (a virus systemic plant disease) which retarded the cane's growth and consequently led to diminished yields.[13] The attempt at eradication was abandoned in 1930 when it was discovered that the disease was endemic in maize and wild grasses and would never be eliminated.[14] In 1925 the Mount Edgecombe Experimental Station had been established to conduct research for the sugar industry. This research resulted in the introduction in the 1930s of four new varieties of cane, namely Co 281, Co 290, Co 301 and POJ. These canes had the advantage of being softer and therefore easier to mill; furthermore, they gave higher yields with a greater sucrose content. Their introduction meant that Uba's predominance was reduced in seven years to 23 per cent of the cane harvested.

Table 4   Varieties percentage of cane harvested 1934–1940[15]

Year	Uba	Co 281	Co 290	Co 301	POJ
1934	97		3		
1935	92		8		
1936	84	2	24		10
1937	54	12	28		6
1938	32	21	35	1	11
1939	30	28	30	3	9
1940	23	38	28	3	8

The cane yield increased by 42,8 per cent from 19 tons per acre in 1932 to 27 tons per acre in 1940. There was a 37,3 per cent increase between 1937 and 1939 which coincided with the increase in the proportion of Co 281 and Co 290 being harvested. Thus increases in yield can be ascribed to the introduction of new varieties as there were no major changes in the management of estates in that period.[16]

Table 5   Average yield per acre 1932–1940[17]

Year	Tons	% Increase	Year	Tons	% Increase
1932	19,29		1937	23,75	11,7
1933	20,24	4,7	1938	27,37	15,2
1934	20,84	2,8	1939	30,22	10,4
1935	20,10	−3,4	1940	27,55	−8,8
1936	21,27	5,8			

During the inter-war years sugar production was affected by three major disputes within the industry. Each of these disputes led to a request for government intervention. The first arose from the perception amongst growers that millers were making disproportionate profits in the boom following the cessation of hostilities in 1918. This led to the appointment of the Sugar Inquiry Commission under the chairmanship of W.D. Baxter which presented its report in 1922.[8] The commission found that the growers received 50 per cent of mill proceeds, rather than the 33,35 per cent which growers mistakenly believed they received. The government only implemented two of the commission's recommendations: those concerning the abolition of the Mozambique concession in 1923; and the establishment of a sugar experimental station in 1925.

The second dispute resulted in the Board of Trade and Industries Report on the industry in 1926,[19] and was the consequence of dissatisfaction with the importation of sugar into the Union, the organisation of the export market, and the payment basis for cane. The intervention by government led to the Fahey Agreement of 1926 by which the basis of payment for cane was changed from weight to sucrose content. The planters agreed to participate in the export market by sharing the costs involved, while the millers were to participate in the export market on a pro rata basis in accordance with their output. The government granted the industry increased protection and in return obtained the industry's consent to fix the retail price of sugar.

In the 1930s the world sugar market remained depressed and in terms of the Fahey Agreement growers and millers shared the costs of exports. There were, however, a few millers who were not party to the 1926 Agreement and who had been able to increase their share of the domestic market without having to bear the costs of the export market. Furthermore, growers' output after 1926 had risen by 50 per cent while miller-planters had increased their output by 100 per cent. This placed an unfair burden upon the independent growers who had to share the costs of increased exports. These grievances led to the third enquiry, and to the Board of Trade and Industries Report of 1935.[20] The findings were extensively discussed within the industry before being incorporated in the Sugar Act of 1936. The Act of 1936 provided for the self-government of the industry through the Sugar Industry Central Board that was to be responsible for the settlement of disputes, the administration of quotas and the testing of cane.[21]

Production control was introduced with maximum quotas for each mill which were then sub-divided amongst the growers supplying each mill.[22] The grievance of the small growers was addressed in that they were allowed to exceed their quota by 3 500 tons at the expense of the larger growers attached to their mill.[23] In the 1936–37 season, production was limited by the government to 476 888 tons and was increased by the supplementary agreement of September 1938.[24] A new system of payment, known as the marginal formula, was also introduced. This, although still based on sucrose content, gave growers a larger share of the proceeds.[25] The formula took into account the cost both of growing cane and of milling it with reasonable efficiency. The production of new varieties of cane was also promoted through the introduction of premium prices for such cane.[26] Furthermore, all the mills had to share the domestic and export markets on a pro rata basis.[27] The government required the industry to introduce

Grade 2 sugar at a lower price in exchange for this restricted self-government.

In terms of the Fahey Agreement of 1926 and the Sugar Act of 1936, the costs of exports were shared between the millers and planters. This, as noted previously, caused a great deal of resentment in the 1930s when the world market was depressed. The local price of sugar, in the 14 years between the 1927–28 and the 1940–41 seasons, declined by 19,7 per cent and the export price declined by 28,7 per cent. This meant that the average price of sugar declined by 24,1 per cent. These price reductions, however, did not curb output as the protected local market financed the losses sustained in the export market. Furthermore, compared to many other producers the local industry was well off.

Table 6   Prices obtained for South African sugar 1927/28–1940/41[28] (£ per ton)

Season	Local price	Export price	Average price
1927/28	17,3	12,9	16,2
1928/29	16,8	12,2	15,5
1929/30	15,2	9,8	12,8
1930/31	14,6	7,7	11,2
1931/32	13,6	7,1	10,4
1932/33	15,0	5,7	10,3
1933/34	15,4	7,1	11,4
1934/35	15,9	6,2	12,5
1935/36	15,6	6,4	10,8
1936/37	15,2	6,4	11,6
1937/38	14,8	7,2	11,4
1938/39	14,7	6,6	11,5
1939/40	13,9	8,1	11,5
1940/41	13,9	9,2	12,3

Exports

South African exports grew from 2 790 tons in 1910–11 to 308 763 tons in 1939–40 and absorbed an increasing proportion of production. The exportation of sugar can be divided into three periods. In the first one, from 1910–11 to 1918–19, exports constituted less than 10 per cent of total production. The 1918–19 season is significant because it was the first time in the history of the industry that production exceeded consumption. In the second period, from 1919–20 to 1927–28, exports accounted on average for 22,7 per cent of production. However, the average was reduced by the

8,4 per cent recorded in 1924–25 as a result of the drought. In the third period, from 1928–29 to 1939–40, exports averaged 45,4 per cent of production.

South Africa's major export market was Britain, following the institution of an imperial preference of 4s. 3d. in 1919. The country's proportion of Empire sugar imports rose from 2,4 per cent in 1919 to 3,5 per cent in 1925.[30] Britain continued to be the predominant market for South African sugar exports until the Second World War. Exports to Britain rose from 51 931 tons in 1926–27 to 206 381 in 1938–39 and, on average, accounted for 75,8 per cent of total exports (excludes 1937–38, for which figures are not available). Canada also became an important export market and absorbed on average 28,6 per cent of total sugar exports between 1929–30 and 1936–37. Canada played a crucial role in 1932–33 and 1933–34 when British imports declined, possibly as a result of the Ottawa Agreement which gave all Empire sugar producers equal access to the British market. In the export market South Africa was insulated from the world sugar crisis through its preferential access to Britain and Canada.

Table 7   South African exports to Britain and Canada 1926/27–1938/39[31]
(tons 2000lb.)

Season	Britain	% Total	Canada	% Total
1926/27	51 931	77,6	8 740	13,1
1927/28	61 267	88,8		
1928/29	85 559	88,5		
1929/30	108 078	85,5	18 262	14,6
1930/31	143 563	68,2	49 852	23,7
1931/32	113 697	71,3	46 420	29,1
1932/33	80 322	44,8	99 000	55,2
1933/34	72 711	38,1	118 135	61,9
1934/35	104 157	86,0	17 015	14,0
1935/36	174 802	82,3	37 700	17,7
1936/37	146 357	86,3	21 000	12,4
1938/39	206 381	92,2	17 398	7,8

In terms of the International Sugar Agreement of 1937, South Africa undertook to export no more than 230 380 tons.[32] This quota was subject to increase in accordance with the increase in British consumption. The quota in the 1937–38 and 1938–39 seasons was divided into an 'A' and a 'B' pool, and in the 1939–40 season a 'C' pool was added. The institution of quotas did not have a detrimental effect upon the local industry as production quotas had been introduced locally prior to the implementation of international restrictions.

Furthermore, exports in the 1939–40 season increased by 84 979 tons as a result of representations by the Ministry of Food for Great Britain.[33]

Table 8   South Africa's quotas in accordance with 1937 Agreement[34] (tons)

Season	Total exports	'A' Pool	'B' and 'C' Pool
1937/38	258 047	229 476	28 571
1938/39	223 784	189 533	34 251
1939/40	308 763	203 386	105 377

Imports

Sugar imports prior to the 1918–19 season were significant and constituted, on average, 16,9 per cent of total local consumption. The two major sources of sugar imports were Mozambique and Mauritius. This was acceptable as domestic production only surpassed local consumption for the first time in 1918–19. Imports then declined to 0,8 per cent of total consumption in 1919–20 and rose to 2 per cent in 1920–21. The extent of this decline can be ascribed to strong world demand following the end of the First World War. Imports then surged to over 10 per cent of consumption in 1921–22 and 1922–23 in response to the surplus on the world market. In 1923–24 imports again declined to 0,3 per cent of consumption with the termination of the Mozambique preference.

Imports from Mozambique for the eleven years from 1910–11 to 1920–21 constituted, on average, 46,2 per cent of total sugar imports. Mozambique achieved this through the 1909 Convention with the Transvaal which allowed Mozambique's sugar duty-free access to the latter's market.[35] Furthermore, Mozambique sugar was cheaper than South African sugar because of its lower production costs. This preferential access to the Transvaal caused considerable resentment in the local industry,[36] but the agreement had been signed prior to Union and was binding. Following the Baxter Commission report, the concession was removed in 1923 when the new trade and labour convention was concluded with Mozambique.[37]

Table 9   Sugar imports from Mozambique 1910/11–1920/21[38]

Season	Tons	% Imports	Season	Tons	% Imports
1910/11	3 105	9,6	1916/17	3 545	44,0
1911/12	6 184	22,9	1917/18	16 760	100
1912/13	4 991	21,1	1918/19	9 230	87,9
1913/14	9 745	37,7	1919/20	43	3,2
1914/15	11 428	72,6	1920/21	848	41,4
1915/16	4 018	67,9			

In 1928–29 sugar imports rose to 11,3 per cent of domestic consumption as a result of low world prices; in particular the dumping of sugar by Czechoslovakia on the local market.[39] The large-scale importation of sugar continued in the 1929–30, 1930–31 and 1931–32 seasons, with American sugar being landed for 2 shillings less than the local wholesale price.[40] This led the industry to ask Government for further tariff protection, which was granted.[41] In the seasons from 1932–33 to 1939–40 sugar imports never exceeded 1 per cent of total local consumption as a result of tariff protection.

The duty on imported sugar was raised progressively in order to counter the threat to the domestic industry. The duty was increased on five occasions from 3s. 6d. per 100 lb. in 1910 to 16s. 1d. per 100 lb. in 1932, an increase of 447,2 per cent in 22 years. The protection given to the local industry clearly minimised imports and ensured its growth and prosperity in the inter-war period.[42] However, the cost to the domestic economy of protecting the sugar industry was estimated at £1,9 million in 1935 and at £2,2 million in 1939.[43]

Table 10   Duty on imported sugar[44]

Year	Per 100 lb.
1910	3s. 6d.
1915	6s. 0d.
1926	7s. 0d.
1931	12s. 1d.
1935	16s. 1d.

Consumption

The per capita consumption of sugar in South Africa rose from 32 lb. per annum in 1915 to 47 lb. per annum in 1940, an increase of 46,9 per cent. Britain's per capita consumption in contrast grew by only 15,8 per cent between 1900 and 1937, although from a higher base.[45] South African consumption only declined during the depression years, when it slumped to 37 lb. in 1935, a fall of 15,9 per cent. Consumption between 1935 and 1940 increased by 27 per cent as a result of the improved economic conditions and the introduction of Grade 2 sugar.

Table 11   South African per capita consumption of sugar 1915–1940[46]

Year	lbs.	% Increase
1915	32	
1920	37	15,6
1925	39	5,4
1930	44	12,4
1935	37	–15,9
1940	47	27,0

In August 1936, a new sugar known as Grade 2 was introduced to the market.[47] The idea originated within the government and was accepted by the industry as it offered them an opportunity to broaden their product base.[48] Grade 2 sugar was sold at 2,5d. per lb. and was positioned in the market to cater for the needs of poorer consumers, who could not afford 3,5d. per lb. for refined sugar.[49] In the 1938–39 season the 19,7 per cent increase in local consumption was attributed to the increasing demand for Grade 2 sugar.[50] The industry encouraged this trend by initiating an intensive advertising campaign amongst the African population.[51]

The introduction of price control also influenced the consumption of sugar on the domestic market. Price control was first introduced on a voluntary basis with the outbreak of the First World War as a result of discussions between the industry and government.[52] The price was fixed in August 1914 at 17s. per 100 lb. and was raised the following month to 20s.[53] In April 1917 the sugar price rose to between £34 and £39 a ton as a result of the industry dropping its voluntary control.[54] The government, faced with an escalating sugar price, introduced price control in May 1917, with the producer price fixed at 26s. per 100 lb. Thereafter, the price was fixed in accordance with market trends, first under the Moratorium Act and then under Act No. 13 of 1922.[55] Price control was abolished in June 1923 when the latter Act expired. Deregulation could then be allowed because the world sugar price had slumped and the domestic price of sugar was no longer escalating.

Table 12 Price control of sugar 1917–1923[56] (per 100lb.)

Date	Producer	Wholesale	Date	Producer	Wholesale
5/1917	26s. 0d.	27s. 9d.	6/1920	41s. 0d.	43s. 0d.
6/1917	26s. 0d.	27s. 9d.	8/1920	51s. 0d.	53s. 6d.
5/1918	26s. 0d.	27s. 9d.	8/1921	31s. 0d.	33s. 8d.
12/1918	21s.10d.	23s. 7d.	10/1921	29s. 0d.	31s. 8d.
1/1919	23s. 0d.	24s. 6d.	5/1922	25s. 0d.	27s. 6d.
6/1919	26s. 0d.	27s. 9d.	4/1923	30s. 0d.	33s. 0d.
11/1919	29s. 3d.	31s. 3d.			

The deregulation of sugar prices in 1923 led to intense speculation in the sugar market. The industry, as a result of this speculation, requested governmental regulation in 1926 and this led to the institution of price control in terms of the Sugar Prices Act.[57] The maximum retail price was fixed at 3,75d. per lb. for refined sugar and 3,5d. per lb. for mill white.[58] The retail price remained at this level until 1932 when prices were reduced to 3,5d. and 3,25d. respectively in terms of Act No. 25.[59] This reduction was made in order to protect the domestic consumer, following the increased tariff protection granted to the industry. The 1936 Sugar Act retained these maximum prices and required that Grade 2 be sold at 2,5d.[60] The price was only increased again in October 1946, due to the low world sugar prices.[61]

The manufacturing sector's consumption of sugar became an increasingly important component of the sugar market, as its consumption increased by 316,1 per cent between the 1916–17 and 1939–40 seasons. The demand for sugar in this sector originated in the Cape Province where the canning and spirits industries were located, and was augmented by the confectionery trade's requirements. In the 12-year period between 1916–17 and 1926–27, consumption in the sector rose by 76,4 per cent. Consumption then declined as a result of the depression by 2 367 tons to 22 475 tons in 1931–32. In 1933 there was an upturn in demand for sugar from the fruit canneries of the South Western Cape.[62] Manufacturing's consumption of sugar then continued to escalate until 1939–40, when the sector absorbed 44 522 tons.

Milling

The milling sector of the industry was subject to continued consolidation between 1906 and 1940, with the number of mills in operation being reduced from 33 to 22. This decrease was the result of company mergers and the high capital cost of the machinery used. The large capital expenditure is illustrated by the fact that the value of machinery and plant in the 1915–16 season in 31 factories was estimated at £1 253 000, and increased to £2 144 000 in the 1921–22 season despite the reduction in the number of mills to 28.[63] Therefore, the average investment per mill rose from £40 419 in the 1915–16 season to £76 571 in the 1921–22 season.

Table 13   Number of sugar mills 1906–1940[64]

Year	Mills
1906	33
1915	31
1920	29
1925	27
1930	24
1935	23
1940	22

The objective in milling was to extract the greatest possible amount of sucrose from the cane, and the mills therefore operated between May and December when the sucrose content was at its optimum.[65] The efficiency of mills in this regard is measured by means of the sucrose extraction, boiling-house recovery and overall recovery rates. A comparison of the rates for the 10-year periods between 1925–34 and 1935–44 shows that the average mill performance did improve by 6,2 per cent in terms of the overall recovery rate. This can be ascribed, in part, to the investment in plant and the research conducted into better extraction methods.

Table 14   Average mill performance[66] (percentage)

Years	Sucrose extraction	Boiling-house	Overall recovery
1925–34	89,83	83,67	75,12
1935–44	92,05	88,36	81,34

However, the efficiency of the mills was limited by the composition of the cane and the cane-to-sugar ratio. There was only a slight improvement between 1925–34 and 1935–44, which limited the overall improvement of mill efficiency. The improvement that did occur can be ascribed to the utilisation of new varieties in the 1930s which contained more sucrose and less fibre. The effect of more efficient milling on the industry as a whole was to improve its profitability.

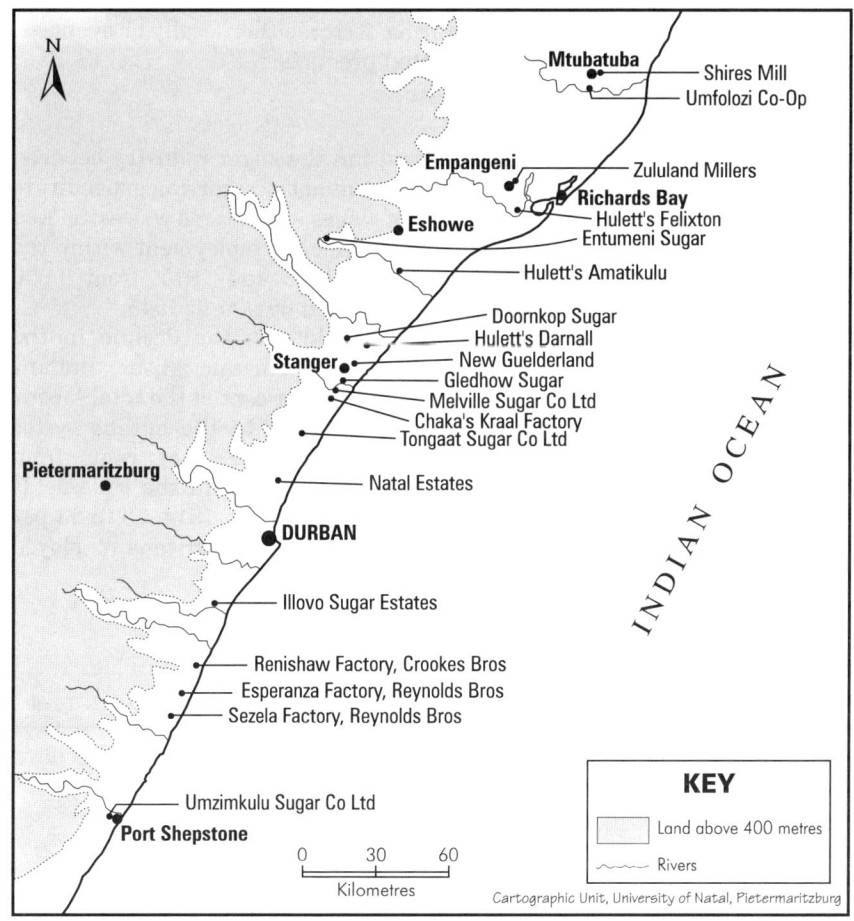

Map 1   Sugar mills in Natal/Zululand, 1948

Table 15   Composition of cane[67]

Years	Sucrose % Cane	Fibre % Cane	Cane-to-Sugar ratio
1925–34	13,19	15,78	9,64
1935–44	13,53	15,30	8,73

The sugar mills produced three by-products from the crushed cane, namely bagasse, filter-press cake and molasses.[68] Bagasse was made up of fibre and was used to fuel the mill boilers. The fuel value of bagasse was 15 per cent of the fuel value of coal and a ton of cane produced 0,33 tons of bagasse which was the equivalent of 100 lb. of coal.[69] Bagasse enabled the mills to reduce their running costs and utilise a by-product in the process. The residue left in the filter-press after the sap passed through it was known as filter-press cake and was used as a fertilizer on the cane fields.[70] Molasses was sold to the manufacturing sector, either locally or overseas, which used it to produce alcohol-related products.[71]

Labour

Labour was an important component within the sugar industry between 1910 and 1940, as it accounted for 50 per cent of the recurring expenditure within the industry.[72] In 1937 the cost of wages and rations was estimated to amount to £2 million annually.[73] Furthermore, employment within the industry increased by 8,5 times between 1905 and 1945; from 8 000 workers in 1905 to 40 589 in 1929 and reached 68 000 in 1945.[74]

The major change within the labour field was the decline in the importance of Indian labour and the rise of African labour. Indians employed in the cane-fields decreased from 56 per cent of the total labour force in 1914 15 to only 7 per cent in 1944–45. In the milling sector the number of Indians employed declined by 28 per cent, from 4 028 in 1925 to 3 190 in 1934.[75] Africans employed in the cane-fields increased from 44 per cent of the total labour force in 1914–15 to 93 per cent in 1944–45. In the milling sector the number of Africans employed increased from 4 189 in 1925 to 4 823 in 1934.[76]

Table 16   Number Indians and Africans employed in the cane-fields[77]

Season	Indians	% Total	African	% Total
1907/08	10 924	82	2 484	18
1914/15	11 745	56	9 357	44
1924/25	9 500	36	16 473	64
1934/35	4 908	12	33 283	68
1944/45	4 500	7	55 778	93

African employment within the agricultural sector of the industry was a complex process with different recruitment areas for Natal and Zululand.

African labour was employed either as casual labour on a monthly basis and recruited locally, or as migrant labour recruited on a 180-shift contract from outside the province. There was a tendency to use the casual labour for planting and cultivation, and the migrants for cane-cutting, although the converse could also apply. The industry was dependent throughout the period upon migrant labour for at least 40 per cent of its requirements.[78] This dependence on migrant labour was the result of what the Farm Labour Committee described as poor housing, feeding and the lack of medical attention.[79] The larger estates provided brick housing but on the smaller estates workers often had to erect their own accommodation. The rations provided for the African labour force consisted on average of: 90 lb. of maize meal, 8 lb. of beans, 2 lb. of sugar, 4 lb. of meat and 4 lb. of salt per month, which they had to prepare themselves.[80]

Beinart maintains that Africans viewed the work on sugar estates as hard and the wages as low, which made the mines a better prospect.[81] In 1913 the wages paid to Africans on the gold-mines were 73,3 per cent higher than those paid by the sugar industry, while the Natal coal-mines paid 46,3 per cent more. Furthermore, the wage figures for gold and coal are based upon 26 shifts and those for sugar upon 30 shifts. In 1937 the position had become even worse with the two sectors paying 94,7 per cent and 60,3 per cent more than sugar. Wages in the sugar industry for the period 1913 to 1937 increased by 25 per cent, but from a very low base. Clearly, the sugar industry did not offer the same financial rewards as the other industries. In addition, the wages paid in Natal were higher than the wages in Zululand. Actual wage figures are only available for Zululand in 1939, when the difference amounted to 10 shillings or 25 per cent. The farmers maintained that this was due to the smaller size of production units in Zululand and the higher transportation costs which reduced margins, and therefore wages.[82] These factors may have contributed to this trend but the major reason was the presence of migrants from Mozambique, who were prepared to work for lower wages. The farmers often complained about the quality of the migrant labour which they employed and maintained that they obtained those migrants who had been rejected by the mines.[83] In view of the way the industry was perceived by Africans and the lower wages paid, it is quite possible that the farmers' assertion was correct.

Table 17   African wages for gold, coal and sugar 1913–1939[84]

Year	Gold	% Increase	Coal	% Increase	Sugar	% Increase
1913	52s. 0d.		43s. 9d.		30s. 0d.	
1921	58s. 7d.	12,9	57s. 6d.	31,2		
1932	57s. 7d.	−1,7	49s. 4d.	−13,5	40s. 0d.	25,0
1937	58s. 4d.	1,2	48s. 1d.	− 2,6	30s. 0d.	−25,0
1939					40s. 0d.	25,0

Note: In the Witwatersrand gold and Natal coal industries, wages are for 26 shifts, while in the sugar industry wages are for 30 shifts.

Table 18   South African sugar production, exports, imports and local consumption 1910/11–1939/40[29] (ton 2000lb.)

Season	Production	Exports	Exports % production	Imports	Imports % consumption	Total local consumption	Manufacturing consumption
1910/11	82 000	2 790	3,4	32 321	29,0	111 531	
1911/12	92 000	2 036	2,2	27 055	23,1	117 019	
1912/13	96 000	2 303	2,4	23 617	20,1	117 314	
1913/14	92 153	2 073	2,2	25 939	23,4	116 019	
1914/15	102 653	2 859	2,8	15 744	13,6	115 538	
1915/16	113 358	3 893	3,4	5 920	5,1	115 385	
1916/17	114 709	4 047	3,5	7 978	6,7	118 640	14 085
1917/18	104 921	4 039	3,8	16 760	14,2	117 642	16 152
1918/19	150 214	12 898	8,6	10 498	7,1	147 805	17 848
1919/20	189 183	27 495	14,5	1 359	0,8	163 047	19 059
1920/21	143 680	42 725	29,7	2 050	2,0	103 005	16 898
1921/22	148 275	36 652	24,7	17 667	13,7	129 290	13 735
1922/23	159 362	39 181	24,6	13 506	10,1	133 687	15 330
1923/24	203 350	36 452	17,9	583	0,3	167 491	18 016
1924/25	161 250	13 558	8,4	791	0,5	148 483	19 698
1925/26	239 851	70 602	29,4	6 075	3,5	175 324	20 710
1926/27	242 662	66 910	27,6	4 091	2,3	179 843	22 351
1927/28	247 273	68 978	27,9	5 292	2,9	183 587	23 919
1928/29	295 934	96 681	32,7	25 261	11,3	224 514	24 842
1029/30	298 635	126 340	42,3	15 746	8,4	188 041	24 217
1930/31	393 205	210 632	53,6	6 004	3,2	188 577	22 664
1931/32	325 899	159 517	48,9	4 154	2,4	170 536	22 475
1932/33	358 905	179 322	50,0	820	0,5	180 403	23 028
1933/34	391 173	190 846	48,8	1 500	0,7	201 827	25 421
1934/35	358 738	121 172	33,8	1 139	0,5	238 705	29 692
1935/36	417 318	212 507	50,9	1 334	0,6	206 145	30 814
1936/37	446 409	169 599	38,0	1 404	0,5	278 214	32 422
1937/38	507 210	258 047	50,9	1 709	0,7	250 872	37 330
1938/39	522 732	223 784	42,8	1 377	0,5	300 325	37 414
1939/40	595 556	308 763	51,8	960	0,3	287 753	44 522

The payment for a shift in the case of cane-cutters depended upon the completion of the 'standard', which was 1,5 tons of cane cut, trashed and loaded. In the case of burnt cane the 'standard' was increased to 2 tons as there was no trashing. Furthermore, the cane-cutters were paid a bonus of 1d. for every 100 lb. above the standard.[85]

The Natal sugar industry obtained most of its African migrant labour from Mpondoland. The industry was able to attract this labour prior to 1921 because of the system of advances, whereby the migrant could obtain cattle and/or cash in advance of commencing work.[86] The advance system was curtailed with the introduction of the Native Advance Regulation Act of 1921. This was the result of representations by the Chamber of Mines, whose recruitment had been detrimentally affected, and because of widespread abuse of the system. Mpondo labour was also attracted to the sugar industry because the work was above ground and the contract was relatively short – involving 180 shifts.[87] The industry's position was further strengthened by the malaria epidemic of 1929 to 1932, as Mpondo labourers were not allowed north of the Thukela for fear of their being infected.[88] Mpondo labour remained vital to the industry in Natal and constituted between 10 and 60 per cent of the labour force in 1939.[89]

In 1912 it was already recognised that the sugar industry in Zululand would require labour from Mozambique.[90] This was because Zululand required malaria-tolerant labour which Mozambique possessed. In 1925 the government prohibited the recruitment of Mozambican labour, except for the mines on the Rand.[91] This led to an outcry by the industry which recognised that labour from Mpondoland and Basotholand would readily succumb to malaria.[92] The industry's view was vindicated by the malaria epidemic between 1929 and 1932 which led to a decline in Transkei labour and a ban by Basotholand on recruitment for Zululand.[93] Zululand farmers continued to make use of illegal Mozambican labour after 1925, and this accounted for 50 per cent of those employed in South Africa in 1930.[94] The revised Mozambique Treaty of 1934 made no provision for recruitment by the sugar industry but, following representations by the industry to the government, recruitment of Mozambican labour for the Zululand sugar industry was allowed from the end of 1935.[95] In 1939 Mozambican labour accounted for 40 per cent of the industry's requirements in the region but there was still an estimated labour shortage of between 20 and 25 per cent.[96]

Conclusion

The South African sugar industry became a net exporter between 1910 and 1939, and was not as severely affected by the crisis in the international sugar trade as many other producers. The industry could not have flourished to the extent it did, had it not been for government protection and assistance which provided it with a captive home market. This captive home market allowed the industry to finance its export market, which was aided by the preferential access that the industry enjoyed in Britain and

Canada. Internally the industry was characterised by an uneasy relationship between growers and millers, who were forced to co-operate through their mutual need. The government intervened whenever this relationship became too strained, but in exchange obtained sugar at a fixed price and, in the 1930s, the introduction of Grade 2 sugar. The government, however, always placed the needs of gold-mining before those of sugar with regard to labour requirements. By 1939, the industry had established itself on a sound economic footing through the protection it enjoyed domestically.

REFERENCES

I would like to acknowledge the assistance of the Human Sciences Research Council whose grant enabled me to complete much of the research undertaken for this paper.

1. A. Graves and P. Richardson, 'Plantations in the political economy of colonial sugar production: Natal and Queensland, 1860–1914', *Journal of Southern African Studies*, 6, 1980, pp. 214–29; P. Richardson, 'The Natal sugar industry, 1849–1905: an interpretative essay', *Journal of African History*, 23, 1982, pp. 515–27; P. Richardson, 'The Natal sugar industry in the nineteenth century' in W. Beinart, et al. (eds), *Putting a plough to the ground: accumulation and dispossession in rural South Africa, 1950–1930*, (Johannesburg, Ravan Press, 1986), pp. 129–75.

2. M. Tayal, 'Indian indentured labour in Natal, 1890–1911', *The Indian Economic and Social History Review*, 14, 1977, pp. 519–47.

3. R. Barnett, 'The Natal sugar industry' (unpublished M. Econ. thesis, UNISA, 1938); I. Behrmann, 'A study of the economics of sugar-cane production in Natal', (unpublished D. Phil. thesis, University of Natal, Pietermaritzburg, 1959); A. van der Merwe, 'Die suikerindustrie van Natal/Zululand' (unpublished M.A. thesis, University of Stellenbosch, 1939).

4. J. D. Beall and M. D. North-Coombes, 'The 1913 disturbances in Natal: the social and economic background to "Passive Resistance"', *Journal of Natal and Zulu History*, 6, 1983, pp. 48–77; W. Beinart, 'Joyini inkomo: cattle advances and the origins of migrancy from Pondoland', *Journal of Southern African Studies*, 5, 1979, pp. 199–219; M. Swan, 'The 1913 Natal Indian strike', *Journal of Southern African Studies*, 10, 1984, pp. 239–58.

5. Richardson, 'Sugar in the nineteenth century', p. 148.

6. S. S. Brand, 'The contribution of agriculture to the economic development of South Africa since 1910' (unpublished D. Sc. Agric. thesis, University of Pretoria, 1969), p. 19.

7. J. J. Stadler, 'Die bruto binnelandse produk van Suid-Afrika, 1911–1959' (unpublished D. Com. thesis, University of Pretoria, 1962), p. 522.

8. Standard Bank Archives (SBA), general manager's office, Half-yearly Report, 5 February 1913, p. 61.

9. *Ibid.*, 12 February 1917, p. 76.

10. *Ibid.*, 31 March 1921, p. 84; 31 March 1925, p. 121; Annual Report, 31 March 1932, p. 149; Barnett, 'Natal sugar industry', p. 62, cites cause of reduction in 1924–25 and 1931–32 as floods rather than droughts.

11. SBA, general manager's office, Annual Report, 31 March 1935, p. 159.

12. Barnett, 'Natal sugar industry', p. 39; Board of Trade and Industries (BTI), report no. 298, *The South African sugar industry – review*, (Cape Town, Government Printer, 1947), p. 76.

13. W. K. Buchanan, 'The sugar industry' in H. R. Burrows (ed.), *Agriculture in Natal: recent developments*, NRS, vol. 13 (Cape Town, Oxford University Press, 1959), p. 49.

14. *Ibid.*

15. BTI, report no. 298, p. 74.

16. RP 96–1970, *Report of the commission of inquiry into the sugar industry of South Africa*, p. 6.

17. BTI, report no. 298, p. 76.

18. UG 22–22, *Report of the sugar inquiry commission*.

19. BTI, report no. 66, *Report on the sugar industry* (Cape Town, Government Printer, 1926).

20. BTI, report no. 194, *The sugar industry: working of conference agreement and future organisation* (Pretoria, Government Printer, 1935).

21. BTI, report no. 298, pp. 29–33.

22. *Ibid.*, p. 32.

23. *Ibid.*

24. SBA, general manager's office, Annual Report, 31 March 1937, p. 179; 31 March 1939, p. 136.

25. BTI, report no. 298, pp. 32, 34, 36.

26. *Ibid.*, p. 35.

27. *Ibid.*, p. 36.

28. Behrmann, 'Economics of sugar-cane', p. 42.

29. BTI, report no. 66, pp. 3, 52; BTI, report no. 194, p. 10, BTI report no. 298, pp. 21, 51; *Official year book of the Union of South Africa*, 9 (1926–27), p. 78; *South African Sugar Journal Annual* (SASJA), (1925), p. 33; *South African Sugar Journal* (SASJ), 23(7), 1939, p. 375; *South African Sugar Year Book and General Directory* (SASYB & GD), 5, 1934, p. 71; *South African Sugar Year Book and General Directory* (SASYB & GD), 12, 1941–42, pp. 204, 206; The various sources give conflicting figures, particularly with regard to imports, and the reader should therefore approach the figures with caution.

30. C. J. Robertson, *World sugar production and consumption* (London, Croom Helm, 1934), p. 44.

31. SBA, inspection report, Durban branch, December 1933–March 1934, p. 14h; November 1935–April 1936, p. 16; April–June 1940, p. 14h; general manager's office, Annual Report, 31 March 1937, p. 179.

32. *SASYB & GD*, 12, 1941–42, p. 206.

33. SBA, general manager's office, Annual Report, 31 March 1940, p. 166.

34. *SASYB & GD*, 12, 1941–42, p. 206.

35. UG 22–22, *Sugar inquiry commission*, 1922, p. 30.

36. See, for example, SBA, general manager's office, Half-yearly Report, 3 August 1910, p. 56.

37. BTI, report no. 66, p. 3.

38. UG 22–22, *Sugar inquiry commission*, 1922, p. 30; *SASJA*, 1920–21, p. 207.

39. SBA, general manager's office, *Annual Report*, 31 March 1929, pp. 142–43.

40. *Ibid.*, 31 March 1932, p. 150.

41. *Ibid.*

42. *Ibid.*, 31 March 1934, p. 156.

43. Behrmann, 'Economics of sugar-cane', pp. 36–37.

44. BTI, report no. 106, *Increased customs duty on imported sugar and co-ordination of the sugar industry* (Pretoria, Government Printer, 1930), p. 1; BTI, report no. 119, p. 2; BTI, report no. 194, p. 8.

45. G. N. Johnstone, 'The growth of the sugar trade and refining industry' in D. J. Oddy and D. S. Miller, *The making of the modern British diet* (London, Bale and Danielson, 1976), p. 62.

46. RP 96–1970, *Inquiry into sugar industry*, 1970, p. 61.

47. *SASJ*, 20(8), 1936, p. 469.

48. *Ibid.*

49. SBA, general manager's office, Annual Report, 31 March 1937, pp. 179–80.

50. *Ibid.*, 31 March 1938, p. 135.

51. *Ibid.*, 31 March 1939, p. 136.

52. *SASYB & GD*, 1, 1930, p. 151.

53. *Ibid.*

54. *Ibid.*

55. *Official yearbook of the Union of South Africa*, 6, 1910–22, p. 537.

56. *Ibid.*

57. *Official yearbook of the Union of South Africa*, 17, 1934–35, p. 470.

58. *Ibid.*

59. *Ibid.*

60. *Official yearbook of the Union of South Africa*, 21, 1940, p. 787.

61. BTI, report no. 298, p. 18.

62. B. Ingpen, 'The coastwise shipping industry of southern Africa' (unpublished M.A. thesis, University of Port Elizabeth, 1983), p. 65.

63. *SASJ*, 8(9), 1924, p. 645.

64. *Ibid. SASJ*, 9(1), 1925, p. 78; *SASJA*, 1925, p. 27; *SASYB & GD*, 3, 1932, p. 137; *Official yearbook of the Union of South Africa*, 17, 1934–35, p. 469; *Official yearbook of the Union of South Africa*, 22, 1941, p. 728.

65. *Official yearbook of the Union of South Africa*, 6, 1910–25, p. 451.

66. RP 96–1970, *Inquiry into the sugar industry*, 1970, p. 13.

67. *Ibid.*

68. *SASJ*, 14(9), 1930, p. 609.

69. *Ibid.*

70. Van der Merwe, 'Suikerindustrie', p. 88.

71. *SASJ*, 14(9), 1930, p. 609.

72. *Report of the native farm labour committee, 1937–1939* (Pretoria, Government Printer, 1939), p. 60.

73. *SASJ*, 21(2), 1937, p. 67.

74. N. Hurwitz, *Agriculture in Natal, 1860–1950*, NRS, vol. 12 (Cape Town, Oxford University Press, 1950), p. 44.

75. *Joint memorandum of South African cane growers' association and the Natal sugar millers' association*, presented to Board of Trade and Industries, October 1934, p. 60.

76. *Ibid.*

77. A. G. Choonoo, 'Indentured Indian immigration into Natal, 1860–1911, with particular reference to its role in the development of the sugar industry' (unpublished M.A. thesis, University of Natal, Durban, 1967), p. 176.

78. R. H. Smith, *Labour resources of Natal*, NRS, Report no. 1 (Cape Town, Oxford University Press, 1950), p. 42.

79. *Native farm labour committee*, p. 63.

80. Van der Merwe, 'Suikerindustrie', p. 59.

81. Beinart, 'Joyini inkomo', p. 211.

82. *Native farm labour committee*, pp. 63–64.

83. *SASJ*, 9(11), 1925, p. 741; *SASJ*, 12(5), 1928, p. 269; *SASJ*, 13(12), 1929, p. 801.

84. Van der Merwe, 'Suikerindustrie', p. 58; *Native farm labour committee*, pp. 60–61; S. T. van der Horst, *Native labour in South Africa* (London, Oxford University Press, 1942), p. 58; Beall and North-Coombes, '1913 disturbances', p. 60.

85. Van der Merwe, 'Suikerindustrie', p. 58.

86. Beinart, 'Joyini inkomo', p. 212.

87. *Ibid.*, p. 211.

88. Personal correspondence with A. de V. Minnaar, HSRC-IHR, 14 May 1987.

89. *Native farm labour committee*, p. 61.

90. Beall and North-Coombes, '1913 disturbances', p. 83.

91. *SASJ*, 14(3), 1930, p. 153.

92. *SASJ*, 9(11), 1925, p. 741.

93. *Native farm labour committee*, p. 61; Van der Horst, *Native labour*, p. 288.

94. *SASJ*, 14(3), 1930, p. 153.

95. Personal correspondence with Minnaar, HSRC-IHR, 14 May 1987.

96. *Native farm labour committee*, p. 61.

ABSTRACT

The search for field workers in the aftermath of the ending of the Indian indentured labour system led to the revival of oscillating migrancy as the dominant labour form on Natal's sugar estates. Despite protracted efforts to institutionalise foreign labour recruitment, sugar-producers had to resign themselves to competition with other employers of coastal labour. Consequently, trade on the market for estate labour manifested itself as the resolution of two pervasive struggles. On the one hand, employers sought to win the initiative over potential labour recruits who had alternatives to estate work as a livelihood; their endeavours having encompassed the use of the lure of wages paid in advance. On the other hand, large and small estate-owners competed against each other, largely *en bloc*, for labour; a contest which came to revolve around the Natal Coast Labour Recruiting Corporation and its recruitment strategies. The outcome of these struggles displayed a distinctly regional pattern, with the larger employers south of the Thukela River finding succour in Pondoland's labour resources, and the small Zululand employers developing a dependence on labour from southern Mozambique. Thus, by the end of the inter-war period employers of sugar estate workers had succeeded in resurrecting a system of migrancy which had previously functioned towards the end of the nineteenth century to supplement supplies of indentured Indian labour. The institutionalisation of migrant sugar estate labour in this fashion would not have been accomplished without the state having intervened in the coastal labour market and, more importantly, without the fortunes of the coastal African populace having undergone profound change.

*T*HE ZULULAND SORE: MIGRANT SUGAR-ESTATE LABOUR IN NATAL 1914–1939

David Lincoln

Mid-October 1913 marked the beginning of the general strike by Indian workers in Natal. As far as Indian sugar workers along the coast of Natal were concerned, it was a climacteric event. From the moment that they laid down their cane knives, the Indian sugar workers were set to withdraw their labour from the sugar industry on a massive scale. Their employers were deeply perturbed by the turn of events. Two years before the strike, the government of India had terminated the flow of its subjects to South Africa; now the employers were being robbed of any hopes they might have entertained of prolonging the indentured labour system indefinitely by recourse to the numerous Indian workers who remained in coastal Natal.[1] And having trebled the volume of sugar production over the previous decade,[2] they had compelling reason to seek out novel methods of protecting their investments from the effects of the strike.

In their ensuing endeavour to establish a viable lasting alternative to the Indian indentured labour system, the employers of sugar workers might have looked back to earlier times for inspiration. Apart from its implementation of the indentured labour system, the sugar industry had, towards the end of the nineteenth century, experienced four decades of reliance on migrant labour from the eastern and the northern Transvaal, southern Mozambique, and Zululand. Indeed, that experience had reflected 'the origins, development and decline of one of the first organised forms of migrant labour in southern Africa'.[3] When labour migrancy along the sugar belt had then receded at the turn of the century, the employers' dependence on local (Natal) African workers and, more particularly, on indentured as well as 'time-expired' Indian workers had intensified. Now, with the dismantling of the indentured labour system in the offing, the employers were motivated to consider resurrecting the system of migrancy which had previously stood them in good stead. An attempt is made in this chapter to trace chronologically the process by which the employers of field workers in the sugar industry did, in the event, resurrect the migrant labour system.

It was a complex process: classes at various stages of formation, as much as groups within the differentiated agrarian bourgeoisie, were pitted one against the other; the state was periodically obliged to make direct interventions; and ecological influences were brought to bear on it.

177

Moreover, during the quarter of a century which separated the outbreaks of the two World Wars, sugar capital was beset by repeated marketing crises of a twofold nature. On the one hand, the prospects for uninterrupted capital accumulation were severely hampered by war-time restrictions, by global overproduction in the mid-1920s, and by instances of low-priced foreign sugars again being dumped on the domestic market in the early 1930s. On the other hand, and until the passage of the 1936 Sugar Act, growers and millers were locked in a dispute over the distribution of the fluctuating proceeds from sugar sales. Notwithstanding intercession by the state to eliminate this twofold tension, the distribution crisis and producers' conflicts served to aggravate the employers' frustrations in their pursuit of field workers.[4] Besides the overbearing frustration of having to engage in an intense struggle for labour, the most testing moments in that struggle arose out of the employers' conflicting material interests. A salient theme therefore of the employers' pursuit was diversity in the routes they took to reach a solution to the common 'labour problem'.

*   *   *   *   *

Heterogeneity amongst sugar estate-owners was the main reason for diversity in the conditions under which workers were drawn onto Natal's cane-fields. In the first instance, there was a fundamental dualism within the ranks of the contenders to the priceless verdant tapestry of coastal cane-fields. This dualism had its origins in the rise of the millers-cum-planters at the turn of the century.[5] Not only did the ascendant millers-cum-planters have greater and more varied labour requirements than independent growers, but they also had considerably larger resources with which to secure labour.

A second factor accounting for heterogeneity amongst sugar estate-owners stemmed from the statutory restraints which prevented miller-cum-planter operations from spreading into Zululand when the territory was opened to white settlers in 1905.[6] Although Zululand's first sugarmills were erected by successful millers-cum-planters from across the Thukela, these were central sugarmills: the holders of milling concessions in Zululand could not also grow cane there, and their mills crushed cane supplied exclusively by white settler-farmers. These settlers were on the whole relatively smaller growers than the independent growers and millers-cum-planters south of the Thukela. They also differed from their southern neighbours in that they were never as dependent on Indian workers – indentured or free – for the cultivation of cane.

Given these particular regional differences, it stands to reason that the 1913 Indian strike did not have an immediate and uniform impact on all growers. The brunt of the strike itself was borne by millers-cum-planters and other estate-owners in the oldest sugar-producing areas of Natal.

Ultimately, every grower – south or north of the Thukela – was to feel the strike's indirect consequences. Those owners who became directly embroiled in the strike, followed up the use of extreme force against striking workers with an appeal to the government for assistance to rally labour in order to reduce cane losses.[7] Their appeal, via the Natal Sugar Association (NSA), received a swift reaction through the agency of Natal's Chief Native Commissioner, R. H. Addison, who asked the employers to furnish him with additional information. Although Addison had been instructed by his superiors to render aid to the estate-owners, he was to do so subject to their fulfilment of certain conditions. It was of special concern to the government that African workers who might be recruited through tribal chiefs and headmen should be paid wages which were as 'high as possible to compete with Rand agents', and that measures should be taken to guarantee recruits against being 'turned adrift' once the strike had ended.[8]

Encouraged by the prospect of governmental aid, and notwithstanding that cane losses were already a *fait accompli*, the NSA immediately responded to Addison on 1 December 1913 with the announcement that its Committee was 'most anxious to consider means whereby the supply of Native Labour to the Planters can be permanently increased'.[9] Leaving little doubt as to the level of the employers' anxiety, the NSA was meanwhile urgently canvassing its members and compiling a report which was dispatched to Addison within six days of his request for information. Although it was noted in the report that 'owing to the crushing season being now so near its end, very few planters are in immediate want of labour', this second missive included a specific requisition for workers direly needed by three of the NSA's members. It also outlined the terms of employment which recruits in general could expect.[10]

It was a significant document in that it articulated a commitment to a wide-ranging programme. The assurance was given that African recruits would not be prejudiced by the termination of the Indian strike; 30s. plus lodgings and rations was accepted as the normal monthly payment for adult male recruits; and the NSA membership was pronounced 'willing to forthwith erect accommodation so that the Natives can establish their women-folk on the Estates, and to employ both women and children – former at 10s. per month plus food, latter according to size and age'.[11] There was also a narrower concern expressed by the NSA with regard to the 180 workers urgently requisitioned by the three employers from the Tongaat district, two of whom were millers-cum-planters. The NSA's opinion was that if these workers could be recruited and employed 'in the main centres of disaffection the moral effect upon the Indians would be enormous and would do much towards breaking the present strike'.[12]

By furnishing the necessary information, the NSA had given Addison the signal to commence the recruitment drive. Yet no sooner had the rapidly executed preparations set the administrative machinery in motion than the wheels of officialdom seemed to lose their momentum. This was not entirely due to inherent bureaucratic impediments; initially it was simply that no workers came forth in response to the offers transmitted to tribal chiefs and headmen via local magistrates.[13] When the employers in the sugar industry then renewed their appeal, they sensed a certain obduracy on the government's part.

The renewed appeal was made when two millers-cum-planters, one from the south coast and the other from the north coast, represented the NSA at a meeting with the Director of Native Labour on 15 December 1913. They argued the case for government intervention in the labour market with a view to securing a continuous supply of workers under the terms which the NSA had earlier outlined to Addison. The government was expected to intervene, principally, by proscribing touting for non-sugar workers in a 50-mile-wide coastal zone between Pondoland's southern border deep in the Transkei, and northern Zululand; and by enabling estate-owners to recruit foreign workers from north of latitude 22°S. It turned out to be a futile appeal, for the employers gained nothing more from it than the Director of Native Labour's pledge to support the idea of recruiting 'a trial batch of tropical labourers', and his promise to convey their proposals to the Prime Minister.[14]

*   *   *   *   *

In their clamour for labour the employers were striving to gain access to distant sources; they also wished to see touting abolished locally. Neither objective could be reached without the government's assistance in affording employers in the sugar industry a relative advantage over other employers of African labour, notably those Witwatersrand mine-owners who recruited African labour along the coast. This constituted a formidable predicament, and the sugar-producers persevered with their representations to the highest levels of government.[15] These endeavours were mostly in vain, and the employers in the sugar industry were forced to accept that they had been left largely to their own devices.

If the estate-owners bemoaned the success enjoyed by the Witwatersrand mining houses in siphoning labour from what they regarded virtually as their own labour reservoir in the coastal districts, they appear not to have been brought to their knees for want of labour. Government officials may not have responded to their every plea, but the state at large ensured – not least of all through the 1913 Native Land Act – that the general conditions for the development of capitalism in agriculture were favourable. Thus even if labour shortfalls were experienced, the estate-owners were presented with ways of offsetting the rapid decline in the number of Indian workers in the sugar industry. Some employers did, as the following evidence illustrates, absorb limited numbers of African tenants who were caught in an incipient proletarianisation process along the sugar belt. Most of them, it is subsequently shown, adopted a more aggressive mode of recruiting wage labour.

Proletarianisation along the sugar belt was a process which during the inter-war period encompassed the pressures of dispossession and the institution of labour tenancy.[16] South of the Thukela River, dispossession could involve the direct and personal uprooting of Africans by estate-owners or their proxies, as the manager of Hulett's Tinley Manor estates explained before the Beaumont Commission in mid-1914:

> Every day Europeans are reclaiming land for sugar planting and it means moving kaffirs off the land; already a big number have moved backwards . . . The native is a peculiar man to deal with, he will move from his patch of ground – his private land – if he sees the reason you desire him to shift; for instance, if you are putting cane down near him. I have moved a lot on account of taking up their land for sugar.[17]

While there were Africans who were being dispossessed of their land, or denied continued access to already alienated land, others were being drawn into arrangements which obliged them to render labour service to white land-owners on whose farms they resided. In his evidence before the Beaumont Commission, Col. F. Addison, the owner of a large sugar estate situated between Durban and the Thukela, succinctly described the nature of labour tenancy on his property:

> I get latterly a good many (workers) from my own place, but I employ anybody who offers. We own a considerable amount of land and we have a number of kraals on the farms. It is only of late that they give labour; formerly they paid rent and worked where they liked. I have no farms, however, outside the cane area. It is not the practice for planters to own land outside of the cane area for labour purposes.[18]

Addison proceeded by according recognition to the value which a resident reserve platoon of labour had for employers like himself:

> In consideration for letting them squat on my land I have a number of men whom I can fall back upon. When the (1913 Indian) strike was on I had 150 and I think it was due to that fact that my coolies did not strike.[19]

Occasionally dispossession and labour tenancy successively impinged on the same coastal African community. Such an incidence of Africans being dispossessed of their land and then becoming 'squatters' was sketched out by W. Campbell, another large employer who was, unlike Addison, the owner of a 'labour farm':

> Our labour farm is 700 acres; we have not more than 30 kraals there now, of probably about a hundred souls. I do not suppose we get more than 20 natives at the outside from there. We pay them exactly the same as we pay any other native. We only call on them in times of stress, such as the Indian strike recently. They do not belong to the location, they come from farms that have been taken up for sugar lands.[20]

To the north of the Thukela, in Zululand, the occupation of land by white cane-farmers amounted to much the same thing for the resident Africans, but on a much smaller scale. Although the Zululand employers appeared neither to be in a position to boast of access to 'labour farms' nor to have many Africans on their lands, some evidently laid store by labour tenancy. Tenants, it was pointed out by one of the Zululand growers, were 'welcome to stay, provided they work, and white occupation does them no harm'.[21] Lower Umfolozi's magistrate was obviously of the opinion that Africans would have been unreasonable to refuse the growers 'welcome': those relatively few Africans who remained on the sugar farms as tenants, and earned 30s. to £2 a month when their labour was required, were considered by him to be 'quite well off'.[22]

Tenancy along the sugar belt was on the whole based upon the receipt of wages and household residence rights, rather than the productive use of land. As the lands under sugar-cane expanded and dispossession proceeded apace, the possibilities for domestic agriculture by tenants would have shrunk, and there was certainly no place on an estate for tenant pastoralism on any significant scale. Such a system of wage-tenancy may have served as a stop-gap for some employers but it came nowhere near to meeting their labour requirements. In short, dispossession and labour tenancy along the sugar belt were symptomatic of expanding estate agriculture; they were both transitional phenomena and of limited impact.

The demise of the indentured labour system meant then that the estate-owners had perforce to submit to the vagaries of the labour market. In this market, as in any other infused with the spirit of capitalism, there was a tendency for the strongest bidders to reap the greatest rewards; however, its specific terms of trade precluded none of the competitors from sharing the risks of paying for a commodity which might only be partly, or possibly never, delivered.

The estate-owners' deeper immersion in the market for wage-labour was accompanied by the adoption of an aggressive style of recruitment. This was manifested in the payment of wages in advance becoming the *sine qua non* of labour recruitment along the sugar belt.[23] Advances, as government officials frequently lamented, bred discontent amongst employers and wily opportunism amongst workers. Writing on the matter early in 1918, Natal's Chief Native Commissioner observed that:

> These advances are in various sums of money – of from £5 upwards. In the cases brought to my notice the agreement was to work off these sums in the usual monthly wages varying from 15/- to £2. The chief complaint was as to the constant absence of the Natives from the service of farmers and planters – constant absence which often necessitates the arrest and punishment of the Natives. In other cases Natives have borrowed money and disappeared to Johannesburg. Advances which should take say 6 to 9 months to work off often extend to double that period. One Sugar Planter in particular told me that he had as much as £500 in advances to Natives and had 60 Natives in his books, but he considered himself lucky if he had 15 or 20 of these men at work.[24]

Tensions caused by the use of advances rose highest in Zululand, where it was clear that the workers were unimpeded by the legal devices which were designed to limit rather than to enlarge their capacity to bargain with employers. The Zululand growers were in a sense being held to ransom by African workers. In the Lower Umfolozi district, for example, advances commonly ranged from £5 to £10; and with some workers playing the field, by having several employers extend them advances, it was hardly surprising that 'in many cases trouble arises between master and servant, in the working off of advances'.[25] The relevant officials, egged on by anxious local growers, expended considerable effort on tightening up as well as clarifying existing controls on the practice of advancing wages.[26] Unimpressed by that effort, the Zululand Planters' Union (ZPU) sought revisions to the Pass Laws and constraints on the advances system in order to render the local labour market more amenable to their own ends.[27]

Left to their own devices, the sugar-producers (primarily those north of the Thukela) had become doleful spectators of the costly exhibition of agility put on for them by partly proletarianised coastal labour. Some (primarily those south of the Thukela) evidently managed to avoid the spectacle. This they did by supplementing locally recruited African workers with *inter alia*, re-indentured Indian workers (albeit in ever-diminishing numbers) tenants, workers tapped from 'labour farms', or foreign workers.[28]

The quest for foreign workers continued unabated, and late in November 1917 the NSA's representatives were to be found trying to convince the Minister of Native Affairs that sugar-producers should be permitted to import labour. They hoped to win his sympathy by telling him of the success enjoyed by certain sugar-producers who had recently employed 'some 400 Rhodesian Natives who work for about six to nine months and have not been inoculated. They come over the border voluntarily from Amalanga District. They are entirely satisfactory and their health is good'.[29] Their proposal was in the event immediately rejected by the Minister.[30]

Within a fortnight the two NSA representatives, W. Pearce and D. Eadie, were repeating their case in subtly different terms before Natal's Chief Native Commissioner, C.A. Wheelwright. Their purpose on this occasion was to discuss the objectives of the newly formed Natal Coast Labour Recruiting Corporation (NCLRC). The NCLRC had been floated as a limited liability company, with a board of management comprising the NSA's executive committee.[31] Some of the NSA's grander ideals for the NCLRC, Wheelwright was told, included the introduction to Natal of workers from the British and Portuguese colonies in the south-eastern tropics; the absorption of workers rejected by the Witwatersrand's Native Recruiting Corporation; and the stationing of a recruiter in Zululand. Ever-sensitive to the politics of agrarian capital, they viewed circumstances south of the Thukela as being 'more delicate' than in Zululand, making it necessary to confine recruiting in Natal 'to areas where farms will not be touched'.[32]

Talk of Zululand becoming a NCLRC target was quickly removed from the realm of ideals. Within three weeks of Wheelwright's meeting with the NSA pair, he was informed of well-advanced plans to establish a NCLRC labour depot at Empangeni, where recruits would be lodged and fed while awaiting allocation to an estate. The NSA had no illusions about some of the difficulties that might be encountered in attempting to attract workers to the depot. It was on the one hand perceived that 'the natives appear to find it possible to subsist on a minimum of labour for the planters and others'; on the other hand, employers in Zululand were considered guilty of having promoted through the system of advances, 'a state of affairs in which the native practically dictates his own terms as to time and period of working'.[33] Clearly, the NSA had identified a prominent role for Wheelwright in the elimination of those obstacles.

Exactly four years had passed since the NSA's abortive venture with Wheelwright's predecessor, Addison, to recruit local workers on a large scale. Was it not a case of foolhardy optimism for the NSA now, under the NCLRC mantle, to be attempting to enlist the support of the Chief Native Commissioner in a similar venture? Evidently not. In the first place, the NCLRC had the financial means to undertake systematic recruiting. Shares in the NCLRC were issued according to the buyers' labour needs; each subscriber being theoretically entitled to a recruit per share held in the Corporation. Thus, whereas the NSA was neither constitutionally nor financially competent to function as a recruiting organisation, the NCLRC had the wherewithal to employ recruiting agents, set up depots, and perform the relevant administrative tasks, not least of which was the regulation of wages.

Secondly, Zululand offered an irresistible nearby source of labour, and the NSA was willing to court internecine conflict in order to wrest the initiative from workers in Zululand who were, it was said, dictating their own terms as to time and period of working. A strategy of combining encroachment on its Zululand brethren's territory with more distant recruiting, backed by the NCLRC's resources, could enable the NSA to accomplish what it had failed to do four years earlier; Wheelwright's co-operation could expedite the NSA's mission.

*   *   *   *   *

With the advent of the NCLRC, all the ramifications of heterogeneity amongst estate-owners were cast in stark relief. In Zululand the growers were affiliated to the ZPU through six district associations, all of which were hard put to dislodge labour recruits (who in any event could generally command higher wages outside Zululand) from the local reserves. Their rickety financial and organisational resources made them no match for the predatory forces from the south, namely the millers-cum-planters and their largest independent growers who constituted the bulk of the NSA's membership. By virtue of its members' omnipotence in the orbit of cane pricing and sugar marketing, and as the representative organ of the largest and most highly capitalised employers in the sugar industry, the NSA wielded considerable power. It was therefore to be expected that the Zululand growers should have harboured doubts about their own capacity to withstand the threat posed by the NCLRC.

As a preliminary gesture, before striking into Zululand, the NCLRC threw open its doors to growers in the Empangeni district, the overwhelming majority of whom had not earlier bought shares in the corporation. Those who declined were to know that the 'recruiting operations . . . will be gone on with independently of the number of members in Empangeni district'.[34] The smug attitude of the NSA/NCLRC executives was counterpoised by alarm and anger amongst the Zululand growers. Apart from its aggressive wording, the NCLRC's letter to the Empangeni growers was an affront to the handful in the district who had earlier joined on the understanding that the corporation's efforts were to be directed towards the recruitment of Rhodesian workers. There was no question as to the threat constituted by the NCLRC's unexpected shift. Thus, with cane lands expanding in the district, while 'every good mealie harvest for the natives decreases the number who will go out to work', the Empangeni growers were moved to lodge a strong protest with the Chief Native Commissioner about the NCLRC's action.[35]

Pressure was again mounting on the government to take matters in hand, and a meeting in January 1918 between the NCLRC representatives and the Prime Minister precipitated the announcement that an official investigation would be made into the alleged labour shortage in Natal.[36] If the announcement that a (Native Affairs) Departmental Committee would conduct its inquiry in mid-1918 subdued the animus amongst sugar-producers, it did not of course eliminate their problem.

In its continued search for contract workers, the NCLRC found significant openings in the Cape (Pondoland and the Transkei), and lesser ones elsewhere (Swaziland and the northern Transvaal). The opportunity of recruiting in the Cape enabled the corporation to make a proposition to its members. To ensure the scheme's viability, some 1 000 workers would have to be requisitioned for a minimum contract of 210 shifts. The workers in question would be 'youths of from 16 to 19, a certain number of older men not suitable for mining work, and a percentage of men who prefer agriculture to mine work'. Married women would also be supplied if accommodation could be provided for them and their recruited spouses. For the privilege of being supplied with these workers, some of whom were not the most likely candidates for estate work, a fee of £3 5s. was payable to the corporation for every male and a pound less for every female recruited for 7-month terms; £3 15s. was the fee set for 9-month (270-shift) male recruits. The discrepancy in recruiting costs, which was explained by the absence of capitation fees for women, was replicated in the wages set for the recruits: a ticket of 30 shifts would be worked for £2 in the case of men, and 'at a lower rate' in the case of women.[37] All told, these workers would be more expensive to recruit than others, as their employers were not spared having to advance them £2. However, the adoption of a ticket system meant that each worker would be paid less for a day's work than one who was paid £2 per month.

A ticket system was also a means of cancelling the losses usually incurred by employers on days when workers did not appear for work; nevertheless, it appears not to have inflated attendance rates. Frequent absences from work, notably on Mondays and Tuesdays, and 'desertions' were prevalent; and advances, if they were not altogether lost, were seldom recouped in the shortest possible period. While there were some who attempted to curb the workers' manipulation of the advances system by offering cattle instead of cash as a recruiting incentive, the employers were virtually impotent when it came to policing the system. The sugar-producers' dependence on the risky advances system was exacerbated (particularly for those who did not belong to the NCLRC) by the low numbers of workers who were resident on the estates and therefore vulnerable to tighter control. Although some Zululand growers found it impossible to provide accommodation for a full complement of workers, those growers in Zululand and elsewhere who had erected compounds complained of low occupancy. Togt and weekly-paid labour was becoming more widespread, with increasing numbers of women and children being employed especially by Zululand growers. Young boys were also becoming preponderant amongst the declining number of Mpondo workers on the south coast. It was against the background of this largely qualitative rather than quantitative labour shortage that on the one hand, the NCLRC's schemes succeeded; and that, on the other, employers pleaded the need for more active police involvement in rounding up 'deserters'; for systematic corporal punishment – 'Lack of the lash tends to shortage'; and for modifications to the Pass Laws that would restrict the mobility of workers.[38]

In the eyes of the law African estate-workers were not 'Native Labour'. Like other agricultural workers they were not recruited in terms of the 1911 Native Labour Regulation Act, nor were they necessarily registered in labour districts or subject to all the other strictures imposed on African workers in mining and the manufacturing industry. But if their status as 'Servants' within the ambit of Masters and Servants legislation afforded them opportunities to escape capture by the net intended for 'Native Labour', estate-workers were no longer in firm command over the pace at which they worked.

Diminished estate-workers' autonomy in this respect stemmed from the evolution of piece-work, which was an elaboration of the employers' controls embedded in the ticket system. The employment of workers at piece-rates was by mid-1918 widely accepted amongst the sugar-producers, notably those to the south of the Thukela. In some cases this method of remuneration incorporated the payment of bonuses, and in isolated instances the levying of penalties, depending upon whether the stipulated daily task was exceeded or unfulfilled. This sophistication of control over the workers' productivity during the crucial cutting season presupposed the availability of a weighbridge, and was consequently not applied ubiquitously. Where piece-work was the norm, it was usual for the basic task of a cutter to be set at 2 000 lb. per day, with 1d. per 100 lb. being the standard bonus (or penalty).

Whether or not workers were paid according to piece-rates, the productivity of any estate's work-force was ultimately a function of human strength and endurance. Patriarchy, too, entered into the productivity formula, and women were likely to have experienced tension between the demands of wage labour and those of household obligations. Although cane-cutting was conventionally done by men, when women were called on to perform the task – a not uncommon occurrence in Zululand especially – the employers' expectations were not as high. Thus women cutters doing piece-work were usually paid by the 100 lb. rather than according to a stipulated daily minimum. Boys, although widely employed, were seldom assigned to cane-cutting. Clearly, the employers had different expectations of workers according to age and sex, and the regional patterns of estate labour therefore suggested considerable variation in productivity from one part of the sugar belt to another. Of the almost 10 000 Indian workers who were still employed by the members of the NCLRC in mid-1918, 15 per cent were women; while only 115 women and boys were included amongst their 4 794 African workers.[39] In Zululand, by contrast, African boys constituted almost 17 per cent of the growers' total workforce of 6 622; and a prominent grower from the Gingindlovu district admitted that:

> had it not been for the women we would have been absolutely wiped out this year . . . Three of us (in the district) employ over 150 women and girls. They go back to the Location every afternoon. It is growing; we have no other labour. I reduce the task of a woman one-third. They get the same pay as a man, and two feeds a day. I am paying little youngsters 1s a day, to save my cane . . . 'Picanins' get 6d. a day. When I am planting they carry the cane along; they are not strong enough to hoe. We should like a method of indenture for these boys. I pay 'umfaans' up to 15/- a month. We don't want outside competition for our 'umfaans'.[40]

Just as the expected levels of productivity varied according to the composition of the workforce, so too did wages. Advances of amounts ranging from £2 to as high as £20 were now being made to entice the bulk of estate-workers, and with a wage ceiling of £2 per month effectively covering the entire workforce, they were generally held in a state of indebtedness. Togt labour, and women in general, commonly received 1s. a day, and boys about 6d. This wage structure was not radically altered by the inception of piece-work, as workers mostly treated the prescribed task as their maximum daily stint. This was of course the beauty of piece-rates as far as employers were concerned: without additional expenditure, every worker could be compelled (or, according to the growers, encouraged) to perform the assigned tasks and a day's output could be predicted on the basis of the number of workers reporting for work.[41]

In the course of its investigation into the alleged labour shortage along the sugar belt, the Departmental Committee found cause for concern in the fact that very few workers showed any interest in the bonuses, small as they were. As an interim corrective measure the Department of Native Labour put out a notice in the Zulu-language newspaper *Ilanga lase Natal* which urged chiefs and headmen to spread 'the propaganda of Labour' by drawing attention to potential bonuses and to the inviolability of contracts.[42] Yet, when their Report was gazetted in December 1918, the Departmental Committee construed the labour question 'with less apprehension than many of the witnesses have expressed'.[43] Substantial material incentives and sympathetic management on the estates were identified as the missing ingredients required for a stable labour market.

Apart from their specific criticisms of the sugar-producers for providing inadequate housing, rations, and monetary incentives, the Departmental Committee furnished a telling (and ideological) account of the deleterious consequences of the advances system. Their proffered remedy hinged on a conservation/dissolution approach to the culture and economy of traditional Zulu society. Thus on the one hand they condemned communal agriculture on the grounds that it 'neutralises individual ambition and militates against progress'; the 'magic of ownership', it was declared, 'is an axiom of political economy and in its absence in the native polity lies the secret of his lack of ambition'.[44]

On the other hand, their critique of the advances system came with a dose of moralism and an implicit denial that the acceptance of advances by workers reflected either 'ambition' or 'progress'. Advances, it was claimed:

> are almost invariably for initial payments in respect of 'lobolo' or other matters more or less connected with sexual relations, such as the fee for 'vula mlomo' or for compensation for seduction. Not only is the advance system pernicious on general grounds but it lends itself to sex immorality, as the security it affords to natives encourages a laxity of sex relations, admitting as it does to payment (at the expense of the employer) for transgressions of the moral code.[45]

If these concerns were hardly likely to have been at the forefront of the individual employers' thinking on the matter of advances, the intimation that official curbs on the system were in the offing, and the support expressed for institutionalised recruiting, evoked widespread interest amongst sugar-producers. The level of interest in the report and its recommendations was unsurprising considering that approximately 90 per cent of permanent workers in the sugar industry were now in receipt of wages paid in advance.[46] However, if large-scale recruiting was encouraged by the report, its recommendations concerning state intervention were not given immediate effect, and advances remained part and parcel of exchange on the local labour market.

Large-scale recruiting on the basis of advances could influence the patterns of migrancy within Natal quite markedly. During the three-month period ending on 31 May 1919, for example, the south coast millers-cum-planters, Reynolds Bros, took into their employment 235 of the 604 workers signed on in Zululand by their recruiting agent. The total amount advanced to the 604 was £3 558 18s. An outlay of such magnitude, to which rail fares, monthly wages of £2, and the agent's monthly salary of £25 would ultimately be added, was quite beyond the reach of a typical Zululand grower. But far more pertinently, the risks and subsequent losses taken by Reynolds Bros. meant that there were 369 potential workers who were unlikely to submit to work on Zululand estates in the immediate future.[47]

While the Zululand growers were smarting under the blows meted out by large recruiters, magistrates were experiencing difficulties in collecting hut tax from the indebted recipients of advances.[48] The use of large advances had obviously become an endemic worry for employers and officials in every corner of Natal: in the north it induced Zululand growers to consider recruiting in Pondoland;[49] in the south it drained the Ixopo farmers' labour reservoir;[50] and in the midlands it had the owners of coal-mines scuttling to Wheelwright for protection.[51]

It is highly probable that there was a correspondence between surges of localised advances-induced trauma, and the activities of large recruiters. The likelihood of that correspondence is difficult to gainsay in the light of the text of a spirited homily penned in August 1920 for the NCLRC's board by the corporation's superintendent. Parkin, the NCLRC's chief recruiting official, revealed that despite their having raised wages by 10s. to £2 2s. for 30 shifts, the members had only obtained some 1 700 recruits through the corporation between mid-1919 and mid-1920; 1 500 fewer than the previous year.[52] A shortfall of these proportions would have been passed on through the advances system from the large to the small employer.

Growers in Zululand were the chief victims in the disparate struggle for labour by millers-cum-planters and small estate-owners, but competition by means of advances was not the only source of friction between the two groups. If the misgivings of one of the Baxter Commission's deponents are anything to go by, African workers recruited by sugarmillers were first put to field work and registered as agricultural labour, and then later moved into the sugarmills without being accorded their rights as industrial labour.[53] Would the propaganda of labour be sufficient to eliminate the inequities between large and small employers, and to eradicate the malign effects of the advances system (which one grower had ingeniously dubbed the 'Zululand sore')?[54]

Zululand's affliction, according to the diagnosis made in 1922 by the Baxter Commission, was more complicated than a rash of advances. The commission observed that whereas cane grown on hilly lands generally had a 13 per cent sucrose content, 'flats' cane had a sucrose content of 10,5 per cent.[55] The topography of large parts of Zululand was seen to be disadvantageous in this respect, although lower sucrose content in Zululand might well have been a function of the habitual burning before cutting to overcome the difficulties of trashing Uba cane. More significantly, cane yields were on the decline in Zululand; this being put down to poor cultural methods and mismanagement. The commission could thus point out that 'those planters have done well, some of them very well, who have worked their farms energetically, to their full extent and with proper methods of cultivation and who knew how to handle labour'.[56] Most, however, could not rid themselves of their complicated affliction.

What the Baxter Commission had in mind when referring to the 'handling' of labour is not clear, but contemporary investigations into employment practices along the entire sugar belt left no doubt that labour was being treated in anything but a beneficent manner.[57] Workers did not complacently adapt to the rigours of estate life, and magistrates in the Transkei bore testimony during their 1924 conference to the growing resistance by men in the territory to taking up employment on the sugar estates. At the conference, mention was made of signs that housing for sugar workers had improved, but attention was also drawn to poor rations, 'strong indications of cruelty', and a noticeable deterioration in the health of estate-workers returning to the Transkei.[58] Health officials were equally aware of the situation, but their attempt in 1925 to revise the 'distinctly unsatisfactory' medical facilities for sugar workers were thwarted by dissenting employers.[59] Later in the year, the Chief Native Commissioner and the state's Durban-based Assistant Health Officer saw fit to remark that 'conditions of employment may in many respects be regarded as fairly satisfactory'.[60] This was an uncharacteristic and oddly less than precise remark coming from these two officials; all the more so because at about the same time the ZPU tacitly acknowledged that workers were being abused by voicing its condemnation of 'employers of Native Labour who use methods of coercion and punishment other than those recognised by the Law'.[61] It is inconceivable that the improvements alluded to by official commentators had made a profound impression on sugar workers.

Mounting opprobrium and concern for the plight of sugar workers coincided with the beginnings of a dramatic expansion in cane production. Between 1924 and 1932 the area under cane in Natal was increased by 50 per cent.[62] This expansionary phase straddled the crisis in the world market for sugar, when South Africa's large crop contributed to global overproduction. One of the local responses to the crisis was the government-orchestrated Fahey Conference Agreement, which was struck between millers and growers in 1926. The agreement embodied principles of protection for both parties, and it promised greater efficiency in production and greater equity in the disposal of revenue from sugar sales. In the seven seasons following the Fahey Conference, the tonnage of cane produced by independent growers and millers-cum-planters increased by 53 per cent and 110 per cent respectively.[63] Voluminous increases in production obviously betokened the enlargement of lands under cane, but they were also indicative of the success of experimentation in cane varieties. An experimental station had been founded in 1924 on the recommendation of the Baxter Commission, and Uba had begun to be gradually ousted by mosaic-free varieties with higher sucrose levels and milling qualities.

Expanded cultivation and output were undoubtedly also encouraged by the fact that the sugar-producers had greater cause for confidence *vis-à-vis* labour supplies. The capitation fees payable to recruiting agents had dropped somewhat to between 45s. and 50s.,[64] and although the agents occasionally ran foul of officials in the Transkei in the late 1920s and early 1930s for the 'irregular recruitment' of juveniles,[65] Pondoland was reliably established as the principal external source of contract labour. Moreover, prolonged drought and the effects of the Great Depression were releasing a country-wide flood of unemployed Africans, to the extent that by April 1931 Natal's employers of agricultural labour were confronted with an estimated surplus of 10 000 workers.[66] Faced with this fortuitous surfeit of potential recruits, the NCLRC went into voluntary liquidation later in the same year.

$$*\qquad*\qquad*\qquad*\qquad*$$

The demise of the NCLRC confirmed the institutionalisation of oscillating migrancy whereby field workers were recurrently contracted for the seven months every year during which cane harvesting and milling were carried out. But while this represented a triumph for the millers-cum-planters and the larger independent growers, the Zululand growers had not been relieved of the difficulties they experienced in recruiting labour. Relative weakness in the recruiting stakes was compounded for the Zululand growers by local ecological and economic conditions: they operated in a territory where levels of food production in the reserves were not so low as to force great hordes of Africans into wage labour on the growers' terms, and where malaria was endemic.

The case for Zululand's growers to be assisted in the procurement of labour was given impetus by Swellengrebel's 1931 report on malaria.[67] The report was published during a devastating spate of malaria outbreaks which claimed thousands of lives throughout Natal, but particularly in Zululand, between 1929 and 1932.[68] Swellengrebel adduced seemingly incontrovertible evidence in support of his major recommendation that only workers who were deemed 'malaria tolerant' be permitted to work in areas such as Zululand where malaria was endemic. However, it was to be a few years before effect was duly given to the recommendation.

Of the almost 40 000 workers who were reported to have been employed in the fields sector of the sugar industry in 1934, no more than 12 per cent were now classified as Indians.[69] An indeterminate but probably minor number of the 33 000 African field workers came from Mozambique. The frequent illegality of the Mozambican workers' presence would explain their absence from the sugar-producers' records.[70] In any event their ranks were set to swell after the terms of the Mozambique Convention were renegotiated towards the end of 1934.[71] Under the revised terms, workers were formally allowed entry into Zululand from Mozambique, a country of malarial endemicity. As was to be expected, the arrangement found favour amongst the Zululand growers, and 'malaria intolerant' field labour previously drawn from Pondoland, Basutoland, and elsewhere was immediately threatened with displacement from Zululand.

The displacement of distant migrants from Zululand was completed in the wake of an official inquiry into the Zululand growers' labour affairs in 1935. All the magisterial districts where cane was grown in Zululand were included in what was defined in September 1935 as a 'malarial area', and in which only local labour and workers from regions of high malarial endemicity could be employed.[72] Although this proclamation effectively added the final touches to the map of the sugar belt's geography of labour, it did not signal the inception of greater uniformity in employment conditions.

When the Report of the Native Farm Labour Committee was published in 1939 its authors were obliged to acknowledge the absence of either precise or current statistics on field labour in the sugar industry. Estimates were nevertheless made as to the origins of the bulk of the estates' workforces; suggesting that 40 per cent of field workers in Zululand now came from Mozambique, and 10 to 60 per cent of those employed by the various sugar producers in the rest of Natal were from Pondoland. Such a contrast was emphasised by the observed regional differences in employment conditions and productivity. Zululand's manifold shortcomings were attributed to its employers being of a 'poorer class'; to the depressive effect of imported labour on wages; and to the relatively low productivity of inefficiently managed labour. Whereas in Zululand the basic wage was generally 30s. per 30 shifts, higher wages and marginally superior accommodation and rations were provided for workers who were employed south of the Thukela. The report also conveyed the impression that the latter workers were now being subjected to a far more scientific form of management than their counterparts in Zululand. Gledhow Sugar Estates, for example, paid cutters £2 per 30 shifts and a bonus of 1d. per 100 pounds over the specified daily task, which varied according to whether or not the cane was burnt prior to being cut. An even more elaborate specification of tasks was devised by Reynolds Bros, according to the varieties of cane being cut.[73].

A pronounced imbalance in class forces – between agrarian bourgeois and dispossessed peasant – had led to the emergence of oscillating migrancy as the preponderant labour form on South Africa's sugar estates in the aftermath of the ending of the Indian indenture system. The rhythm of trade on the market for migrant field labour was consonant with agrarian underdevelopment in the Natal Reserves, in the Transkeian territories, and in southern Mozambique, as much as with the beat of the mining and manufacturing sectors. In other words the sugar-producers had become immersed in the political economy of the national labour market; a process which had been closely monitored, though not completely attended to by the state.

Unlike the situation which had prevailed in the latter half of the nineteenth century, sugar capital had not had the sway over the Union government to effect an easy transition from one labour form to another. To be sure, sugar capital had enjoyed periods of fruitful representation in Parliament, but neither under the Smuts administration nor after 1924 were sugar-producers unambiguously assisted by the state. It goes without saying, that a capitalist state does not of necessity commit its every apparatus to the direct and unequivocal service of each of the multiplicity of groups within the bourgeoisie, agrarian or otherwise. In this instance, millers-cum-planters had been reasonably assisted as manufacturers and distributors yet, as employers, they and independent growers on both sides of the Thukela had made little headway without a struggle. Out of the estate-owners' own differentiation there had arisen situations which elicited different responses from respective agents and branches of the state. These state organs had nevertheless been consistent in one respect: they had combined a favourable disposition towards the estate-owners as agrarian producers with a scepticism of their specific demands as employers. Against this backdrop, the resurrection of migrancy was for the employers a happy outcome of their quest for a predictable and reliable alternative to the Indian indentured labour system.

In another sense, the institutionalisation of migrancy represented a redefinition of the terrain upon which agrarian workers would engage sugar capital in a continuing struggle over the fruits of their labour. That this struggle would be difficult was certain; for one thing, the terrain was deeply scarred by the employers' controls to which the migrant labour form and the nature of estate production lent themselves. For another, the Thukela River retained the semblance of a barrier to unity between differently endowed employers as well as between differently exploited workers of diverse regional origins.

REFERENCES

1. There were thousands of Indian workers who still toiled in the sugar industry under first, second, and sometimes subsequent terms of reindenture. See M. Swan, *Gandhi: the South African experience* (Johannesburg, Ravan, 1985), pp. 273, 286–87.

2. South Africa's production was 33 787 short tons in 1903; 19 238 in 1904; and 92 153 for the 1913–14 season. See *South African Sugar Year Books*. For an analysis of sugar milling in the post-war period, see D. Lincoln, 'Employment practices, sugar technology, and sugar mill labour: crisis and change in the South African sugar industry, 1914–1939' in B. Albert and A. Graves (eds), *The world sugar economy in war and depression, 1914–40* (London and New York, Routledge, 1988).

3. P. Harries, 'Plantations, passes and proletarians: labour and the colonial state in nineteenth century Natal', *Journal of Southern African Studies*, 13, 1987, pp. 372–99.

4. The state's intervention initially came in response to repeated appeals by sugarmillers and growers to have the domestic sugar price raised. The consequent 1922 (Baxter) Commission of Inquiry into the sugar industry was followed by another official investigation which yielded its own report; viz. Board of Trade and Industries (BTI), Report no. 66, *Report on the sugar industry*, 1926. The latter report paved the way for the 1926 Fahey Conference out of which came an agreement between millers and growers on the economics of sugar production and income disposal. Shortly before the terms of the Fahey Agreement had run their 10-year course, another report was compiled on the basis of a further investigation; viz. BTI, Report no. 194, *The sugar industry: working of conference agreement and future organization*, 1935. See also

I. Behrmann, 'A study of the economics of sugar-cane production in Natal' (unpublished D. Phil. thesis, University of Natal, Pietermaritzburg, 1959), A. H. Duminy, 'The Natal sugar interest and the Smuts government, 1919–1924' in P. S. Thompson (comp.), *Natal and the Union, 1909–1939*, (History Workshop Papers, Department of Historical Studies, University of Natal, Pietermaritzburg, typescript publication, 1978), and R. F. Osborn, *Valiant harvest: the founding of the South African sugar industry, 1848–1926* (Durban, South African Sugar Association, 1964).

5. See P. Richardson, 'The Natal sugar industry, 1849–1905: an interpretative essay' in Bill Guest and John M. Sellers (eds), *Enterprise and exploitation in a Victorian colony: aspects of the economic and social history of Natal* (Pietermaritzburg, University of Natal Press, 1985). Also see D. Lincoln, 'An ascendant sugarocracy: Natal's millers-cum-planters, 1905–1939', *Journal of Natal and Zulu History*, 11, 1988, pp. 1–39.

6. Colloquial and even official references to Natal after Union did not always acknowledge Zululand as a constituent part of the province. I've used the Thukela River (the original Natal/Zululand border) as a constant means of reference, to distinguish what some after 1910 used to term 'Natal proper', from Zululand. References to the north coast do not apply to Zululand, but only to the coast between Durban and the mouth of the Thukela River.

7. See NAD, CNC 2035, CNC to Burgess, 28 November 1913.

8. *Ibid.*, Campbell to Dept. of Native Affairs, 25 November 1913.

9. *Ibid.*, Fowler to CNC, 1 December 1913.

10. *Ibid.*, Fowler to CNC, 5 December 1913.

11. *Ibid.*

12. *Ibid.* Although relevant statistics are not easy to come by, the situation amongst Indians along the sugar belt towards the end of the strike was as follows:

	Working	On Strike	Gaoled
North Coast	11 060	302	810
South Coast	7 864	154	92
Zululand	1 400	–	–

Source: TAD, GG 898, Gov.–Gen. to Sec. of State, 11 December 1913.

13. NAD, CNC 2035, CNC's circular to magistrates, 9 December 1913; CNC to Fowler, 11 December 1913; Lower Umfolozi magistrate to CNC, 12 December 1913; Pinetown Asst. magistrate to CNC, 18 December 1913; Inanda magistrate to CNC, 14 February 1914. An interesting remark was made by Mtunzini's magistrate, to the effect that he did not 'anticipate that any natives will go down to the Natal Estates (from this part of Zululand) as he had 226 Indain [sic] Male strikers arrested in this Division and natives were employed to keep the Mills going'. (*Ibid.*, Mtunzini magistrate to CNC, 11 December 1913).

14. TAD, GNLB 81, Rough notes on meeting between Dir. of Native Labour and representatives of the sugar planters, 15 December 1913.

15. See for example NAD, CNC 348, Representations by the ZPU requesting that the Division of Hlabisa be closed to all outside recruiting for labour, February–April 1914; TAD, GNLB 81, Notes of meeting between Prime Minister and representatives of the Natal Labour Assoc., 16 March 1914.

16. For an appropriate contextual discussion of dispossession and tenancy during this period see W. Beinart and P. Delius, 'Introduction', in Beinart et al. (eds), *Putting a plough to the ground: accumulation and dispossesion in rural South Africa, 1850–1930* (Johannesburg, Ravan Press, 1986). See also H. Slater, 'Land, labour and capital in Natal: the Natal Land and Colonisation Company, 1860–1948', *Journal of African History*, 16, 1975, pp. 257–83.

17. UG 19–1916, *Report of the Natives' land commission*, vol. II, p. 449.

18. *Ibid.*, pp. 450–51.

19. *Ibid.*

20. *Ibid.*, pp. 446–47.

21. *Ibid.*, pp. 461–62.

22. *Ibid.*, pp. 459–61.

23. For a detailed exposition of the advances system see W. Beinart, *The political economy of Pondoland, 1860 to 1930* (Johannesburg, Ravan, 1982), pp. 55–69.

24. NAD, CNC 36, CNC to SNA, 7 January 1916.

25. *Ibid.*, Tanner to CNC, 31 October 1916.

26. See for example NAD, CNC 2132, Snr. Inspector of Native Reserves in Zululand to CNC, 20 December 1916.

27. For some background information on the ZPU, which was established in 1909, see A. G. Hammond, *South African Cane Growers' Association: the first 50 years* (Durban, South African Cane Growers' Association, (SACGA), 1977).

28. See for example correspondence regarding Umfolozi's employment of 5 men from Nyasaland (accompanied by 3 of their wives) (NAD, CNC 1847, Passes inward, 1916); and NAD, CNC 2105, Natal Estates' application for 140 'tropical' workers, 11 April 1917.

29. NAD, CNC 2118, Notes of interview with Minister of Native Affairs by representatives of Natal sugar planters, 22 November 1917. Of course, the workers in question were not necessarily from Rhodesia at all, but possibly from much further north or east and having made their way 'along the stop-go labour route to the south by a series of well-planned desertions' (C. van Onselen, *Chibaro: African mine labour in Southern Rhodesia 1900–1933* (Johannesburg, Ravan, 1980), p. 230). In any event, the NCLRC's members believed that workers from Mozambique and the Rhodesias were 'the most suitable labourers . . . for this class of work' (TAD, GNLB 252, NCLRC to Dir. of Native Labour, 3 January 1919). That certain employers managed to continue recruiting them was evident from the observation that W. A. Campbell had 'employed 200 to 300 Makalangas some little time back who arrived looking like skeletons and went back pig fat. He had never had a finer type of labourer. Man for man they were the equal at the end of their term of the Indian. They came for 12 months and stayed 15 and would have stayed longer but for the Influenza Epidemic which frightened them away' (TAD, GNLB 308, Notes on meeting, 26 November 1919).

30. NAD, CNC 2118, Notes of interview, 22 November 1917.

31. NAD, CNC 2117, Eadie to CNC, 6 December 1917. The NCLRC's draft articles of association were sent to Wheelwright on 8 December, apparently immediately after the Saturday afternoon interview, (*Ibid.*, 8 December 1917).

32. *Ibid.*, Minutes of Eadie, Pearce and Wheelwright meeting, 8 December 1917. During 1912, the Mtunzini and Lower Umfolozi magisterial divisions were closed to outside recruiters. See Hammond, *Cane Growers' Association*, p. 19; and TAD, GNLB 253, Acting Director of Native Labour to Tongaat Sugar Co. manager, 8 February 1918.

33. NAD, CNC 2118, Eadie to CNC, 28 December 1917.

34. *Ibid.*, SNA to CNC, annexed NCLRC memo., 2 February 1918.

35. *Ibid.*, Dent to CNC, 24 January 1918. They were also alleged to have hatched a strategy to obstruct the NCLRC, and there were indications that an alternative, local recruiting organisation had been considered (*Ibid.*, NCLRC to SNA, 14 February 1918).

36. *Ibid.*, Acting Dir. of Native Labour to CNC, 1 February 1918; CNC to SNA, 8 February 1918; CNC to Dent, 14 February 1918; CNC to NCLRC, 16 February 1918.

37. *Ibid.*, NCLRC instructions and requisition form, *c.* May 1918.

38. *Ibid.*, Report of evidence taken at Stanger, 19 August 1918. See also *ibid.*, Résumés of evidence taken at Gingindlovu, 24 and 25 June 1918.

39. *Ibid.*, Résumé of evidence taken at Durban, 21 and 22 June 1918.

40. *Ibid.*, Dent to CNC, 31 August 1918; Résumés of evidence taken at Gingindlovu, 24 and 25 June 1918.

41. See NAD, CNC 2118, Résumés of evidence to Shortage of Native Labour Committee, June-August 1918.

42. *Ibid.*, Davidson to SNA, 10 October 1918.

43. UG *Government Gazette*, 13 December 1918.

44. *Ibid.*

45. *Ibid.* See also the observations on the recommendations, made in NAD, CNC 2118, Dept. Native Affairs to minister, 28 November 1918.

46. *Ibid.*, Eadie to CNC, 21 January 1919; Dent to CNC, 2 February 1919; Johnson to CNC, 24 March 1919; CNC to SNA, 2 June 1919.

47. *Ibid.*, Jackson to CNC, 31 May 1919; CNC to Jackson, 5 June 1919; Jackson to CNC, 13 June 1919; CNC to SNA, 23 June 1919; CNC to Hill, 24 June 1919.

48. See for example *Ibid.*, Mtunzini magistrate to CNC, 4 June 1919; CNC to Mtunzini magistrate, 11 June 1919; Ingwavuma magistrate to CNC (telegram), 26 August 1919; CNC to Ingwavuma magistrate, 27 August 1919.

49. *Ibid.*, Owen to CNC, 1 September 1919; CNC to Owen, 11 September 1919.

50. *Ibid.*, Stone to Natal Provincial Administrator, 29 September 1919.

51. *Ibid.*, Royston to CNC, 30 September 1919.

52. TAD, GNLB 253, 'The native labour problem of the NCLRC', 21 August 1920.

53. *Ibid.*, SNA to Dir. Native Labour, 23 October 1919.

54. *Ibid.*, Extracts from a paper read at a meeting of the ZPU executive, 12 June 1918.

55. Union of South Africa, *Report of the sugar inquiry commission*, Cape Town, 1922, pp. 8–9.

56. *Ibid.*, p. 11.

57. See for example TAD, GNLB 308, Central coastal area Native Affairs Dept. Inspector to Dept. of Native Labour, 23 August 1921. As late as 1934, the Dept. of Public Health found that 'some of the larger estates' had built workers' quarters which did not meet the Dept.'s regulations, on the assumption that no action would be taken against them once the buildings had been erected (Department of Public Health, *Annual Report* for 1935, p. 53).

58. House of Assembly, Annexure 268 of 1926, Papers relating to labour conditions on the sugar estates, letter from office of Chief Magistrate of Transkeian Territories to SNA, 9 June 1924.

59. Department of Public Health, *Annual Report* for year ending 30 June 1925.

60. House of Assembly, Annexure 268 of 1926, Memo. on plantation labour in Natal, 5 October 1925.

61. *Ibid.*, ZPU Sec. to SNA, 25 November 1925.

62. Behrmann, 'Economics of sugar-cane production', p. 34. Spreading cane fields contributed to the migration of 306 African families from coastal and northern Natal into Zululand between 1926 and 1928, 12 per cent of which were from the Lower Thukela district. (U.C.T. Library, Herbst Papers, D 16, Natal CNC to SNA, 24 September 1928).

63. Behrmann, 'Economics of sugar-cane production', p. 34.

64. BTI, *Report on the sugar industry*, p. 10.

65. U.C.T. Library, Herbst Papers, D 7.9, 'Natlab' to 'Natives', 28 May 1931.

66. *Ibid.*, D 7.7.1, Schedule showing the estimated labour position, April 1931.

67. U.G. *Report on investigation into malaria in the Union of South Africa 1930–31*, Pretoria, 1931.

68. See R. M. Packard, 'Maize, cattle and mosquitoes: the political economy of malaria epidemics in colonial Swaziland', *Journal of African History*, 25, 1984, pp. 189–212.

69. Employment statistics for the South African sugar industry in 1934 were as follows:

		African	Indian	White
Millers' employees:	Mills	4 823	3 190	1 132
	Fields	13 283	3 908	342
Growers' employees:	Fields	20 000	1 000	1 251

Source: *South African Sugar Journal*, 19, 1935, pp. 201–3. A small number of the Indian workers were still serving indentures, and it was not until his *Report* for the year ending 31 Dec. 1936 that the Protector of Immigrants could record that there were no indentured workers in Natal.

70. See A. Jeeves, 'Migrant labour and South African expansion, 1920–1950', *South African Historical Journal*, 18, 1986, pp. 75–6.

71. See S. T. van der Horst, *Native labour in South Africa*, (London, Oxford University Press, 1942), p. 288.

72. G.N. no. 1312 of 6 September 1935, cited in U.G., *Report of the Native farm labour committee, 1937–39*, Pretoria, 1939, p. 61.

73. *Ibid.*, pp. 60–64.

ABSTRACT

The importation of indentured Indian labour was terminated in 1911. Within sixty years Natal's Indians were thereafter transformed from an economically undeveloped community with a high rate of illiteracy that was engaged predominantly in agriculture, mining, manual labour and trade into an urbanised, educated group which was actively involved in all sectors of the regional economy. There was a steady drift to the towns, prompted by population increase, limited access to land and investment capital, urban expansion into peri-urban market-gardening areas and a growing preference for less expensive African labour on the part of sugar estates. In the urban areas Indians again found themselves in competition with Africans for unskilled jobs, and with whites for semi-skilled and skilled posts from which they tended to be excluded in terms of the 'civilised labour' policy. Significant industrial growth after the Second World War forced the abandonment of the pro-white bias of the 1930s and 1940s, providing many more job opportunities for the Indian community. Indian involvement in retail and wholesale trade, dating back to the 1870s, continued to expand in the post-Union period, while movement into other sectors of commerce and into the professions became evident following the availability of secondary and tertiary education and a change in attitude towards the employment of women outside the home. Improved educational standards were achieved through persistent effort on the part of the Indian community and have led to a dramatic upliftment of its economic and social condition. Better education and employment opportunities for Indian women have contributed towards later marriages, the gradual breakdown of the extended family system, a declining birth-rate and higher standards of living. The poverty which was so rife among Indians in Natal during the first half of the twentieth century nevertheless still persists in some areas, particularly in the smaller towns and countryside, and is aggravated by the shortage of land available for Indian housing as a result of legislation passed since the 1940s.

198

AN ECONOMIC TRANSFORMATION: THE INDIAN COMMUNITY IN NATAL

Joy Brain

In 1911, when the importation of indentured labour from India came to an end, there were approximately 113 000 Indians in Natal, including the passenger group who were predominantly traders. At about this time, those free men and women who, having completed their indenture, had re-indentured for a further period – some 23 900 in all – were about equal in number to those who were serving their first period of indenture (22 500).[1] The remainder, indeed the majority, were able to establish themselves in business or agriculture or sell their labour in Natal or across its borders. Restrictions imposed during the pre-Union era prevented Indians from settling in those parts of northern Natal that had been ceded to the colony in 1902, in the Orange Free State, which had restricted the entry of Indians from as early as 1881, and in the Transvaal. They could, and some did, move into the Cape Province but most remained within Natal and Zululand. Although some of the free Indians were engaged in trade of one kind or another, the largest number turned to agriculture as this was seen not only as a way of acquiring stability but also as a sensible way of using their tried and tested methods of intensive farming. In addition, land could provide occupation and a living for the members of the extended family and, as Sugden points out, the burning desire to own land amongst the earliest settlers, who came from landless communities, was passed on to succeeding generations, and landownership became a status symbol of some importance.[2]

Indentured men had worked in considerable numbers in the agricultural and other sectors of the economy since 1860 and their distribution in 1911 is given in table 1.[3]

Table 1   Distribution of indentured men in 1911

	Indentured %	Re-indentured %	
Sugar estates	29	53	(incl. tea)
General farming	24	8	
Coal mines	14	14	
Tea estates	7		see sugar above
Railways	10	13	(incl. public bodies
Domestic service	8		(incl. in general category)
General	8	12	

The largest number of Indians, both free and indentured, were to be found in the rural areas. The illiteracy rate was high, especially among women who were often not sent to school even when schools existed. Apart from some women employed as labourers on the plantations, they were engaged predominantly in domestic duties. In the next fifty years there was to be a remarkable metamorphosis in the social and economic position of all classes of Indians in Natal.

Indians had begun to purchase smallholdings in the vicinity of Durban and Pietermaritzburg and along the north coast as early as 1866. Before long they had established a monopoly of the fruit and vegetable markets and, in the inland areas, were making a success of grain, beans, tobacco and other crops. Yet after Union there was a steady drift to the towns. A number of reasons have been given for this movement which, in view of the attitude to land, was unexpected. Arable land was expensive in Natal and holdings were therefore small to begin with, while families were usually large, so that before long the land could not provide for them all. Drought and plant disease could be disastrous and, with no reserves, the only recourse was to wage labour. No agricultural colleges existed, nor exist now, for Indians and they were often not able to mechanise because of high costs so that their farming operations became steadily less competitive. The traditional system of inheritance led each son to expect a portion of the farm on the death of the father and it was not long before subdivision made even the prosperous smallholding incapable of providing a subsistence income. In such circumstances wage labour could often be obtained on sugar and other estates so that it might, in time, be possible to build up a small amount of working capital. Work in the towns was the alternative.

With the growth of Natal's urban centres, industrial land was required in increasing amounts after 1936. Peri-urban areas were incorporated and this drove market gardeners off the land, especially in the South Coast Junction and Umgeni districts outside Durban. Not all the displaced farmers could re-establish themselves; those who could not sought work in the towns. Finally, legislation prevented the sale of land from one population group to another without special permission; this effectively closed the land market to Indians except for the subdivision of existing Indian-owned property into units which soon became too small to be viable.

Although Indians had long been the mainstay of the sugar estates, after 1915 they were steadily replaced by African workers. The extent to which this took place in the period to 1965 is shown in table 2.

The reasons for the replacement of Indian labour with African are complex and can only be explained in terms of the interests of all three groups, i.e. employers, Indian and African employees. The cane growers were faced with heavy competition in world markets and were seeking ways of reducing costs. More than ever they looked to paying the lowest wages for the highest productivity, and also to minimising demands for housing large families and for imported food such as rice and dahl. The Indian labourer, who, after the repeal of the £3 tax, could sell his labour

Table 2 Indians and Africans employed on the sugar estates

Year	No. of Indians	%	No. of Africans	%
1907–08	10 924	82	2 484	18
1914–15	11 745	56	9 357	44
1924–25	9 500	36	16 473	64
1934–35	4 908	12	33 283	88
1944–45	4 500	7	55 778	93
1953–54	3 900	5	62 942	95
1964–65	3 450	3	124 000	97

Table 3 Regular labour employed on Natal farms 1911–1946

Year	White	Black	Indian	Other	Total
1911	9 296	45 499	26 030		80 825
1925	10 412	101 288	16 255	644	128 599
1930	11 122	106 352	14 221	651	132 346
1936	11 759	120 198	16 198	862	149 017
1946	12 760	140 102*			

*Includes Indian and Other, not separated in 1946.

Source: Union Agricultural Census 1911–1936 and Union Yearbook 1946.

freely and to best advantage, was now far more expensive and independent than the indentured worker had been. The African labourer became increasingly available after the passing of the 1913 Land Act and, as local industry was in an early stage of development, the demand for unskilled labour in the towns was limited. Many Africans found it necessary to accept the agricultural jobs they had refused a few years earlier. This can be clearly seen in table 3.

Indians did not desert the sugar estates altogether and continued to work in considerable numbers in the sugar mills, where housing conditions and wages were generally better. The wages offered to field workers on the sugar estates compared unfavourably with those in the industrial sector. In 1915, for example, when the move away from the cane-fields was gaining momentum, the average wage offered in the sugar estates was £21 per annum as compared with £40 in the metal industry and £52 in the printing industry.[5]

The move from field to mill began early and wages quoted in 1872 for mill workers with five years' experience varied from £1 2s. 6d. per month for a mill sirdar to £4 for a vacuum-pan operator. The mill worker was a skilled or semi-skilled man and his wages reflected the difficulty the miller would experience in replacing him.[6] Indian mill workers remained in demand throughout Natal and in 1944 the mill or sugar factory was still the largest single sphere of industrial employment.[7] In that year there were 3 500 Indians employed in sugar mills, of whom 230 were described as skilled, 340 as semi-skilled in responsible positions, 1 330 semi-skilled in less responsible positions and 1 650 unskilled. After 1953 mill workers no longer received free housing or rations; nevertheless, with improved wages and general conditions in the industry this does not seem to have made any noticeable difference to the number of Indians employed. In 1952, for example, mills which produced 96 per cent of Natal's sugar preferred Indian sirdars, drivers and clerks, and also employed over 3 300 field workers and 2 075 mill workers.[8]

The last group of Indian agriculturalists to be considered is the independent cane-growers. In 1952 there were about 1 400 Indian and 1 500 African sugar-planters who together produced about 8 per cent of the total output. It is obvious, then, that most of them operated on a small scale. Woods estimates that there were about 50 important growers at this time; 300 made a reasonable living and the rest were subsistence farmers.[9] The most prominent cane-grower in the first two decades of the century was an ex-indentured farmer, Baboo Bodasingh, who acquired land on the north coast. His family have continued as cane-growers with considerable success. In 1964 Indian producers were responsible for 6,4 per cent of the total production of sugar and held 9,5 per cent of the utilised land. About this time many market gardeners had switched from fruit to sugar. This was due partly to the fall in the price of bananas and partly to the increase in the sugar price. Some of these men continue to grow both vegetables and sugar by the inter-crop method and, although this practice is frowned on by the Mill Group Boards, some find it profitable. The amount of land held by Indian sugar growers in the Tongaat-Verulam areas, as given by Maasdorp, is not large (88 per cent holding less than 50 acres and 73 per cent less than 30 acres). With land units of this size it is obvious that many of the smallest growers cannot make an adequate living and many have other sources of income or are managing farms on behalf of an extended family who share the costs.[10]

Since Indian sugar producers could claim a much larger share of the sugar industry, what is it that prevents them from doing so? Up until 1965, when Land Bank loans became available to them, it was a chronic shortage of capital that held them back, and even after that only large landowners could provide the necessary security. Capital is also necessary for improvements, for mechanisation and to tide the grower over the lean years. Lack of agricultural education and expertise, and the determination to stick to traditional methods, which are not best suited to cane-growing, have caused the small farmer to ignore modern scientific methods of agriculture. Finally, the Asiatic Land Tenure and Indian Representation Act of 1946 had the effect of limiting the amount of land available for purchase; since then scarcity has increased the price and made it necessary for farms to be subdivided, many becoming too small to be profitably developed.

It was not only Indians who began to drift to the towns after 1910. 'Poor whites' had been leaving the rural districts since the South African War and now large numbers of Africans were joining them. De Kiewiet's description of the plight of the 'poor white' applied to the Indian as well:

> In the towns as upon the land they were caught between the upper and nether millstones of two classes. In the country they had been extruded from the ranks of the landowning and prosperous farmers; in the town they could not enter the ranks of the skilled and well-paid workers, for they had no skill of their own.[11]

Table 4 shows the extent of urbanisation in the 1904–80 period.[12]

Table 4   Degree of urbanisation in Natal 1904–1980

| | Urban % of each racial group | | | | |
Year	White	Indian	Coloured	African	Total Population
1904	60,5	24,1	56,4	4,0	11,1
1911	63,9	38,1	38,1	3,8	12,8
1921	59,3	21,3	28,1	4,8	11,9
1936	76,4	61,8	67,1	8,2	20,5
1946	82,4	65,9	75,8	12,3	26,2
1951	85,8	74,0	81,0	15,9	31,9
1960	88,9	80,7	86,0	19,1	36,2
1970	90,0	84,6	89,5	22,1	37,8
1980	91,5	90,2	90,2	23,3*	56,6

*Zulu only

By 1946 over a quarter of Natal's population was living in towns and, in the case of Indians, the figure was two out of three. In the whole of South Africa an estimated 72,8 per cent of Indians were town dwellers in 1946, rising to 86,6 per cent in 1970 and 90,5 per cent in 1980.[13]

For Natal, with its undeveloped industrial and manufacturing sector, the problem of urbanisation was particularly difficult. In 1901, for example, there were only 625 establishments listed in the Industries, Manufacturing and Works category of the *Natal Statistical Yearbook* and these included the large industries such as sugar mills, brick and tile works, and tea and coffee factories which were situated outside the towns. Altogether the 625 enterprises employed 28 109 people, of whom 11 822 were Indians. Nor did the situation improve in the next decade. The deep depression that settled over South Africa after 1904 saw the demise of many of the smaller establishments, leaving the position in 1910 no better than it had been in 1901. It took the 1914–18 war to encourage industry, but by then thousands more of all races had migrated to the towns and were seeking work in industry and commerce. Initially, many Indians had an advantage in that they could engage in one of the arts and crafts which had been part of their lives in India. As early as 1891, the census returns list Indian men working in the informal sector as potters, goldsmiths, tinsmiths and tailors. A further advantage was that under the extended family system they could expect food and lodging until they found some kind of job. Hostility towards Indians, which had long been present, was aggravated by the large numbers of unemployed persons arriving in the towns, leading to overcrowding and slum conditions and eventually to enquiries into Indian 'penetration'.

The First World War had the long-term effect of accelerating industrialisation and strengthening the economy in all parts of South Africa. With thousands of white men drawn into the forces, openings occurred for other races when protective policies were temporarily relaxed. This was particularly fortuitous for the Natal Indian worker who was being edged out of agriculture, mining and the sugar estates. Statistics reveal that from 1911 to the end of 1921, Indians employed in agriculture declined from 36 238 (34,3 per cent) to 19 625 (31,7 per cent), while the number employed in commerce rose from 9,8 per cent to 21,5 per cent. The vague category 'indefinite and unspecified' showed an increase from 1,9 per cent in 1911 to 19,1 per cent in 1921.[14] There was an unexplained drop in the number of Indians engaged in manufacture from 20,7 per cent in 1911 to 8,9 per cent in 1921, and this may have been associated with the industrialisation process involving the increased use of machinery which the small manufacturer could not afford.

The first official industrial census was taken in 1915 and showed 3 638 establishments in the whole of South Africa. After the war there was significant growth in the manufacturing sector and this provided jobs for Indians and blacks, in the lean years of the 1920s and 1930s, as unskilled or semi-skilled workers. By 1946–47 there were 9 999 establishments and the number of Indians employed in them had risen from 7 361 in 1921 to 17 620 in 1946; comprising 5,3 per cent of the total labour force in the manufacturing industry in 1921 but only 3,6 per cent in 1946. Arkin suggests that Indians entered industrial employment in this period because of the way in which manufacturing techniques were being broken down and simplified, thus requiring workers with less training. Division of labour enabled workers to become skilled in a single operation and it was in these semi-skilled jobs that large numbers of Indians found employment.

After the war the new industries encouraged white immigration from overseas. Forty thousand white settlers arrived in Natal between 1921 and 1931, of whom 48 per cent were male. At the same time state-aided emigration had encouraged a number of Indian families to return to India and in 1936, for the first time since 1903, there were more whites than Indians in Natal.[15] Combined with the increasing number of whites, the Pact government's 'civilised labour' policy, which gave preference to white labour in all fields, made it increasingly difficult for Indians and Africans to obtain employment. The educational qualifications laid down in the Apprenticeship Act of 1922 put a skilled job out of reach of most of the unemployed. With African workers preferred for most of the unskilled jobs, and whites in competition for semi-skilled posts, Indian workers were in an unfortunate position during the 1920s and 1930s.

The 1920s also saw the establishment of the first Indian trade unions under the auspices of the Natal Indian Congress led by Albert Christopher. Trade unions were set up for laundrymen, tinsmiths, metal workers, tobacco workers, printers, hotel employees, bakers and workers in the biscuit, sweet and furniture industries.[16] The idea behind the formation of trade unions was that, since Indians were not permitted to join white unions, their own unions would organise for them.

The expansion of manufacturing, actively promoted by the government, was providing work by 1935 for 115 971 whites and only 149 877 blacks. Natal at this time had 1 294 factories employing white and black staff but, whereas the manufacturing industry played a significant role in solving the 'poor white' problem in the 1930s, it certainly did very little to reduce unemployment among the other races. It was only after the Second World War that secondary industry really began to make rapid progress. The steady decline in whites and the increase in the number of Indians employed in industry can be gauged from table 5 and it is evident that, overall, the number of Africans employed was increasing more rapidly than that of other racial groups.[17]

Table 5   Racial composition of the labour force, Durban/Pinetown/Inanda
(percentage)

Year	White	Coloured/ Asian	Black	Total no.
1959–60	20,2	31,0	48,8	76 409
1967–68	16,9	35,2	47,9	130 914
1970	15,3	36,3	48,4	148 139
1972	14,2	35,5	50,3	152 903
1976	13,5	36,7	50,0	186 767

In certain specific industries, in which Indians had long been active, there is no indication that they were being replaced by African workers.[18] The most important of these are shown in table 6.[19]

The two manufacturing sectors in which the percentage of Indians decreased significantly are leather and leatherware, where the percentage employed fell from 65,3 per cent in 1960 to 52,3 per cent in 1976, and textiles where, after a steady growth from 1917, there was a decline from 28,2 per cent in 1960 to 17,7 per cent in 1976.

Several attempts have been made to explain the apparent trend away from Indian labour in the Durban/Pinetown/Inanda area. Douwes-Dekker and Watts in their 1964 study on the attitudes of white employers concluded that 'viewed overall the Indian worker tends to be regarded less favourably than the African worker'.[20] They also claimed that the employment of African workers was not a consequence of the shortage of available Indian labour and pointed out that the rate of unemployment among Indians was high and had been since 1958, even when economic growth

**Table 6   Coloured/Asian proportion of sectoral labour forces,
Durban/Pinetown region** (percentage)

Year	1917	1936	1946	1960	1976
Food	6,4	38	27	48	39,7
Textiles	2,8	20	26	28,2	17,7
Clothing	*	*	*	78	81
Footwear				63	70
Wood				23	25
Furniture	3	5	7	47	55
Paper				33	42
Printing	2,3	3,8	5,3	28	40
Chemicals	1 0	3,5	4,2	8,2	16
Leather	1,1	5,3	10,5	65,3	52,3
Metal production	5	8	6,6	20	22

*Clothing and textiles are combined for these years.

was buoyant. Russell and Allen held the view that Indians were preferred in all industries requiring manual dexterity; in those industries where they were being replaced by Africans the explanation was to be found not in the psychological attitudes of the employer, but in the more mundane circumstance that automatic and semi-automatic machines were being installed and that these could be as efficiently operated by semi-trained African workers as by the more dextrous Indian.[21] Bell, however, found that in the 1959–60 to 1976 period, the percentage of Indians in the labour force in the Pinetown/Durban/Inanda region tended to increase rather than decline, while the percentage of blacks in the same period and the same region rose from 48,8 per cent to 50 per cent. It was the percentage of whites that declined from 20,2 per cent in 1959–60 to 13,5 per cent in 1976, reflecting, in Bell's view, a substitution of Indians for whites while the growth in the number of blacks employed has not been at the expense of Indians. Inter-sectoral differences in the preference for Indian or African labour were, in Bell's view, 'related mainly to the level of skill-intensity, with Blacks being more substitutable for Indians the lower the general level of skill required by the industry'.[22]

At the present time there can be no doubt that Indian workers play a vital part in the industries of Natal. This has developed steadily over the years and can be attributed, partly at least, to the strong economic growth of South Africa as a whole since 1945, and of Natal in particular. This has forced the abandonment of the pro-white bias of the 1930s and 1940s. But without education and the changed attitudes towards women, which will be discussed later, the Indian community could not have been absorbed into the economy in the way it has.

Urbanised Indians have also entered commerce in considerable numbers. Traders, mostly from north-western India, had been establishing businesses in Durban and Pietermaritzburg from the late 1870s. From there they spread widely into the country towns and settlements, establishing trading stores to supply the basic necessities of the rural white and African communities. It was these traders who roused the bitter opposition of the colonial storekeeper, although recent research has indicated that the extent of their trade competition has been exaggerated.[23] The number of licences held by Natal's Indian traders or Dukawalas is given as 393 in 1895 rising to 1 008 in 1908. After Union there was a steady increase in the number of licences issued to Indians as compared to whites, as the statistics for Durban given in table 7, show:[24]

Table 7   Trading licences held by whites and Indians

	Whites (no.)	%	Indians (no.)	%
1914	1 357	72,5	515	27,5
1930	3 931	76,0	1 164	22,5
1938	5 449	58,34	3 767	40,3
1946	6 731	54,29	5 327	42,9
1955	9 617	53,83	7 728	43,3
1963	10 913	53,75	8 661	42,7
1975	12 191	56,44	8 834	40,9

There is no indication in these bare statistics of the size of the businesses in terms of the income generated or number of persons employed, and the commercial world is generally reluctant to disclose details of income. Census returns, however, show clearly that more and more Indians are being employed in commerce and that the employment choices have broadened and continue to broaden. It is clear from the number of licences issued to traders in Durban over the years that the general dealer is still the most popular type of enterprise among Indian traders, who hold 37 per cent of the licences issued. Indians hold 90 per cent of the hawkers' licences, and fruit and vegetable dealers hold 94 per cent.[25] With the opening of the central business districts to all races it is likely that Indian traders will take advantage of the new opportunities offered to extend their activities. In the rural areas and small towns Indian traders held 54,16 per cent of licences by 1947, and there is no sign that this figure is declining.[26]

Apart from the traditional trading occupations, both retail and wholesale, Indians are increasingly moving into other sectors of commerce. Professional training available at the technical colleges, technikons and universities has enabled considerable numbers to qualify as accountants and bookkeepers, as company secretaries and marketing and personnel managers, and in the new field of labour relations. Some of these are self-employed. Typists, clerks, salesmen and shop assistants are employed everywhere in the urban centres of Natal. The following statistics give an indication of the extent to which economically active Indians have been employed in commerce and manufacturing since 1921. By 1946 commerce had become the second largest employer, with 24 per cent of all employed Indians. By 1951 the percentage had risen to 50 per cent and in 1970 commerce and manufacturing provided jobs for 70 per cent of Indians of both sexes.[27]

Since Union, the number of Indians entering the professions has also increased dramatically and is directly related to the availability of secondary and post-secondary education and the changing attitudes towards the employment of women outside the home. This is shown in table 8:[28]

Table 8   Indian men and women in the professional and technical sectors

Year	Total	Men	Women	% Women	
1921	391	347	44	11	(Natal)
1924	468	398	70	14	(Natal)
1936	582	512	70	12	(Natal)
1946	1 914	1 647	267	14	(Natal)
1980	15 782	11 610	4 172	26	(Natal)

Although Indians had been heavily engaged in railway construction and in coal-mining in the 1880–1910 period, the number employed in these two sectors has shown a steep decline since then. The Natal Government Railways imported skilled and semi-skilled construction workers from India in the 1880s and 1890s to work on the main line to Johannesburg and the branch lines, and were the largest single employers of indentured labour prior to 1910. After Union some Indians were transferred to the South African Railways, but the number declined significantly as a result of the 'civilised labour' policy of the 1920s and the slowing down of railway construction. In 1971 Indians made up only 0,5 per cent of the labour force of the railways and harbours sector.[29] The public sector, including central, provincial and local government, employed 15 000 Indians in 1960, making up about 8 per cent of their labour force, and this figure had increased to 25 631 by 1981.[30]

Coal-mining had never been popular with Indian labourers and underground work was particularly disliked. After 1910 African labour replaced Indian in unskilled and semi-skilled work and whites took over the skilled jobs. The number of Indians employed on Natal's coal-mines dropped from 4 466 in 1911 to 488 in 1945, i.e. from 38,53 per cent to 2,62 per cent of the total work-force.[31] The number of Indians on the coal-mines in 1973 had dropped to 252 of a total work-force of 74 793 and in 1980 represented 0,55 per cent of the work-force.[32]

Apart from the political conditions prevailing in South Africa, nothing has made as much difference to the social and economic position of the Indian community as their increasing educational attainments. As has already been shown, education has opened doors not only to skilled occupations in industry and commerce but also in the professional sphere. Although, even among the indentured Indians, there were always those who were literate in English as well as in one or more Indian language,

The M.L. Sultan Technikon has, since 1956, played an important part in improving the skill levels of Indians employed in industry.

these were in the minority. The Indian community had to struggle long and hard to obtain government-aided education and even in recent times has had to bear most of the costs of buildings, books and teachers' salaries. Not until 1899 was schooling beyond standard four provided and only in 1917 did it become possible for the first time to study beyond standard seven. At the time of Union, 3 284 Indian children were at school in the whole of Natal, of whom only 324 were girls and, overall, 50 per cent had not yet reached standard two.

The 'upliftment' clause in the Cape Town Agreement led to the appointment of an Education Commission in 1928 and two educationists were brought from India to advise. One of these experts, K.P. Kichlu, made a survey of the existing educational facilities in Natal for all races. He reported to the commission that although schools for white and coloured children were financed by both the central and the provincial governments, no funds were allocated to Indian education by the Natal Provincial Council and that even the funds provided by the central government for Indian education were not fully utilised.[33]

The recommendation of the Education Commission was that each year facilities be provided for 1 000 more children so as to gradually reduce the considerable backlog. However, the high birth rate among the Indian community made this plan ineffectual and, in any case, the economic depression of the early 1930s made urgent demands on financial resources while at the same time reducing these resources drastically. The newly appointed agent-general, V. Srinivasa Sastri, took the initiative in raising funds from the wealthier members of the Indian community for the educational needs, and also for the general upliftment, of the community. It was through his efforts that Sastri College was established in 1930. It was opened as a high school for boys, offering both academic and professional training and was to have a significant effect. Not only did it provide opportunities for able boys to acquire an education equal to that of their white counterparts, but the whole community was given new confidence that their future might indeed be more promising. Indian girls continued to attend Dartnell Crescent Indian School which later became the Durban Indian Girls' High School.

By 1936, 75 per cent of Indian boys and 30 per cent of girls of school-going age were attending school. In the following year the Broome Commission, appointed to enquire into education in Natal, was critical of Indian schooling and its short duration. The majority left after standard six to find jobs in order to augment the family finances; the rest remained until they had passed their standard eight examination. It should be pointed out that white children of the lower income groups were in exactly the same position, with only the minority matriculating.

By 1958, when education for Indian children was generally available except in the most rural areas, there was considerable 'bunching' in the primary grades and only 1,4 per cent in standards nine and ten, revealing that the majority of Indian children were still leaving school at the end of standard six or eight. By 1970 the number in standards nine and ten had risen to 4,7 per cent and in 1977 the percentage was 5,9 per cent.

Education was made compulsory for all Indian children between the ages of seven and fifteen years in 1977.[34]

As a result of the Broome Commission's recommendations, the Natal Provincial Administration agreed to pay one-third of the cost of buildings, raised to one-half in 1943. The platoon system and double-shift classes were introduced to overcome the shortage of classrooms and even in 1960 a considerable number of children still attended platoon classes.[35] Despite its drawbacks the system enabled the literacy rate to be considerably increased. It is also noteworthy that the efforts that parents had to make to provide education for their children have resulted in a respect for education and for the teaching profession among the Indian community.

Technical education was provided in the 1930s in a small way, but not until 1950 was the Hugo Commission appointed to enquire into this important sphere. As a result of its findings the M.L. Sultan Technical College was opened in 1956 at a time when over 13 000 untrained Indians were employed in industry. This was the turning-point for Indian education and was followed in 1960 by the opening of the University College for Indians on Salisbury Island, now the resited and renamed University of Durban-Westville.

From the foregoing account it is to be expected that the educational qualifications of Indians in industry should show a steady rise after 1956 when technical education became available. This should be reflected also in the number of skilled and semi-skilled workers and the decline in the percentage of unskilled. Arkin[36] defines a skilled worker as one occupying a position which requires some post-matriculation training, a semi-skilled requiring some high school education and an unskilled a primary education or less. The following statistics show the extent to which the percentage in each category has altered since 1904. In that year only 1 per cent of Indians were in the skilled category as were 30 per cent of whites; 10 per cent of Indians and 57 per cent of whites were semi-skilled; and 89 per cent of Indians and 13 per cent of whites were unskilled. Of the skilled Indian group nearly 70 per cent were teachers. No accurate figures are available for African workers. Thompson[37] points out that at this time free Indians filled the gap between the limit of available African labour and 'the lower limit of the European's condescension'. Free Indians at the turn of the century were no threat to whites or Africans in the labour field; the situation was very different in 1970, especially in the semi-skilled category, and the competition for jobs was increasing as Africans qualified for more and more jobs in industry.[38]

Table 9   Skill percentages of workers 1970

	Skilled		Semi-skilled		Unskilled	
	M	F	M	F	M	F
Indian	3,5	4,0	57,2	42,3	39,3	53,7
White	14,0	8,9	82,9	89,9	3,0	1,2
African	0,2	0,2	11,8	17,3	88,0	82,5

The general literacy rate of Indian employees also shows a substantial rise after 1970, as does the length of time spent at school. Table 10 shows the increase in educational attainment of whites, Indians and Africans for 1981 compared with 1970.[39]

Table 10   **Educational attainment of the economically active population** (percentage)

	Indians		Whites		Africans	
	1970	1981	1970	1981	1980	1981
No education	7,89	1,1	0,62	0,1	49,57	40,5
Primary	35,86	23,6	2,82	1,5	36,58	43,9
Std. 6–9	46,89	59,4	54,97	51,3	12,57	14,9
Std. 10	5,03	10,1	25,62	30,3	0,39	0,5
Degrees, diplomas	4,36	5,8	15,97	16,8	0,89	0,2

By 1981 the structure of educational attainments of Indians was closer to that of whites than to that of any other group and a comparison of the 1971 figures with those for 1981 shows clearly that compulsory education had reduced the number of workers with no education at all; the most significant change, however, was in the number who had entered high school and remained until standard nine.

Arkin, in a comparison between education levels of the economically active Indian population in 1960 and 1970, shows that the professional and technical group enjoyed the greatest increase. In 1960, 39,5 per cent of the men in this group had had more than 12 years' education, rising to 61 per cent in 1970; 13,8 per cent of women of the professional-technical group had over 12 years of schooling in 1960 and this figure had risen to 34,4 per cent in 1970.[40]

The changing attitude to women and their gradual entry into the labour market has been a marked feature of Indian life since the 1940s. The number of girls receiving education has increased steadily until now they receive the same opportunities as boys in most homes. Sugden[41] suggests that the reasons for the move away from the traditional attitudes to women are their increasing emancipation, the displacement of agriculture as a primary source of employment, urbanisation, and the changing attitudes towards children and the family. This has already been shown in table 8 in the increase of women in the professional and technical fields. The increased level of education has led to greater employment opportunities and greater earning power. This in turn has meant that girls tend to marry later and have fewer children. All population groups are finding it difficult to retain a reasonable standard of living on one salary only and this is forcing married women into the labour market while smaller families have made it unnecessary for single girls to be kept at home to care for younger brothers and sisters.

The population of the Indian community in Natal was given as 299 068 in 1951 and the annual growth rate as 3,4 per cent. It was generally predicted in the 1950s that this tendency was likely to persist and that the typical Indian family would remain much larger than the white, with the Indian population in Natal soon leaving the white far behind. This was expected to have far-reaching effects on housing, employment and the provision of services.[42] In fact this has not happened and there has been a persistent decline in the birth-rate, which was estimated at 2,4 per cent in the late 1970s.[43] This tendency can be ascribed primarily to urbanisation followed by efficient family planning, better education among Indian women and employment outside the home. It must also be ascribed to higher expectations among Indian families and the desire to limit the number of births in order to provide the best possible advantages for existing children.

Despite important changes since Union, poverty and poor living conditions, which were rife in the first half of the century, certainly still exist in some areas. Although local authorities in Durban and Pietermaritzburg have given some attention to slum clearance and have provided council houses and flats at sub-economic rentals, many more are required. In rural areas and smaller towns, very little has been done to improve general living conditions. Low incomes make it impossible for the occupants to do much to improve their dwellings and landlords are often unwilling to do so in view of the low return they receive on their investment. The whole situation has been aggravated by the shortage of land available for Indian housing. This is a result of legislation passed since 1940 to prevent Indian 'penetration' into white areas, as well as the Group Areas Act. There are indications now that this situation is changing, yet even if it does the number of families living below the poverty datum line will have to be drastically reduced before the problems of poverty, of which housing is only one, can be alleviated. Pillay and Ellison found, in their 1969 study of the Indian domestic budget, that between 50 and 60 per cent of the families in their sample had incomes below the cost of living minimum.[44] Butler-Adam and Venter, in their sample of 1979–80, found that, despite improved educational and employment opportunities in the previous decade, about 40 per cent of the families were living very close to poverty, with incomes below or within R50 of their minimum living levels. They are under the impression that the position was much the same in 1986.[45]

In conclusion it should be recognised that the Indian community in Natal has grown within the past 50 or 60 years from an economically undeveloped community with a high rate of illiteracy, engaged predominantly in agriculture, mining, manual labour and trade, into an urbanised, educated, enterprising group which plays an important part in all aspects of the economy. As a consequence of improved educational opportunities at every level and a degree of westernisation, they have become integrated into Natal society, whereas formerly they had remained on the periphery, unable to compete successfully in the wider economy. It would be true to state that the Indian community has undergone a transformation rather than evolutionary development in the social and economic sphere.[46]

REFERENCES

1. NAD Indian Immigration Papers, II/1/179, 14/1911.

2. M. A. Sugden, 'Membership of the South African labour force' in B. Pachai (ed.) *South Africa's Indians: the evolution of a minority* (Washington, University Press of America, 1979), p. 285.

3. Compiled from the *Report of the Protector of Indian Immigrants 1911*, and the *Report of the Indian Immigration Commission* (Clayton), 1909.

4. A. G. Choonoo, 'Indentured Indian immigration 1860–1911, with particular reference to its role in the development of the sugar industry (unpublished M.A. thesis, University of Natal, 1967), p. 176.

5. V. Padayachee et al., *Indian workers and trade unions in Durban, 1930–1950* (Durban, Institute for Social and Economic Research, University of Durban-Westville, 1985), p. 24.

6. Choonoo, 'Indentured Indian immigration', p. 206.

7. R. H. Smith, *Labour resources of Natal*, NRS, Report no. 1 (Cape Town, Oxford University Press, 1950), pp. 77–78.

8. C. A. Woods, *The Indian Community of Natal: their economic position*, NRS, vol. 9 (Cape Town, Oxford University Press, 1954), pp. 25–27.

9. *Ibid.*, p. 28.

10. G. G. Maasdorp, *A Natal Indian community: a socio-economic study in the Tongaat-Verulam area*, NRS, Additional report no. 5 (Durban, Department of Economics, University of Natal, 1968), pp. 91–106.

11. C. W. de Kiewiet, *A history of South Africa, social and economic* (London, Oxford University Press, 1968), p. 196.

12. *South African statistics* 1978, 1980 (Pretoria, Government Printer, 1978, 1980), section 1.13.

13. *South African Statistics* 1970, 1980.

14. A. J. Arkin, *Contribution of the Indians to the South African economy, 1860–1970* (Durban, Institute for Social and Economic Research, University of Durban-Westville, 1981), p. 141.

15. Natal Chamber of Industries, *Fifty years of progress: the development of industry in Natal* (Durban, The Chamber of Industries, 1956), p. 31. The number of Indians who left South Africa in the 1914–40 period is estimated at 37 905.

16. *Natal Mercury*, 20 September, 26 October, 17, 26, 29 November, 4, 11, 17 December 1928.

17. R. T. Bell, *The growth and structure of manufacturing employment in Natal* (Durban, Institute for Social and Economic Research, University of Durban-Westville, 1985), p. 37.

18. *Ibid.*, p. 39.

19. *Ibid.*, p. 39; *Industrial census*, 1917, 1936, 1946.

20. L. Douwes-Dekker and H. L. Watts, 'Certain attitudes of White industrial employers in Durban towards the Indian worker in contrast to the African worker', *Humanitas*, 2(2), 1973, p. 119.

21. Quoted in Bell, *Growth and structure of manufacturing employment*, pp. 35–36.

22. *Ibid.*, pp. 36, 41.

23. See, for example, A. J. Arkin, 'The contributions of Indians on the economic development of South Africa, 1860–1970: an historical-income approach' (unpublished Ph. D. thesis, University of Durban-Westville, 1981), pp. 70–81.

24. Arkin, 'The contributions of Indians', pp. 169, 293.

25. *Ibid.*, p. 294.

26. *Ibid.*, p. 298.

27. *Ibid.*, p. 288.

28. Census 1921, 1936, 1945, 1980.

29. Sugden, 'Membership of the South African labour force', p. 284.

30. *Ibid.*, p. 284; *South African Statistics*, 1982, pp. 7, 20–21.

31. *Reports of the Government Mining Engineer* 1911–1945; *South African Statistics*, 1978, 1982.

32. *South African Statistics*, 1982, section 7.9.

33. K. P. Kichlu, Memorandum on Indian education in Natal (Pietermaritzburg, 1928), pp. 26–27.

34. RP 38/1977, Report of the Department of Indian Affairs 1975/76.

35. S. R. Maharaj, 'Primary and secondary education' in Pachai (ed.), *South Africa's Indians*, pp. 358–62.

36. Arkin, 'The contributions of Indians', p. 321.

37. L. M. Thompson, 'Indian immigration into Natal' *Archives Yearbook for South African History 1952* (Pretoria, Government Printer, 1952), p. 53.

38. Arkin, 'The contributions of Indians', p. 321.

39. Bell, *Growth and structure of manufacturing employment*, p. 54.

40. Arkin, 'The contributions of Indians', p. 283.

41. Sugden, 'Membership of the South African labour force', p. 264.

42. Woods, *The Indian community of Natal*, p. 6.

43. Sugden, 'Membership of the South African labour force', p. 230.

44. P. N. Pillay and P. A. Ellison, *The Indian domestic budget: a socio-economic study of incomes and expenditures of Durban Indian households*, NRS, Additional report no. 6 (Durban, Department of Economics, University of Natal, 1969), chap. 6.

45. J. F. Butler-Adam and W. M. Venter, *Indian housing study in Durban and Pietermaritzburg*: vol. 1, Metropolitan Durban (Durban, Institute for Social and Economic Research, University of Durban-Westville, 1980), pp. 76–77.

46. I am grateful to Professor John Butler-Adam and Mr Vishnu Padayachee for their comments, and also to Professor J. St. E. Pretorius.

```
┌─────────────────────── ABSTRACT ───────────────────────┐
```

It is widely assumed that agricultural methods in KwaZulu are primitive and that output and yields are low. An analysis of that territory's agricultural industry in the period 1957–73 indicates that its annual rate of growth during those years was 1,4 per cent compared with South Africa's national average of 2,7 per cent. However, field crop production in KwaZulu grew at the same rate as in South Africa, although operating at lower output yields, while the output of animal husbandry declined at an annual rate of 0,5 per cent compared with a growth rate of 1,2 per cent in South Africa. In 1957 KwaZulu's livestock enterprises contributed nearly two-thirds of the gross value of its agricultural output, but by 1973 they had declined in relative importance to share equally in the value of total output with crop production. Qualitatively KwaZulu's agricultural land compares favourably with the rest of South Africa, but quantitatively it is very scarce relative to the numbers employed on it. During the 1957–73 period cereals, in particular sorghum and maize, remained the predominant crop but there was a shift in emphasis towards the cultivation of legumes, vegetables and fruit, and an increase in the area put under sugar-cane. The output of main staple crops was more or less static whereas there was sustained progress in horticulture and in the production of sugar, KwaZulu's main cash crop, which has a high growth potential but is restricted by the traditional system of land tenure and insufficient investment capital. Customary investment in cattle ensured that KwaZulu's livestock numbers remained practically unchanged though they continued to be excessive in relation to the carrying capacity of the land, which resulted in further veld erosion as well as a declining marketable output. Attempts to improve the state of animal husbandry by encouraging the sale of stock, introducing better breeding policies and enforcing compulsory culling met with little or no success. The situation demands much more active governmental intervention in pursuit of a total development strategy for the country as a whole.

DEVELOPMENT OR STAGNATION? AGRICULTURE IN KWAZULU 1957–1973[1]

Giuseppe Lenta

CROP PRODUCTION

The pattern of land use

From a quality point of view, the land of KwaZulu compares favourably with the rest of the land of South Africa. Some 14 per cent of total land in the homeland is arable, compared with approximately 12 per cent of white-owned South African land and 15,7 per cent of the white areas of Natal. The relative amount of land suitable for pasture in KwaZulu (roughly 77 per cent of the total) does not differ significantly from the national average (81,3 per cent).[2]

In terms of quantity, however, land as a factor of production, in particular arable land, appears to be very scarce relative to the numbers employed in the agricultural sector.

Table 1   Labour force and land-labour ratios in the agricultural sector KwaZulu 1960 and 1970

	1960	1970
Land		
Total area of farm land (Ha.)	2 994 000	3 160 000
Area of arable land (Ha.)	384 000	454 000
Labour force	229,000	320 000
Hectares of all farm land per worker	13,1	9,8
Hectares of arable land per worker	1,7	1,4

Sources: *Land* – Bantu Administration and Development, Division of Agriculture, Natal, *Annual Reports*, 1960 and 1970.

Labour force – 1970: Farm and Forestry Workers, Zulus in KwaZulu. Population Census 1970, Department of Statistics. Bantu – Age, Occupation, Industry, School Standard, Birthplace, Report 02–02–02, Government Printer, Pretoria, 1973, Table B.13.

Labour force – 1960: Estimated on the assumption that the proportion of farm workers (39 per cent) in the economically active rural population (46 per cent of the total rural population) has remained constant between the census years. Data on the 1960 rural population from Bantu Administration and Development, Division of Agriculture, Natal, *Annual Report*, 1960.

217

As can be seen from table 1, in 1960 13,1 ha. of all farm land and 1,7 ha. of arable land were available to each worker in the rural sector of KwaZulu. In contrast, according to estimates made by Brand[3], in that year some 69 ha. of total farm land and 7,76 of cultivated land were available to each worker in the modern agricultural sector of South Africa. The land-labour ratio prevailing in KwaZulu, which was low by white farm standards in 1960, deteriorated further over the years; although arable land increased at an annual rate of 1,6 per cent between 1960 and 1970,[4] the estimated labour force grew at the rate of 3,8 per cent per annum. Consequently the availability of improved land per worker decreased from 1,7 to 1,4 hectares.

Paradoxically, not all arable land available in KwaZulu was cultivated. For example, only 80,5 per cent of all arable land was under cultivation in 1965, and only 73,3 per cent in 1972.[5] While part of the land left uncultivated was in this state because of fallow requirements, it would appear that factors which are often beyond the control of a homeland farmer are partly responsible for this pattern of land usage.[6]

Very little KwaZulu land was under irrigation; approximately 1 600 ha. of land was irrigated in 1957, which represented less than half a per cent of total arable land. While 15 years later the amount of total irrigated land had nearly doubled, it still stood at less than 1 per cent of total arable land. At any one time between 1957 and 1973, some 15 to 20 per cent of irrigated land was left idle.[7] Agricultural officers attributed this partly to apathy on the part of farmers and partly to tribal friction in the Msinga district – where most of the irrigated land was located – which has prevented the use of some 250 ha. of irrigated land for many years.

The pattern of crop specialisation

The uses to which arable land was put over the period under review are shown in table 2 where changes in the pattern of crop specialisation are also indicated.

In terms of land used, the cereals ranked highest in the cropping pattern of KwaZulu. In 1957–59 some 86 per cent of the specified area planted was taken up by maize and sorghum production; the relative figure for 1971–73 was 84 per cent. Legume and root crop cultivation accounted, on average, for roughly 11 per cent of the given area. The amount of land under sugar-cane, the only cash crop of any significance in the territory, grew from 2,4 per cent at the beginning of the period to 3,9 per cent in 1971–73.

It is interesting to note that over the 16-year period, significant changes took place in the utilisation of arable land. While cereals remained the predominant crop and accounted for 73 per cent of the marginal increase in arable land which took place during the period, a change in emphasis occurred from the production of cereals – sorghum in particular – to the production of legumes. Vegetable and fruit cultivation became more popular, land under these crops increasing on average by 50 per cent. Though the hectarage under these crops was still small in 1971–73

Table 2 Pattern of crop specialisation
KwaZulu crop years 1957–1959 and 1971–1973

Crops	Averages 1957–1959 Area planted to given crops		Averages 1971–1973 Area planted to given crops		Marginal changes in area planted to given crops		Percentage increase in area planted to given crops 1957–1959/ 1971–1973
	Ha.	%	Ha.	%	Ha.	%	
Cereals	253 260	86,2	292 757	84,1	39 497	73,0	15,6
Legumes	20 697	7,0	27 507	7,9	6 810	12,6	32,9
Root crops	11 798	4,1	12 601	3,6	803	1,5	6,8
Vegetables	1 015	0,3	1 663	0,5	648	1,2	63,8
Sugar cane	7 129	2,4	13 463	3,9	6 334	11,7	89,0
	293 899	100,0	347 991	100,0	54 092	100,0	18,4

Source: Bantu Administration and Development, Division of Agriculture, Natal, *Annual Reports,* 1957, 1958, 1959, 1971.

Department of Agriculture and Forestry, KwaZulu, *Annual Reports*, 1972, 1973.

relative to total arable land (1 per cent), this marginal change in land usage affected significantly the size and value of the agricultural product, as will be shown later.

A further indication of crop specialisation was given by the increase in the quantity of land under sugar-cane. The area planted to the crop almost doubled and 11,5 per cent of new arable land was used for cane production.

If the pattern of crop specialisation is analysed on a regional basis, however, it appears that there was still a strong tendency among KwaZulu farmers to produce those staple crops which immediately satisfied their food requirements, without sufficient consideration being given to the possibility of earning higher incomes in the longer term by altering the traditional pattern of production. The proportion of land under maize and sorghum cultivation was fairly even among the regions, with the exception of the southern coastal region which seemed to display a greater degree of specialisation: the area planted to root crops, vegetables and sugar-cane was well represented. There would appear to have existed among farmers a reluctance to consider the question of which combination of crops best suited the local environment. For example, in experts' opinion,[8] there was in the Zululand region a comparative advantage in the production of cotton; the popular tendency, however, was towards the cultivation of maize, a crop unsuited to the hot, lowveld areas of the region.

Crops

An attempt has been made in this section to cover all crop production irrespective of the form of organisation and of whether the crops were consumed by the producers or sold. Rural household services, covering the processing, storage, transportation and distribution of their own primary output are not, however, included in the production boundary of the agricultural sector.

The validity of the estimates which follow depends, of course, on the accuracy of production figures used and on the right choice of prices. Most production figures have been extracted from the Annual Reports of the Department of Bantu Administration and Development, Agriculture Division, which later became the Annual Reports of the Department of Agriculture, KwaZulu Government.[9] The data are estimates; as the reports point out, no exact assessment of agricultural output can be made in a predominantly subsistence economy. The reliability of these estimates has been tested, however, against the data of two Agricultural Censuses (1960 and 1965) conducted by the Department of Statistics.   The comparison between the two sets of data shows that while discrepancies exist between the figures for minor crops, there appears to be fairly close agreement between the two estimates for the most important crops. In view of the fairly strong similarity between the two independent estimates, it is felt that the data used in this study must be offered as a reasonably good guide, or at least, the best available, towards the evaluation of the agricultural activity in KwaZulu.[10]

The appropriate choice of prices for the evaluation of the output presented certain problems. In theory, the prices to be applied to output sold or consumed by the producers should be the price at which the producer sells, or, if he does not sell, those at which producers of similar products sell in the same or neighbouring localities. In practice, however, it proved difficult to collate a reliable set of producer prices ruling in the various districts of KwaZulu over a 16-year period for the whole range of crops produced. It was therefore decided that use would be made of producer prices ruling on selected markets in Natal or in South Africa as a whole; the choice depended on the availability of figures.

The overall view of crop production in KwaZulu for the period 1957–73 is given in table 3. The general picture that emerges is that field production in the homeland was characterised by two trends, displaying opposite tendencies. The first was to be observed in the production of staple crops – grain, legumes – which occupied the largest share of land input, output and gross value. The performance in this division was consistently disappointing. The second, and more hopeful and dynamic trend, occurred in the production of the main cash crop and in horticulture.

Food Crops
Because of the high rating of cereals and legumes in the cropping pattern of KwaZulu – some 92 per cent of total arable land – the way in which the crops (particularly maize) performed becomes, to a great extent, an index

of the performance of agriculture as a whole. During the period 1957–73 the production of these crops met with only moderate success.

Maize output increased by approximately 2 per cent per annum, while land allocated to the crop increased by 1 per cent per annum. This implies that the yield per unit of land increased marginally from an average of 3,2 bags per hectare at the beginning of the period to 3,8 bags at the end of the period. In the case of sorghum, the physical output showed little change between 1957 and 1973; though land allocated to the crop increased marginally over the years (0,07 per cent per annum), output declined slightly at a negative rate of 0,08 per cent per annum.

In contrast, maize production in South Africa between 1957 and 1968 increased at an average rate of 5,1 per cent per annum.[11] The production of sorghum on white farms more than doubled over the same period.[12] If the comparison is conducted in terms of yields, the difference in productivity between the two agricultural systems becomes even greater. In the crop year 1964–65, for instance, the average yields obtained on white-owned farms were approximately four times as great as those obtained on African-owned farms. The difference was at its highest in the Zululand region, where, against 11,3 bags per hectare on white farms, only 2,1 bags were harvested on African farms.[13] The economic significance of the comparison seems to be fairly clear: differences in yields cannot be accounted for by ecological factors alone. Poor farming techniques, indiscriminate choice of land and meagre factor inputs were probably responsible for the lower yields on KwaZulu farms.[14]

In contrast to the static situation in the output of the main staple crops, sustained progress was recorded over the years in horticulture. Bulb and tuber production, for example, was particularly good. While the area planted to these crops was not in itself very large (an amount of some 12 000 hectares) and increased by only a moderate 0,5 per cent per annum between 1957 and 1973, output doubled over the years from approximately 12 000 to 25 000 tons. Similarly, vegetable production showed an annual rate of increase of 17 per cent per annum; as against some 700 tons of vegetables grown in 1957, 9 000 tons were harvested in 1973. Partly responsible for this progress in the diversification of land usage and in productivity were the special efforts made over the years by the agricultural authorities in KwaZulu to encourage horticulture in an attempt to diversify the diet of the inhabitants, increase the yield of the land and provide a new source of cash income. Demonstration plots at schools and the creation of 'community gardens' assisted in making horticulture more popular; community gardens, established in many villages, consisted of small allotments of land, set aside for vegetable growing, which were fenced, subdivided into small plots and apportioned among local farmers. Irrigation often took the form of an adjacent earth dam provided by the Department of Agriculture from which water was carried to the gardens. The success of these community gardens is shown by the fact that within the short period 1967–71, the number of peasant farmers growing vegetables increased from 6 400 to 16 102.

Despite these apparently encouraging trends, however, it must be

Table 3   Land under cultivation, output and gross value of output of given crops KwaZulu 1957–1959 and 1971–1973

Crops	Average 1957–59				Average 1971–73			
	Area planted Ha. (1000) (a)	Output 90 kg. Bags (1000) (b)	Yield Bags/Ha.	Gross value of output R (1000) (c)	Area planted Ha. (1000) (a)	Output 90 kg. Bags (1000) (b)	Yield Bags/Ha.	Gross value of output R (1000) (c)
1. Food crops								
Maize	206	668	3,2	1 797	245	931	3,8	3 231
Sorghum	47	139	2,9	404	47	137	2,9	509
Legumes	20,7	43	2,1	329	27,5	75	2,7	1 027
Oilseeds	1,1	2,1	2,0	19	1,5	4,1	5,2	53,6
Bulbs and tubers	11,8	135	12,1	603	12,6	271	21,5	1 820
Vegetables	1,1	6,6		31	1,7	86,7		612
	1,1	21,7		105	1,5	81,6		580
2. Industrial crops								
Sugar cane	7,1	170*	23,8	712	13,5	380*	28,2	2 199
Cotton	1,1	0,25*		31	0,26	0,09*		12
Tobacco	0,01	4,1**			0,02	5,2**		1,9
Fibres	0,1			1,1	3,3	1,7**		177

* Metric tons
** Kilograms

Sources: (a) and (b) *Agriculture, Annual Reports,* 1957–1973. Detailed figures for each crop and each crop year are given in Appendix B of G. Lenta, *The economic structure of KwaZulu, a South African homeland* (Ph.D., University of Natal, Durban, 1976).

(c) The sources of prices used in the evaluation of each crop are given in Lenta, 'Economic structure of KwaZulu', Appendix B.

admitted that, as in the case of maize production, yields in horticulture, and, in particular, yields obtained per unit of land under root crops in KwaZulu, were extremely low when compared with yields obtained on white-owned farms in Natal. For example, in the crop year 1964–65, a hectare of land under potatoes yielded an average of 464 pockets on white farms, while the same unit of land yielded 29 pockets on African farms, i.e. a ratio of production of 15:1. In the case of sweet-potatoes the ratio was 4:1.[15]

Industrial Crops

SUGAR-CANE

The cultivation of sugar-cane was introduced to the areas then known as the African reserves of Natal at the turn of the century. After disappointing results in the first few decades,[16] the sugar industry went on to become a relatively successful undertaking, given the general pattern of agricultural enterprises in the homeland. It provided KwaZulu farmers with their only cash crop of any economic significance.[17]

As table 4 shows, the area planted to cane increased between 1957 and 1973 at the rate of 4 per cent per annum and more than doubled. Output increased at a slightly higher rate – 5,2 per cent per annum – and the growth index in 1973 stood at 247 against the 1957–59 average yearly production. The increased volume of production, assisted by an upward movement of the cane price at the rate of 2,1 per cent per annum, boosted the cash income provided by this crop from R0,5 million in 1957 to R2,5 million in 1973.

**Table 4   Sugar cane production
KwaZulu 1957–1973**

Periods (3 year averages)	Area planted (a)	Output (b)	Yield	Gross value of output (c)	% of South African production (d)
	Ha.	M. tons (1000)	Tons/ Ha.	R (1000)	
1957–59	7 129	170	23,8	712	2,1
1963–65	9 039	176	19,5	869	1,7
1968–70	13 530	340	25,1	1 657	2,2
1971–73	13 463	380	28,2	2 199	2,4
Annual growth rate (%)	4,05	5,16		7,30	

Sources: (a) and (b) *Agriculture, Annual Reports*, 1957–1973
(c) (Sugar-cane prices) and (d) *The South African Sugar Year Book*, 1957–1973

Compared with the total production of sugar-cane in South Africa, cane output in KwaZulu increased at an annual rate slightly higher than that of the rest of the country – 5,16 per cent as against 4,12 per cent. It must be emphasised, however, that while in the late 1950s the territory's production amounted to approximately 2 per cent of the total output for the country, in 1973 the percentage stood at 2,5. It appears therefore that either circumstances or deliberate policy did not allow KwaZulu to acquire over the years a significantly greater share of the sugar industry of South Africa.

Cane yields obtained by African growers in all regions were disappointing. The average annual yield per hectare over the period 1957–73 amounted to approximately 22 tons while the highest yield ever recorded was only 32 tons. In contrast, over the same period, yields obtained on white-owned farms averaged 46 tons per hectare.[18] Land under sugar-cane in KwaZulu, therefore, produced somewhat less than half the industrial-average yield. Had land been operated at the industrial average, potential output would have yielded another R1,2 million gross earnings to KwaZulu sugar farmers, an increase of approximately 50 per cent on actual earnings.

The growth potential of the sugar industry in KwaZulu is high. According to estimates made by the Sugar Association, the South African sugar industry, in 1973, was faced with having to increase its annual production by 30 per cent by 1980 to meet increasing local demand,[19] and would be hard put to meet the challenge. On the other hand, a survey conducted by the Department of Agriculture, KwaZulu, in 1973 indicated that KwaZulu had about 100 000 ha. of land suitable for sugar production within economical transport distance of established mills. Only 13 per cent of this land was used for the purpose for which it was best suited. On the strength of this evidence, the central government released 4 000 ha. of new quotas to KwaZulu in 1974. A further 2 800 ha. which was held in reserve by the sugar industry Central Board was also made available to KwaZulu growers. This release of 6 800 ha. of quota represented a 50 per cent increase on existing plantings.[20]

Two factors, however, appeared to handicap the long-term exploitation of the cane-growing potential of the homeland. First, the traditional land-tenure system which has divided the land into a great number of small allotments, would have had to be changed substantially to make provision for the establishment of 10 ha. plots, estimated to be the minimum size for an economically viable sugar farm.[21] Assuming it was possible to redistribute land – or to introduce a communal-farm type of operation into an improved land-tenure system – so as to bring under cane the 100 000 ha. suitable for sugar production, some 10 000 families could have been settled on the land as full-time farmers.

The second obstacle in the way of the full development of the sugar industry was the magnitude of the capital required. The Sugar Association estimated that to establish a 10 ha. plot would involve, at 1974 costs, an expenditure of some R4 500. On this basis, if provision was made for expenditure on infrastructures, the overall sugar development scheme would have required an injection of capital into KwaZulu in the region of R50–60 million.

The returns, of course, would have been high; apart from creating the new employment opportunities just mentioned, a fully developed sugar industry, operating at the industrial average yield, would have earned KwaZulu, at 1973 prices, some R28 million per annum. This would have provided the average sugar farmer with a gross annual income of approximately R2 500. This income from sugar farming could have been supplemented by other farming activities, such as small-scale animal husbandry and horticulture.[22]

FIBRE CROPS

In an attempt to provide work for non-farming Africans and to test the possibility of introducing new cash crops in KwaZulu, in the late 1950s the Bantu Administration Department established plantations of fibre crops – *Furcraea* and *Phormium tenax*. The former proved an unsuccessful crop; slow growth, low yields and uneconomic market prices for the fibre brought its cultivation to an end in 1965, and it was replaced by sisal. *Phormium tenax*, on the other hand, proved to be a useful fibre. Its output, which was a mere 50 tons in the first harvest year (1959), rose to over 3 700 tons in 1973, yielding the Bantu Trust a gross revenue of R177 000 from its fibre sale to the Butterworth Bag Factory in Transkei. The number of fibre plantations in 1973 amounted to 11, located in 7 districts.[23]

Forestry products

Forestry in the economy of KwaZulu ranked fairly low in importance among the enterprises of the primary sector. Commercial forestry contributed only marginally to the value of product of that sector; forestry activities were almost entirely confined to the production of timber for fuel and for other non-commercial purposes.

In 1971 approximately 10 500 ha. were under wattle cultivation; government plantations accounted for one-third of the total. If a similar amount of land planted to other trees is taken into account, it would appear that only 0,6 per cent of the total land area of KwaZulu was used for afforestation.

It was estimated[24] that the forestry industry in KwaZulu could have been expanded to five times its size; at least 100 000 ha. of land appeared to be ideally suited to afforestation. However, there were necessarily great difficulties encountered in the establishment of forestry as a cash-income producing industry within the area. The first was that forestry had to compete, in a land-shortage situation, with livestock, for the farmers' attention. Given the special attachment to cattle, which is capable of overriding most economic considerations – as will emerge clearly from the discussion on animal husbandry – it was clear that in the majority of cases the possibilities of forestry would be dismissed.

It must be remembered, too, that forestry is a crop; within the spectrum of crop production, it may well have appeared unattractive to many farmers whose main motive for crop choice was the satisfaction of domestic needs.

The fact that many Zulu farmers, despite the suitability or otherwise of the land, selected maize as their major crop, further supports this theory.

ANIMAL HUSBANDRY

It will appear from the following discussion that animal husbandry in KwaZulu displayed certain features which, while characteristic of other African economies, are alien to the Western mode of agricultural production. A few introductory observations on the attitude of African farmers to livestock are therefore necessary in order that what may appear absurd in terms of purely financial considerations, may be understood as natural within the framework of the customs and social values of KwaZulu.

The social system of the African community is bound up in the closest possible manner with livestock ownership. Livestock, and cattle in particular, fulfil certain functions which are probably even more important than the obvious economic ones of acting as a source of income and a factor of production; livestock is regarded as a store of wealth and as a medium of exchange. Acquisition of livestock is probably the most important form of private investment in the homelands of South Africa and is the customary method of amassing wealth. Precluded from buying land and often unable to canalise their savings into industrial or commercial enterprises, Africans indulge in excessive investment in stock, often preferring number to quality; the possession of livestock in itself gives weight and dignity to the owner. The productive capacity of the stock is often of little significance.

Livestock population

The relevant statistics concerning the size and composition of the livestock of KwaZulu are summarised in table 5.

Two main points emerge from the data in the table. Firstly, during the period 1957–73 the numbers of livestock in KwaZulu remained practically unchanged. Apart from minor yearly fluctuations, total animal units decreased by a mere 0,01 per cent per annum, from 1 509 million units in 1957–59 to 1 508 million in 1971–73. In 1972, for example, the livestock population was almost identical to that of 1957.

Secondly, the size of the herd in KwaZulu has always been excessive in relation to the carrying capacity of the land. In 1957, for example, with an estimated average carrying capacity of 2,52 ha. of land per L.S.U., the optimum stock population should have been 1 129 627 units. The actual population amounted to 1 494 599 units, representing a rate of overstocking of 32 per cent. In years of favourable weather, e.g. 1961–64, the overstocking rate rose as high as 38 per cent; in more recent years, due to land increase and a cyclical contraction in stock numbers brought about by years of lower rainfall, the surplus decreased somewhat, and in 1973 the rate of overstocking stood at 21 per cent.[25]

Table 5 Livestock population and estimated surpluses KwaZulu 1957–1973

Periods (3 year averages)	Livestock (1000)				Total LSU[1] (1000)	Estimated surplus (1000)	Over-stocking[2] %
	Cattle	Sheep	Goats	Equines			
1957–59	1 247	252	663	109	1 509	341	29
1963–65	1 342	241	655	90	1 581	408	34
1968–70	1 222	239	638	94	1 463	261	21
1971–73	1 246	268	694	101	1 508	274	22
Annual growth rate (%)	–0,01	0,39	0,29	–0,48	–0,01	–1,35	

Notes: (1) A LSU (Large Stock Unit) is taken as one mature beast, or six goats or sheep, or two yearling beasts, or four cows under eight months, or one donkey or horse.

(2) Actual LSU as a percentage of optimal livestock population based on the estimated carrying capacity of the land.

Source: Agriculture, Annual Reports, 1957–1973.

The economic consequences of overstocking are evident. In a situation where free access to communal grazing exists, the practice has had heavy social costs as it leads to veld erosion and to constant deterioration of the community's land resources. From the individual farmer's point of view, overstocking may well have equally high private costs. An example of this is provided by the heavy stock losses suffered by KwaZulu farmers each year – losses which are, to a great extent, the result of the tendency in the livestock population to gravitate to the maximum number which the land will bear. Between 1959 and 1973 cattle losses in KwaZulu averaged nearly 9 per cent of the cattle population.[26] In 1959–60, for which comparative figures are available, losses stood at 7,4 per cent in the African reserves of Natal as against 3,9 per cent on white farms in the province.[27] Cattle losses due to diseases and malnutrition in KwaZulu far exceeded the reduction in numbers through sales and slaughtering. For example, in 1970, 66,2 per cent of the yearly reduction in cattle number was accounted for by losses; sales and slaughter only represented one-third of the total decrease. It follows that in that year, for every animal that was used for commercial gain, two died from disease, old age, or hunger and thirst. Some commentators[28] have agreed that the prevalent tendency among African farmers to accumulate cattle should be recognised as a sign of an impressive willingness and capacity to save; investment in livestock has provided a higher rate of return than the few alternatives open to African farmers and should therefore be regarded as a rational type of investment and not a 'quaint tribal custom'. Be that as it may when investment in livestock is excessive, the marginal product of live-stock tends to decrease not only in absolute terms but relative to the product of other inputs. In such a situation, an intra-sectoral reallocation of investment would be conducive to the attainment of a higher agricultural output and to an even more rational use of given resources. A change in investment decisions, however, presupposes a substantial change in the motivation of the decision maker; figures at our disposal (table 5) seem to prove that such a transformation had not yet taken place by 1973.[29]

Attempts at a solution of the overstocking problem
The administration attempted for years to improve the state of cattle husbandry in KwaZulu by means of a two-pronged policy: (a) by encouraging the sale of stock and the rate of meat consumption, which would both decrease the stock surplus and increase income to rural households, and (b) by enforcing regulations concerned with compulsory stock limitation and by introducing sound breeding policies. The sale of cattle has always been regarded as the only effective long-term solution to overstocking.

CATTLE SALES AND PRIVATE SLAUGHTERING
Sales figures presented in table 6 indicate that the efforts of the administration were rewarded with only marginal success. While auction sales increased at an annual rate of 0,2 per cent and showed significant improvement in 1973, sales to abattoirs and butcheries declined, with the result that the total volume of sales decreased by 0,25 per cent per annum between 1957 and 1973. On average, the proportion of cattle marketed amounted to 2,1 per cent of the total cattle population and never exceeded 2,8 per cent. Auction prices, which rose at the rate of 6,8 per cent per annum, had only a modest effect on inducing owners to send a larger proportion of their cattle to sales-pens.

Revenue derived from the marketing of cattle, which showed an annual rate of increase of 6,5 per cent, rose from approximately R750 000 in 1957 to nearly R4 million in 1973. Over the period under review, cattle sales did not show any sustained trend; yearly fluctuations were fairly pronounced.

This inconsistent marketing activity was probably related to fluctuations in the level of output in the food sector of agriculture; there appears to have been a negative correlation between the volume of cattle sales and the level of output of the main food crops. The size of the cattle herd, on the other hand, does not appear to have been a determinant of sales. As the numbers of cattle increased steadily between 1960 and 1964, the level of sales was low; as the numbers contracted after 1964, due to a sequence of years of unfavourable weather conditions, sales increased, always directed, in their yearly fluctuations, by the trend of maize output. It appears logical, therefore, to infer that the volume of sales was determined neither by the numbers of stock on hand nor by prices. The marketing of cattle in KwaZulu appears to have occurred as an ancillary function to crop farming; cattle were retained as a store of wealth and only a small

Table 6   Cattle, physical volume and gross value of sales and private slaughtering KwaZulu 1957–1973

Year	Sales				Private slaughtering			
	Number	Growth index (1957–59 = 100)	% Cattle population	Gross value R (1000)	Number	Growth index (1957–59 = 100)	% Cattle population	Gross value R (1000)
1957	22 852	84	1,8	731	28 132	81	2,3	928
1965	32 812	121	2,5	1 345	49 770	143	3,8	1 991
1970	29 710	110	2,4	1 634	35 806	103	2,9	1 898
1973	27 233	100	2,2	3 902	32 200	93	2,6	4 121
Annual growth rate (%)	−0,24			6,52	−0,49			5,75

Source: Agriculture, Annual Reports, 1957–1973.

proportion of this wealth was realised every year to maintain a past level of income and to offset losses of income experienced in other sectors of agriculture.[30]

The numbers of cattle slaughtered for direct consumption were considerably higher than those of cattle marketed; between 1957 and 1973 they averaged 3,2 per cent of the total cattle population as against 2,1 per cent for total sales. Estimated beef consumption, as table 6 shows, remained fairly constant over the years. However, given a yearly increase in the value of stock of 6,2 per cent, gross income to rural households from private slaughtering increased from an estimated R0,9 million in 1957 to R4,1 million in 1973.

The rate of meat consumption appeared to follow fairly closely the size of the herd and its rate of change. The greater the rate of increase in the number of cattle, the greater the propensity to consume, and vice versa.

The rate of turnover (number of cattle marketed and consumed as a percentage of the herd) prevailing in the cattle husbandry of KwaZulu was approximately a third of the turnover rate of the modern agricultural sector of South Africa where the turnover rate is estimated at 16 per cent.[31] The average rate in KwaZulu between 1957 and 1973 was 5,4 per cent. Taking 1973 as an example, it is interesting to speculate that had KwaZulu farmers operated on a turnover rate of 16 per cent of a smaller herd – reduced to its optimum number in terms of the carrying capacity of the land – gross revenue at prevailing market prices would have amounted to some R16 million against the R4 million of the actual estimated earnings. Income from cattle husbandry would thus have risen from R3.20 to R15.50 per cattle unit.

COMPULSORY STOCK LIMITATION

The second aspect of the administration's policy towards stock reduction consisted of compulsory culling of cattle and the introduction of a better breeding policy, aimed at persuading stock owners to prefer quality to numbers.

In the scheduled areas of the territory, where the Department could not exercise direct control over the use of land,[32] no stock culling could be enforced except where, upon the agreement of tribal authorities, wards had been declared 'betterment' areas. But even in such cases direct control over the number of cattle could not be achieved until betterment areas were divided into grazing camps, provided with the necessary water-points and generally equipped for efficient grazing control. By the end of 1970, only 203 000 ha. (or 8,6 per cent of the total grazing area of KwaZulu) was so organised,[33] implying that the necessary stock reduction to effect complete stabilisation had only been carried out on a very small portion of the land. The introduction of a sound breeding policy was hampered by the traditional practice of common grazing which made it practically impossible to isolate improved stock from inferior herds. As the Department's annual report of 1959 put it:

To permit the application of a progressive breeding system which aims at larger animals, higher production and greater fertility, the qualitative and quantitative deficiencies of the environment prevailing in the Bantu areas must first be lifted. The hereditary qualities in the progeny of the improved sires supplied by the Trust were denied full expression under the prevailing conditions. Add to this the extremely low standard of management and one is faced with a most complex problem.

Minor enterprises within the livestock industry

Despite the large numbers of cattle in the territory there was no dairying or hides industry as such. Various attempts were made to introduce commercial dairying to African farmers; co-operative societies were formed by the administration and assistance was given with the provision of dairying equipment and the finding of profitable outlets for the produce, such as creameries, condensaries and hospitals. The results were discouraging. Between 1957 and 1973 the number of commercial dairying schemes decreased from 42 to 8 and the number of participants from 402 to 51. Output in 1972 stood at 15 per cent of the 1957 level; gross revenue dropped from its highest level of R17 652 in 1958 to R6 176 in 1973.[34]

The productivity situation in the hide industry was equally disappointing. African stock-owners did not appear to appreciate the potential income that could be derived from the marketing of hides. The volume of hides sold through brokers, traders and speculators between 1957 and 1973 averaged approximately 44 per cent of total available hides. Revenue from sales fluctuated from approximately R118 000 in 1959 to R330 000 in 1962; the estimated value of sales in 1973 stood at approximately R104 000.[35]

Similarly, in spite of the fact that the sheep population in KwaZulu averaged over the years some 250 000 units, wool output was negligible. It varied from 110 tonnes in 1972, when the highest clip was recorded, to 8 tonnes in 1963. Revenue from the sale of wool never exceeded R54 000 per annum and in 1963 it only amounted to about R6 000. The low economic value of sheep, in terms of wool production, was to a great extent attributable to the quality of sheep reared in the homeland. They were of a nondescript type, being mostly of mixed breed; only about 30 per cent were woolled sheep. In contrast, 94 per cent of total white-owned sheep in Natal were Merino or wool-producing sheep.[36] In consequence, wool production in the territory was low, erratic and of little economic significance.

A similar situation prevailed in the husbandry of goats. A very small proportion of the goat population was of the Angora type;[37] consequently, mohair production was practically non-existent. The only recorded sales of mohair amounted to 2 149 kg. in 1969 and 34 kg. in 1970, yielding a gross revenue of R558 and R28 respectively. This is a surprising trend in the animal husbandry of KwaZulu, considering that some areas of the territory, namely the Drakensberg region, have ecological features similar to those of Lesotho where the mohair industry, despite its low productivity, marketed in 1969 an output of approximately 1,1 million kg.[38]

Few sheep or goats were ever sold. Hardly any were auctioned at stock sales and comparatively little stock was offered for sale to abattoirs and butcheries. In 1969, for example, 9 612 head, the highest number ever recorded, were sold to controlled markets; this represented 1,1 per cent of the total sheep and goat population of that year.[39] Far greater numbers of small stock were slaughtered for private consumption; in 1972 approximately 46 000 units were consumed directly as against 3 000 units sold. Commercial and domestic slaughter in that year represented 5,1 per cent of the combined sheep and goat population. The volume of sheep and goat skins sold between 1957 and 1972 was negligible both in number and in the gross revenue earned; against approximately 19 884 skins sold in 1957, only 16 255 were used for commercial gain in 1972.[40]

CONCLUSION

Our review of the state of the agricultural industry in KwaZulu over the period 1957–73 is summarised in table 7 where value estimates of all output, including that of activities not specifically mentioned in the discussion, are given; figure 1 offers a visual sense of the situation. At constant price evaluations, the gross value of output increased by 25 per cent at an annual rate of 1,4 per cent.

If the overall performance of agriculture in KwaZulu is compared with that of South Africa as a whole, the rates of real growth obtained in the homeland were considerably lower than the national average. This, in fact, amounted to 2,7 per cent per annum between 1958 and 1973.[41] It must be pointed out, however, that hardly any difference existed in the rates of growth in the crop husbandry division; although operating at lower yields of output, field-crop production in KwaZulu grew at the same rate as in South Africa.[42] The growth differential was particularly pronounced in the livestock farming sector; against an annual growth rate of 1,2 per cent for South Africa, the output of animal husbandry in KwaZulu declined at an annual rate of 0,5 per cent. This lopsided pattern of development in KwaZulu's agriculture is further indicated by the changes that occurred in the relative importance of the various industry groups within the sector. While in 1957 nearly two-thirds of the gross value of the output was contributed by livestock enterprises, the relative importance of the industry declined over the years and by 1973 it shared equally in the value of total output with crop production.

The encouraging development that took place in crop production did not materialise in the field of animal husbandry, being inhibited by the survival of a sense of the value of livestock proper to a pastoral people, but inappropriate by that time.

The question to be asked is why so little progress was made in KwaZulu towards the adoption of production techniques which could increase substantially the volume of output, standards of living and the level of employment.

Official reports, commenting on this matter, attributed the results obtained to the demonstration effects of cultivation plots established by

Table 7 Gross value of agricultural and forestry production at constant (1973) prices KwaZulu 1957–1973 (R1000)

Year	Field Products				Livestock and pastoral products				Total crops and animal products	Livestock changes (7)	Forestry (8)	Total gross value	Index of gross value (1957/59 = 100)
	Field crops (1)	Horticulture (2)	Industrial crops (3)	Total	Cattle (4)	Sheep and goats (5)	Pigs and poultry (6)	Total					
1957	4 059	1 398	776	6 233	7 972	424	1 453	9 849	16 082	–	611	16 693	89
1958	4 018	1 121	1 087	6 226	10 600	688	1 463	12 751	18 977	+ 470	594	20 041	106
1959	3 513	1 276	1 147	5 936	9 967	563	1 430	11 960	17 896	+1 342	563	19 801	105
1964	4 741	1 364	1 090	7 195	14 224	698	1 193	16 115	30 339	+3 042	485	33 866	180
1965	3 664	1 473	991	6 128	12 324	488	1 183	13 995	26 319	–6 375	488	20 432	108
1966	4 950	2 056	766	7 772	10 548	563	1 017	12 128	22 676	–7 227	487	15 936	85
1971	5 877	3 080	1 932	10 889	10 535	605	1 139	12 279	23 168	+3 209	532	26 909	143
1972	5 861	3 583	2 896	12 340	7 238	598	939	8 775	21 115	– 902	545	20 758	110
1973	4 337	3 596	2 673	10 606	9 024	593	1 093	10 710	21 316	+1 529	587	23 432	124
Annual growth rate (%)	2,06	6,41	5,87	3,88	–0,39	0,43	–1,95	–0,53	1,36		–0,37	1,39	

(1) Includes – Maize, sorghum, legumes, groundnuts
(2) Includes – Tubers, vegetables, fruits
(3) Includes – Sugar-cane, cotton, tobacco, fibres
(4) Includes – Sales, private slaughtering, sale of hides, milk consumption
(5) Includes – Sales, private slaughtering, products marketed and consumed
(6) Value of consumption
(7) Includes – Cattle, sheep and goats
(8) Includes – Sales and firewood consumption

Sources: Output: Agriculture, Annual Reports, 1957–73.
Prices: The sources of prices used in the evaluation of each item are given in Lenta, 'Economic structure of KwaZulu', Appendix B.

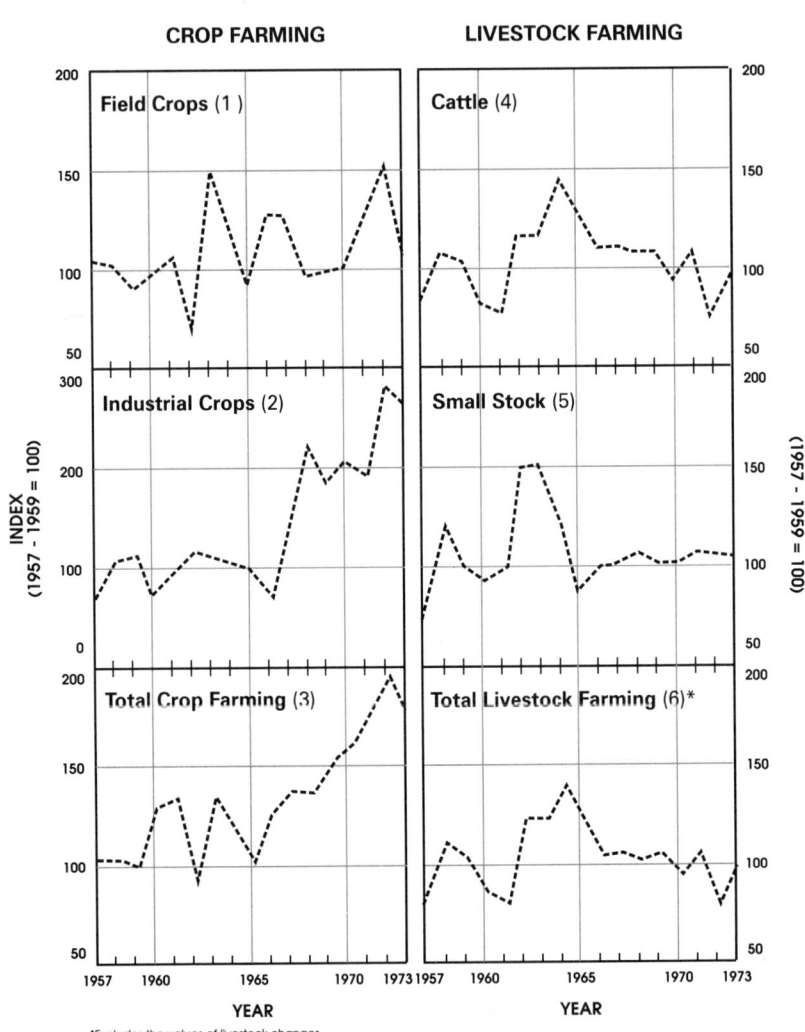

Figure 1   Real gross value of agricultural products

government officials on which the use of the new inputs, accompanied by progressive cropping techniques, yielded high output. The lack of further progress therefore can, to a large extent, be explained by the inadequacy of the extension work carried out in KwaZulu. Demonstration officers were in short supply; in 1965 the ratio of officers per landed household was 1:1420. Given the nature of rural life in the region, the fact that a large proportion of the population was illiterate and therefore unreachable by propaganda literature, and that economic and other conditions made travel difficult for farmers, it seemed essential, if farming methods were to be influenced at all, that officers with educational functions be employed in far larger numbers. Even on the basis of 1965's conservative estimate, each household could receive only a quarter of a day per year of contact with a district officer. While it is not the function of this study to suggest suitable educational methods, it is asserted that an unfilled potential for development existed, and continues to exist, in this area.

Further difficulties experienced in the diffusion of the new technology were the lack of facilities for transporting fertilizer to the farm and the lack of adequate supplies of seed due to the almost total absence of marketing facilities for this type of input.[43]

In addition, no credit facility of any significance, or subsidy grant, had ever been made available to the Zulu farmer for the acquisition of current inputs[44] – in contrast to the easy credit at the disposal of white farmers. Under these conditions, growth and productivity differentials between the two sectors become more easily understood. The willingness of the Zulu farmer to adopt new production techniques, to bear new risks and to implement what the advisory worker demonstrated as something more profitable, was dampened by factors often beyond the control of farmer and adviser alike.

It seems likely that the impetus for the central government to embark on educational programmes, and to provide economic stimuli to agriculture, was lacking because of misunderstandings about the attitudes of KwaZulu farmers to change.

It was claimed[45] that the low productivity of agriculture

> stems mainly from the method of land tenure, overpopulation and tribal customs . . . Very little use can be made of mechanisation and due to their [farmers'] beliefs and customs the use of good seed, fertilizer and crop spraying is ignored. For at least the coming decade very little improvement in productivity is to be expected, but if it is to improve, agriculture cannot become a significant source of new work.

This view, presupposing as it did, that the advantages of modern agricultural technology had been made clear to the KwaZulu farmer in a manner that took into consideration levels of education and experience among the farming population, appears on the evidence presented in the present study, to have been entirely inadequate. It assumed that irrational resistance to change on the side of the farmer formed the main impediment to development, whereas, in fact, changes had taken place despite the shortage of assistance to the farmer.

It is true that the extent of change was small. But the fact that, despite the difficulties handicapping farmers who wished to improve production, significant changes occurred, suggests that there existed in the KwaZulu community an interest in development and a willingness to learn. Yet the position still remains substantially the same. Demonstration officers are in short supply; scarcity of professional and technical manpower reduces the capacity of the region to absorb capital. It is evident that future development will be obstructed until the government makes adequate provision in this field.

It may well be that the solution to the problem of how to transform the agricultural sector cannot be sought in isolation from a total development strategy for the whole country. The link between migration and agricultural stagnation is clear, but the tide of migration cannot be induced to flow back into the rural areas so long as they remain relatively undeveloped. It is clear, too, that central government must intervene far more actively to develop agriculture, not only in KwaZulu, but in South Africa as a whole.

REFERENCES

1. I should like to express my gratitude to the Director and staff of the Department of Agriculture of the KwaZulu Government for their kindness in making available to me much of the information on which this study was based. This paper is a shortened version of one published as *Occasional Paper no. 7 (1978)* by the Department of Economics, University of Natal, Durban, whose permission to publish here is gratefully acknowledged.

2. Department of Statistics, *Report on Agricultural and Pastoral Production 1964–65*. Agricultural Census no.39, Part 1, Report no.06–01–07 (Pretoria, Government Printer, 1965), tables 3.1 and 3.2.

3. S.S. Brand, 'The contribution of agriculture to the economic development of South Africa since 1910' (unpublished D.Sc. Agric. thesis, University of Pretoria, 1969), p.205.

4. Arable land in 1960 and 1970 was estimated at 384 418 ha. and 451 643 ha. respectively. Bantu Administration and Development, Division of Agriculture, Natal, *Annual Reports*, 1960 and 1970.

5. *Annual Reports*, 1965 and 1972.

6. D. Hobart Houghton, in a survey on the agricultural activities in an African area, found that the hectarage ploughed in any year depends upon the adequacy of the rainfall, the condition of draught animals and the availability of able-bodied men to do the ploughing. D. Hobart Houghton and E.M. Walton, Keiskammahoek Rural Survey vol.2, *The economy of a native reserve*, (Pietermaritzburg, Shuter and Shooter, 1952).

7. Bantu Administration and Development, Division of Agriculture, Natal, *Annual Reports*, 1950, 1951 and 1965. Department of Agriculture and Forestry, KwaZulu, *Annual Report*, 1973.

8. Department of Agriculture and Forestry, KwaZulu, *Annual Report*, 1973.

9. For the period 1957–67, production figures were extracted from unpublished annual reports of the Agriculture and Forestry Division of the Department of Bantu Administration and Development; from 1968 to 1971, use was made of published (mimeographed) annual reports from the same source. For the years 1972 and 1973 statistics were taken from the annual reports of the Department of Agriculture and Forestry of the KwaZulu Government. From now on the annual reports will be referred to as 'Agriculture, *Annual Reports*'.

10. Merle Lipton, in comparing volumes and yields attained in the production of maize in the homelands – as indicated by official estimates – with those prevailing in other parts of the developing world, casts serious doubts on the validity and reliability of the official statistics. Production levels in the homelands, according to these estimates, appear incredibly low, even inferior to those obtained in some of the most arid regions of the African continent. This gives rise to a suspicion that the official estimates have either overstated the land area under the cultivation of the crop or have been too conservative in their calculation of output, or both. A survey conducted by Gill Westcott into agricultural methods in three locations of the Transkei where maize yields were found to be in the region of 6,5 bags per ha. – as against an average of 3,4 for KwaZulu over the period 1957–73 – seems to lend credibility to the Lipton contention. A *caveat* must therefore be entered in interpreting the figures used in this study. It is important to point out, however, that if the underestimation of production in the official reports has been applied with consistency over the years, growth trends and other indices of change would still remain valid.

    Merle Lipton, 'South Africa: two agricultures?' and Gill Westcott, 'Obstacles to agricultural development in the Transkei' in F. Wilson, A. Kooy and D. Hendrie (eds), *Farm labour in South Africa* (Cape Town, David Philip, 1977).

11. RP 84/1970, *Second Report of the Commission of Enquiry into Agriculture* (Pretoria, Government Printer, 1970), p. 127.

12. Department of Agricultural Economics and Marketing, Division of Agricultural Marketing Research, *Supplementary Data to the Abstract of Agricultural Statistics of the Republic of South Africa* (Pretoria, Government Printer, January 1969), table 13.

13. Department of Statistics, *Report on Agricultural and Pastoral Production, 1964–65*, Agricultural Census no. 39, Part 2, Report no. 06–01–07 (Pretoria, Government Printer, 1965), tables 2.5, 3.2, 6.2, 7.1, 10, 11.

14. For a comparison of factor endowments and factor utilisation between KwaZulu's and white agriculture, see Part II.

15. Department of Statistics, *Report on Agricultural and Pastoral Production, 1964–65*, Report no. 06–01–07 (Pretoria, Government Printer, 1965), tables 10, 11.

16. See E. H. Brookes and N. Hurwitz, *The native reserves of Natal*, NRS, vol. 7 (Cape Town, Oxford University Press, 1957), p. 108.

17. Besides sugar-cane, two other cash crops featured in the production pattern of the private sector of KwaZulu, viz. cotton and tobacco. They were minor crops both in absolute terms and relative to overall production. Their production declined steadily over the years and the combined gross value of output in 1973 merely stood at some R14 000 (see table 3).

18. *The South African Sugar Year Book*, 1957 to 1973.

19. *The Daily News*, 30 January, 1973.

20. Agriculture, *Annual Report*, 1973, p. 6.

21. This and following estimates were obtained from interviews with officials of the Sugar Association.

22. The immediate prospects of developing the newly released 7 800 ha. of quota appeared favourable. In 1973 the Sugar Association established a Small Cane Growers Financial Aid Fund, amounting to R5 million, aimed at providing financial assistance to sugar growers whose annual cane deliveries to a mill had not exceeded, over the two preceding years, 1 000 tons. Almost all KwaZulu growers fell into this category. Loans, granted to small farmers for a maximum of 10 years, could be repaid by cession of cane sales proceeds to a mill at low interest rates; this was to establish a system of revolving credit. The Association also provided extension facilities to African cane growers with the establishment of three training centres at which seminars, lectures and discussions on sugar-cane farming were held.

23. Capital expenditure undertaken by the government for the development of the 11 projects stood, at the end of 1973, at R315 000. Permanent employment in that year was provided for 390 people, with an approximately equal number employed as occasional labourers for a quarter of the year. (Unpublished information kindly supplied by the Department of Agriculture, KwaZulu.)

24. See A.J. Raubenheimer, 'The consolidated plans for KwaZulu and the economic potential of the homeland' in *A resume of the proceedings of a national conference on the development of Natal* (Durban, National Development and Management Foundation, November 1973), p. 36.

25. It would appear that the strong tendency of local farmers to overstock their land has always presented one of the greatest obstacles to agrarian development. Agriculture, *Annual Report*, 1959 comments: 'That the great majority of the Bantu Areas in Natal are overstocked out of all proportion requires no introduction (sic). That livestock in these areas have (sic) been and are existing on resource-capital is a known fact; overstocking remains the problem of the Bantu economy and merits top priority.' The Minister of Agriculture of the KwaZulu government in his policy speech to the Legislative Assembly in 1978 stated: 'Many tens of thousands of hectares of potentially good veld have been totally destroyed by overstocking and overgrazing . . . If we do not stop this abuse of our land, we will turn our country into a desert.' *Policy Speech*, 1978.

26. Agriculture, *Annual Reports*, 1959–1973.

27. RP 10/1964, Department of Statistics, *Report on Agricultural and Pastoral Production 1959–60*, Agricultural Census no. 34, no. 3, (Pretoria, Government Printer, 1960).

28. Merle Lipton, 'South Africa: two agricultures?'; G. Rutman, 'A test of the uneconomic culture thesis', *Journal of Development Studies*, July 1973.

29. Had cattle owners in KwaZulu been willing to market their cattle surplus, the volume of cash injection into the economy of the territory would have been substantial. In 1973, for example, estimated cattle surplus sold at current market prices would have yielded an income of approximately R20 million. Total stock would at the same time have decreased to the optimum number of 1 million units, still representing an investment in cattle of approximately R119 million. According to the Minister of Agriculture, KwaZulu, in 1977 only 9 400 head of cattle were sold out of a population of 1,4 million. 'Just to stabilize the cattle population the number of cattle marketed should have been in the vicinity of 100 000.' *Policy Speech*, 1978.

30. See Agriculture, *Annual Report*, 1962: 'The Departmental Stock Sales are hardly touching the livestock disposal problem, in that only 0,9 per cent of the total stock is marketed annually, whereas it is necessary to market 15 to 20 per cent if numbers are to be maintained at a level which can be adequately supported by the land. The question of revenue for the people is also involved, as it is quite wrong that people should suffer malnutrition, and inadequate income, while the revenue-earning capacity of the livestock remains unexploited.'

31. RP 84/1970, *Second Report of the Commission of Enquiry into Agriculture* (Pretoria, Government Printer, 1970), p. 135.

32. As opposed to Trust Farms, where, in terms of Proclamation no. 116 of 1949, the Department acquired full control and allowed no overstocking or overgrazing.

33. Agriculture, *Annual Report*, 1970.

34. Agriculture, *Annual Reports*, 1957 to 1973.

35. *Ibid.*

36. Department of Statistics, *Report of Agricultural and Pastoral Production 1946–1965*, Agricultural Census no. 39, Part 3, Report no. 06–01–07 (Pretoria, Government Printer, 1965).

37. 311 out of a given goat population of 577 357 in 1964–65. Department of Statistics, *Report on Agricultural and Pastoral Production 1964–1965*, Census no. 39, Part 3, Report no. 06–01–07 (Pretoria, Government Printer, 1965), table 4.1.

38. See J. C. Williams, 'Problems and prospects of the economic development of agriculture in Lesotho' (unpublished Ph. D. thesis, University of Natal, 1970), pp. 82–85.

39. Agriculture, *Annual Report*, 1963 commenting on the marketing of small stock, reports: 'The marketing of small stock still defies solution.'

40. Agriculture, *Annual Reports*, 1957 to 1973.

41. Gross value of agricultural production deflated by producers' price indices of agricultural products. Department of Statistics, *South African Statistics 1974*, pp. 9.32 and 8.23.

42. 3,76 per cent per annum in South Africa as a whole; 3,88 per cent per annum in KwaZulu.

43. Agriculture, *Annual Report*, 1973 remarks, 'Unfortunately the drive to use more fertilizer has also brought its problems. These mainly centre around the difficulty farmers experience in having supplies of fertilizer transported. This applies particularly to agricultural lime. In the high rainfall areas heavy applications are needed (1 ton to 1 acre as a minimum application) and these quantities of lime require an efficient system of distribution. It is certain that still greater quantities of fertilizer and lime would have been used by farmers if transport had been available. During the past season some difficulty was experienced in obtaining sufficient quantities of seed potatoes. This crop is increasing in popularity and seed may become a problem.'

44. With the exception of credit facilities made available to sugar farmers by the South African Sugar Association in the early 1970s.

45. J. Adendorff, 'Problems in the creation of infrastructure and techniques applied in the development of Zululand', (unpublished mimeograph, Durban, Institute of Social Research, University of Natal, February 1972), p. 1.

ABSTRACT

In 1910 the majority of white farmers in northern Natal were engaged in cattle and sheep farming. By 1936 the latter activity had expanded at the expense of the former, and a significant number of those who continued to run cattle had switched from beef production to dairying. As white ranchers developed better quality livestock they tended to exercise closer control over the size and movement of herds belonging to African tenants. The most intensive farming operations in the region were those conducted on the wattle and cotton plantations that emerged in isolated areas. As these had no space for labour tenants they were reliant upon the recruitment of wage-labourers. Plantation owners experienced acute shortages in competing with other employers for the services of local African rent and labour tenants during their 'free' periods, and in trying to raise labour from further afield. By contrast, livestock farmers were able to draw upon a huge rent and labour tenant population that was resident on their properties, though labour relations in the region were changing. By 1936 cash wages for labour tenants were the norm west of the Buffalo River and restrictions on labour tenant rights had become much more severe in an effort to convert them into wage labourers. Formal control of labour tenants was increased by legislation but farmers continued to be frustrated by the state's inability to control the movement of labourers, not least that of young Africans who were moving permanently off the land. By 1936 labour tenancy had changed very little east of the Buffalo River, where cash wages were still rare but tenants enjoyed almost unrestricted rights in land and livestock, and service obligations were not unduly burdensome. While the market economy had made a substantial impact on the 'system' of labour tenancy in northern Natal its effect had been very gradual. The 'system' had demonstrated a considerable resilience in the face of various pressures, with squatting still widespread on white-owned farms.

CHANGING FORMS OF AGRICULTURAL LABOUR ON WHITE-OWNED FARMS IN NORTHERN NATAL 1910–1936

Verne Harris

Between 1910 and 1936, the great majority of Africans living in the rural areas of northern Natal[1] were resident on white-owned farms.[2] The balance lived on one or other of the following categories of land: African-owned land, mission stations, Crown land, or 'reserve' land. In the latter areas African peasants[3] retained access to the means of production and, although income from migrant labour became increasingly important to the sustenance of peasant families, their ultimate security lay in the land which they worked. But the striking feature of social relations in the northern Natal country-side in the period under review, and what sets them apart from those in other regions of Natal, is the resilience of Africans in retaining their access to land on white-owned farms. At a time when white South African agriculture was rapidly becoming capitalist, and despite state attempts to curb squatting,[4] African rent tenants and labour tenants more dependent on rights in land and livestock than on wages made up the bulk of the African population on white-owned land.[5] This essay is concerned with examining and accounting for this phenomenon.

The capitalisation of agriculture, vital to the development of rural social relations, was perforce a gradual process in northern Natal. Markets in the region were small and access to outside markets limited. Moreover, in terms of farming potential, the region is predominantly marginal. Much of the land is suitable only for semi-intensive and extensive operations; and it is faced with disaster as a consequence of heavy grazing, and cultivation without irrigation, fertilization or the implementation of soil-conservation methods. Even today, farmers utilising advanced farming methods are frequently defeated by the environment when trying to intensify their operations.

Between 1910 and 1936, much of northern Natal's soils and grasses were exhausted by inexperienced, careless or overcrowded farmers, both white and African. Farmers, whether landlords or tenants (even the former having little access to modern technology) ignored the limits laid down by nature at their peril. In 1910 the vast majority of the region's white farmers conducted cattle- and sheep-farming operations, primarily for beef and wool. Maize, 'kaffir-corn', oats and wheat were grown for feed and labourers' rations. Kaffir-corn, which thrives in dry climates, was the

241

only crop which produced high yields. Maize, which flourishes in areas of laterite and lateritic red earths, with good rainfall and little frost – elements seldom found together in northern Natal – produced yields often half those of the Natal midlands.[6] In most parts of the region, maize cultivation had to be pursued carefully and with restraint if the soil were not to be exhausted. Even today, with the wider availability of fertilizers, hybrids and irrigation, maize cultivation remains a precarious pursuit.[7]

The period 1910–36 saw two noteworthy developments in livestock farming in northern Natal. Firstly, due largely to the prevalence of east coast fever in the sandy sourveld areas,[8] sheep farming expanded at the expense of cattle ranching.[9] Secondly, increasing numbers of farmers, particularly in Bergville and Klip River, switched to dairying.[10] In Bergville operations were semi-intensive, and milk was produced primarily for industrial purposes. In the rest of Klip River County,[11] with a lower rainfall and sparser grasses, operations were more extensive and the main product was butterfat for creameries.[12] In both instances, the development led to a squeeze on rent and labour tenants; with better quality herds to sustain and protect, white farmers sought a tighter control over the size and movement of tenant herds.

A high proportion of northern Natal's ranchers were Free State and Transvaal farmers who had purchased farms in the region for winter grazing and as a source of labour. In addition, a significant number of wealthier farmers in the highveld areas of northern Natal owned farms in the lowveld for the same purposes. At the beginning of every winter thousands of cattle and sheep were driven down into the lowveld; some indication of the scale of this annual migration is given by the Ngotshe magistrate's 1912 estimate of between 60 and 70 thousand sheep being moved into his district annually.[13] The evidence suggests that a substantial number of highveld farmers who owned properties in the lowveld used bywoners[14] to supervise them and to care for their sheep and cattle in the winter months.[15] But there were other categories of bywoner in northern Natal as well. There is evidence of farmers (particularly Afrikaans-speaking farmers) with large properties apportioning land to landless whites. As Professor Boshoff remembers of his childhood in Utrecht:

> . . . daar was na 1910 nog heelwat bywoners. In die omgewing waar ek groot geword het was daar enklikes wat ek goed kan onthou. By ons op die plaas was daar 'n bywoner het en met 1924.[16]

It also appears that many farms were wholly occupied by white share-croppers.[17] By the 1930s bywoners, more so than African tenants, began to feel the squeeze. In Dundee, for example, the extension of farming operations saw the elimination of virtually all the district's bywoners in the decade before the Second World War.[18] However, in certain districts the practice endured well into the post-war era. As Hurwitz noted in 1957:

Farms on the 'shares system' are mostly concentrated in the northern districts, especially Utrecht, Vryheid and Newcastle. This is mainly due to share croppers, who have not entirely disappeared.[19]

Given the evidence referred to above, it is uncertain why the *Report of the Carnegie Commission on the Poor White Problem in South Africa* (1932), which devoted a complete volume to rural impoverishment, failed even to mention the presence of *bywoners* in northern Natal.[20]

While ranching and dairying were the dominant white farming operations in the region, the most intensive were those conducted on the wattle and cotton plantations which emerged in isolated areas. The only areas suitable for wattle in northern Natal are in the districts of Vryheid, Babanango and Paulpietersburg.[21] They are on the escarpments with an aspect precluding conditions that are too hot and too dry. In 1904 there were only 889 acres under wattle in the region;[22] by 1936, 30 550 acres were under timber and wattle.[23] An important feature of the wattle plantation is that space does not allow for labour tenants: wattle farmers relied almost wholly on recruited cash labourers.[24] Like the wattle plantations, the cotton plantations of Ngotshe required a large labour force and were unable to employ labour tenants.[25] Cotton was grown for the first time in Ngotshe in 1919 and, after initial difficulties, covered 24 471 acres in 1926. Thereafter, despite the establishment of several state-aided irrigation schemes, cultivation was steadily reduced, and by 1936 no more than 196 acres were under cotton.[26]

Precisely because the operations of the cotton and wattle growers were more efficient than those of northern Natal's other farmers, their problems in securing an adequate labour force were most acute. Their attempts were directed towards employing local cash labourers, and African rent and labour tenants during their 'free' periods. Their endeavours brought them into direct competition with the towns, the coal-mines and the Rand employers (particularly the gold-mines), and they met with very little success. The Kambula Farmers' Association, which represented wattle-growing interests, complained to the Native Farm Labour Committee (1937–1939):

> The Zulu boys are too rich and do not want to work today . . . The local boys do not want to work on a farm, even for £2. 0s 0d a month.[27]

And a cotton grower informed the same committee:

> Today we are employing about 300 boys, 230 shangaans and 70 Zulus. We have tried to force the local natives out to work but nothing helps.[28]

Both wattle and cotton growers were forced to rely on recruited labour from the Transvaal, Basutoland and Mozambique. However, confronted by restrictions on recruiting and prohibitive recruiting fees, both often experienced acute labour shortages. In 1937, for example, the Kambula

Farmers' Association employed 300 labourers at a time when their work load required 2 000.[29] The growers petitioned the government repeatedly to relax restrictions on recruiting in Mozambique, and at the same time ignored them. This was particularly true of the cotton growers, who required labourers resistant to malaria and used to extremely hot weather:

> We employ many Portuguese natives without registration . . . There are also men recruiting illegally there. People must have labour and they will do anything to get labour. We want to regularise the recruiting of P.E.A. [Portuguese East African] natives.[30]

While wattle and cotton growers struggled to establish an adequate labour pool, northern Natal's livestock farmers could call on a huge rent and labour tenant population. In the period under review, this population found its rights in land and livestock increasingly encroached upon and faced greater demands from landlords to provide labour. Nevertheless, and despite the operation of the 1913 Natives' Land Act, a significant proportion was able to avoid anything more than slight labour obligations through 1936. The Natives' Land Act did not demand the eviction of squatters in Natal, merely the control of all future squatter transactions. However, there were an unusual number of evictions in certain parts of Natal at the time the Natives' Land Act was passed, and there is evidence of farmers using the Act to put pressure on tenants to yield labour services. As the Natives' Land Commission (1916) was informed by the Dundee magistrate:

> I cannot say that there have been really more evictions owing to the Act. When the Act was first promulgated there was a kind of alarm, as some farmers threatened the natives therewith, but not many, I think, actually turned them off, but since then things have calmed down.[31]

It was to the 'not many' that Chief Sandanezwe referred when he told the Commission:

> Even as I am speaking here there are many natives homeless in the veld with their bundles. Two years were mentioned as the time in which things would be rectified, but things have become worse . . .[32]

Witnesses from Klip River, Newcastle, Utrecht, Bergville and Paul-pietersburg also mentioned an increase in the number of evictions.

No doubt many of the farmers carrying out evictions were under the impression that the Act demanded this of them, or at least they were afraid the moratorium on evictions in Natal would be lifted soon and they were therefore attempting to avoid being caught unprepared. However, many evictions, perhaps most of them, were not directly related to the Natives' Land Act. As the Bergville magistrate informed the Natives' Land Commission:

I do not know of a single eviction having taken place in my district since the Act came into force which was due to the Act.[33]

As white farmers attempted to use their land more efficiently, squatters were beginning to feel the squeeze, but this remained comparatively slight in the period 1910–36. The capitalisation of agriculture in northern Natal was slow and uneven, while the Natives' Land Act's restriction on squatting was relatively easy to avoid. That it was avoided in Natal as a whole is made plain by the Natal Agricultural Union's request to the Government in 1925 to 'enforce the Law of 1913 relative to native renters on farms',[34] and in the following year to take 'drastic action' against landowners leasing land to African rent tenants.[35]

Before examining squatting on white-owned farms in northern Natal, it is important to define the categories of African rural-dweller which demand attention. Firstly, there is the African rent tenant who dwelt on land not occupied by its white owner. Most of this land was owned by individuals, specifically livestock farmers, the great land companies of the colonial period being in a state of rapid decline by 1910. In that year a mere 47 608 acres was owned by land companies in Klip River County.[36] This form of squatting was known to farmers and to the Native Affairs Department as 'kaffir farming'. Closely related to it was a form of labour tenancy which utilised 'labour farms'. In the words of R. H. Smith:

> One of the forms of labour tenancy . . . is scarcely distinguishable from kaffir farming. When the farmer owns two farms, for example, he may abandon one entirely to Native agriculture; and in return for such occupation, the Native residents pay a rent not in money or kind but in labour.[37]

In order to qualify as farm labourers in terms of the Natives' Land Act these residents were obliged to provide the landowner with at least ninety days of service in each calendar year. This requirement was met only infrequently, and in many instances 'kaffir farms' were labelled 'labour farms' in order to avoid the Act's restrictions on squatting. Thirdly, there is the African rent tenant who dwelt on land occupied by its white owner. This was not common in northern Natal. Also uncommon was a fourth category, the labour tenant who paid rent in kind or cash, in addition to the labour he provided, for the privilege of dwelling on land occupied by its owner. No reference to African share croppers in the region could be found.

Given the exceptional character of the latter two categories and the difficulties entailed in quantifying them, the most useful measures of squatting are the number of Africans dwelling on farms owned but not occupied by whites and the extent of these farms. Precise figures for the whole of northern Natal could only be found for 1916 (gathered and compiled by the Natives' Land Commission).[38] They suggest that squatting was particularly extensive in Helpmekaar, Ngotshe and Dundee, and slight in Bergville and Paulpietersburg. However, it is plain that the commission regarded white-owned farms occupied by whites for only part of the year as being in the category of land owned and occupied by its owner. Consequently, their figures underestimate the extent of squatting, which was extensive on farms occupied by whites only during the winter. Confronted by the paucity of statistics on squatting, the researcher is forced to rely on the collation of impressions given by farmers and magistrates in order to trace its development between 1916 and 1936. What follows is an impressionistic account of the position in each of northern Natal's magisterial districts.

According to the Natives' Land Commission squatting was rare in Bergville by 1916. Yet the 1910 *Blue Book on Native Affairs* quotes the local magistrate as saying that 'the system known as "kaffir farming" is carried on to a considerable extent'.[39] The Natives' Land Commission was told by the same magistrate that there were a 'good many' squatters in Bergville, most of whom dwelt on farms owned by Free State farmers who used them for grazing their stock in winter.[40] In theory these farms were labour farms, but according to the local magistrate most of the African tenants on them were rent tenants.[41] The only acceptable explanation for the disparity between this impression and that given by the Land Commission report is that the latter regarded white-owned farms occupied by whites for the winter as land owned and occupied by whites. That the bias this introduces is considerable becomes plain when it is considered that the practice outlined above was common in all the lowveld areas of northern Natal. In the opinion of the Bergville Native Commissioner the practice remained common in Bergville through 1934.[42]

The Elandslaagte Farmers' Association of Klip River informed the Native Farm Labour Committee that there were 'many kaffir farms' in the district, rents in most instances being collected in the guise of dipping fees.[43] A similar use (or abuse) of dipping fees was common in Helpmekaar.[44] Farmers interviewed in Dundee by the Native Economic Commission (1930–32) spoke of 'kaffir farming' as the 'curse of the district'.[45] George Pringle, who farmed in the Dundee district from 1931, remembered that most of the 'kaffir farms' were owned by Free State farmers who demanded rent in the form of cattle.[46] According to the magistrate of Ngotshe, in 1916 very few farms in his district were occupied by their owners, most of whom lived in the Free State, Utrecht, Wakkerstroom and Dundee.[47] This held throughout the 1930s, figures supplied by the 1930 Inter-Departmental Committee on the Labour Resources of the Union suggesting that the African population on farms unoccupied by whites in Ngotshe had increased slightly since 1916.[48]

'Kaffir farming' was rare in both Utrecht and Paulpietersburg, but labour farms were common. There is no evidence from these districts of pseudo-labour tenancy, and it seems that the labour demands placed on the tenants changed very little between 1916 and 1936. In the Vryheid/ Babanango district, where 'kaffir farming' strictly defined was also rare, there is abundant evidence of pseudo-labour tenancy. In 1925 the magistrate of Babanango referred to 'the fact that certain large land owners still allow numbers of Natives to squat without rendering much service for the privilege . . .'[49] A decade later the Native Farm Labour Committee heard from most of the farmers interviewed in the district that the practice, which they labelled 'kaffir farming', was still rife. As one farmer complained:

> Die groot moeilikheid so ver arbeid in hierdie distrik betref is die hoeveelheid kafferboere. Die kaffers plak hulself neer op die plase en lewer min of geen dienste nie. Hulle betaal 4/- per bees per jaar dip-fooi.[50]

The same pattern is evident in Newcastle, although figures supplied to the Chief Native Commissioner in 1936 show the African population on unsupervised white land to be 295 (compared to 1 382 in 1916).[51] Official figures failed to reflect the fact that squatting remained a problem for commercialising farmers in the district, as is evident from the following complaint by a Newcastle farmer in 1930:

> . . . there are evasions going on to a considerable extent under this squatting business . . . Of course, it is due to the fact that the whole of the country is under-policed . . . we know perfectly well what is going on. Farmers' meetings too have raised this matter, but it does not help . . . kaffir farming is just becoming as rampant again as it ever was. There was a check put on it in 1913 under the Act, but not [sic] it has increased again.[52]

It is plain, then, that the Natives' Land Act made no significant impact on squatting on white-owned land in northern Natal. While it was not a dead letter, the capitalisation of agriculture rather than its operation explains any squeeze on squatters before 1936. The capitalisation of agriculture also explains the squeeze exerted on northern Natal's labour tenants in the period under review. The mid-1930s saw increasing numbers of farmers eroding their labour tenants' rights in land and livestock in an attempt eventually to convert them into wage labourers. By 1936 the ultimate security of a significant number of nominal labour tenants lay not in their rights in land and livestock but in the wages (in cash and in kind) they received from their employers.

In giving evidence to the Native Economic Commission and the Native Farm Labour Committee, northern Natal's white farmers vigorously debated the advantages and disadvantages of the labour tenant system. They were almost unanimous, as never before, that the system was 'inefficient' and 'wasteful', and some eagerly looked forward to its demise. As one Newcastle farmer informed the Committee:

> Dit sal my gelukkigste dag wees as my plaas skoon is van plakkerdiensbodes, en ek sal bly wees om £2 0s 0d of meer te betaal vir voltydse arbeiders. 'Jim Fish' kan werk waar hy wil.[53]

In saying this he spoke for the wealthier, commercialising farmers. But most of those who gave evidence, while conceding its relative inefficiency, did not wish for fundamental change. In defence of this view they listed several advantages of the system: it protected a way of life treasured by Africans and which promised best to promote healthy relations between whites and Africans; it enabled farmers, most of whom possessed little liquid capital, to weather the competition of mines, towns and plantations; and it was suited to the irregular labour demands of extensive stock farming. But by far the most frequently mentioned factor was the fierce resistance staged by labour tenants against any attempts to erode their rights in land and livestock.

Writing in 1931, C.H. Neveling, in his study of farm labour in South Africa, noted that

> many prominent and progressive farmers have already endeavoured to introduce a system of cash wages in lieu of land, but without success . . . the Native holds out for a piece of land which he may call his own . . .[54]

This was certainly true of northern Natal. Initial resistance took the form of refusals to accept increased wages in return for reduced rights in land and livestock, and refusals to abide by landowners' limitations on the latter.[55] The final step was to leave and search for a farmer prepared to offer more attractive terms or, more desirably, a landlord who would not demand any labour services. Two examples illustrate the many complaints about this phenomenon made by northern Natal farmers after 1930:

> A farmer is always keeping down the amount of native stock on his farm and a progressive farmer does his utmost to keep it down. But there is a limit; as soon as he gets it well down the native refuses to stay.[56]

And again:

> . . . only two miles away the natives get little or no wage, but they get grazing and lands, just as they desire, and were I to attempt to bring any of these over to my farm on cash wages I would fail. They are very happy and contented.[57]

With the growing squeeze on labour tenants, the phenomenon became increasingly commonplace. According to the magistrate of Klip River it contributed significantly to the 'constant movement of native kraals from place to place' noted by him in 1934.[58]

But the system of labour tenancy was not only being eroded by white farmers. It was also being threatened by the rebellion of young African men and women against their elders. The latter assumed absolute control over the labour power of the former, the kraal head contracting with the farmer on behalf of the whole kraal.[59] In their free periods young men and women were either required to work the kraal's land, labour for additional wages under the farmer, or were permitted to seek work on the mines or in the towns. The last alternative frequently led to complications, labourers often breaking the contracts entered into by their elders by arriving back at the farm late. However, the period 1910–36 saw the growth of a far more serious complication – increasing numbers of young men and women deserted the farms either for long periods of time or permanently. The Native Affairs Department commented on this with regard to South Africa as a whole in its 1926 report:

> A further cause of the bitter complaint by the employer is the readiness of the young and serviceable native to absent himself, often for years, from the obligations undertaken by him or on his behalf, while cheerfully leaving his family or dependants to enjoy the benefits of the contract.[60]

Complaints by farmers in northern Natal were heard as early as 1910;[61] judging by a number of complaints presented to the Native Economic Commission, Native Farm Labour Committee and Chief Native Commissioner after 1930, the phenomenon became more widespread from the late 1920s.[62]

Why did young men and women abandon their elders to probable eviction? Africans interviewed by the Native Economic Commission and the Native Farm Labour Committee presented a wide range of reasons, but three principal factors can be identified. Firstly, the impoverishment of elders caused by farmers' limitations on labour tenants' livestock constituted a threat to the ability of young men to acquire wives. They were therefore forced to look elsewhere for sufficient wealth. The Revd Africa of Dundee referred to this when he listed the following point as one explanation for the labour shortage experienced by some farmers:

> Stock not being allowed on the farms. Some farmers do not allow any sheep or goats and only a very limited number of cattle, about 6 head. The young men have to run away to earn money to pay lobolo when they want to get married.[63]

The relatively high wages on the mines and in the towns, particularly those of the Rand, were most attractive. Secondly, the mines and towns presented Africans with a vastly different environment. In it they developed new values which further undermined the authority of their elders. As Newcastle clerk P. Mtembu told the Native Economic Commission:

> . . . many of our people abandon their homes and go to towns, the mines, and to many other places. So our people who have in that way got away from tribal influence have now begun to grow up in an entirely newer environment, and are becoming an entirely different people . . . We find that our girls who go to town marry all kinds of people – all sorts of nationalities. The parents have little power to control their children in these circumstances.[64]

In this new environment the young African enjoyed greater independence, was able to purchase more consumer goods, and had greater access to formal education. Commenting on the latter, Industrial and Commercial Workers' Union member, Tembe, told the same commission:

> As soon as those children grow sufficiently old they run away from the farm and they go to towns, where they can get work . . . and they may perhaps also be able to get some schooling.[65]

Thirdly, desertions tended to snowball. If a young man failed to return for his period of service, the farmer would require his brother (or other adult member of the kraal) to supply the required services. That brother would probably have just completed his own period of service, which would mean his being tied down on the farm for a long period of time. The temptation for such a person to desert was great, especially if he worked for a farmer who offered no cash wage during the period of compulsory service.[66]

The state's inability to control the movement of labour tenants was a constant source of frustration to northern-Natal farmers. Dissatisfaction with the pass system increased during the period under review, the efflux of labour tenants increasing despite repeated legislative enactment. Too weak to trace pass-offenders effectively, and confronted by sustained resistance from Africans and urban and industrial employers, state machinery for control was further debilitated by the uncertain legal standing of labour tenant contracts. These were concluded between farmer and kraal head, and were usually verbal, of indefinite duration, and committed most members of the kraal to some form of service. The validity of these contracts was uncertain until specified in the Masters and Servants Law (Transvaal and Natal) Amendment Act of 1926 and the Native Service Contract Act of 1932. Until then each magistrate drew his own inferences from the existing laws, with the result that, as the Newcastle magistrate pointed out in 1925, 'both masters and servants find different rulings in different districts'.[67] However, as a rule, farmers found it extremely difficult to secure the conviction of contract-breakers, something which often caused acute resentment against magistrates.[68]

Between 1910 and 1932 the Natal Agricultural Union, attempting to meet the demands of both commercialising farmers and those protecting labour tenant pools, repeatedly called on the Government to make written contracts compulsory and to recognise the validity of contracts entered into on behalf of minors and wards.[69] Northern Natal's farmers, with a few exceptions, opposed the introduction of compulsory written contracts. While they conceded the desirability of such a measure in theory, they argued that the state was not strong enough to enforce it in the face of African resistance. Tenant resistance to written contracts certainly was fierce in northern Natal. A comment by the Babanango magistrate in 1925 illustrates this:

> As to written contracts, the natives seem unwilling to enter into them . . . I have heard of an instance where natives who had begged, and even paid fines to a farmer, to be allowed to remain on a farm, left at once when he decided to introduce a written contract.[70]

Why were tenants opposed to written contracts? Unfortunately the evidence consulted for this essay is largely that furnished by educated Africans (especially ministers of religion). However, despite this hiatus, it is reasonable to suppose on the basis of this evidence that tenant objection was essentially threefold: they resented tighter control; they feared the exploitation of their illiteracy by the farmers; and, being illiterate, they were wary of the written word. Tenant opposition ensured that by 1936 only a few northern Natal farmers had succeeded in introducing written contracts.

The legal recognition of verbal contracts made by kraal heads on behalf of their kraals was therefore vital for the control of labour tenant movement. But South Africa's employers of wage labour, seeking to bolster their uncertain labour supply, were opposed to such a step. Their influence was probably responsible for the attempt to include a prohibition on contracts between farmers and entire kraals in the 1917 Native Administration Bill,[71] and for the 1926 Masters and Servants Law (Transvaal and Natal) Amendment Act's specific rejection of all labour tenant contracts except those between farmers and individual tenants.[72] In terms of the latter a kraal head was still able to make a contract on behalf of a minor (a child under sixteen years of age), but was required to give his services at the same time.[73] The Native Service Contract Act ameliorated the 1926 Act (in the eyes of farmers employing labour tenants) by recognising contracts made by kraal heads on behalf of persons under eighteen years of age and by establishing that verbal contracts were as binding as written contracts.[74] From 1932, then, the farmer's hold over his labour tenants, at least formally, was far greater. However, he remained dependent on the efficient wielding by the state of the tools provided by legislative enactment, and his dissatisfaction with the state's control of labour tenant movement was as profound in 1937 as it had been in 1930.

Subject to both internal and external pressures, the system of labour tenancy in northern Natal was undergoing important changes. But precisely what impact did the market economy have on it? The remainder of this essay examines the position in each of northern Natal's districts in turn. The Bergville magistrate reported in 1910 that 'practically the whole of the labour on private farms is supplied by Native tenants under agreements to contribute labour in lieu of paying rent'.[75] On farms occupied by their white owners this usually involved six months' labour from each adult male (apart from the aged and kraal heads); labour obligations were not as onerous on the many labour farms in the district owned by Free State farmers. With the growth of dairying during the 1920s, white farmers increasingly restricted labour tenant rights and attempted to obtain more labour from their tenants. The Native Economic Commission reported in 1932 that the average labour-tenant kraal in Bergville was allowed four to five acres for cultivation and grazing for ten head of large stock or their equivalent of small stock.[76] This compared unfavourably with the rights enjoyed by most labour tenants in other districts. A Bergville farmer commented in 1937 that this was an important factor behind the drain of young Africans from the district.[77] Some farmers were forced to prohibit their labour tenants from leaving the farms during their free periods, while there is evidence of a growing use of casual labour by 1936.[78] Very little evidence could be found on wages, but it seems probable that Bergville farmers were in a position to offer higher cash wages to both labour tenants and casual labourers than could be offered by livestock farmers elsewhere in the region.

Labour tenancy arrangements were more diverse in Klip River than they were in Bergville. In 1910 the six-months-on/six-months-off arrangement was prevalent, and remained so through 1936.[79] However, pseudo-labour tenancy, particularly on the labour farms of the 'thorn district',[80] was widespread,[81] while the practice of calling out labour tenants on an irregular basis, for no wages and with no set obligations, the *lekelela* system, was common on farms owned by Afrikaans-speaking farmers.[82] At the same time, a small but growing number of farmers succeeded in effectively transforming their labour tenants into wage labourers with limited rights in land and livestock.[83] As early as 1918, casual labour was being utilised by some farmers during peak periods (this was widely available when the hut-tax drive began each year),[84] but the evidence suggests that it was never more than supplementary labour. Restrictions on labour tenant rights increased on most farms between 1910 and 1936, particularly on the smaller farms and on those converting to dairying. Although by 1930 a significant number of farmers still placed little restriction on livestock, there are also instances of farmers who allowed each labour-tenant kraal only three acres for cultivation and ploughed the land for their tenants.[85] Wages varied considerably. Throughout the period under review there were farmers who offered no cash wage at all. Those who did offered adult males between five and ten shillings a month and adult females and children around two and a half shillings a month.[86] There was no increase between 1910 and 1936. Those who worked for the farmer outside the period of compulsory service could expect a cash wage of as high as thirty to forty shillings a month in some cases.[87] Most male casual labourers received one shilling per day in 1918, and by 1937 this wage had not changed.[88]

As in Klip River, the system of six months' labour per year held sway in the Dundee/Helpmekaar district. As in Klip River, by 1936 an increasing number of farmers were supplementing their tenant labour with casual labour. Restrictions on labour tenant rights varied from farm to farm although, on the whole, they seem to have been markedly stricter than in Klip River. This was especially true in Helpmekaar. The Helpmekaar magistrate recorded in 1937 that labour tenants' land rights ranged from six acres per hut to as much as they wished to cultivate, while livestock rights ranged from five head of cattle per male labourer to no restriction at all.[89] By as early as 1918, some farmers had begun lending their oxen to labour tenants for ploughing,[90] and in 1937 the Dundee Agricultural Society claimed that this practice had been adopted by most farmers in the district.[91] However, it is worth noting that George Pringle, who was farming in the area in the 1930s, only began ploughing for his labour tenants in the 1950s.[92] Wages were substantially the same as those offered in Klip River, although the evidence suggests that women and children frequently received more than two and a half shillings a month and up to six shillings a month.[93]

According to the Newcastle magistrate, in 1910 labour tenancy arrangements on white-occupied farms in his district ranged between six months' labour every year and twelve months' labour, alternating with twelve months of freedom.[94] There were also many labour farms in Newcastle, owned by Free State farmers, who usually demanded both rent and labour from tenants.[95] Developments on these farms probably explain the presence of the *lekelela* system in the district in 1930,[96] and arrangements of three months' labour in the year in 1937.[97] However, by the latter date six months' labour in the year was the most common arrangement.[98] No evidence could be found of farmers employing casual labour before 1930, but figures submitted to the Native Farm Labour Committee by the Newcastle magistrate suggest that this practice was common by 1937.[99] Little evidence could be found of labour tenant rights in land and livestock in the district – the impression given is that strict limitations only began to be enforced after about 1930, and that even then they were not widespread enough to precipitate a significant increase in the number of evictions.[100] However, there were farmers who allowed only five head of cattle per kraal and outlawed sheep and goats altogether.[101] Unlike Klip River and Dundee/Helpmekaar, Newcastle had only a handful of farmers who offered no cash wages to labour tenants. Those who did offered substantially the same as those in Dundee/Helpmekaar, although those who demanded rent in addition to labour paid wages of up to £2 a month.[102]

In both Paulpietersburg and Utrecht the number of labour farms was high. It is unclear to what extent this labour pool was exploited in the early part of the period under review, but by 1930 the six-months-on/six-months-off system was the most common in both districts.[103] Some farmers preferred either three-month or twelve-month periods of service. In 1937 the Utrecht magistrate informed the Native Farm Labour Committee that 'squatter labour is employed exclusively'.[104] However, from other evidence presented to the same committee, it appears that some farmers with relatively small farms (and thus unable to keep a large labour-tenant population) were forced to hire casual labourers at certain times of the year.[105] No evidence could be found of this practice in Paulpietersburg. Neither could evidence be found of farmers reducing labour-tenant rights in the two districts. These rights appear to have been appreciably more generous in Utrecht, where the farms were generally larger than those in Paulpietersburg. No cash wages were offered labour tenants in the two districts, although some farmers would give small cash gifts at the end of the period of compulsory service.[106]

The district of Vryheid/Babanango was characterised by extensive labour farming. Africans dwelling on labour farms were frequently called up for far less than three months' service in the year. On farms occupied by white farmers the six-months-on/six-months-off system was predominant throughout the period under review.[107] In addition, as early as 1910 certain farmers were relying on casual labourers at peak periods,[108] and with the expansion of the wattle industry wage labour became a common feature of the area. As stated above, the wattle growers were wholly reliant on recruited labour, and resented what they saw as the 'locking up' of labour by farmers utilising tenant labour.[109] Restrictions on labour-tenant rights were slight, even in the 1930s. This, together with the prevalence of farms unoccupied by whites, explains the fact that African cattle holdings were on average higher in Vryheid than elsewhere in northern Natal.[110] The district's large farms enabled farmers to offer tenants relatively generous terms. The following statement by the repre-sentative of the Brakwal Farmers' Association in 1937 illustrates this:

> We give the natives approximately 80 acres, free dipping and their stock grazes with ours. Our limit is more or less 10 head of cattle and 15 small stock. This is per working adult.[111]

Early on, increasing numbers of farmers lent their oxen and ploughs to their tenants.[112] Cash wages, when given to labour tenants, were lower than those in Klip River County, ranging between one and ten shillings a month.[113] The evidence suggests that in 1936 a majority of farmers still paid their labour tenants no cash wage at all. Wage labourers could earn anything between ten shillings a month (in addition to food and quarters) [114] and seven shillings a day (doing piece-work on the wattle plantations).[115] Most labourers on the wattle plantations earned from two to three shillings a day.[116]

As in the other districts of northern Natal east of the Buffalo River, Ngotshe contained many labour and 'kaffir' farms through 1936. It is unclear how much labour was extracted from the tenants on the former and on farms occupied by white farmers. However, it is probable that the six-months-on/six-months-off system, which one farmer described as being common in the district in 1917,[117] was only implemented by farmers resident on their farms. There is also evidence of landowners demanding both rent and labour from their tenants.[118] The labour demands of most farmers were too slight and the tenant population too large for there to be any need for farmers to employ wage labour. However, the district's cotton plantations, like the wattle plantations of Vryheid/Babanango, employed only recruited labour. Given the extensive nature of most farming opera-tions and the large size of farms in the district, it is not surprising that very little restriction was placed on labour-tenant rights and, as in Utrecht and Paulpietersburg, the paying of cash wages to labour tenants was extremely rare.[119]

Between 1910 and 1936, forms of labour on white-owned farms in northern Natal were far from static. This was especially apparent west of the Buffalo River, where by 1936 cash wages for labour tenants were the norm, restrictions on labour-tenant rights were increasingly severe, and the use of casual wage labour was becoming more common. The labour tenant's independence outside the period of compulsory service was probably most tenuous in Bergville, where by 1941 African cattle holdings were down to 4,5 head per family of six.[120] The system of labour tenancy was also being transformed by the growing tendency for youngsters to work elsewhere in their free periods (and frequently never to return) and by the increasingly widespread practice of white farmers lending their oxen and ploughs to their tenants. However, east of the Buffalo, labour tenancy changed very little between 1910 and 1936. Outside the wattle and cotton plantations, which were not extensive, tenants were still able to enjoy almost unrestricted rights in land and livestock and service obligations which seldom amounted to as much as six months in the year. Cash wages were rare. So, while the market economy had made a substantial impact on the system of labour tenancy in northern Natal before 1936, the

Map 1   Magisterial districts of northern Natal

striking feature remains the system's resilience in the face of wide-ranging pressures. Moreover, squatting remained widespread in the region during the 1930s, not so much on Crown land, mission stations and land-company held land as on farms owned by white farmers. In short, white-owned land in northern Natal in 1936 was characterised by the resilience of squatting and pre-capitalist forms of agricultural labour. Any attempt to describe the transformation of social relations in the South African countryside or the capitalisation of South African agriculture must account for the position in northern Natal, and in other regions, where the impact of the market economy was extremely gradual.[121]

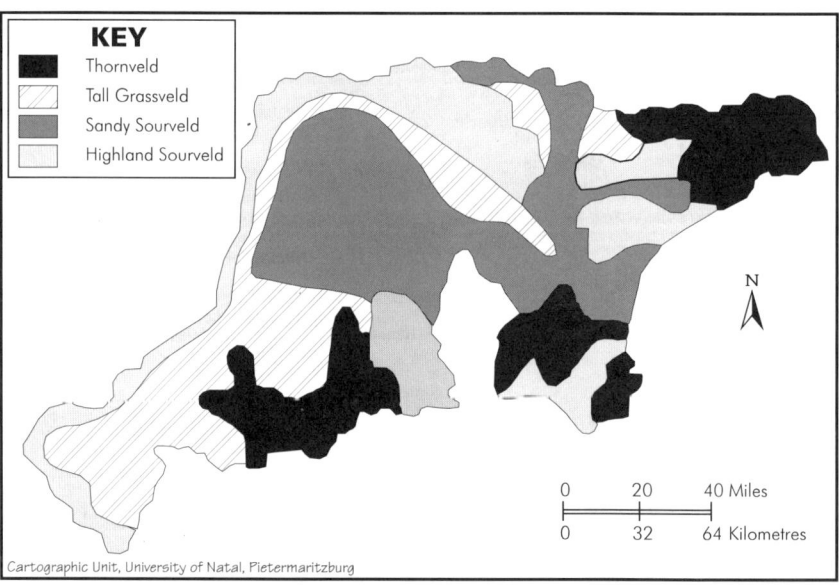

KEY

Thornveld
Tall Grassveld
Sandy Sourveld
Highland Sourveld

N

0   20   40 Miles
0   32   64 Kilometres

Cartographic Unit, University of Natal, Pietermaritzburg

Map 2   Northern Natal veld types

REFERENCES

1. By northern Natal is meant that region comprising the portion of Bergville district south of the Thukela River, and Natal north of the Thukela, but excluding Zululand. See map 1.

2. 169 737 out of 205 260 in 1916, and 187 405 out of 240 300 in 1936. UG 19–1916 *Report of Natives' Land Commission* (hereafter cited as NLC), p. 5, and UG 21–1938. 1936 Population Census, 1, pp. 96–99.

3. The use of the word 'peasant' here is consistent with the definition of J. S. Saul and R. Woods: '. . . peasants are those whose ultimate security and subsistence lies in their having certain rights in land and in the labour of family members on the land, but who are involved, through rights and obligations, in a wider economic system which includes the participation of non-peasants.' J. S. Saul and R. Woods, 'African peasantries' in T. Shanin (ed.) *Peasants and peasant societies* (Harmondsworth, Penguin, 1971), p. 105.

4. A squatter was defined by the state as either a rent tenant (on white-owned or Crown land) or a labour tenant providing less than ninety days' service in the year.

5. In his 1979 study *The rise and fall of the South African peasantry* (London, Heinemann), C. Bundy labels rent and labour tenants as squatter-peasants.

6. Hurwitz, *Agriculture in Natal 1860–1950*, NRS, vol. 12 (Cape Town, Oxford University Press, 1957), p. 66.

7. Interview with G. Pringle, Dundee, 18 January 1984.

8. Sandy sourveld covers large parts of Dundee, Newcastle, Utrecht, Vryheid, Paulpietersburg and Ngotshe. See map 2.

9. *Agriculture in Natal: recent developments*, NRS, vol. 13 (Cape Town, Oxford University Press, 1957), pp. 36–37.

10. Hurwitz, *Agriculture in Natal*, p. 88 and T. J. D. Fair, *The distribution of population in Natal*, NRS, vol. 3 (Cape Town, Oxford University Press, 1955), p. 51.

11. The triangle of land between the Drakensberg, the Buffalo River, and the Thukela River.

12. Hurwitz, *Agriculture in Natal*, p. 91.

13. TAD Archives of the Secretary for Native Affairs, (NTS), 280, 7396/F 684, Ngotshe magistrate to Chief Native Commissioner (CNC), 13 March 1912.

14. By *bywoner* is meant a landless white person dwelling on another man's property in exchange for a share in his profits, produce or labour.

15. This practice was referred to by a number of correspondents and interviewees who farmed in northern Natal in the 1920s and 1930s. See also NTS 280, 7396/F 684, Ngotshe magistrate to Secretary for Native Affairs (SNA), 1912, and NAD Archives of the Secretary for Native Affairs, 2/5/6, NA 2680/13/814, Minute, 29 April 1916.

16. Correspondence with J. Boshoff, 26 September 1983.

17. Hurwitz, *Agriculture in Natal*, p. 24.

18. Interviews with M. Z. J. Pringle, Dundee, 18 January 1984, C. Henderson, 'Balbrogie', near Wasbank, 18 January 1984, and H. Langley, 'Langleydale' near Dannhauser, 19 January 1984.

19. Hurwitz, *Agriculture in Natal*, p. 24.

20. J. F. W. Grosskopf, *Report of the Carnegie Commission on the Poor White Problem in South Africa*, vol. 1, *Rural impoverishment and rural exodus* (Stellenbosch, Pro Ecclesia-Drukkery, 1932). Grosskopf's work constitutes the first volume of the Report, and according to a map in it (between pp. xiv and xv) evidence for the Report was gathered in the district of Utrecht. However, no analysis of bywoners in this district could be found in Grosskopf's text.

21. Agriculture in Natal: recent developments, p. 79.

22. Hurwitz, *Argiculture in Natal*, p. 24.

23. UG 18–1939, Union Agricultural Census, 1936–1937.

24. TAD, Record of Evidence of Native Farm Labour Committee, 1937–1939, 4, Evidence of Kambula Farmers' Association, Vryheid.

25. *Ibid.*, Evidence of R. A. Rouillard, Ngotshe.

26. Union Agricultural Censuses.

27. NFLC, 4, Evidence of Kambula Farmers' Association.

28. *Ibid.*, Evidence of R. A. Rouillard, Ngotshe.

29. *Ibid.*, Evidence of Kambula Farmers' Association.

30. *Ibid.*, Evidence of R. A. Rouillard, Ngotshe.

31. UG 22–1916, NLC, Record of Evidence, p. 613.

32. *Ibid.*, p. 600.

33. *Ibid.*, p. 603.

34. Natal Agricultural Union Records, Resolutions passed at Annual Congresses of NAU, 1924–1944, 1925 Congress, Resolution 13.

35. *Ibid.*, 1926 Congress, Resolution 18.

36. A. J. Christopher, 'Natal: a study in colonial land settlement' (unpublished Ph. D. thesis, University of Natal, 1969), p. 313.

37. R. H. Smith, 'Native farm labour in Natal', *The South African Journal of Economics*, 9, 1941, p. 168.

38. UG 19–1916, NLC, appendix 3, p. 5.

39. UG 17–1911, *Blue Book on Native Affairs*, 1910, p. 262.

40. UG 22–1916, NLC, p. 603.

41. *Ibid.*

42. NAD, Archives of the Chief Native Commissioner (CNC), 21, N2/9/2, CNC 22/1, Bergville native commissioner to CNC, 17 August 1934.

43. NFLC, 4, Evidence of Elandslaagte Farmers' Association, 1937.

44. TAD K26, Native Economic Commission (NEC), Record of Evidence, 16, Evidence of Helpmekaar magistrate, 1930.

45. TAD K26, NEC, 4, pp. 1263–1318.

46. Interview with G. Pringle, Dundee, 18 January 1984.

47. UG 22–1916, NLC, p. 625.

48. The Committee gave the number of adult male Africans living on such farms as 2 500 (Report of the Inter-Departmental Committee on the Labour Resources of the Union, 1930 (Ann. 89, Parliamentary Library), p. 17). According to the Natives' Land Commission, the total number of Africans living on such farms in 1916 was 10 086 (UG 19–1916, NLC, appendix 3, p. 5).

49. NAD, Archives of the Babanango magistrate, 17/14/2, Annual Report for 1925.

50. NFLC, 4, Evidence of A. L. Pretorius, Vryheid, 1937.

51. CNCb 15, N2/10/2 (x), CNC 22/683, List entitled 'Native Population on Native Owned Farms'.

52. TAD K26, NEC, 4, p. 1184, Evidence of A. Wood, Newcastle, 1930.

53. NFLC, 4, Evidence of C. K. Aveling, Newcastle, 1937.

54. C.H. Neveling, 'Farm labour in South Africa', *Journal of the Economic Society of South Africa*, 4(2), 1931, p. 32.

55. See, for example, NFLC, 4, Evidence of Elandslaagte Farmers' Association, Ladysmith, 1937, and UG 22–1916, NLC, p. 611, Evidence of M.J. Gregory, Utrecht, 1916.

56. TAD K26, NEC 4, pp. 1292–93, Evidence of Dundee and Glencoe Farmers' Associations and Dundee Agricultural Society, 1930.

57. *Ibid.*, p. 1318, Evidence of W. Stein, Dundee, 1930.

58. CNCb 21, N2/9/2, CNC 22/1, Klip River magistrate to CNC, 6 September 1934.

59. A labour-tenant kraal usually consisted of the kraal head, his wife/wives, their unmarried children, and sometimes their married sons, daughters-in-law and grandchildren.

60. UG 14–1927, Report of the Native Affairs Department, 1922–1926, p. 9.

61. UG 17–1911, *Blue Book on Native Affairs*, 1910, p. 233.

62. See, for example, TAD K26, NEC 4, p. 1180: NFLC, 4, Vryheid evidence, 1937; and CNCb 21, N2/9/2, CNC 22/1, Paulpietersburg magistrate to CNC, 29 September 1934.

63. NFLC, 4, Evidence of the Revd Africa, Dundee, 1937.

64. TAD K26, NEC, 4, pp. 1360–61.

65. *Ibid.*, p. 1214.

66. CNCb 21, N2/9/2, CNC 22/1, Ngotshe magistrate to CNC, 12 September 1934.

67. TAD, Archives of the Secretary for Agriculture, (LDB), 1758, R 2989 II, Newcastle magistrate to SNA, 17 December 1925.

68. See, for example, SNA 2/5/5, Second Committee, Evidence of D.C. Uys, Dundee, 1917.

69. Natal Agricultural Union Records, NAU Proceedings, 1906–1912, and Resolutions passed at Annual Congresses of NAU, 1924–1944.

70. LDB 1758, R 2989, II, Babanango magistrate to Vryheid magistrate, 19 December 1925.

71. SC 6A/1917, Select Committee on Native Affairs, 1917, p. 48.

72. *Union Government Gazette*, 1 June 1926, section 1(1), p. 2.

73. SNA 1/4/27, Notes headed 'Legal Relationship between European Owner and Native Squatter', p. 5, no date.

74. *Union Government Gazette*, 30 May 1932, section 3, p. 40, and section 5(2), p. 42.

75. UG 17–1911, *Blue Book on Native Affairs*, 1910, p. 233.

76. UG 22–1932, NEC, p. 193.

77. NFLC, 4, Evidence of C.G. Dicks, Ladysmith.

78. *Ibid.*

79. NEC, Record of Oral Evidence, University of South Africa (Acc. 177), 4, p. 2457.

80. See Map 2.

81. NFLC, 4, Evidence of Elandslaagte Farmers' Association, Ladysmith, 1937.

82. TAD, Departmental Committee appointed to Inquire into the Alleged Shortage of Native Labour in Natal, 1918, Record of Evidence, Secretary for Native Affairs, vol. 233 (DC), Evidence of Klip River assistant magistrate, 1918.

83. NFLC, 4, Evidence of Klip River magistrate, Ladysmith, 1937.

84. DC, Evidence of Klip River assistant magistrate, 1918.

85. NEC (Acc.177), 4, p. 2475.

86. UG 17–1911, *Blue Book on Native Affairs*, 1910, p. 237; UG 28–1932 NEC, p. 193; and NFLC, 4, Evidence of Klip River magistrate, Ladysmith, 1937.

87. NFLC, 4, Evidence of Klip River magistrate, Ladysmith, 1937.

88. DC, Evidence of W. Pepworth, Ladysmith, 1918, and NFLC, 4, Evidence of Piet Afrikaans, Ladysmith, 1937.

89. FLC, 4, Evidence of Helpmekaar magistrate.

90. DC, Evidence of D. C. Pieters, Dundee, 1918.

91. NFLC, 4, Evidence of Dundee Agricultural Society, 1937.

92. Interview with G. Pringle, Dundee, 18 January 1984.

93. UG 22–1932, NEC p. 193; and TAD K26, NEC, 16, Helpmekaar magistrate to NEC, 15 September 1930.

94. UG 17–1911, *Blue Book on Native Affairs*, 1910, p. 264.

95. UG 22–1916, NLC p. 431, Evidence of F. A. R. Johnston, Newcastle.

96. UG 22–1932, NEC, p. 194.

97. NFLC, 4, Evidence of C. J. W. Adendorff, Newcastle, 1937.

98. *Ibid.*

99. NFLC, 7, Evidence of Newcastle magistrate, 1937.

100. CNCb 21, N2/9/2, CNC 22/1, Newcastle native commissioner to CNC, 11 September 1934.

101. NFLC, 4, Evidence of C. J. W. Adendorff, Newcastle, 1937.

102. SNA 2/5/4, First Committee, Evidence of J. Parks, Newcastle, 1917.

103. TAD K26, NEC 16, Report by Paulpietersburg magistrate, 24 September 1930; and UG 22–1932, NEC, p. 194.

104. NFLC, 4, Evidence of Utrecht magistrate.

105. *Ibid.*, Evidence of Flentershoek Boerevereniging.

106. UG 22–1916, NLC, p. 611; CNCb 21, N2/9/2,CNC 22/1, Utrecht magistrate to CNC, 17 August 1934; and NFLC, 4, Evidence of Alpheus Sibisi, Paulpietersburg, 1937.

107. SNA 2/5/4, First Committee, Evidence of S. E. Henwood, Vryheid, 1917; UG 22–1932, NEC, p. 192; and NFLC, 4, Vryheid evidence, 1937.

108. SC 3/1910, Select Committee on Native Affairs, 1910–1911, p. 414.

109. NFLC, 4, Evidence of Kambula Farmers' Association, 1937.

110. Smith, 'Native farm labour', p. 175.

111. NFLC, 4, Evidence of G. M. Spoelstra, Babanango, 1937.

112. SC 3–1910, Select Committee on Native Affairs, 1910–1911, p. 412.

113. UG 17–1911, *Blue Book on Native Affairs*, 1910, p. 241; and NFLC, 4, Evidence of Vryheid magistrate, 1937.

114. UG 22–1932, NEC, p. 192.

115. TAD K26, NEC, 4, p. 1540.

116. NFLC, 4, Evidence of Kambula Farmers' Association, 1937.

117. SNA 2/5/4: First Committee, Evidence of D. J. Louw, Louwsburg, 1917.

118. UG 22–1916, NLC, p. 626: Evidence of the Revd Bang, Ngotshe, 1916.

119. UG 22–1932, NEC, p.54.

120. Smith, 'Native farm labour', p.175.

121. More regional and local studies than have thus far been published are required to substantiate the contention of both Mike Morris and Bundy that South African agriculture became capitalist in the 1920s and 1930s. M. Morris, 'The development of capitalism in South African agriculture: class struggle in the countryside', *Economy and Society*, 5, 1976, pp.292–343, and Bundy, *Rise and fall*, pp.232–33.

┌──────────────── *ABSTRACT* ────────────────┐

Prior to the 1920s, influx control and segregation were
imposed only to a limited extent in Durban. The city was still
in an early stage of urban growth, Africans comprised less
than one-third of its population, and a large part of its
work-force was made up of unskilled male migrants who lived
in municipal 'barracks' or in private compounds. Urban
migration had not yet become a prominent feature of the
regional economy, though the foundations of the 'Durban
system' of control over the physical and occupational mobility
of Africans were laid in the form of a curfew and a system of
registration and identification passes. These policies were
intensified between 1920 and the mid-1930s as the stream of
impoverished reserve-dwellers and evicted tenants migrating
to Durban increased in response to deteriorating conditions in
the rural areas and improved job opportunities in the city. The
purpose of influx control was to limit the African presence in
Durban according to labour needs and thereby satisfy police
and ratepayers' demands, which also included the implementation of strict residential segregation. A series of segregation
proclamations forced many Africans out of the city's central
residential areas into the shack settlements emerging in Cato
Manor and on the southern periphery, or into the new Lamont
township. The political economy of Durban and its hinterland
changed significantly between the mid-1930s and early 1950s
as rural poverty and industrial growth gathered momentum,
while increasing numbers of Africans became permanently
settled in and around the city. However, during the 1940s this
did not result in a more stringent implementation of influx
control owing to Durban's fluctuating labour needs. A much
greater nationwide uniformity and tightening of the mechanisms that controlled the movement of Africans followed the
accession to power of the National Party in 1948. This was
accompanied by a much more vigorous implementation of
urban segregation than had characterised the 1940s. The 1950
Group Areas Act was indicative of an increasing centralisation
of power at the expense of municipal autonomy but, in the case
of Durban, complete residential segregation was imposed
upon a local authority that was by no means unwilling to
co-operate.

└───┘

262

THE EVOLUTION OF URBAN APARTHEID
INFLUX CONTROL AND SEGREGATION:
IN DURBAN, c. 1900–1951

Paul Maylam

There has evolved over the years in South Africa a phenomenon that can loosely be called 'urban apartheid'. The essential objectives of urban apartheid have been to regulate the number of Africans living in urban areas, and to exercise tight control over the daily lives of urban Africans. Underlying these essential objectives have been further fundamental concerns: to maintain the supply of labour at sufficient levels to meet the needs of capital; to ensure that the demand for different types of labour is met, whether it be migrant, unskilled or skilled; and to allay the paranoia and fears of an urban middle class who felt their health and safety threatened by the large numerical presence of the black underclasses.

The history of urban apartheid in twentieth-century South Africa has been marked by the efforts of government, central and local, to achieve these often contradictory objectives, and by the struggles of the black underclasses to resist the imposition of controls. Over the years two mechanisms have been devised by the state as the chief components of the urban apartheid system: influx control and segregation. Much has been written about both of these instruments of control. For instance, work has been done on the evolving legislative framework of urban apartheid.[1] Hindson has produced an important analysis of the influx control system, showing how its major functions changed over time.[2] In recent years studies in local urban history have proliferated, and some of these have been concerned with the issues of influx control and segregation.[3] There has, though, been virtually no attempt to trace and analyse the development of influx control and segregation over time in any specific local urban context. Part of the purpose of this essay is to attempt such an examination, looking at how these mechanisms evolved in Durban through the twentieth century up until the beginnings of the 'group areas era' in the early 1950s.

It will clearly be insufficient to provide a mere catalogue of control measures. The local, regional and national context in which influx control and segregation were implemented will have to be examined. Influx control and segregation measures in Durban can only be understood in terms of demographic trends and the changing political economy of the city. Attention must be paid to the many forces that shaped local-government policy: the demands of capital; the dictates of the central government; pressure exerted by local ratepayers; the perceptions and policies of key local administrators; and the struggles of Durban's black underclasses.

At various times segregation measures in Durban have affected Africans, Indians and 'coloureds'. The main focus of this essay is the way in which certain forms of urban apartheid operated against Africans in Durban. The time-span covered can be broken down into three main phases: the first runs to about 1920; the second from 1920 until 1936–37; and the third from 1936–37 until the early 1950s.

Before the early 1920s, influx control and segregation were imposed only to a very limited extent in Durban. This was because the economic, social and demographic make-up of the town did not seem to demand such controls at the time. The town's economy still rested very largely on commerce and shipping. Its industrial base was minuscule, in spite of some expansion during the South African War and the First World War. Moreover, Durban was still in the early stage of urban growth at the beginning of the century. In 1900 its total population amounted to about 55 700, and by 1921 it was still only 90 500. Africans made up less than one-third of the total population; in 1921 there were an estimated 28 400 Africans living in Durban.[4]

The vast majority of this African population was male. In 1921 the African male:female ratio was 6,6:1.[5] Many of these males were migrant workers living in so-called barracks (single-quarters hostels) or in private commercial compounds. This preponderance of male migrants reflected the central position of the docks in the local economy. The docks required a flexible labour supply to cope with fluctuations in shipping and the seasonal demand for labour. Thus the docks came to rely on casual, togt labour, supplied largely by unskilled African migrants.

In 1911 a member of the Natal Manufacturers' Association stated, quite bluntly, his vision of an ideal labour supply: 'The essential requirements are: 1. That the labour should be cheap. 2. That it should be constant. 3. That it should be controllable.'[6] Casual, togt labour did not really satisfy these requirements. As Hemson has shown, togt workers at the Durban docks enjoyed a certain degree of independence and could command relatively high wages.[7] The point was not lost on either local employers or the police. Durban's Superintendent of Police, R. C. Alexander, proposed his solution in giving evidence to the South African Native Affairs Commission in 1904: 'I would put my Natives in barracks and let them march into the town as they do with soldiers. That has been my ambition for 25 years, and I have not altered it.'[8]

Alexander's lament about the lack of regimentation and segregation arose out of what he saw as the laxity of the corporation in failing to provide controlled accommodation for casual workers. Since 1878, when the first barracks had been built, he had pestered the corporation to build more:

> Then it took me from 1878 to 1894 worrying the Corporation every year to build some barracks.
> Then they built the old barracks down at the Point . . .

Then it took me from 1894 to 1904 to get them to put up these other barracks. At the same rate of progress, the next barracks will not be put up during my life.[9]

A Native Locations Act, passed by the Natal legislature in 1904, opened up the possibility of urban segregation. The Act enabled Durban and Pietermaritzburg to establish segregated urban locations for Africans. But it was no more than enabling legislation, and the Durban municipality did not act on it. The town council was neither willing to provide the necessary finance, nor able to agree on a site for such a location.[10] In the early 1900s there continued to be much debate and discussion among local capitalists and officials about the pros and cons of herding Africans into a segregated location.[11] But the municipality stuck with the practice of providing limited barrack accommodation for single workers. In 1914 about 5 850 Africans, including 1 000 women, were housed in municipal barracks or hostels.[12] The first municipal housing for African families did not become available till 1916 when Baumannville was opened; and this comprised a mere 120 so-called cottages.

Just as the imperative to establish segregated locations in Durban was not all that strong before the 1920s, so was the machinery available to limit African mobility and urban migration not all that awesome. The political economy of both Durban itself and the rural hinterland simply did not demand rigid controls. The rural economy was still sufficiently resilient to prevent urban migration from being the vital necessity it became for millions of Africans in later generations. However, controls restricting the physical and occupational mobility of Africans in Durban existed from the nineteenth century. In 1869 a 9 p.m. – 4 a.m. curfew was introduced.[13] A law passed by the Natal legislature in 1888 provided for the registration of all African workers. From 1891 it was enforced in Durban, not very effectively, with a view to excluding from the town 'native deserters, idlers and vagabonds'.[14] This represented an early attempt on the part of the local municipal authority to limit the African presence in Durban to labour needs. This was to be the essence of the future influx control system.

A further step towards such a system was taken with the enactment of another Natal measure in 1901. This required all African workers in the colony to obtain an identification pass, which had to be carried at all times and produced on demand.[15] By 1904 Police Superintendent Alexander was making full use of this control mechanism: '. . . I have a Pass Book with a counterfoil, and every Native who comes into the town to transact business, such as purchasing goods, visiting friends, or looking for work, goes straight to the Police Station. He cannot go an inch without that pass.' What is more, Alexander saw the identification pass, not as a restrictive control, but as a ticket to liberty: 'I think the identification pass one of the grandest things they could have. They can show their pass, and say: "I am so and so; there is my pass, I am a free man."' Curious notions of freedom reigned among officialdom in early twentieth-century Durban.

The system of registration and identification passes was consolidated and tightened in by-laws passed by the Durban Town Council in 1916. J.S. Marwick, the manager of Durban's newly established municipal Native Affairs Department (later changed to Native Administration Department), was soon expressing his delight at the immediate impact of the by-laws. Desertion and crime were being curbed. The by-laws, together with the new local government apparatus for 'native administration', offered the prospect of much tighter control being exercised over Durban's African population.[17] This was the foundation of the 'Durban system'. Largely on the basis of profits derived from the municipal beer monopoly, the Durban corporation was creating administrative machinery that would serve as a model when national policy-makers and legislators embarked in the early 1920s on formulating urban areas legislation for the country as a whole.

Thus towards the end of the first phase, the period up to about 1920, local government in Durban was developing apparatus for controlling the black underclasses. But the degree of control being exercised at this stage was only very limited. Durban was still in an early phase of industrialisation. It did not contain a vast black proletariat. Indeed, early control measures were rather directed at semi-proletarianised migrants. Moreover, these measures were adopted largely at the Durban Corporation's own volition, with no prompting or pressure from central government.

During the second phase, from about 1920 to the mid-1930s, there were both an intensification of pre-1920 trends and some new developments. Durban's vast rural hinterland, where a fairly buoyant farming economy had sustained African reserve-dwellers as well as tenants on white-owned land, gradually became more impoverished during the 1920s. The reserves wilted under the pressures of overpopulation, overstocking and drought, giving rise to migration. Also, African tenants were squeezed off their plots as white farmers, keen to put more of their land to direct productive use, terminated quasi-feudal or leasing arrangements with their tenants. The natural drift of impoverished reserve-dwellers or evicted tenants was towards the urban areas, and an emerging city like Durban was an obvious destination.

In the 1920s Durban was still a place where there were open spaces to be occupied and opportunities to be exploited. Africans could rent backyard rooms or outhouses in central areas, or they could occupy the vacant sites of land not far from the city centre. There they could participate in the lucrative 'illicit' liquor traffic or some other informal-sector activity. Alternatively, they could find work in the growing formal sector. During this second phase Durban enjoyed sporadic industrial growth. After a recession in the early 1920s, Durban's industry recovered in the mid-1920s. Following on the Great Depression of the early 1930s, industry in the city had entered a major period of growth by the mid-1930s.

In these circumstances it was not surprising that the African population of Durban should have been growing in numbers. In 1921 about 46 000 Africans lived in Durban; by 1936 the figure had risen to about 71 000.[18] The question at once arises, how did the central government and the Durban municipal authorities respond to this growing African urban presence? The form that this response should take was, in fact, a matter of debate. One side in the debate favoured official recognition of the growing stabilisation and permanence of the African labour force in urban areas. This position was expressed in the 1932 report of the Native Economic Commission, and in the 1935 report of a Department of Native Affairs sub-committee (the Young-Barrett Committee). The latter argued that the issue of African urbanisation could not be resolved '. . . by expelling them [Africans from urban areas] as soon as they have served the white man's purpose; . . . there is a duty on Enlightened Authority . . . to concern itself with the betterment of Native social conditions.'[19] The Young-Barrett Committee was responding specifically to the earlier report of the Transvaal Local Government Commission (the Stallard Commission). The Stallard Report, issued in 1922, reflected the other side of the debate in its oft-quoted conclusion that Africans should only enter urban areas to minister to the white man's needs.[20]

Which side prevailed in this debate? There is no clear-cut answer to this question. It is probably true to say that official thinking at the central government level was veering more towards the Young-Barrett view in the 1930s. However, this point needs to be qualified in two ways. First, it would be wrong to suggest that the stabilisation of African workers and the Stallardist view, preferring the continuation of migrant labour, were stark alternatives. As Hindson has shown, state policy increasingly became geared towards sustaining a system of differentiated labour-power, balancing the requirements of different capitalist sectors for either stabilised or migrant labour.[21]

The second qualification is that the debate might have a different outcome in different urban centres. This was possible because in the 1920s and early 1930s local government still enjoyed a considerable degree of autonomy from central government. It is true that the central state was beginning to intervene more in the sphere of urban African management from the 1920s. This intervention was embodied most clearly in the 1923 Natives (Urban Areas) Act. However, this measure had a very limited impact on Durban. Some of the provisions of the 1923 Act, such as the introduction of the municipal beer monopoly and the native revenue account, had already long since been in operation in Durban. At the same time the Act was largely enabling legislation, which imposed few obligations on municipalities. Some of these non-obligatory clauses the Durban municipality chose to ignore, at least until the late 1920s. For instance, the Act provided for the possible establishment of 'native advisory boards'. Durban did not create one of these until 1929. The Act also provided for the construction of segregated African townships. It was only eleven years after the passing of the Act that Lamont Township, to the south of the city, was opened for occupation.

In Durban, municipal policy in the 1920s tended towards the Stallardist position. This was partly made possible by the city's geographical location. Durban's proximity to the reserves facilitated labour migrancy, which was the basis of Stallardism. Moreover, the limited development of Durban's manufacturing sector meant that the demand for semi-skilled stabilised labour was not all that great, so that structural factors made Stallardism possible. But it was also very much encouraged and sustained by a key figure in the local administrative apparatus. C.F. Layman was the manager of Durban's Native Administration Department from 1921 until 1936. During his time at the helm he developed a reputation for being authoritarian and unapproachable. In 1931 Durban's Native Advisory Board, a body that was not accustomed to expressing forceful opposition, passed a vote of no confidence in Layman.[22] More significant was Layman's persistent support for the Stallardist line. In 1923 he expressed his views to the parliamentary select committee examining the Natives (Urban Areas) Bill. Layman was critical of some aspects of the original bill. For instance, he expressed his strong disapproval of the bill's provision for African freehold tenure in urban areas: 'The natives will cease to recognise that they are in the urban area primarily for employment, and once they become owners in freehold the stimulus to good behaviour which is maintained by the possibility of their leasehold tenure being forfeited, will cease to operate.' Layman's voice may have carried some weight, as the provision for freehold was taken out of the final bill. Layman also fiercely objected to the growing tendency of African families to settle in urban areas like Durban: if 'encouraged' this tendency 'will lead to a state of affairs in which the control at present exercised over the native population in the town will disappear'.[23] Far better, he contended, that 'those natives who wish to maintain touch with their homes in the country should receive every possible facility and encouragement to do so'.[24]

The Stallardist line was consistently expounded by the likes of Layman, though a rigid Stallardist policy was never practicable. It could not be fully enforced, as Africans ignored or evaded the controls restricting their movement. By the mid-1930s a 'differentiated' labour-force was becoming more and more of a reality in Durban. A rapidly declining male:female ratio was clear evidence of family settlement and the growing permanence of a large section of Durban's African population. However, this did not prevent the Durban corporation from using controls to contain the process of stabilisation.

The consistent, fundamental objective of these controls was to restrict the African presence in Durban according to labour needs. As we have seen, such controls had been in operation in Durban since the nineteenth century. In the 1920s there were efforts to systematise the controls even further. One of the concerns of the 1923 Urban Areas Act was to consolidate regulations restricting African movement into urban areas. But these consolidated regulations would only come into force in particular urban areas after such areas had been proclaimed by the Governor-General. Durban became a proclaimed area in 1928, thereby bringing into operation the controls laid down in the 1923 Act. As a result of the proclamation African work-seekers and other visitors coming to Durban had to report to a registering officer within twenty-four hours of arrival. Work-seekers could remain in a proclaimed area for a maximum of six days. All those who did find work had to be registered; and they were bound by a service contract which gave employers considerable control over their workers. The service contract was, in effect, a form of pass that had to be carried at all times and be produced on demand.[25] It obviously suited Layman. In 1930 he was calling for 'a systematic inspection of all Native Registration passes' in Durban. He gained the backing of the city council. And his hand was further strengthened by a 1930 amendment to the Urban Areas Act, providing for the deportation from towns of Africans considered to be 'idle, dissolute or disorderly'. Armed with these weapons, Layman's department was able to organise the expulsion from Durban of over 1 000 Africans in 1930 alone.[26]

The tightening of influx control measures in Durban was a response to the growing African influx into the city, brought on by a deterioration in the material position of rural Africans and by the expansion of Durban's industrial sector. The essential objective of influx control was to limit the size of the African influx without endangering the labour supply. It was thus geared to meet capital's need for labour, and to satisfy police and ratepayers' demands for social control by keeping out of Durban those Africans who were surplus to labour requirements.

Social control, however, could not be achieved just by limiting urban immigration. Control still had to be exercised over those Africans whose labour was required in the city. One of the key mechanisms developed to achieve such control was racial residential segregation. In the early 1930s the Durban corporation came under considerable local pressure to implement segregation. The pressure did not come from capital. Indeed, strict residential segregation was often not in the best interests of employers who liked to have their workers living close to the work-place. Rather, the pressure emanated from the local police and middle-class ratepayers. In the forefront of the demands for segregation was Chief Constable Whitsitt. He complained that Africans of the 'won't work, illicit liquor-selling class' were being 'harboured' all over the borough.[27] Whitsitt was supported by strong representations from various ratepayers' associations. In 1933 and 1934 the Bluff, Mayville and Umbilo associations, among others, demanded that their areas be segregated, complaining particularly about the presence of African liquor-dealers in their areas.[28]

The upshot was a series of segregation proclamations, applied successively to specific areas of the city, culminating in the proclamation of the whole borough in 1937. The intent of the measures was to prohibit any householders in the proclaimed areas from accommodating on their premises any Africans except domestic workers or those exempted under the 1923 Act. As Whitsitt put it, 'The whole idea of having an area proclaimed is to get rid of the Native inhabitants with the exception of domestic servants.' The effect of the proclamations was to force many Africans out of the central residential areas of Durban to the emerging shack settlements in Cato Manor and the southern periphery of the city.[29]

This was perhaps the first official manifestation of the group areas approach, of which the Durban local authority was to be such an enthusiastic proponent in the following decades. This early segregation drive did not, though, develop into a concerted programme of segregation. It was essentially a foretaste of what was to follow in the 1950s. In the 1930s wholesale segregation was prevented by a legal loophole. The 1923 Act laid down that in order to evict an urban resident, a municipality must first be able to provide alternative accommodation for the evicted person. This condition placed the onus on the Durban corporation to provide more housing for Africans. It was in this context that Lamont township was constructed, to the south of Durban, and opened for occupation in 1934. But the building of Lamont was a mere drop in the ocean. The corporation was unwilling to provide the finance to embark on a substantial programme of African housing. Moreover, it was not yet entirely committed to the principle of constructing African townships, which in themselves amounted to an implicit recognition of labour stabilisation. Rather was Durban's housing policy coming to be based on a dual system: township accommodation for 'stabilised' families, and single-quarters for migrant workers. This was a housing policy that reflected the growing shift towards a system of 'differentiated labour-power' in Durban.

During this phase, from about 1920 until the mid-1930s, the issues of influx control and segregation figured more often on the agendas of both the central government and the Durban corporation. Measures were adopted that were to form the basis of urban apartheid. In the third phase, from the mid-1930s until the early 1950s, the political economy of Durban and its hinterland changed significantly. This change was to lead ultimately to a more intensive implementation of influx control and segregation. The end of this phase was also to see a change of government in South Africa. Many have ascribed the intensification of urban apartheid in the 1950s to the newly elected Nationalist government. This assumption needs to be seriously questioned. The Durban corporation, which was not controlled by a Nationalist city council, was to show itself to be an enthusiastic proponent of urban apartheid.

From the mid-1930s those trends that had begun to change the face of Durban during the previous twenty years or so gathered momentum. The city's manufacturing sector, which had enjoyed occasional phases of growth before the mid-1930s, now began to develop significantly. The Second World War provided a major stimulus. The metal and engineering industries assumed special importance during wartime, and demand for locally produced clothing rose as the war drastically curtailed imports. While the manufacturing sector was growing, Durban's rural hinterland was, for various reasons, providing a less and less stable material existence for African communities. The reserve economies continued to deteriorate under the growing burdens of overpopulation, overstocking and soil exhaustion. The 1936 Land Act rendered ever more precarious the position of labour tenants on white farms.

Rural poverty had the effect of driving more and more Africans away from the countryside. Industrial expansion, and the accompanying growth in labour demand, made Durban a natural destination for rural emigrants. The estimated size of Durban's African population rose from 63 457 in 1936 to about 150 000 in 1949.[30] Moreover, the composition of this population increase gave an irreversible demographic impetus to stabilisation in the form of a changing male:female ratio. Between 1936 and 1946 Durban's African female population doubled from about 14 200 to about 28 000. Over the same period the ratio of African males to African females declined from 3,46:1 to 2,65:1.[31]

These are clear indicators of a trend towards stabilisation, though the proportion of African migrants to permanent city-dwellers still remained very high in Durban in the mid-1940s. According to an official government estimate for the year 1946, about 74 per cent of Durban's African population were migrants. However, an unofficial estimate for 1953 reckoned that about 50 per cent were migrants.[32] It is unlikely that such a significant shift in the balance had occurred over a mere seven years. Rather, the disparity between the figures is a reflection of the difficulties involved in achieving accurate estimates and in making a rigid distinction between migrants and non-migrants. Many Africans seem to have been weekly commuters between Durban and the reserves; to classify them would have been problematic.

Whatever the exact proportion of migrants to non-migrants, the 'differentiation of labour-power' was becoming a demographic reality in Durban in the 1940s. It was a reality that neither the central government nor the Durban municipal authority could try to wish away. Central government thinking was reflected in the reports of the Smit Committee and the Fagan Commission in the 1940s, both of which acknowledged the inevitability of African urbanisation and the irreversibility of labour stabilisation. The Minister of Native Affairs, P. van der Byl, stated the position clearly in a meeting with the Durban City Council in November 1945:

> The influx of families is the result of industrial development. It is a penalty of all-round prosperity. Industry requires a permanent labour force – stabilised labour – which gives greater efficiency. It will pay higher wages for a man who will stay on the job all the year round with an annual two or three week holiday. Therefore the Native no longer goes home every six or nine months. But he is not prepared to sacrifice his family life so he brings his family to town and houses them where he can.[33]

This also seems to have been the dominant line of thinking in the Durban corporation in the 1940s. It was partly a case of coming to terms with realities, though Durban's departure from the older approach may have been made easier by the retirement of the ardent Stallardist, Layman, in 1936 and his replacement by T.J. Chester as manager of the municipal Native Administration Department. Chester seems to have been more of a benevolent paternalist. Even A.W.G. Champion had some good words to say about him: 'The Administration of the present Manager's predecessor [Layman] was just the opposite of what we gladly enjoy today [under Chester].'[34] No doubt Chester's rejection of a rigid Stallardist line partly explains his relative popularity.

It would, however, be wrong to assume that the Durban corporation's abandonment of Stallardism also implied a relaxation of the controls exercised over the city's African population. Both the central government and the Durban corporation retained a fundamental concern to limit the African urban influx to labour needs. Towards this end the influx control system was tightened, intermittently rather than progressively, from the late 1930s. A key measure was the 1937 Native Laws Amendment Act. This legislation strengthened the influx control and expulsion powers of local authorities. No African could enter an urban area without the necessary permission. Illegal entrants could be removed. Local authorities could refuse entry to any African if there was a surplus of labour in the urban area concerned. Furthermore, in order to determine whether such a surplus existed or not, each local authority would be required to conduct a biennial census, supplying details of African population and employment levels.[35]

The central government in the late 1930s was alarmed at the growing African urban influx and was determined to curb it.[36] Thus the 1937 Act was followed by an intensified implementation of pass controls and a rapid increase in prosecutions for pass offences. Influx control was tightened even further by a proclamation issued in 1940. This restricted the right to enter urban areas, under the control of certain local authorities, to those Africans seeking or taking up employment or on a *bona fide* temporary visit.[37]

By 1940 it appeared that a trend was developing towards a more rigorous and repressive influx control system, prefiguring the pattern of the 1950s and 1960s. However, during the 1940s the pattern was interrupted, particularly in Durban. There were two main, interconnected reasons for this. First, an ever more stringent implementation of influx control was not always in the interests of a city like Durban. The Durban economy tended to be subject to fluctuations in labour demand. These could be short-term and seasonal, depending on shipping levels and the holiday trade, or of a longer-term nature, depending on wider business conditions. Such fluctuations required a more flexible implementation of influx control. This can be illustrated for the late 1930s. As we have just seen, the central government was tightening influx control at this time. But in 1938 Durban was enjoying a low unemployment level. Its 1938 census revealed that only 2 per cent of African males in the city were unemployed. Chester was concerned that influx control might endanger the city's labour supply: 'The present labour requirements of the City indicate that the present influx of Natives to take the place of those returning to their homes should not be restricted, as the percentage of unemployed is infinitesimal.'[38] The following year Chester was urging that native commissioners throughout Natal be asked not to discourage Africans from coming to Durban to obtain work.[39]

The second factor inhibiting the implementation of influx control was the outbreak of the Second World War. Durban was a key contributor to the country's war effort. During the war the city's economy boomed. At the same time, the drain of personnel to the war effort placed a severe strain on the state apparatus. It was largely in order to relieve pressure on the police that the government decided in 1942 to relax the pass laws in the major urban areas. Passes could now only be demanded from Africans suspected of criminal activity.

The combined effect of Durban's wartime boom and the relaxation of the pass laws was to bring Africans flocking into the city. In time the influx began to exceed the demand for labour, with the result that from 1944 key figures and bodies in local government began to call for the full re-implementation of the pass laws. Early in 1944 a conference was held on the 'Alleged increase of Native Crime in Durban'. The participants at the conference – the chief magistrate, district commandant, the local native commissioner, the town clerk, and city council representatives – called for the reimposition of the pass laws to check crime.[40] Chester complained that since the relaxation of pass controls, 'Durban had become the refuge for a considerable number of workshy and dissolute natives and under the existing conditions it was not possible to deal expeditiously with these undesirables.'[41]

The Durban corporation was caught in a contradiction. It needed the labour to service the city's growing economy, but local officials were unhappy with the urban influx, which seemed in their view to exacerbate the social problems that they associated with the African presence. As Chester put it, 'we wanted their labour, and either we had to sabotage our war effort by turning them out of town, or tolerate them where they were at Cato Manor. We took the lesser of the two evils.'[42] In order to manage the contradiction as best it could, the local authority continued to direct its efforts towards regulating urban migration in accordance with labour demand. However, this exercise remained problematic as labour demand continued to fluctuate and the calculation of demand tended to be uncertain and inexact. These variables militated against a consistent implementation of influx control and made for the kind of vacillation and hesitancy that characterised the Durban corporation's policy in the 1940s. The municipal records reveal the corporation's concern that the administration of influx control be as flexible as possible and allow for fluctuations over time and changing local needs.

Such flexibility may have been possible for most of the 1940s because the central government had not yet firmly imposed its stamp on urban policy. This, though, began to change after the accession to power of the National Party in 1948. The Nationalist government showed itself to be less prepared to make concessions to meet particular local needs, and more concerned to achieve a greater centralisation and uniformity in urban policy. One of the new government's immediate concerns was to remove 'surplus' labour from urban areas. Thus the Durban corporation received a telegram from the Department of Native Affairs in May 1949 stating that the Minister was 'perturbed at high percentage of unemployed [Africans in Durban]. Steps should be taken to remove unemployed from urban area.'[43] The government also applied itself eagerly to the task of standardising and tightening the mechanisms that controlled and restricted the movement of Africans. Amended registration regulations, aimed at African work-seekers or temporary visitors to urban areas, were promulgated in 1949.[44]

The Natives (Abolition of Passes and Co-ordination of Documents) Act was passed in 1952, consolidating existing pass laws and introducing a standard pass book for Africans. In the same year a new Native Laws Amendment Act further strengthened the influx control apparatus. The aim and effect of this measure was to reinforce the growing differentiation between the stabilised African proletariat and temporary migrants. The right to permanent urban residence depended on strict qualifications being met. The access of temporary migrants to urban areas was to be restricted according to labour requirements.[45]

It is beyond the scope of this essay to probe in any detail the growing centralisation of urban policy under the Nationalists in the 1950s and the impact of this process on Durban. It can be said that this growing centralisation may have introduced a new uniformity and rigidity into influx control; and it would have limited the possibilities for the flexible implementation that the Durban corporation had desired in previous years. However, the approach of the Nationalist government did not represent any radical new departures from earlier urban policies. The underlying features of state policy continued to rest on the basic objectives of the pre-1948 era: to limit the African urban presence according to labour requirements, by excluding or removing people surplus to those requirements; and to secure a differentiation in status among those whose labour was required – a differentiation between 'stabilised' proletarians and temporary migrants. Moreover, this basic approach of the Nationalist government was not out of line with the Durban corporation's thinking on influx control. Although there had, over the years, been some shifts in this thinking, it had consistently been rooted in those same basic concerns which shaped goverment policy in the 1950s and beyond.

A similar picture of compatibility and congruity between the policies of the Durban corporation and the central government becomes apparent when examining the second main theme of this chapter, urban segregation, for the period from the mid-1930s to the early 1950s. We have already seen how a segregationist drive against Africans was launched in Durban in the early 1930s. In the 1940s a similar drive was directed against Indians. Many whites had been agitating against the growing 'penetration' of Indians into predominantly white-owned residential and trading areas. In 1943, under pressure from the Durban City Council, the Government appointed Mr Justice F.N. Broome as a one-man commission to investigate the extent of Indian 'penetration' in Durban. His report, which indicated that 'penetration' was on the increase, was followed by restrictive legislation. The Trading and Occupation of Land (Transvaal and Natal) Restriction Act, commonly known as the 'Pegging Act', was passed in 1943. It was a temporary measure designed to restrict property transfers between whites and Indians in Durban for three years. This was followed in 1946 by the Asiatic Land Tenure and Indian Representation Act, or 'Ghetto Act', a wider, more permanent measure that applied to the whole of Natal. Among its provisions was one creating controlled and uncontrolled areas. In the uncontrolled areas there were to be no racial restrictions on property transfers; but in the controlled areas inter-racial property transfers would be prohibited, except by ministerial permit.[46]

This assault on Indian property-owners was part of a larger segregationist blueprint that was being formulated in Durban in the 1940s. In 1943 the city council's Post-War Development Committee, believing that it was in the interests of each racial group to be housed in separate areas, recommended that a system of racial zoning be introduced in Durban. The city's Valuator and Estates Manager had submitted a broad plan, according to which certain areas of Durban would be set aside for particular race groups. This formed the basis of the committee's recommendation. The segregationist map of Durban envisaged by the Valuator and Estates Manager was based on the projected growth of the city's industrial areas to the west and south of the harbour. Segregated residential zones would therefore have to be established 'for the four races to serve the Old Borough Area and also, for the four races to serve the industrial area'. A remarkable feature of this plan was the extent to which it prefigured the pattern of segregation that came to be formally implemented under the Group Areas Act from the 1950s.[47]

While key figures in Durban local government were thinking more and more along these segregationist lines in the 1940s, the corporation was not carrying the blueprint through. Implementation of the blueprint would have involved a considerable financial commitment from Durban, particularly for the provision of African township housing. The corporation was not prepared to make this commitment. It is true that there was some expansion in the provision of formal accommodation for Africans from the late 1930s, best illustrated by the opening of Chesterville in the mid-1940s. But this limited expansion was never sufficient to keep pace with the rapid growth of the city's African population. Thus by the late 1940s vast shack settlements had grown in and around Durban – a trend hardly in keeping with the segregationist blueprint which could not permit such uncontrolled residential expansion.

Moreover, in the 1940s the Durban corporation was under no pressure from the central government to implement wholesale segregation. Indeed, the Durban corporation seems to have been ahead of the central government in its thinking on this issue in the 1940s. Rather was the Department of Native Affairs in Pretoria at this time preoccupied with trying to devise ways of reducing the cost of African housing. Department officials were stressing the need for mass housing for Africans to meet the backlog: this would inevitably involve the construction of individual housing units of poorer quality. Cut out the 'frills', use cheaper building materials, and employ African labour on construction schemes – these were some of the cost-saving proposals. The idea of Africans building their own homes in controlled village settlement schemes was also given favourable consideration.[48]

The accession to power of the Nationalist government in 1948 was followed by a more vigorous and forceful pursuit of an urban segregation policy, as embodied in the 1950 Group Areas Act. It has sometimes been suggested that the group areas policy was inflexibly imposed by a monolithic central government on some non-Nationalist municipal authorities (such as Durban) that did not accept the group areas principle. This was certainly not the case with Durban. It is true that the Durban corporation might not have implemented a wholesale segregation scheme without the push from the Nationalist government and the element of compulsion inherent in the Group Areas Act. Nevertheless, it remains equally true that the Durban corporation was an enthusiastic supporter of the group areas principle, from the inception of the legislation. The Group Areas Act was passed in 1950. Its immediate effect was to restrict transfers of property between members of different racial groups. Much more significant was its longer-term objective. The Act created the machinery, in the form of the Group Areas Board, for the demarcating of group areas. The Board would advise the Government as to which areas should be demarcated for the exclusive ownership or occupation, or both, of a particular racial group. Such demarcation could then be enforced by proclamation.[49]

The Durban corporation's enthusiasm for the group areas model is borne out by the report of the city council's technical sub-committee, appointed in November 1950 to consider the racial zoning of Durban. The report came out firmly in support of the principle of racial residential segregation, the necessity for this arising 'primarily from the desire of persons of the same group to live in the same neighbourhood'.[50] But it was not just a case of keeping people of different races apart. In some draft notes produced by the technical sub-committee a bizarre justification was presented for separating white properties and Indian smallholdings. The argument went like this: both whites and Indians kept dogs and chickens, but while whites confined their chickens to coops and let their dogs roam free, Indians chained their dogs and let their chickens free. The result was that white dogs attacked Indian chickens, and relations between the two communities deteriorated.[51]

The sub-committee's support for segregation did not, of course, arise out of a concern to protect Indian-owned chickens. The sub-committee had a clear idea of how the demarcation of group areas could facilitate the social and political control of the black underclasses in Durban, without endangering the labour supply. It realised, for instance, that it would be simpler for the police and military apparatus to deal with large, racially homogeneous areas than with a racial patchwork. It urged that segregation be as complete and effective as possible. Zones should be so demarcated that members of one racial group should not have to travel through the zone of another group, and racial zones should be separated by effective boundaries. Natural features, such as rivers, valleys or hills, formed ideal barriers, in the sub-committee's view, while belts of industrial or commercial development served as the most effective artificial barriers. Such belts also formed another important thread in the segregation pattern. Group areas planners deemed it essential that residents in segregated areas should have easy access to their place of work. Thus the demarcation of racial zones in Durban would take into account the main centres of employment for each racial group.[52]

It is beyond the scope of this essay to examine the details of the eventual group areas demarcation in Durban. The technical sub-committee first

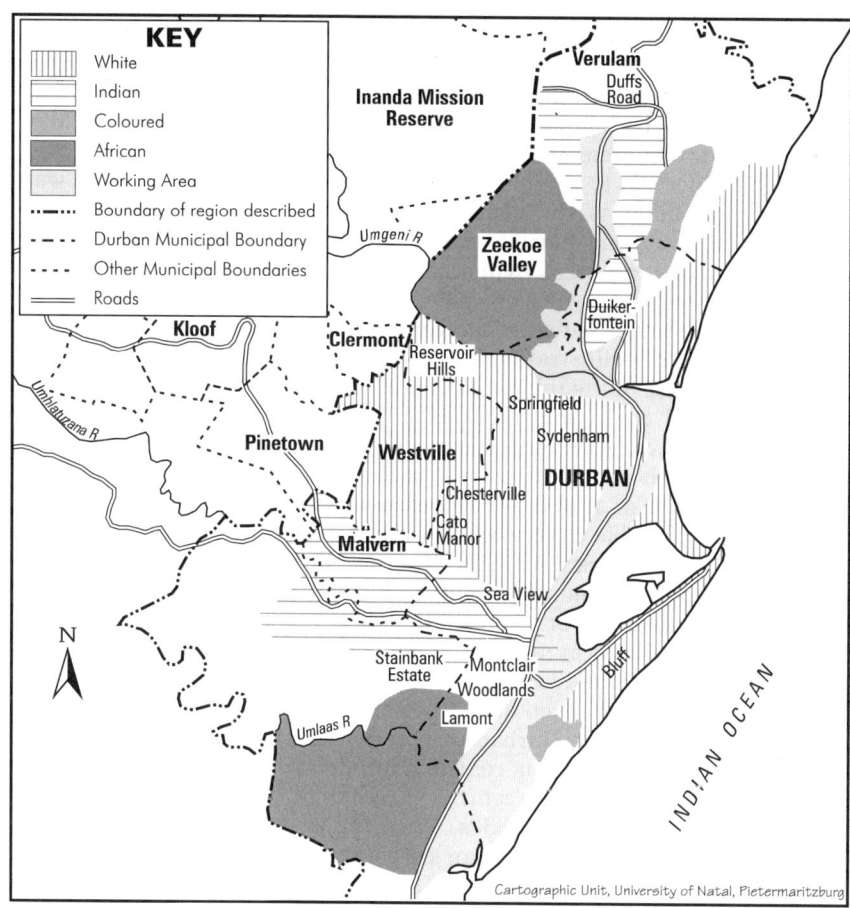

Map 1   Racial zoning as proposed by the technical sub-committee of the Durban City Council, 1951

drew a set of particular proposals. In their basic outline these followed the segregation plan put forward by the 1943 sub-committee. But in some respects the proposals of the 1951 sub-committee were too far-reaching even for the Durban City Council. The sub-committee recommended, for instance, that the main residential area between the Umbilo and Umgeni Rivers be reserved for whites. This would have involved the large-scale displacement of thousands of Indians from Sydenham and Springfield. When the city council eventually considered the sub-committee's proposals it was not prepared to endorse such a massive displacement. It accordingly suggested that those areas of Sydenham and Springfield occupied by Indians should remain an Indian zone. But the city council largely accepted the sub-committee's basic proposal for the demarcation of African zones. These would fall in two main areas, to the south and north of Durban.[53] It seems that the Durban corporation had particularly strong feelings about the belt of land owned or occupied by Africans and Indians to the west, namely Cato Manor and Chesterville. The objection was that this belt 'cut off' the inland white residential areas like Westville. In May 1951 a deputation from Durban, including the mayor and city officials, voiced this objection to the Minister of Native Affairs. The minister was not as sympathetic as the deputation would have liked, and perhaps expected. He could not permit immediate wholesale removals from the area; and, in the short-term, living conditions in Cato Manor would have to be improved.[54]

This last exchange between the central government and the Durban corporation further illustrates one of the central themes of this essay, namely the nature of the relationship and interaction between the central government and the Durban municipal authority. Some theorists have contended that local government is essentially the arm or extension of the central state. Such a contention is not borne out by this case-study. For the first three decades or so of the twentieth century the Durban City Council enjoyed a considerable degree of autonomy in the way it approached the management of its black underclasses. From the late 1930s, in particular, the central state increasingly began to invade that autonomous sphere; and the accession to power of the Nationalists in 1948 was to be followed over the next decades by a gradual centralisation of power and a corresponding diminution of local autonomy in the management of the black underclasses. However, even as the power of local government was being gradually weakened, the Durban corporation continued to assert its own interests. This study of influx control administration has shown that the Durban corporation and the central government were often out of tune with each other. In the late 1930s, when the central state was trying to tighten influx control, the Durban corporation was calling for it to be relaxed. In the early 1940s, after the Government had suspended the pass laws, Durban officials demanded tighter controls to restrict the African influx into the city.

The passing of the Group Areas Act might also be seen as a symptom of the growing centralisation of state power at the expense of municipal autonomy. In some respects this was so, and in the case of Cape Town very much so. But in the case of Durban it would be entirely wrong to conclude that the group areas model was imposed upon an unwilling and uncooperative local authority. Officialdom in Durban had shown its enthusiasm for urban racial segregation long before the Group Areas Act. In the early 1930s a local segregationist drive gained some momentum, and in the 1940s segregation was still very much on the agenda of municipal policy-makers. So for Durban, the Group Areas Act did not represent any major new departures at the policy level. Its main impact was to spur the corporation into devising and implementing a thorough system of residential segregation. It was the kind of system that Durban officials had been favouring over the years but had lacked the will or the resources to implement.

Influx control and segregation represent two key components in the system of urban management developed in South African cities during the course of the twentieth century. This essay has tried to illuminate the particular local dynamic that lay behind the evolution of this system in the city of Durban. The Durban case-study serves to warn against any simplified view of the central government/local authority relation. It also tries to warn against any reductionist analysis of urban apartheid. Certainly, economic imperatives weighed heavily in the Durban corporation's implementation of influx control and segregation. As we have seen, as the influx control system became more refined so was it supposed to be more closely geared to the labour needs of Durban, and the evolving pattern of segregation tried to ensure a suitable allocation of residential space in relation to centres of employment. However, neither influx control nor segregation can be explained in terms of economic imperatives alone. Both need to be examined in relation to the collective mentality of Durban's predominantly white middle class. In the eyes of the majority of Durban's white residents the African presence in the city has for decades been (and continues to be) closely associated with problems of crime, disease and disorder. Thus a major aim of influx control has been to limit the intrusion of these problems into the city by excluding those Africans who were surplus to labour requirements. Similarly, a significant purpose of urban segregation has been to insulate and immunise middle-class residential areas against these perceived dangers. Ultimately it has been a matter of ensuring the exploitability of labour-power, while maximising the invisibility of the labourers.

REFERENCES

The research for this chapter was made possible by an *ad hoc* grant from the HSRC. This financial support is gratefully acknowledged.

1. See T.R.H. Davenport, 'African townsmen? South African Natives (Urban Areas) legislation through the years', *African Affairs*, 68, 1969; T.R.H. Davenport, 'The triumph of Colonel Stallard: the transformation of the Natives (Urban Areas) Act between 1923 and 1937', *South African Historical Journal*, 2, 1970; T.R.H. Davenport, 'The beginnings of urban segregation in South Africa: the Natives (Urban Areas) Act of 1923 and its background', (ISER Occasional Paper, no.15, Rhodes University, 1973).

2. Doug Hindson, *Pass controls and the urban African proletariat* (Johannesburg, Ravan, 1987).

3. See, for instance, M.W. Swanson, 'The "Durban System": roots of urban apartheid in colonial Natal', *African Studies*, 1976; C.C. Saunders, 'The creation of Ndabeni: urban segregation and African resistance in Cape Town', *Studies in the History of Cape Town*, 1, 1979; E. Koch, 'The destruction of Marabi culture: urban segregation in Johannesburg, 1923–1938' (unpublished paper, History Workshop, University of the Witwatersrand, Johannesburg, 1984).

4. Swanson, 'Durban System', p.161.

5. Gavin Maasdorp and A. S. B. Humphreys, *From shantytown to township* (Cape Town, Juta, 1975), p. 10.

6. Department of Native Affairs (DNA) files, vol. 2067, 138/280, Natal: Native Labour Supply 1911–39, Memorandum by J. Reynolds Tait, 1911.

7. D. Hemson, 'Class consciousness and migrant workers: dock workers of Durban', (unpublished Ph. D. thesis, University of Warwick, 1979) pp. 83–90.

8. *South African Native Affairs Commission*, 1903–1905, Minutes of Evidence, vol. III, Q.28,351.

9. *Ibid.*, Q.28,193.

10. *Ibid.*, Q.28,351; Swanson, 'Durban System', p. 172.

11. See Hemson, 'Class consciousness', pp. 100–109.

12. Paul la Hausse, 'The struggle for the city: alcohol, the ematsheni and popular culture in Durban, 1902–1936', (unpublished M.A. thesis, University of Cape Town, 1984), p. 76.

13. Durban Town Clerk's Files (DTCF), 4/1/2/1173, Native Pass System; Extract from the *Natal Advertiser*, February 1916.

14. DTCF, 4/1/2/1174, Native Registration Bye-laws, Mayor of Durban to Prime Minister, 12 January 1917.

15. DTCF, 4/1/2/1176, Memorandum by Acting Town Clerk, 17 June 1930.

16. *South African Native Affairs Commission*, 1903–1905, Minutes of Evidence, vol. III, Qs. 28,257 and 28,265.

17. DTCF, 4/1/2/1174, Native Registration Bye-laws, Marwick to Town Clerk (TC), 7 February 1917.

18. Maasdorp and Humphreys, *Shantytown*, p. 9.

19. Quoted in Davenport, 'Colonel Stallard', pp. 86–87; see also UG 22–1932, *Report of the Native Economic Commission*, 1930–32, Part III, pp. 72, 77.

20. Davenport, 'Colonel Stallard', p. 77.

21. Hindson, *Pass controls*, pp. 10–11.

22. Durban Native Administration Committee (DNAC), Agenda Book, 27 July 1931.

23. SC 3–23, Select Committee on Native Affairs, 1923.

24. DTCF, 4/1/2/75, Natives (Urban Areas) Bill, Statement by Layman, 3 March 1923.

25. DTCF, 4/1/3/1624, Registration of Natives, Proclamation of Urban Area of Durban under Section 12 of Act No. 21 of 1923; D. C. Hindson, 'The pass system and the formation of an urban African proletariat in South Africa: a critique of the cheap labour-power thesis', (unpublished Ph. D. thesis, University of Sussex, 1983), pp. 86–90.

26. DTCF, 4/1/2/1177, Registration of Natives, Acting TC to Chief Constable, 17 June 1930; Hemson, 'Class consciousness', p. 267.

27. DNAC, Agenda Book, 25 August 1931, Whitsitt to TC, 19 August 1931.

28. See DNAC, Agenda Books, 19 September and 17 November 1933, 16 July and 14 December 1934.

29. DNAC, Agenda Books, 6 February 1936. Layman to TC, 24 January 1936; DNAC, Agenda Books, 28 February 1936, Whitsitt to TC; DNAC, Agenda Books, 15 March 1937, Cllr. Kemp to TC, 1 March 1937.

30. DTCF, subject no. 290 P, Judicial Commission on Native Affairs in Durban, Durban City Council's memorandum, ch. II, p. 1; DNA, vol. 5389, 29/313 G, Durban Municipality: Kaffir Beer, Memorandum by P. Gray, 27 June 1950. Note that the 1936 and 1946 figures are derived from the official government censuses of those years; the other figures are municipal estimates.

31. DTCF, subject no. 290 P, Judicial Commission on Native Affairs in Durban, Durban City Council's memorandum, ch. II, p. 1.

32. DTCF, subject no. 290 P, Report of the Judicial Commission on Native Affairs in Durban, 31 January 1948, p. 18; Iain Edwards, 'Nurturing the soil to protect you from politics: the African proletariat in Durban in the early 1950s' (unpublished conference paper, Oxford University, September 1987), pp. 12–13.

33. DTCF, 4/1/3/1622, Registration of Natives, Minutes of Council-in-Committee, 14 November 1945.

34. DTCF, Native Locations, file 10, Champion to TC, 21 April 1947.

35. Hindson, 'Pass System', pp. 97–101. As it turned out, only one such municipal census was undertaken, in 1938.

36. DTCF, 4/1/3/1618, Registration of Natives, Chester to TC, 8 September 1938.

37. DTCF, 4/1/3/1619, Proclamation no. 39, 1 March 1940.

38. DTCF, 4/1/3/1618, Chester to TC, 8 September 1938.

39. DTCF, 4/1/3/1619, Chester to TC, 8 November 1939.

40. DTCF, 4/1/3/1621, Memorandum by TC, 7 December 1944.

41. DTCF, 4/1/3/1622, Minutes of DNAC, 13 September 1945.

42. Quoted in Paul Maylam, 'The "Black Belt": African squatters in Durban 1935–1950', *Canadian Journal of African Studies*, 17, 1983.

43. DNA, vol. 5389, 29/313 G, Memorandum by P. Gray, 27 June 1950.

44. UG Extraordinary, 30 May 1949; Government Notice 1032, 1 May 1949.

45. Hindson, *Pass controls*, pp. 61–64.

46. *The Durban housing survey*, NRS, Additional report no. 2 (Pietermaritzburg, Department of Economics, University of Natal, 1952), pp. 403–9; Uma Mesthrie, 'From Sastri to Deshmukh: a study of the role of the government of India's representatives in South Africa, 1927 to 1946' (unpublished Ph. D. thesis, University of Natal, 1988), pp. 241–46.

47. Jeff McCarthy, 'Changing the definition of Natal's metropolitan areas: the case of Durban 1930–1987' (unpublished paper, Workshop on Regionalism and Restructuring in Natal, University of Natal, January 1988) pp. 8–13; *Durban housing survey*, pp. 405–8.

48. Examples of such thinking can be found in DNA, vol. 4270, 120/313, vol. 2. DNA memorandum, 'Housing in Urban Native Areas', June 1940; 'Notes on the question of cheaper urban native housing', 20 January 1944; 'Extension of National Housing Scheme with special reference to native housing needs', January 1948.

49. *Durban housing survey*, pp. 409–16.

50. DNA, vol. 5304, 29/313E, Durban – Segregation, First Report of the Technical Sub-Committee on Race Zoning, Part I, June 1951.

51. DNA, vol. 5304, 29/313E, Draft Notes on Some Aspects of the Group Areas Act in Relation to Durban, by the Technical Sub-Committee.

52. *Durban housing survey*, pp. 418–21.

53. *Ibid.*, pp. 431–45.

54. DNA, vol. 5304, 29/313E, Durban – Segregation. Secretary for Native Affairs to Provincial Secretary, 15 May 1951.

ABSTRACT

In 1910, at the end of its 'colonial' phase of spatial evolution, Pietermaritzburg was characterised by white occupation of the original Voortrekker grid layout; an already significant Indian community established primarily in the lower part of the city but also with businesses in the upper Church Street and City Hall areas; and a growing African population resident on the periphery in barracks, hostels or self-erected dwellings. During the 'segregated city' stage of its development (1910–1948) Pietermaritzburg experienced considerable extensions to its built-up area and internal structure despite the absence of any significant economic growth or comprehensive town planning scheme. Residential growth was characterised by suburbanisation, slum growth and increasing segregation. Apart from the city council's earlier opening of Scottsville, suburban expansion was primarily privately initiated and for white residents, the majority of whom lived in the suburbs by 1940. Uncontrolled shack construction on the city's periphery became a source of concern to local health officials but by 1948 the central government had created a comprehensive segregationist apparatus for the regulation of African urbanisation and the curtailment of alleged Indian penetration into white residential areas. During its 'apartheid city' phase of development (post-1948) Pietermaritzburg experienced its first industrial boom after being declared a 'Bantustan Border Industrial Area' in 1963, but was formally divided into racially exclusive areas, separated by buffer zones to minimise contact, in terms of the 1950 Group Areas Act. This obliged many Indian and 'coloured' residents to move from the upper Church Street and Pentrich/ Camps Drift areas and diverted African residents to the Imbali, Ashdown and Edendale townships to the south of the city. Pietermaritzburg is changing relentlessly in character as a result of the gradual relaxation of segregationist legislation during the late 1980s. What is likely to emerge in the future is a 'post-apartheid' city which in many ways resembles colonial Pietermaritzburg at the time of Union.

282

SEGREGATION, SEPARATION AND DESEGREGATION: PIETERMARITZBURG SINCE 1910

Trevor Wills

There is a voluminous, and growing, literature on South African urban history, whilst geographers are compiling a growing body of information on the historical geography of South African cities, after a long period of neglect.[1] In both instances, it can be argued, the major focuses of concern have been the evolution and impact of urban policies imposed by the central government, particularly with respect to Africans. Geographically and historically the main areas of concern have been the major metropolitan centres, particularly those influenced by mining and other major industrial growth. In this essay the evolving social geography of Pietermaritzburg, from the time of Union in 1910 to the present (and the immediate future) is discussed.

Pietermaritzburg, administrative capital of the province of Natal, is not a mining town, nor is there any appreciable mining activity within its immediate hinterland. The capital is also not a major industrial area and, as a metropolitan area, ranks eighth in the country in terms of population.

In many other respects, however, the city is a microcosm of South African urban conditions. Founded by the Voortrekkers, moulded by British colonialism and shaped by South African municipal and central government policies, Pietermaritzburg is today home to roughly equivalent numbers of white and Indian residents (with a small but rapidly expanding 'coloured' population), and being situated adjacent to areas of KwaZulu, is an important focus of African urbanisation.

Following Davies's[2] example, the spatial evolution of Pietermaritzburg can be traced conventionally through a colonial-city phase (pre-Union), a segregated-city phase (1910–1948) and an apartheid-city phase (post-1948), whilst it will be argued that the city is currently on the brink of transition to a post-apartheid form. These phases cannot be rigidly demarcated, but they do reflect distinct periods of change in the social and physical morphology of South African towns.

The widely held prejudice in favour of National Party accountability for the racially segregated nature of the apartheid city of today[3] is under-

283

mined by an examination of the unfolding social geography of Pietermaritzburg. It has been argued that the divide between the segregated city
and the apartheid city is marked by the post-1948 implementation of a
comprehensive national urban model based on the doctrine of separate
development.[4] In other words, the apartheid city that evolved was not
simply characterised by racial segregation, which has a long history, but
by separation. However, prior to the plethora of statutory legislation after
1948, that crystallized the apartheid-city form, the local authority in
Pietermaritzburg (as in most South African towns) was actively involved
in creating a segregated city.

The colonial city: Pietermaritzburg at the time of Union, 1910

At the time of Union, Pietermaritzburg was still quintessentially a
pre-industrial colonial town. All the morphological ingredients of the
British colonial town were present – the military cantonment (in this case
the garrison at Fort Napier); the clustering nearby of the civilian elite (at
the head of the original Voortrekker grid layout, in the vicinity of
Government House); the market square and its surrounding commercial
enterprises; the administrative precinct (more grandiose than one would
expect of a town of Pietermaritzburg's size, after the colony became
self-governing) – all welded together by a thinly spread population of
small tradesmen, craftsmen and artisans. Nuclei of suburban development
had begun to emerge, but the white population was still predominantly
housed within the original grid. A *de facto* 'cordon sanitaire' separated the
colonists from the indigenous African population (with the exception of
those in domestic employment) which was increasingly drawn towards the
town. The African residents were expected to provide their own accommodation on the periphery of the town, although accommodation was
typically provided for certain categories of employee, in the form of
barracks or compounds.

The Indian community formed an important part of Pietermaritzburg
society at the time of Union. The 1911 national census indicates that
21,2 per cent of city residents were 'Asian', compared to the 48,6 per cent
who were classified as 'European'. Indian settlers had begun to arrive in
the town from the early 1860s. Many of the first Indian settlers were
Hindi- or Tamil-speaking Hindus who were attracted by Pietermaritzburg's large irrigated erven in the lower, largely unoccupied, part of the
town's grid layout, and later to smallholdings beyond the original nucleus.
By the 1890s the lower reaches of two of the city's major thoroughfares,
Church Street and Longmarket Street, had acquired a distinctive Indian
flavour, with temples, stores, gabled houses, market gardens and barracks. By 1910 the 'barrack' had become a ubiquitous feature of Indian
residential areas, taking the form of a row of rooms, usually opening
directly onto a veranda on the street side, and onto a yard at the rear with
communal ablution facilities. In many cases, the barracks were organised
in a rectangle with a central courtyard. Barracks are very rare in
Pietermaritzburg today, but now, as then, tend to house the poorest
families in often overcrowded conditions.

In the 1880s an additional Indian component enriched the Pietermaritz-burg townscape when Moslem merchants set up shop in the town in increasing numbers, concentrating in the upper Church Street area, and in the vicinity of the City Hall. These 'Arabs' as they often liked to be called, to distinguish themselves from their ex-indentured countrymen, soon captured the dominant share of the 'native' trade, and to the other sounds of the market place was added the daily call to prayer from the mosque.[5]

Anti-Asiatic agitation has had a long history in the capital. In 1885 the Pietermaritzburg Chamber of Commerce unsuccessfully petitioned the Governor, for several, and severe, restrictions to be placed on Indian traders; in particular that Indians be allowed to live and trade only in designated areas.[6] This echoed Law No.3/1885 of the South African Republic (Transvaal) which restricted Indians to 'Asiatic Bazaars'. In 1897 the *Natal Witness* urged that separate locations for Indians be established, whilst in the same year the Mayor of Pietermaritzburg joined his counter-parts in Durban and Newcastle in petitioning the Colonial Secretary to stop the acquisition of land by Indians.[7]

It has been generally accepted that the first legislation aimed at residentially segregating Indians in Natal was the 1922 Durban Land Alienation Ordinance No.14, permitting the Durban City Council to include an 'anti-Asiatic' clause in the title-deeds and leases of Borough land.[8] However, there is evidence that Pietermaritzburg had taken the initiative some 24 years earlier. In January of 1898, the Finance Commit-tee recommended to the Town Council that a piece of townlands be '. . . offered for sale at an upset price of 20 pounds per acre, and that the non-Asiatic clause be inserted.'[9]

At the same meeting it was recommended that the lease on a quarry on townlands be offered by public competition '. . . with the usual non-Asiatic clause'.

Scrutiny of early street directories reveals that, until 1910, white and Indian households were widely interspersed in the part of town below Retief Street – the 'recognised Indian area'. From that time onwards, however, the pattern that emerged was one of a mosaic of segregated areas outside the city centre (with some exceptions where 'mixed' areas evolved) and Indian enclaves within the central grid (although on the fringes of these enclaves white, coloured and Indian families occupied the same streets).

In colonial Pietermaritzburg, social distinctions were not based on race alone. Among the white colonists social lines were, in the main, drawn in conformity with official standing; with the most obvious cleavage being that between military and civilian. A further distinction was between colonial officials and townsfolk.

Until the turn of the century, the majority of the white colonists of Pietermaritzburg lived within the expansive grid laid out by the Voor-trekkers. Socially, the upper reaches of the grid in the vicinity of the fort (and the Lieutenant-Governor's residence) had been regarded as the most desirable residential areas by the affluent, and the politically powerful. By the time of Union, however, suburbanisation had begun; the most con spicuous example of which was the development by the city council of the garden suburb layout of Scottsville in 1906 in order to raise revenue to pay for a newly installed electric tram system.

In keeping with their colonial counterparts elsewhere in the Empire, local governments in the late nineteenth century were acutely aware of the pressing problems of overcrowding and insanitary conditions facing the industrialised towns of the mother country, and this was coupled to a widely held perception that public health would be prejudiced by the uncontrolled presence of 'natives' in town. One year after its creation in 1854, the Pietermaritzburg Town Council discussed the question of building by-laws to control the erection of buildings of a very low standard. The aim of regulating the quality of buildings within the city did not meet with the approval of all the councillors and it was argued that:

> . . . a portion of Her Majesty's subjects with limited means would be driven from the city, and that newcomers with insufficient means whose services might be necessary for the prosperity of the City would be prevented from settling in the city.[10]

Notwithstanding their protests, building by-laws were introduced in 1856 which, amongst other things, banned buildings made of materials of 'a lower standard than green brick', including wattle and daub, and grass. The by-laws effectively kept those who could not afford conventional brick-built houses from erecting homes within the city proper.

Although legislative attempts to restrict Indians within the capital pre-date measures aimed at segregating the African population, agitation against a 'native' presence in the town proper dates back to the very origins of the dorp. Certainly the Voortrekkers made no provision for the accommodation of the indigenous population; the city was seen as the white settlers' creation and preserve, and no place for Africans (barring servants and other employees). As far as the African population of the city is concerned, the story is one of a largely unsuccessful battle to establish a niche for themselves near the centre of the town, where jobs were, and are, to be found.

In 1848 Surveyor-General Stanger expressed the view that each town should have a portion of its townlands appropriated for the use of Africans engaged in daily labour in those towns.[11] In 1854 it was reported that Africans were squatting on Pietermaritzburg's townlands, and in the following year the borough council accepted a motion that a portion of the townlands be set aside for a 'native' village.[12] This motion was vehemently attacked in a letter to the *Natal Chronicle*:

> The burden of proof lies with the Municipality to show that a Kafir village can be safely and profitably laid out on the Town lands. And councillors, perhaps, would do well to consult ratepayers before they grant any site for that purpose.[13]

Criticisms of the council seem to have had an effect for, apart from a solitary attempt to resuscitate the issue in 1856, it was twenty years before a village in Town Bush Valley was proposed.[14] However, a number of irate residents protested at the proposed site and the Town Lands Committee was instructed to find an alternative. Despite the passing of the Native Locations Act by the Natal parliament in 1904 (which enabled municipalities to establish segregated locations) it was not until separate townships for Africans became enforceable (and fundable) in terms of the 1923 Natives (Urban Areas) Act that the much discussed 'Pietermaritzburg Native Village' became a reality.[15]

Before Sobantu (as the village became known in 1947) was built, municipal housing efforts had been confined to the erection in 1877 of barracks for African employees near the slaughterhouse on the outskirts of town, below the confluence of the Msindusi and the Dorp Spruit; the provision in 1890 of barracks for 'togt' workers nearby; and the building of hostels for males and females in 1914 and 1924 respectively.

The degree of racial segregation in South African towns and cities at the time of Union has recently been quantified by Christopher[16] using data drawn from the first post-Union census in 1911. Using population data at the enumeration tract level, indices of segregation and dissimilarity were calculated for all towns with a population of over 2 000.[17] Not surprisingly, given the varying policies with respect to enforcing segregation, pursued by the four colonial administrations, the levels of segregation varied significantly between individual towns. Levels of segregation in Pietermaritzburg at the time of the census are shown relative to those in a sample of other South African towns in table 1.[18]

Table 1 Indices of segregation and dissimilarity for selected South African towns, 1911 Population Census

Town	Indices of segregation			Indices of dissimilarity		
	White	Black	Coloured*	White/ Black	White/ Coloured	Black/ Coloured
Cape Town	48.0	58.3	48.0	63.3	48.1	61.5
Stellenbosch	13.7	24.5	13.4	26.7	13.6	22.7
Port Elizabeth	57.6	71.8	50.1	79.5	51.6	68.7
Grahamstown	74.0	81.2	58.3	83.1	54.6	81.2
Johannesburg	66.8	70.4	61.1	70.8	56.8	74.2
Pretoria	51.1	48.9	68.8	49.9	69.6	70.2
Bloemfontein	84.9	86.8	56.7	86.9	37.8	86.7
Harrismith	52.5	51.4	54.1	52.4	56.7	59.9
Durban	52.3	39.2	66.1	41.5	67.9	64.9
Pietermaritzburg	42.7	27.8	54.2	30.3	58.7	50.9

* 'Coloured' includes Indians

Towns in the Western Cape and Natal exhibited lower overall levels of segregation than, for example, towns in the Transvaal and Eastern Cape. The apparent high degree of integration between whites and Africans in Pietermaritzburg, when towns in different regions are compared, contrasts with the relatively higher degree of segregation of 'coloureds' (predominantly Indians in Natal). Whilst these results may well reflect the greater preoccupation of segregationists with the urban Indian population in Natal towns, they should not be seen as reflecting, on the other hand, integrationist policies as far as Africans were concerned. The indices reflect, rather, the greater spatial concentration of Indians within borough boundaries at the time of Union, and the dispersed, yet segregated, pattern of African settlement within the borough. At the time of the 1911 census, the enumerated African population would have been dominated by people in domestic employ (and thus widely dispersed without being socially integrated in any way with the white population), or people housed by their employers or the municipality in compounds, barracks or hostels. The detection of segregation would thus have required a finer spatial resolution than the enumeration tract. In addition, at the time of the 1911 census a considerable proportion of the African daytime population was housed beyond borough boundaries in Edendale and Zwaartkops Location, whilst many of the shack-dwellers within the borough would have escaped enumeration.

The 'segregated city' 1910–1948

Between 1910 and 1948 there were considerable extensions to the built-up area of the city, and changes to its internal structure. These changes had occurred during a period of slow economic growth, and in the absence of any comprehensive town planning scheme. Despite the presentation of a detailed report on the need for a town planning scheme by the City Engineer in 1930,[19] it was not until 1952 that the first draft town planning scheme for Pietermaritzburg was approved by the city council.[20] Planning and development during this period was therefore carried out on an *ad hoc* basis, and to a considerable degree reflected the whims of the city councils, controlled as they were by white ratepayers.

The slow economic growth of the city throughout this period can in part be attributed to national economic conditions, but was also a reflection of the failure of the city to attract significant industrialisation.[21] City council involvement in the promotion of industry began in 1909, when the recession following the South African War and the prospect of losing colonial capital status prompted investigations into ways of improving the prosperity of the borough. In 1918 modest concessions were offered to industrialists willing to locate in the city, and again in 1928 further inducements were offered, but both initiatives were largely unsuccessful. The city also missed out on economic growth stimulated by the Second World War. City councils were not unanimous in their support for industrialisation, and there was strong support for the maintenance of the city as an administrative, educational and market centre. During the

Second World War, for example, the city was led by a mayor and council actively opposed to further industrial growth.[22]

Although the city did not match the doubling in employment in secondary industry enjoyed by the country as a whole between 1921 and 1958, it did share in the marked increase in African urbanisation, sparked, many observers would argue, by the steady decline in the economies of the African reserves.[23] This was reflected not in the official African population growth rate within the borough, which remained at approximately 1,7 per cent per annum from 1911 to 1940,[24] but in the growth in shack communities and in the peri-urban fringe. It was during the 1930s and 1940s that neighbouring Edendale began to lose its village character as immigration produced overcrowding and slum conditions.[25]

The residential growth of the city was characterised by suburbanisation, slum formation, and increasing segregation. With the exception of the initial phase of development of Scottsville by the city council, suburban growth was largely the result of private initiative and involved the progressive subdivision of large small-holdings fringing the original nucleus of the city, aided by the extension of the tramway system and later a bus service. The periodic sale of sections of townlands helped to keep the price of development down. With very few exceptions, the new suburban houses were occupied by white residents, and by 1940 the majority of the white population lived beyond the original Voortrekker nucleus. The pattern of suburban growth that resulted was later to be entrenched by the Group Areas Act.

Slums

The reports of the Medical Officer of Health (MOH) for Pietermaritzburg, throughout the 1920s and 1930s are dominated by one subject above all others, namely the problem of uncontrolled 'shack' housing scattered in pockets around the borough (but 'outside the city proper'). In 1930 the MOH and the Secretary of the Benevolent Society concluded that there was little shortage of housing for 'the poorest class of European', nor much overcrowding. They reported that the houses occupied by these families:

> . . . do not constitute a slum area, but are scattered singly over the northern and eastern sides of town . . . There is in fact no area in the European part of the city which by any stretch of the imagination could be regarded as a slum area.[26]

This is not to deny that in individual cases housing conditions were very poor, or to suggest that poverty did not exist – both are confirmed by the existence of relief work projects employing whites from 1922 onwards.

In contrast, contiguous areas of very poor housing for African and Indian town-dwellers did exist. In his report for the same year the MOH provided detailed information on the desperately poor conditions in two areas in particular: Hathorn's Hill and Camps Drift (Pentrich).

The Camps Drift area, on the immediate outskirts of the city centre, straddled the Msindusi River. It was prone to frequent flooding but this did not appear to deter those who settled there. An earlier report on the same area by the MOH in 1920 described the situation in the following terms:

> Many of these Indians are gardeners who rent one or two acres of ground on a monthly tenancy from the private owners, or from the Corporation, and erect on it their own dwellings, gradually enlarging them in order to take in Native lodgers. As these Indians have no permanent tenure of the ground they cannot be expected to put up proper dwellings. This is probably the principal cause of the existing state of affairs. The by-laws [sic] requiring dwellings to be built in brick has usually been waived by the Corporation in respect of this area, almost all of the habitable houses are built of wood and iron.[27]

The MOH's description of the dwellings in the report submitted a decade later (1930) has a familiar ring to it; the conditions existing in those days being so similar to those prevailing in emerging shack settlements today:

> A great proportion of the dwellings erected are best designated by the word 'shack'. They are constructed of old iron, wood, petrol tins, or mud. They have earthen floors and no windows. They are cold in winter and hot in summer and freely admit the rain and the wind. 97 per cent of these are unfit for habitation. In some of these dwellings a single family only, Indian or Native, is accommodated, but to many have been added additional rooms for accommodating lodgers. These additional rooms are of the same type of construction as the original shack. The number of persons living in one of these shacks, enlarged to take lodgers, is in some cases, twenty or thirty. The lodgers are in most cases Native families.[28]

The central city did not escape the scrutiny of the MOH, and in 1934 a survey of the 105 Indian barracks in the eastern section found that most were unsatisfactory structures physically, and that overcrowding was widespread, with the average occupancy rate over three people per room.[29]

The shack areas, in a ring around the eastern and south-eastern periphery of the borough, were subjected to constant scrutiny by city health officials. The provisions of the Natives (Urban Areas) Act of 1923 and its later amendments, and the Slums Act No. 53 of 1934 gave more power to officials seeking to regulate settlements such as Maryvale, Hathorn's Hill, Camps Drift, Foxon and Maharaj Locations, New Scotland, New England, Fitzsimmons's Location and Slangspruit.

Segregation

The passing of the Natives (Urban Areas) Act in 1923 represented the first major intervention by the central government in directing urban African affairs. Although it was only enabling legislation, it formed the framework upon which later legislation governing African urbanisation was to be based, and by 1948 a comprehensive apparatus for the regulation and control of urban Africans was in place.[30] In response to the passing of the Act the mayor made the following comment:

> The question of native housing in the borough has for many years been one of the thorniest description. A native location or village has been discussed for years, but it has hitherto been impossible to do anything because of the objections of burgesses to allow the village to be formed in some particular part of the borough or the other. The passing of the 'Urban Areas Act' makes it incumbent upon local authorities to deal with the question or the Minister of Native Affairs can step in and apply compulsion.[31]

Section 12 of the 1923 Act allowed the council to declare Pietermaritzburg an area within which Africans had to be registered, while Section 5 allowed an urban area to be proclaimed so that virtually all Africans could be forced to live in a location, hostels or a village. Section 5 was implemented in two phases and in 1931 the entire borough was thus proclaimed.[32]

An amendment in 1931 required the licensing of 'native premises' within the borough, subject to approval by city inspectors, and enabled Pietermaritzburg to be declared an area within which the only Africans permitted to reside were domestic servants and those with special exemptions. However, the existence of a large African peri-urban area beyond the city boundaries (Edendale and Zwaartkops Location) complicated attempts to regulate settlement within the borough, by providing a refuge from authority.[33]

The council's only attempt to provide low-cost public housing for Africans within the borough was Sobantu Village. The major impetus for building such a village came from the MOH who firmly believed that the slum conditions that had developed in peripheral shanty settlements could not otherwise be eradicated.

During 1925 a plebiscite of white municipal voters was held to decide whether to locate the village south of the town, near Mason's Mill and Edendale (favoured by African residents), or on a property on the eastern side of town off the Bishopstowe Road, overlooking the Msindusi River (not favoured by African residents due to its proximity to the town sanitary dump, and its distance from the established African area of Edendale). In an 18 per cent poll the white voters decided by a 2 to 1 majority to build the village at the Bishopstowe Road site, at that stage some three kilometres from the edge of town.[34]

Construction on the first 100 houses, half of them semi-detached, began in 1927. The village was not initially very popular and reports in the *Corporation yearbooks* indicate that an element of compulsion was necessary to get the first phase occupied by people from Mawhelene in Chase Valley, and from the New Scotland area. The first brick houses had earth floors smeared with cow-dung, but these were soon replaced by brick floors. Though sewage disposal was by the bucket system, and only communal bathrooms were provided in the earlier stages, the village and its houses were supplied with electric lighting; a feature that was rare in later such developments. A further 100 houses were added in 1931, intended mainly to house families from the African shack settlement of Hathorn's Hill.

The council's involvement in regulating Africans within the borough did not only encompass housing. In his Mayor's Minute in 1935, the mayor noted with satisfaction that by building 'native' beerhalls and eating houses, the city had taken:

> . . . a step forward in the scheme of moving Africans from the centre of town, but providing them with adequate facilities elsewhere.[35]

In 1939 the provisions of the Natives (Urban Areas) Act were once more invoked to frame regulations prohibiting the 'loitering of natives on the market square' and a circular was issued admonishing Africans to use the sports grounds provided in the lower end of town.

During the period 1910 to 1948, Indian residents of Pietermaritzburg established themselves in enclaves outside the central grid layout, particularly to the north of the town where market gardening was practised on smallholdings, and along the Msindusi valley south of the city. The position at the time of Union in 1910 was that legislative machinery for the compulsory residential segregation of Indians existed only in the Transvaal (while Indians were excluded altogether from the Orange Free State and those parts of northern Natal that had been part of the old South African Republic). The period 1910 to 1946 was marked by strong 'anti-Asiatic' agitation in the Transvaal and Natal, particularly in Durban, and this culminated (after a number of piecemeal attempts to enforce segregation or encourage voluntary segregation) in the 1943 Trading and Occupation of Land (Transvaal and Natal) Restriction Act No. 35/1943 – more commonly known as the 'Pegging Act'. This pegged out the areas occupied by Indians in 1943, and controlled further property transactions between whites and Indians. This act was followed soon afterwards in 1946 by the Asiatic Land Tenure and Representation Act No. 28/1946 (the 'Ghetto Act') which placed absolute limits on the territory which could be occupied by Indians.[36]

The root cause of the hostility between white and Indian residents was said to be the alleged 'penetration' of Indians into formerly white residential areas. The government-appointed Indian Penetration Commission heard evidence that between 1927 and 1940, 512 formerly white-owned properties had been acquired by Indians in Durban, whereas during the same period only 16 complaints had been reported for Pietermaritzburg.[37] However, well before the introduction of any restrictive measures Pietermaritzburg was, in the minds of its officials in any event, clearly divided along racial lines. Hence municipal housing was designated for specific racial groups long before the Population Registration Act (1950) made such racial division mandatory, or the Group Areas Act enforced territorial separation.

To ameliorate the housing position somewhat, the municipality did become involved in providing low-cost housing (spurred by the passing of the Housing Act in 1920), building an initial twenty houses for whites in 1926.[38] Separate low-cost municipal housing for Indians was initiated much later in 1938, when fifty houses for Indians were built in lower Boom Street. Apart from Sobantu Village and the hostels in town, however, it was left up to employers or the people themselves to house Africans.

In the central business area of Pietermaritzburg, Indian trading families consolidated their positions. Redevelopment of the area around the City Hall in the early 1930s removed Indian traders from the core of Pietermaritzburg's trading district, but in upper Church Street and its lower reaches Indian traders and their families were firmly entrenched.[39] Unlike their white counterparts, who traded in the city centre but resided in the growing suburbs or elsewhere in the central city, the Indian traders tended to reside in dwellings above or behind their premises.

What emerged were spatially integrated neighbourhoods with shops on the main street frontages, dwellings above and behind, and schools and mosques occupying the centre of the large city blocks. An example was the upper Church Street area where Indian-owned and occupied land increased steadily to reach a peak in 1940 (map 1). The threats posed by the 'Pegging Act' and the 'Ghetto Act' curtailed expansion thereafter, whilst the enactment of the Group Areas Act in 1950 further threatened survival of the Indian trading areas, and by the time the Act was extended to the city in 1960 Indian landholdings in the upper Church Street area had begun to decline. By 1980 the Indian land-holdings almost replicated those at the turn of the century (map 1).

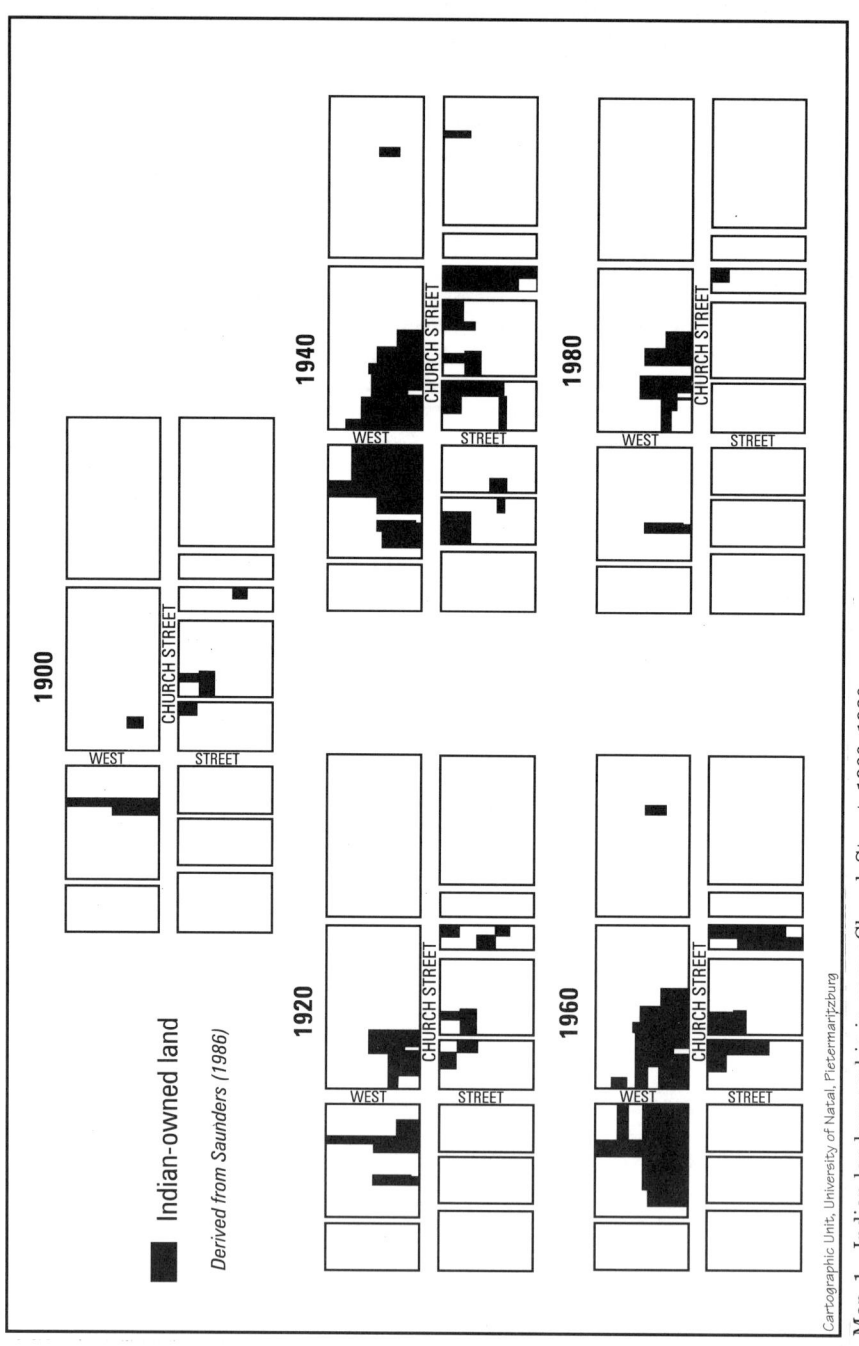

Cartographic Unit, University of Natal, Pietermaritzburg

Map 1   Indian landownership in upper Church Street, 1900–1980

The apartheid city: Pietermaritzburg after 1948

Post-war growth

Using the annual growth rate of the white population as an indicator of business growth, it is clear that the city boomed in the immediate post-war years when compared with the inter-war years. The annual growth rate for the 1918–36 period was 1,6 per cent, whereas the rate for the period 1948–51 was 3,4 per cent.[40] This was despite slow industrial growth.

This expansion of the city coincided with fundamental political change, heralded by the coming to power of the National Party in 1948. Both the territorial partitioning of South Africa into a white 'heartland' and Bantustans or 'homelands', and the translation of a policy of rigid racial separation to the local urban scale, were to markedly and permanently change the face of Pietermaritzburg, and the daily lives of most of its inhabitants.

Aware of the growing threat of economic stagnation, and the demand for employment from a burgeoning peri-urban population, the Pietermaritzburg City Council embarked on a vigorous campaign to attract industry to the city during the 1950s.[41] These efforts were rewarded by the designation of the city as a 'Bantustan Border Industrial Area' in 1963. The border industrial policy was planned to be one of the cornerstones of separate development and the development of the homelands. The idea was to encourage industry in South Africa to decentralise from the dominant economic core regions (e.g. the Southern Transvaal) to locations adjacent to large African rural labour reservoirs, where factories could be sited so as to permit a daily ebb and flow of commuters without the need for urban expansion. The economically acceptable motive of decentralisation was mated, therefore, to a blatantly 'anti-African-urbanisation' policy.

By virtue of Pietermaritzburg's proximity to Edendale and the surrounding African rural areas, generous incentives were offered to industrialists willing to locate or relocate in the city, and this prompted the capital's first significant industrial boom. In 1963, 23 per cent of the local labour force was engaged in industry, and in 1972 this had increased to 36 per cent.[42] In the apparent belief that concessions were no longer necessary to sustain growth in Pietermaritzburg the concessions were withdrawn in 1971. The result was a slump in industrial land sales from which the city has only recently shown signs of recovering, having been declared a 'deconcentration' point in the latest revision of the national physical development plan. During the intervening period, however, the demand for housing and other services from a burgeoning population in metropolitan Pietermaritzburg has continued unabated.

To cope with population growth in the 1950s and 1960s, and the imminent displacement of people by the Group Areas Act, plans were made to construct low-cost housing (with government assistance) on an unprecedented scale. This massive state involvement in the provision of housing occurred in all the major urban centres. It formed part of an attempt to restructure the black urban areas of South African cities, by eliminating informal settlements and racially mixed inner-city slums. The

Indian township of Northdale, the coloured township of Woodlands, and the Grange housing scheme for whites, as well as the first stages of Imbali Township were conceived, and construction begun during this period.[43]

The actual geographical locations of these schemes, such a dominant element in the townscape and social geography of the city today, was to a large degree determined by the provisions of the Group Areas Act passed by Parliament in 1950, but only formally applied to the city in 1960. More than any other single act, the Group Areas Act has changed the face of South African cities, Pietermaritzburg being no exception.

The Group Areas Act and the 'ideal apartheid city'

Long before the Group Areas Act was passed the principle that Africans were temporary sojourners in the 'white' city had been an integral part of urban planning, and the Natives (Urban Areas) Act of 1923 and the Amended Act of 1937 effectively kept African residential areas on the distant fringes of the city.[44] The Group Areas Act now aimed not at *segregating* race groups, because this was largely the case in any event, but at *separating* race groups as defined in the Population Registration Act, in the belief that friction between races could be avoided by minimising points of contact.[45] In his study of Cape Town, Western[46] concluded that: 'All these strategic considerations indicate that group areas planning is not planning for segregation *per se*, but for *domination through segregation.*'

The removal of 'unnecessary points of contact' was to be achieved by dividing cities up into racially exclusive zones, where only one group would be allowed to live and carry out business. It follows then that if such a system of zoning were to be effective, and at the same time allow access by all to the central business quarters and employment opportunities, then a type of sectoral residential pattern would be most appropriate, with the sectors separated (as required by the Act) by buffer zones. By merging this with the already established policy of keeping Africans on the outskirts of town, or in nearby rural areas, it was possible to postulate an 'ideal apartheid city' form (map 2).[47] From 1960 onwards Pietermaritzburg has increasingly come to adopt just such a form. Buffer strips have either been created (an example being the strip of land between Imbali Township and the adjacent white Grange/Westgate housing scheme, from which African families were moved) or were conveniently to hand (a prime example being the municipal cemetery and the railway servitude which separates the coloured group area of Woodlands and the Indian township of Northdale).

The Group Areas Act and the restructuring of Pietermaritzburg.

It is not known with any certainty exactly how many people were forced to relocate as a result of the implementation of the Group Areas Act in the capital but various estimates were made at the time. Motala[48] suggested that about 900 properties were affected, involving over 9 000 people, while municipal estimates were that 700 properties would be affected and

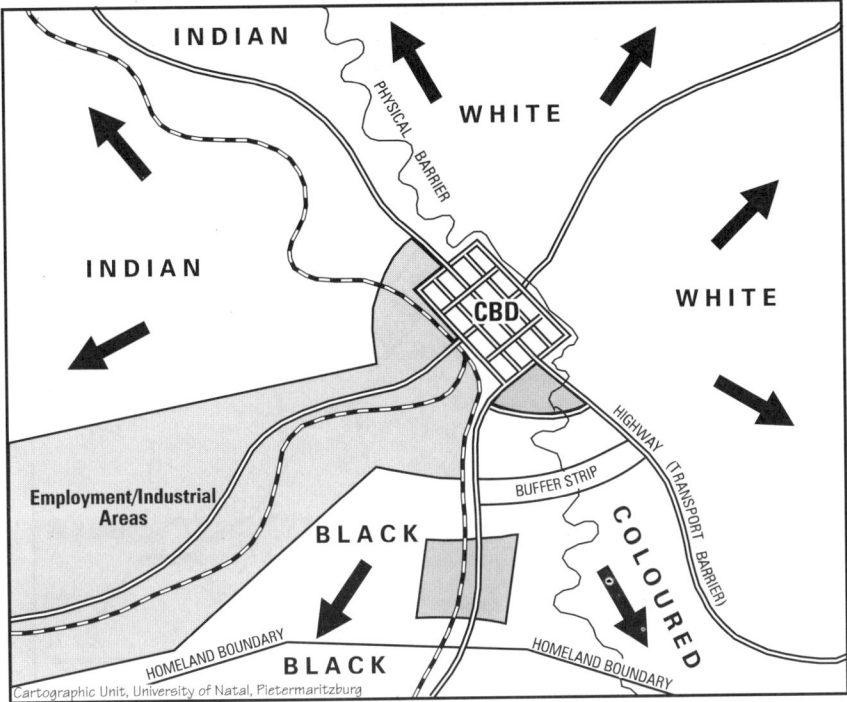

Map 2   An 'ideal apartheid city' model

15 000 people.[49] The Indian community bore the brunt of the changes demanded by the Act, accounting for 76 per cent of those moved. Eleven per cent of the properties affected were owned by coloureds, while a further 12 per cent were African owned. Only 1 per cent of the properties were white owned.[50]

Unlike their Cape Town counterparts, who refused to co-operate with the Group Areas Board and had to be subpoenaed to provide information,[51] the Pietermaritzburg City Council co-operated to the extent that it drew up proposals for the racial zoning of the city (in conjunction with the Natal Local Health Commission). These proposals, and those put forward by a Reference and Planning Committee, together with the counter-proposals proffered by the Natal Indian Organization,[52] were considered by the Group Areas Board (maps 3.1, 3.2, 3.3, 3.4). The Reference and Planning Committee's proposals were the most radical, suggesting that coloured residents be moved *en masse* to Plessislaer, giving up all their properties in the central city and in the suburbs. The city council's proposals were closest to the racial pattern prevailing at the time, with the major exception that they recommended that the south-western section of the central city grid (near the railway station) be zoned for white occupation, notwithstanding the fact that Indians and coloureds had lived there for

Map 3   Pietermaritzburg area zoning plans

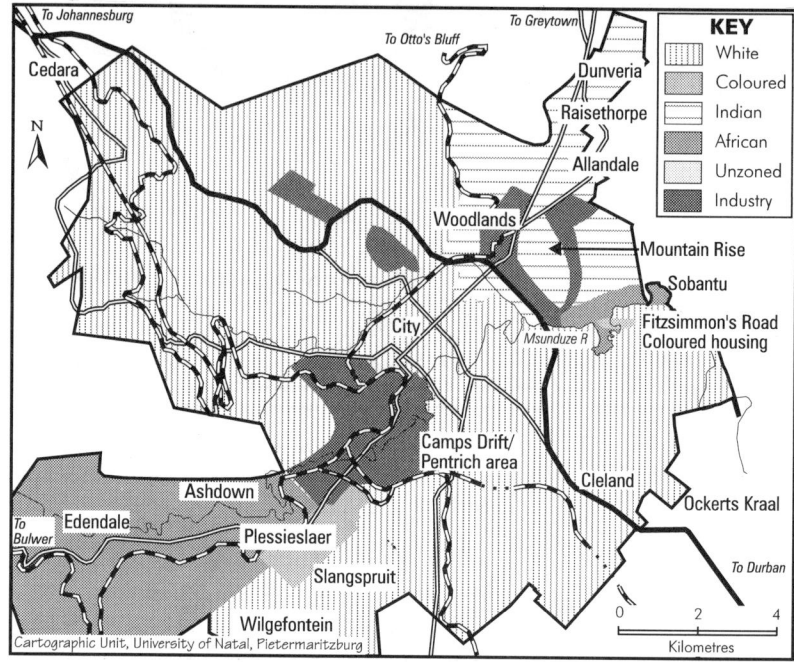

3.1   City Council and Natal Local Health Commission

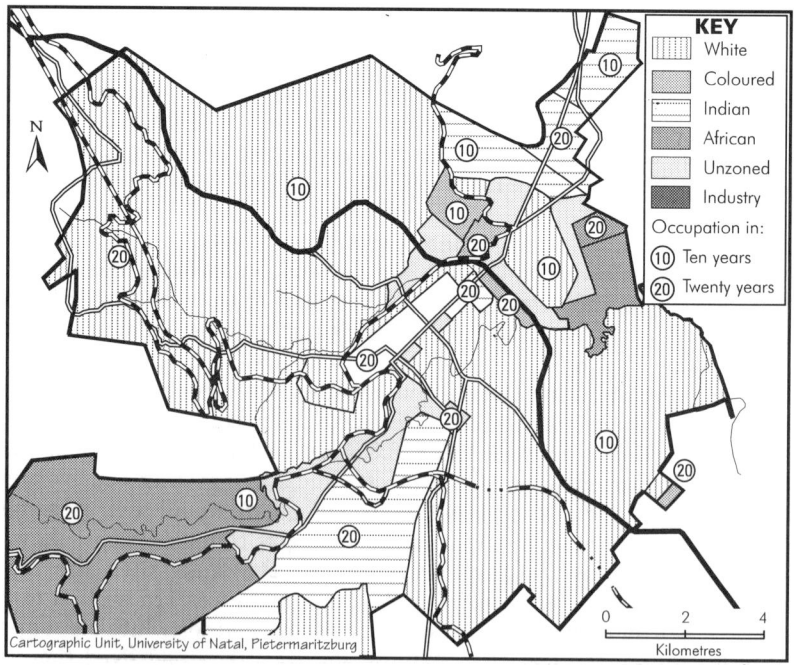

3.2   Reference and Planning Committee

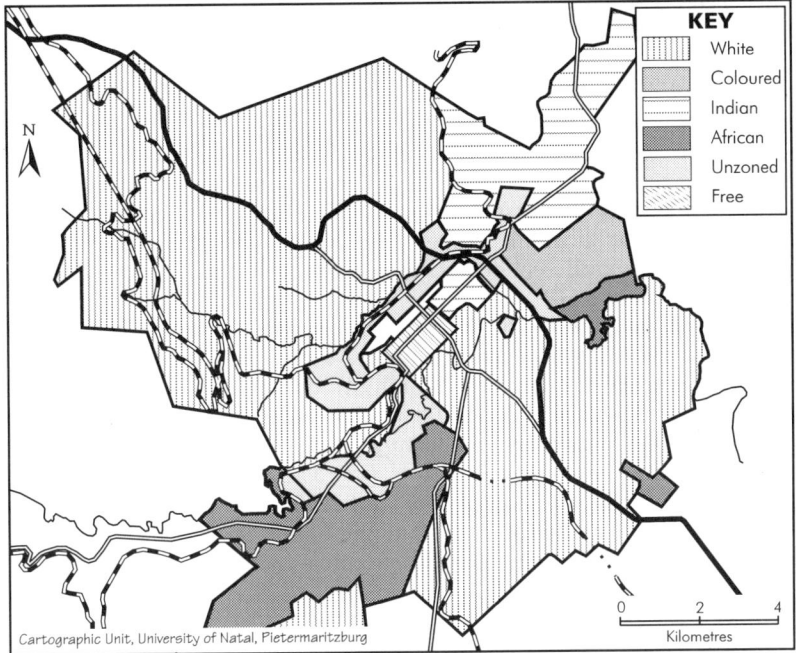

3.3   Natal Indian Organisation

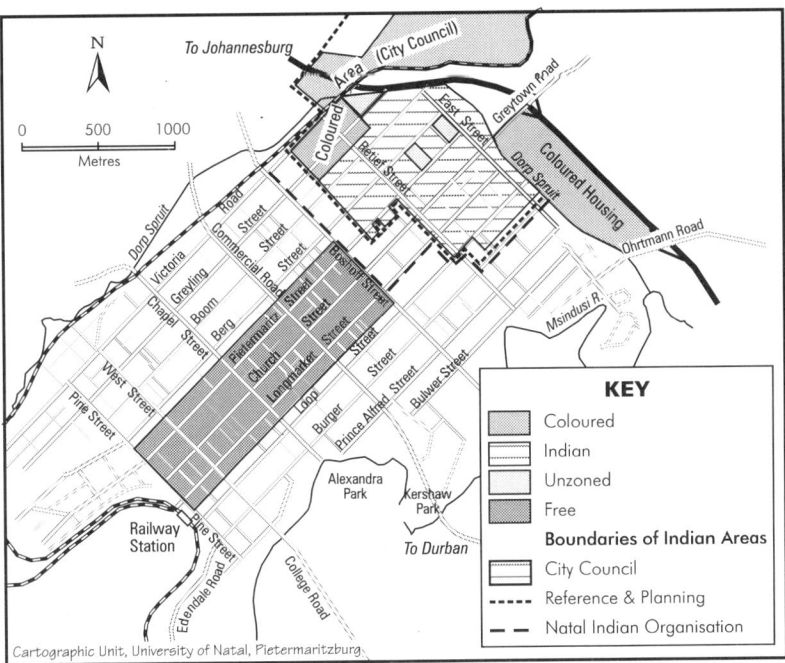

3.4   Zoning proposals for central city area

nearly a century. The Natal Indian Organization recommended that a 'free zone' be created, incorporating most of the business district. Spurned at the time, their recommendation has nevertheless become a reality with the substitution of Section 19 of the Act in 1986, permitting the introduction of the so-called 'free trade zones'.

The group area zoning finally accepted by the Group Areas Board came closer to the recommendations of the Reference and Planning Committee's proposals than the others considered (map 4) although the plan to create a single coloured area at Plessislaer was abandoned in favour of a zone incorporating a small section of the central area and the area formerly known as Hathorn's Hill.

The movement of people precipitated by the Act is summarised in map 4. Perhaps the two most important changes to the face of Pietermaritzburg were the clearance of the upper Church Street area of Indian and coloured residents, and the elimination of Pentrich/Camps Drift. In the former case hundreds of residents were forced to give up their homes, many having lived above or behind their business premises. Nearly 50 traders were disqualified from serving a market they had come to dominate in over 75 years of business. At the time that the upper Church Street area was zoned 'white', shops in the area were being increasingly patronised by

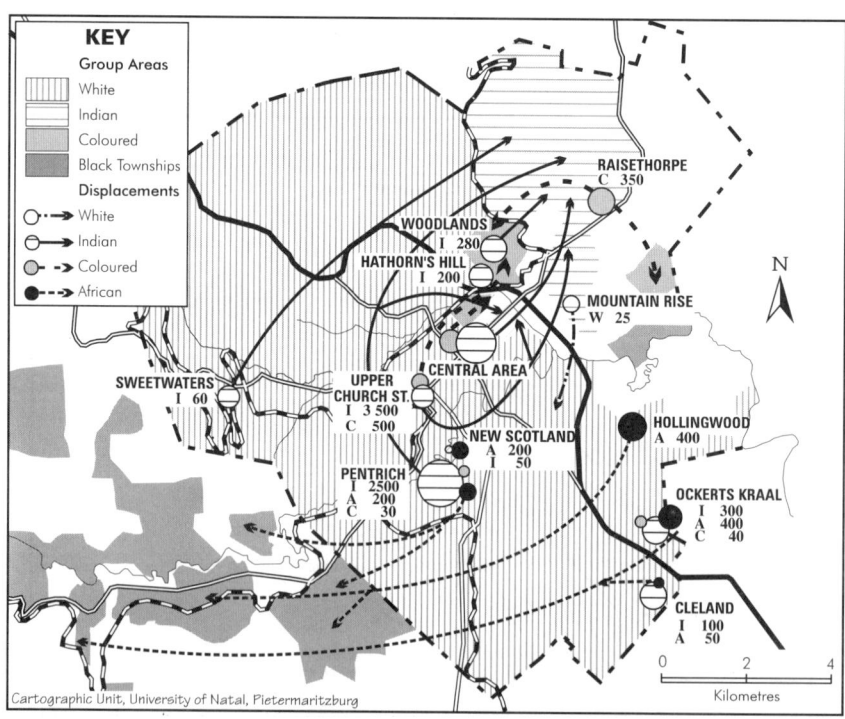

Map 4   Group Areas zoning, showing resulting removals

white shoppers. Ironically, since becoming officially white the district has become overwhelmingly geared towards a black clientele!

Since the earliest years of Pietermaritzburg's existence the Camps Drift area had been home to many Africans, and later, Indians. By 1960 the suburb of Pentrich had developed, and was home to nearly 2 500 Indians, 200 Africans and a few coloured and white families. Not only did all but the white families have to move, but the enforcement of the Act eliminated seven shops, a mosque and four schools. The suburb disappeared from the map of Pietermaritzburg, and until the recent development of the Camps Drift Industrial Scheme, survived as an open buffer strip, separating the black residential suburbs further upstream from the main body of the town.

The division of the city into separate racial zones was unambiguous in the suburbs, and the infrastructure of the city enhanced the 'separateness' of daily life. In the central area the divisions were not as clear, however, and white and Indian properties shared common boundaries in places. A study of the perceptions of group areas zonings held by central city residents was carried out in 1981, with surprising results. A sample of nearly 500 residents were asked to describe where the group areas boundaries were in the central area, and to put this information on a map provided to them. Over half (55 per cent) of the white households interviewed claimed to have 'no idea at all' where the boundaries were, and were unable to fill in anything on the map. In contrast 87 per cent of the Indian residents in the sample filled in the boundaries (the majority of them with great accuracy).

In Pietermaritzburg, the Group Areas Act put paid to any hope of expanding Sobantu Village *in situ*, and African residents of the city were henceforth diverted to the townships of Imbali, Ashdown or Edendale, all south of the city. In the absence of any commuter railway service, commuters have, until recently, had no option but to rely on the bus system (or in a minority of cases, private transport). Today minibus taxis provide a viable alternative for the commuter, and pose a serious threat to the public transport system.[53] As a result of this dependence on public transport, bus termini and their surrounds have become focuses of major importance in the city. The paradox of the South African city, that those who can least afford it are forced to travel the longest distances to work, is very evident within the Pietermaritzburg metropolitan area. Subsidies on transport allow this paradoxical situation to survive.[54]

The demand for housing by Africans in Pietermaritzburg is reflected in the proliferation of backyard 'shacks' and informal extensions to houses in Sobantu and Imbali. These 'llawu' or 'mjondolos' as they are known, house family members, or lodgers taken in to supplement incomes. In some cases they represent the first stage of an upgrading of the basic house by the occupants, and may be superseded by more elaborate structures later, when the family income permits (this is particularly true in Imbali where there is greater security of tenure).

The central area of Pietermaritzburg is home to about 23 000 people. Nearly half live in flats of one sort or another, but the central area does contain tracts of single-family housing in sound to excellent condition. Overcrowding reaches a peak, and physical condition a low point, in the comparatively small areas zoned for Indian and for coloured occupation. Here homes compete for space with shops, warehouses, light industry, schools, temples and mosques. For many white households the central area provides cheaper accommodation than the suburbs, or a temporary home. Others, however, are attracted by the historic character of the core of the city and its many fine, old red-brick homes on tree-lined streets.

The post-apartheid city: Pietermaritzburg tomorrow?

Pietermaritzburg has recently attempted to provide for the future by implementing a strategic plan, based on strategic-planning procedures developed during the past decade in the United States. This has involved identifying and researching five 'key issues', namely: housing, employment, the quality of life, human relations and city finances. The research has brought some sobering statistics to light. The population of the metropolitan area as a whole is likely to exceed 1,2 million by the year 2000 (i.e. double the present population). In the borough alone, over 1 000 houses will have to be built each year to keep up with demand, while in the metropolitan area about 65 000 houses will have to be built by the turn of the century. At the same time it is estimated that over 350 000 new jobs must be created in the same period. Clearly, new low-cost ways of creating employment and housing people will need to be found. This must necessarily lead to deregulation and the acceptance of 'informal' employment and housing of a standard more compatible with Pietermaritzburg's increasingly Third World character. In Pietermaritzburg the planning authorities have already become actively involved in making provision for pavement traders, and in planning future informal 'markets'. Whatever planning strategies are adopted, there is one inescapable fact: in the future a higher proportion of the city's population will be poor.

While the future is being debated, Pietermaritzburg is changing inexorably. This is particularly noticeable in the central area where the emergence of new shopping centres and office complexes is matched by the proliferation of pavement activities on the periphery of the central business district, and increasingly within those precincts as well. In the vicinity of the major bus termini, in particular, Pietermaritzburg assumes the character of cities elsewhere in Africa. Shopkeepers vie with hawkers to tap the crowds thronging the pavements, and the jumble of colours, noises and smells is in sharp contrast to the slickness of the central business district. In 1986 the Group Areas Act was amended to permit the creation of 'free trade areas', within which people of all races can trade, but not reside. Since the declaration of a free trade area within Pietermaritzburg (map 4), there have been signs of a 're-occupation' of their former trading areas by Indian businessmen. Although it is too soon to tell what impact the free trade area amendment will have, it is likely that Indian commercial interests will be represented in the very heart of the business centre to a far greater degree than was permitted in the past.

This transformation of Pietermaritzburg is relentless, but slow. Major political reform will, however, accelerate the change. Influx control no longer inhibits urbanisation, and the fragmented geography of the city has been kept intact primarily by the Group Areas Act and subsidized transportation. The Free Settlement Areas Act (1989) offered the possibility that certain designated areas will be freed from the restrictions of the Group Areas Act. The dangers of opening only selected areas of South African cities was underlined by Schlemmer[55] and Wills et al.[56] The City Engineer of Pietermaritzburg recommended in 1986 that no piecemeal opening up of the city be accepted,[57] and again in 1989 recommended that application be made to have the entire city declared a 'free settlement area'. On the first occasion the report was positively received by the city council, but a change in the balance of power within the council after the 1988 local elections saw the attempt to have the city opened up in its entirety rejected,[58] while an earlier decision not to oppose group areas permit applications was overturned.[59] The process of reform currently in progress, ponderous as it may seem, has inevitably resulted in the further modification, and ultimately the repeal, of group areas legislation. What changes are now likely to occur in Pietermaritzburg?

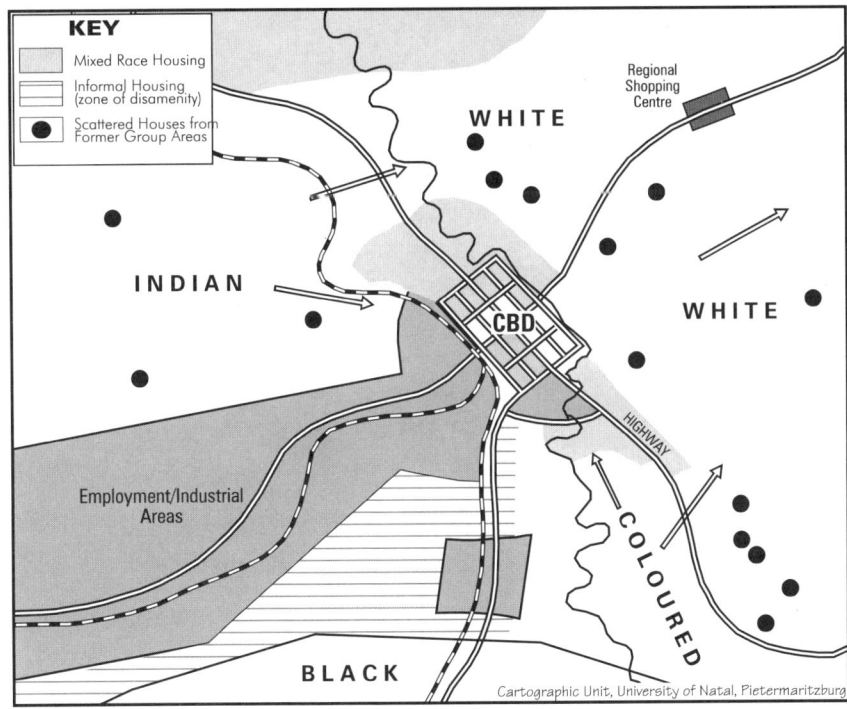

Map 5　A 'post-apartheid city' model

Dewar[60] has asserted that '. . . one of the greatest challenges that will face post-apartheid South Africa is the reconstruction of the fragmented city'. A 'post-apartheid' city model (map 5) recently put forward[61] suggests that there will be an 'implosion' in the present African residential areas, as people use their new freedom to push for housing closer to employment opportunities (and this means the city centre for most). If such housing is not provided by the public or private sectors, they argue, then the people may take the initiative and extend informal housing, currently only in peripheral collars around South African towns, nearer to the city centre. Currently undeveloped 'buffer strips' would be prime targets for such penetration.

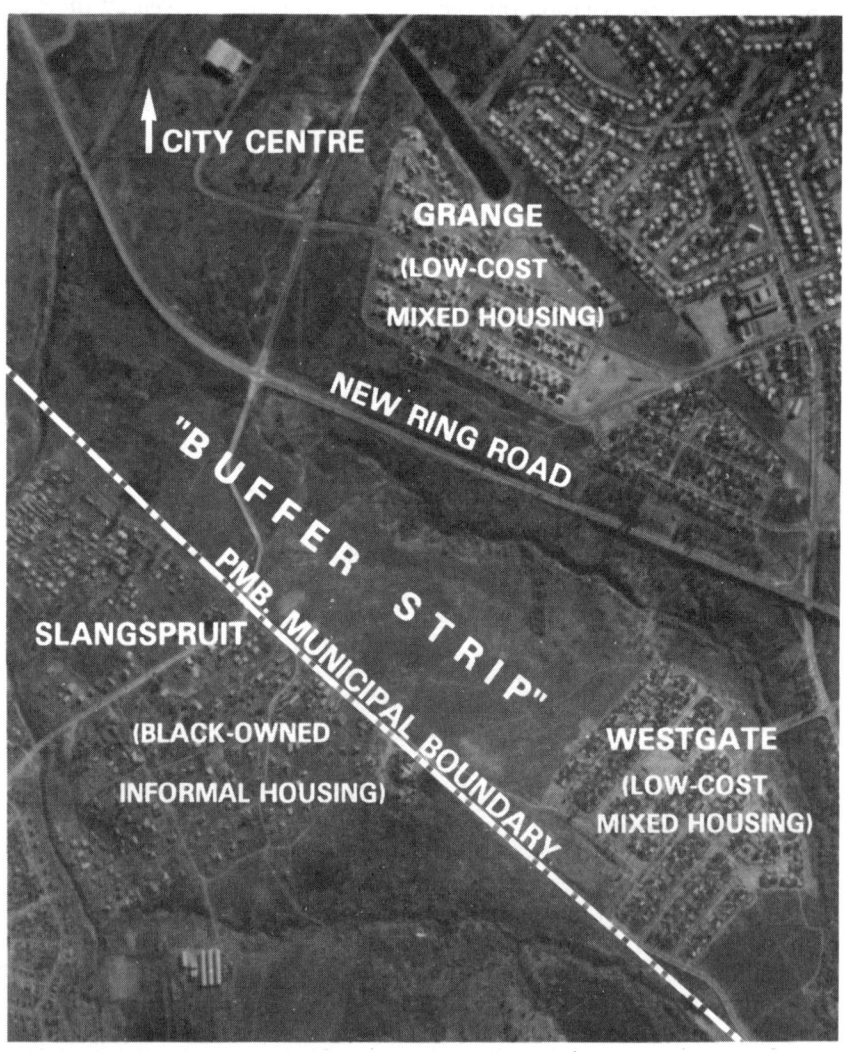

Map 6   A potential conflict zone, post-Group Areas Act

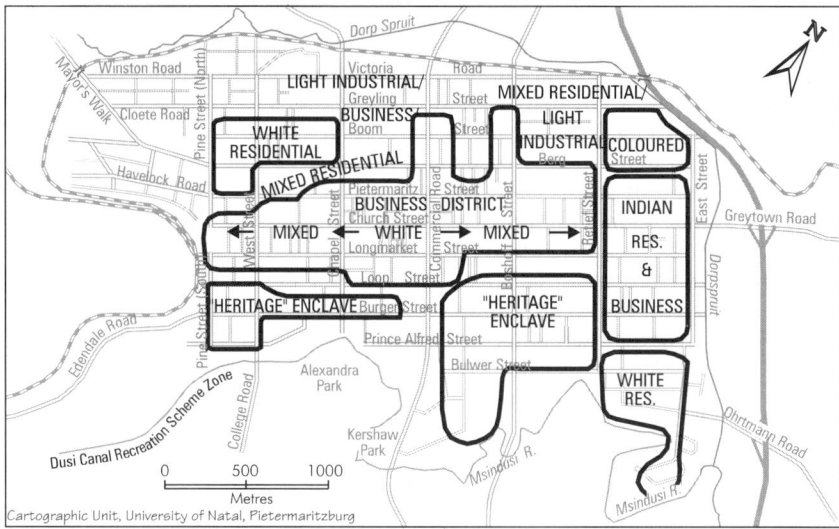

Map 7   Central city area, post-Group Areas Act

This 'implosion' of black urban areas may well be matched by a corresponding 'explosion' of white urban areas, as refuge is sought in suburban areas which, due to the costs of housing, are likely to remain predominantly white. In areas where cheaper housing, currently occupied by white families, lies adjacent to African townships bursting at the seams, and physically separated only by a 'buffer strip', the tendency for the social process of invasion and succession by African families is already more marked, and zones of conflict may emerge. An example of such an area within Pietermaritzburg is the Grange/Slangspruit/Imbali area where apartheid legislation created a social geography ripe for change as the legislative barriers are removed (map 6).

The city centre is likely to witness the most immediate change, as there were many housing opportunities denied to people by the Act, and this is borne out by changes which occurred in the larger cities in advance of legislative reform.[62] A surplus of housing in the present white zones of Pietermaritzburg will rapidly be absorbed by people moving in from elsewhere in the city. The historic core of the city attracts some people because it offers the prospect of cheap temporary housing, others are attracted by the existence of homes with historic appeal in the very heart of the city, while others have lived for generations in the large tracts of modest but sound housing still found in Pietermaritzburg's expansive central grid.

All three groups are likely to be found in the city centre of tomorrow.[63] The central city of tomorrow may then comprise enclaves of predominantly white households zealously defending their neighbourhoods against 'invasion', and enclaves of restored, rehabilitated or 'gentrified' housing, all welded together by a matrix of mixed-race housing and non-residential land-uses (map 7).

In the long-established suburbs, change is likely to be less dramatic as the low incomes of the vast majority of the future city's residents will keep conventional suburban housing out of their reach as it does at present.[64] New suburban developments, constructed after the repeal of the Group Areas Act, will in all likelihood be non-racial in character because there is a dire shortage of modest suburban housing in the present Indian and coloured zones. Removing race restrictions also means that the protection afforded groups as far as public housing is concerned will also disappear, perhaps to the detriment of the poorer families in the Indian and coloured communities. On the city's fringes informal housing is likely to continue to burgeon as urbanisation shows little sign of abating in the near future.

Conclusion

Pietermaritzburg, like other South African towns and cities, started life as a colonial creation in which immigrant-indigene segregation was marked from the very beginning, while relations between white immigrants and other immigrant groups, and people of mixed race, increasingly influenced the social geography of the city.

Political accommodation at Union resulted in Pietermaritzburg losing its status as a colonial capital, but the 'colonial' form of the city lingered on. The period from Union until the coming to power of the National Party in 1948 was characterised by increasing segregation, and the laying down of the foundations of the apartheid geography of contemporary Pietermaritzburg. Suburbs and slums developed simultaneously in different parts of the city. Apart from the direction and powers conferred by statutes such as the Natives (Urban Areas) Act, the Slums Act and the Housing Act, the local authorities dealt with the deteriorating housing position of Africans in and around the city, the suburban growth of the more affluent sectors and industrial growth alike in an *ad hoc* manner. The restructuring of the city that took place from 1948 onwards, resulted from a combination of increasing central government involvement in city planning, and the implementation of co-ordinated town planning at the local level. Long-overdue attention to housing and industrial development on the part of the local authorities coincided with the imposition of new national urban policies enforcing racial separation, and attempting to dictate patterns of economic growth through decentralisation.

Contemporary Pietermaritzburg is changing inexorably in character, and the edges of the apartheid city are becoming increasingly blurred. The speed of change will increase, and sections of the city will be transformed, as major political reform, such as the repeal of the Group Areas Act, is implemented. The form of the 'post-apartheid' city that will emerge from such reform will, however, in many ways resemble on a larger scale colonial Pietermaritzburg at the time of Union.

REFERENCES

1. K. S. O. Beavon, 'Black townships in South Africa: terra incognita for urban geographers', *South African Geographical Journal*, 64(1), 1982.

2. R. J. Davies, 'The spatial formation of the South African city', *GeoJournal*, Supplementary Issue no. 2, 1981, pp. 59–72.

3. S. Parnell, 'Racial segregation in Johannesburg: the Slums Act, 1934–1939', *South African Geographical Journal*, 70(2), 1988, pp. 112–26.

4. Davies, 'Spatial formation'.

5. T. M. Wills, R. J. Haswell, and D. H. Davies, 'The probable consequences of the repeal of the Group Areas Act for Pietermaritzburg', *Report no. 16: Pietermaritzburg 2000* (Pietermaritzburg, City Engineer's Department, 1987).

6. *Ibid.*

7. *Ibid.*

8. G. Maasdorp, and M. Pillay, *Urban relocation and racial segregation: the case of Indian South Africans* (Research Monograph, Department of Economics, University of Natal, Durban, 1977).

9. Minutes of the Borough Council, cited in G. Summers, and D. Meineke, *One hundred years of engineering* (Pietermaritzburg, Pietermaritzburg City Engineer's Department, 1983), p. 33.

10. *Ibid.*, p. 93.

11. *The Natal Witness*, January 1848.

12. Minutes of Borough Council Meeting, 11 September 1855.

13. *The Natal Chronicle*, 19 September 1855.

14. Minutes of Borough Council Meeting, 23 August 1875.

15. H. Peel, 'Sobantu Village: an administrative history of the Pietermaritzburg township' (unpublished BA (Hons) essay, University of Natal, Pietermaritzburg, 1987).

16. A. J. Christopher, 'The roots of urban segregation: South Africa at Union, 1910', *Journal of Historical Geography*, 14(2), 1988, pp. 151–69.

17. The indices range from 0 (no segregation at all) to 100 (complete segregation).

18. Christopher, 'Roots of urban segregation'.

19. Summers and Meineke, *One hundred years*.

20. D. V. Harris, *Industry in the garden city of Pietermaritzburg* (Pietermaritzburg, City Engineer's Department, undated).

21. C. Torino, 'Industrialization, 1838–1987' in J. Laband and R. F. Haswell, (eds) *Pietermaritzburg 1838–1988: a new portrait of an African city* (Pietermaritzburg, University of Natal Press and Shuter and Shooter, 1988).

22. *Ibid.*

23. P. Maylam, 'The rise and decline of urban apartheid' (Paper presented at South African Historical Society Conference, University of Natal, Pietermaritzburg, January 1988).

24. *Urban and rural population of South Africa 1904–1960* (Pretoria, Census Report no. 02–02–01, 1968).

25. S. Meintjes, 'Edendale, 1851–1930: farmers to townspeople, market to labour reserve' in Laband and Haswell (eds), *Pietermaritzburg*.

26. *Pietermaritzburg Corporation Yearbook*, 1929/30, p. 71.

27. Summers and Meineke, *One hundred years*, p. 114.

28. *Pietermaritzburg Corporation Yearbook*, 1929/30, p. 74.

29. *Ibid.*, 1934/35.

30. Maylam, 'The rise and decline of urban apartheid'.

31. *Pietermaritzburg Corporation Yearbook*, 1923/24; Mayor's Minute, p. 33.

32. Peel, 'Sobantu Village'.

33. *Ibid.*

34. *Ibid.*

35. *Pietermaritzburg Corporation Yearbook*, 1934/35; Mayor's Minute, p. 23.

36. Maasdorp and Pillay, *Urban relocation*.

37. *Ibid.*

38. Harris, 'Industry in Pietermaritzburg'.

39. Wills et al., 'Consequences of the repeal of the Group Areas Act'.

40. A. Thorrington-Smith, M. Rosenberg, and L. McCrystal, *Pietermaritzburg 1990* (Planning Report for Pietermaritzburg City Council, 1973).

41. Torino, 'Industrialization'.

42. Thorrington-Smith et al., *Pietermaritzburg 1990*.

43. M. Dubois, 'Aspects of the post-war growth and development of Pietermaritzburg' (Third Year Project, Department of Geography, University of Natal, Pietermaritzburg, 1968).

44. P. Morris, *A history of black housing in South Africa* (Johannesburg, South Africa Foundation, 1981).

45. In the words of the Minister of the Interior, Dr T. E. Donges:

    Now this . . . (the Group Areas Act) . . . is designed to eliminate friction between the races in the Union because we believe, and believe strongly, that points of contact between the races must be avoided . . . (*Hansard*, May 1950).

46. J. Western, *Outcast Cape Town*, (London, Heinemann, 1981) p. 93.

47. R. J. Davies, 'The apartheid city' in P. Adams and F. K. Helleiner, *International geography 2* (Toronto, University of Toronto Press, 1974); J. J. McCarthy and D. Smit, *South African city: theory in analysis and planning* (Cape Town, Juta and Co., 1984).

48. M. M. Motala, 'The Group Areas Act and the effect of the proclamations made thereunder in Pietermaritzburg and environs'. (Paper presented at the Group Areas Conference, January 1961, Pietermaritzburg.)

49. *Pietermaritzburg Corporation Yearbook*, 1960/61.

50. Motala, 'The Group Areas Act'.

51. Western, *Outcast Cape Town*.

52. M. Horrell, *The Group Areas Act: its effect on human beings* (Johannesburg, South African Institute of Race Relations, 1956).

53. T. M. Wills, 'From rickshaws to mini-bus taxis' in Laband and Haswell (eds), *Pietermaritzburg*.

54. E. Voges, *Accessibility, transport and the spatial structure of the South African city: an historical perspective* (Pretoria, National Institute for Transport and Road Research, 1984).

55. L. Schlemmer, 'Apartheid in transition: the collapse of racial zoning', *Indicator SA*, 4(2), 1986.

56. Wills et al., 'Consequences of the repeal of the Group Areas Act'.

57. City Engineer's Department, 'The Group Areas Act' (unpublished Report, Pietermaritzburg, City Engineer's Department, 1986).

58. *The Natal Witness*, 11 March 1989.

59. *Ibid.*, 23 March 1989.

60. D. Dewar, 'City planning and urbanisation strategies: meeting the challenge' in C. Heymans and G. Totemeyer (eds), *Government by the people? The politics of local government in South Africa* (Cape Town, Juta and Co., 1986).

61. Wills et al., 'Consequences of the repeal of the Group Areas Act'.

62. C. Pickard-Cambridge, *The greying of Johannesburg* (Johannesburg, South African Institute of Race Relations, 1988).

63. Wills et al., 'Consequences of the repeal of the Group Areas Act'.

64. City Engineer's Department, *The Group Areas Act*.